Early Southeast Asia
Selected Essays

 Cornell University

Euteen Wolters and O. W. Wolters in 1995
(photograph courtesy of Virginia Hooker)

O. W. Wolters
edited by Craig J. Reynolds

Early Southeast Asia
Selected Essays

SOUTHEAST ASIA PROGRAM PUBLICATIONS
Southeast Asia Program
Cornell University
Ithaca, New York
2008

Cornell Southeast Asia Program Publications
640 Stewart Avenue, Ithaca, NY 14850-3857

Studies on Southeast Asia No. 43

Printed in the United States of America

ISBN-13:   hc 978-0-877277-73-6
ISBN-13:   pb 978-0-877277-43-9

Cover Design: Maureen Viele

TABLE OF CONTENTS

Editor's Note

vii

List of Abbreviations

ix

Sources

xi

The Professional Lives of O. W. Wolters, by Craig J. Reynolds

1

Part I   Southeast Asia as a Region

39

1   Southeast Asia as a Southeast Asian Field of Study

39

2   Early Southeast Asian Political Systems

57

3   China Irredenta: The South

65

Part II   The Long Durée of Malay History

77

4   Studying Śrīvijaya

77

5   Restudying Some Chinese Writings on Sriwijaya

109

Part III   Mainland Mandalas

149

6   Ayudhyā and the Rearward Part of the World

149

7   Jayavarman II's Military Power: The Territorial Foundation of the
      Angkor Empire

165

8   Khmer "Hinduism" in the Seventh Century

177

Part IV   Vietnamese Historiography and Literature

193

9   Historians and Emperors in Vietnam and China: Comments Arising
      out of Lê Văn Hưu's History, Presented to the Trần Court in 1272

193

10   Phạm Sư Mạnh's Poems Written while Patrolling the Vietnamese
      Northern Border in the Middle of the Fourteenth Century

211

11   On Telling a Story of Vietnam in the Thirteenth and Fourteenth Centuries   225

EDITOR'S NOTE

The idea behind this volume is to introduce the work of O. W. Wolters to new generations of scholars entering the field of Southeast Asian history, whether it be of the modern, premodern, or early periods. Given the linguistic skills required for primary research in early Southeast Asian history, it is understandable that few historians take up its study. It occurred to me that one way to encourage new work in the field would be to assemble a volume of essays by Wolters, whose knowledge of Chinese enabled him to reach across the region and write about early Indonesia, early Siam and Cambodia, and early Vietnam.

Before Wolters became a university professor he served in the Malayan Civil Service, and his research into the cultural make-up of precolonial ruling elites thus takes on a particular interest. As someone not born and bred exclusively in academia, he brought to bear on his study of the ancient past his practical experience as a colonial official. For this reason, the nexus between his knowledge of colonial government, the Malayan sultanates, and the histories he wrote of early Southeast Asia after retiring from the colonial service invites questions.

In the course of conceiving of the volume, selecting and editing the essays, and researching the introduction, I corresponded with many colleagues who generously gave of their time and expertise. Barbara Watson Andaya, Leonard Andaya, Haydon Cherry, Tamara Loos, John Miksic, Tony Milner, Michael Montesano, John Seidel, and Eric Tagliacozzo offered enthusiastic support for the feasibility of the project. The advice of Stanley O'Connor and Keith Taylor was particularly helpful in my decision to proceed with the idea. I thank Jacob Ramsay for his views on how the volume should be assembled and for helping to prepare it for publication, as did Nicholas Farrelly. Li Tana kindly helped with Chinese characters, and both she and Thien Do helped with the transliteration of Vietnamese.

Benedict Anderson, John Butcher, David Chandler, Virginia Hooker, John Legge, Bill O'Malley, and Maurizio Peleggi read drafts of the introduction and made valuable comments, as did Mary Kilcline Cody, Mark Emmanuel, Barry Hooker, Ian Proudfoot, and Eric Tagliacozzo. I am particularly grateful to Peter Zinoman, an astute critic of several drafts who pointed out lines of inquiry that had not occurred to me. Virginia Hooker and John Legge shared with me their personal correspondence with Oliver Wolters, and I thank Tim Harper, Hong Lysa, Alaistair MacLaughlan, Michael Montesano, Leon Comber, and Carl Trocki for answering research questions. In a long letter, John Gullick, who had also served in the Malayan Civil Service, put in perspective his own memories of British rule in Malaya. Throughout the project Tony Milner offered insights into the connections between Wolters's careers as a colonial official and as a scholar.

Mrs. Euteen Wolters graciously put up with my numerous inquiries about her life with Oliver Wolters, particularly during the early years in Malaya. I appreciate her forbearance, hospitality, and good nature in answering my questions.

Deborah Homsher, Fred Conner, and the editorial team for the Southeast Asia Program's publications provided timely advice and guided the project to fruition.

My family—Sue Rider, Simon, and Oliver—tolerated the demands on my time of yet another mysterious academic project that seemed to go on forever.

Craig J. Reynolds
June 2007, Canberra

LIST OF ABBREVIATIONS

BEFEO   Bulletin de l'Ecole Française d'Extrême-Orient

BSOAS   Bulletin of the School of Oriental and African Studies

JA   Journal Asiatique

JAS   Journal of Asian Studies

JBRS   Journal of the Burma Research Society

JMBRAS   Journal of the Malayan Branch of the Royal Asiatic Society

JSBRAS   Journal of the Straits Branch of the Royal Asiatic Society

JSEAH   Journal of Southeast Asian History

JSEAS   Journal of Southeast Asian Studies

JSS   Journal of the Siam Society

SOURCES

The essays by O. W. Wolters are reprinted here with minor editorial changes to conform to house style or as otherwise indicated in the text.

Chapter 1: "Southeast Asia as a Southeast Asian Field of Study," *Indonesia* 58 (October 1994): 1-17. Reprinted by permission.

Chapter 2: "Early Southeast Asian Political Systems," in *History, Culture, and Region in Southeast Asian Perspectives*, rev. ed. (Ithaca: Cornell Southeast Asia Program Publications, 1999), pp. 15–19, 23–26. Reprinted by permission.

Chapter 3: "China Irredenta: The South," *The World Today* 19,12 (1963): 540–52.

Chapter 4: "Studying Śrīvijaya," *Journal of the Malayan Branch of the Royal Asiatic Society* 52,2 (1979): 1–32. Reprinted by permission.

Chapter 5: "Restudying Some Chinese Writings on Sriwijaya," *Indonesia* 42 (October 1986): 1–41. Reprinted by permission.

Chapter 6: "Ayudhyā and the Rearward Part of the World," *Journal of the Royal Asiatic Society* 3-4 (1968): 166–78. Reprinted by permission.

Chapter 7: "Jayavarman II's Military Power: The Territorial Foundation of the Angkor Empire," *Journal of the Royal Asiatic Society* 1 (1973): 20–30. Reprinted by permission.

Chapter 8: "Khmer 'Hinduism' in the Seventh Century," in *Early South East Asia: Essays in Archaeology, History, and Historical Geography*, ed. R. B. Smith and W. Watson (Oxford: Oxford University Press, 1979), pp. 427–42. Reprinted by permission.

Chapter 9: "Historians and Emperors in Vietnam and China: Comments Arising out of Lê Văn Hưu's History, Presented to the Trần Court in 1272," in *Perceptions of the Past in Southeast Asia*, ed. Anthony Reid and David Marr (Singapore: Heinemann Educational Books Ltd. for the Asian Studies Association of Australia, 1979), pp. 69–89.

Chapter 10: "Phạm Sư Mạnh's Poems Written while Patrolling the Vietnamese Northern Border in the Middle of the Fourteenth Century," *Journal of Southeast Asian Studies* 13,1 (1982): 107–119. Reprinted by permission.

Chapter 11: "On Telling a Story of Vietnam in the Thirteenth and Fourteenth Centuries," *Journal of Southeast Asian Studies* 26,1 (1995): 63-74. Reprinted by permission.

To conform to the original publication of these essays and to minimize editorial error, the Wade-Giles system for transcribing Chinese characters is used throughout this volume with the exception of some terms in "The Professional Lives of O. W. Wolters" (pp. 1–38).

THE PROFESSIONAL LIVES OF O. W. WOLTERS

PART 1: ENGLAND, MALAYA, ITHACA

By the 1970s, O. W. Wolters was unarguably the most influential historian of early Southeast Asia writing in the English-speaking world. The following selected essays have been chosen for the way they exemplify his geographical and topical range. His curiosity carried him to many parts of the region, and while he was careful in his scholarship to make only warranted statements about the past, he was also fearless in striking off into unfamiliar territory if he thought a problem had been neglected. He had a restless imagination.

For those who had the good fortune to take a university course with Wolters, the unlikely subject of "early Southeast Asia" came alive in the classroom as something fresh and contemporary. What appeared to the uninitiated to be something made impossibly difficult by ancient languages and bewildering scripts became a subject enlivened by new research. At the beginning of the course Wolters would alert his students to the inevitability of discoveries that he would be announcing before the semester ended. Archaeologists were excavating ancient settlements and coastal entrepôts; epigraphers were translating inscriptions and throwing new light on kingdoms that had once dotted the region. News of early Southeast Asia was breaking fast. The impulse to promote the field stemmed from some anxiety about its novice status in the curriculum as much as from his own genuine enthusiasm. So Wolters made it plain from the first day that he believed the study of early Southeast Asia had a definite place in the liberal arts curriculum. It was not a narrow, specialized field of knowledge, and it had as much to offer the humanities as did the more popular courses in American or European history taught by his colleagues. Moreover, its study required methods that might have applicability to other fields, just as Southeast Asian history itself was being invigorated by the disciplines of anthropology, art history, and archaeology. For these reasons he commended its study to undergraduates and graduate students alike.

In this first part of the introduction I will explore the path by which Wolters became a historian. Such a sketch cannot pretend to be an intellectual biography, for the materials are too scanty to allow it. But just as a poet's life has something to do with the poetry that is written out of that life, so the historian's life has something to do with the history that is written. Wolters lived through a dramatic period of Asian history, indeed of world history. He personally experienced the disruption caused by the Japanese occupation of Southeast Asia and the violence and upheaval of the Emergency in Malaya. He witnessed the accession to power of Asian leaders and the dismantling, by force more often than by negotiation, of European colonial establishments. Before he had stepped into the classroom, Wolters had already led a very interesting life—an adventurous life by his own account—with which his scholarship was inevitably entangled. He knew these were epic events. Yet in the backhanded way that he often expressed himself, he said in his memoir about this earlier, adventurous life that he tended to regard what was happening to him as being "of passing importance."[1]

MALAYA, 1938–1957

Wolters began his memoir not with his family history but with a simple declarative statement that he had sailed to Malaya on the P&O steamship *Carthage* in August, 1938.[2] Malaya had changed his life. From the year he arrived, until the country proclaimed its independence from the British in 1957, he was a member of the Malayan Civil Service (MCS). He liked to refer to those two decades when he was "out and about" as among the happiest years of his life. Although he had little to say publicly about his early years, the period he spent in the MCS influenced his academic career in different ways. He acquired language skills in Chinese and Malay, and his work in the MCS during the Emergency from 1948 until he left Malaya in early 1957 brought him into contact with Chinese, Malay, Indian, and British people, many of them officials and community leaders. He gained experience as a government official, mostly in provincial areas of western Malaya where British investment was largely concentrated and where British officers "shadowed" the Malay regime at every level, whatever the proprieties of indirect rule and Malay sovereignty might imply.[3]

Wolters joined the MCS directly after finishing his first degree at Oxford University, where he earned first-class honors in history. He had grown up in an academic family, his father having taught psychology at Reading University where he later served as the Deputy Vice-Chancellor. His younger sister, Gwyneth, eventually pursued an academic career in Russian literature. At Oxford, Wolters lived at Lincoln College where one of his classmates was the late Heinz W. Arndt, the distinguished economist of Indonesia based at the Australian National University.[4] Longevity and Australia would bring the two scholars together towards the end of their careers; they outlived the rest of their Oxford classmates by several years, and Wolters made certain he visited Heinz Arndt on his trips to Canberra. By the time he finished his Oxford degree, Wolters's "eastward-thinking had crystalized," and, declining a research fellowship at Lincoln, he accepted a position in the MCS. He had been intrigued by exotic objects brought home by a family friend who taught in Ipoh, Perak. Also, he had read some Conrad and enjoyed his

---

[1] Wolters, *Some Memories*, unpublished memoir, p. 18. This twenty-five page memoir was found among Wolters's papers at his death and is in the possession of his heirs. On internal evidence it was written in 1999. For biographical information see Stanley J. O'Connor, "Oliver W. Wolters: June 8, 1915–December 5, 2000," *Indonesia* 72 (October 2001): 1–7, which drew on *Some Memories*.

[2] *Some Memories*, p. 1.

[3] Christopher Bayly and Tim Harper, *Forgotten Armies: The Fall of British Asia, 1941–1945* (London: Allen Lane, Penguin Books, 2004), p. 32.

[4] H. W. Arndt, *A Course Through Life: Memoirs of an Australian Economist* (Canberra: National Centre for Development Studies, Australian National University, 1985).

interview at the Colonial Office where, to his relief, one of the interviewers told him there was no reason why he should join any clubs.[5]

As a new cadet, Wolters had been selected to study Chinese, and so he proceeded to Singapore, Macau, and Hong Kong where he spent two and a half years learning the language.[6] His first Malayan appointment was in 1941 in the Labor Department, where many Chinese speakers in the MCS were assigned to handle labor disputes in the tin mines and rubber plantations. Wolters had entered a department of the MCS—the Chinese Protectorate—which was then in the twilight of its existence. Founded during the 1870s in response to a Chinese riot in Singapore, the oddly named Protectorate, later called the Secretariat for Chinese affairs, referred to a bureaucratic office staffed largely by Chinese-speaking officers with the responsibility for overseeing Chinese affairs.[7] The first Protector of the Chinese, William Pickering, had quickly established a reputation for his command of Chinese languages, his down-to-earth way of dealing with difficult issues, and his savvy about just how far the British should try to extend their control.

One of the purposes of the Protectorate was to shield Chinese immigrants from exploitation and abuse.[8] Chinese migrants who arrived in Malaya as debt laborers for the tin mines and rubber estates were easy victims of local Chinese agents and the "brotherhoods," and thus much of the work for the British in the early decades involved battling the secret societies.[9] Of particular concern was the traffic in women and girls, with the Protectorate given legal powers as "Protector under the Women and Girls Protection Ordinance."[10] But it also has to be recognized that the Chinese brotherhoods in British Malaya did not rely primarily on extortion and exploitation for their influence; these organizations also served social and economic ends. They forged bonds of solidarity and mutual assistance in an effort to transcend the divisions of family, region, and language that were the lot of newly arrived Chinese migrants. Recent research shows that British authorities of the time saw the brotherhoods as a police "problem" and failed to recognize the social and economic factors supporting their existence.[11] By the early twentieth century, Protectorate officers had been assigned to the Federated Malay States as well as to the Straits Settlements, and surveillance and registration of secret societies continued up to the

---

[5] Wolters, *Some Memories*, p. 6.

[6] Robert Heussler, *British Rule in Malaya: The Malayan Civil Service and Its Predecessors, 1867–1942* (Oxford: Clio Press, 1981), pp. 160–61. This source gives an account of life in Hong Kong for new cadets studying Chinese there. In 1940, extrapolating from available statistics on population, there was approximately one Chinese-speaking MCS officer for every 40,000 Chinese, in contrast to one Malay speaker for every 15,000 Malays; see Robert O. Tilman, *Bureaucratic Transition in Malaya* (Durham, NC: Duke University Commonwealth Studies Center; London: Cambridge University Press, 1964), p. 26, n. 55.

[7] Rupert Emerson, *Malaysia: A Study in Direct and Indirect Rule* (New York, NY: The Macmillan Company, 1937), pp. 502–4.

[8] Heussler, *British Rule in Malaya*, pp. 150–51.

[9] The conditions of recruitment of Chinese laborers in the late nineteenth century are described in Chai Hon-chan, *The Development of British Malaya, 1896–1909* (London and Kuala Lumpur: Oxford University Press, 1964), pp. 108–112.

[10] Victor Purcell, *The Chinese in Malaya* (London, New York, Toronto: Oxford University Press, 1948), p. 177.

[11] Carl Trocki, *Opium and Empire: Chinese Society in Colonial Singapore, 1800–1910* (Ithaca, NY, and London: Cornell University Press, 1990), pp. 14–15, 21–22, 235–236.

Japanese Occupation. Because of communist infiltration of the secret societies, the courts after the Second World War treated the Malayan Communist party as a secret society.[12]

Although Chinese speakers in the MCS were highly valued for their work with the Chinese population before the war, when Wolters joined, this had not always been the case; even a generation earlier things were different. Specializing in language study could damage an officer's career prospects, though there has been some debate among historians about this point. When Victor Purcell first entered the colonial service in 1921, for example, he was mocked for volunteering to study Chinese. As a "specialist," he was told, he would never rise very high in the colonial administrative hierarchy.[13] He refused to be put off by this pessimistic prediction and went on to become Assistant Director of Education (Chinese) and, after the Japanese Occupation, Principal Adviser on Chinese Affairs to British Military Administration. There may also have been prejudice against Chinese-speaking MCS officials, who were regarded by their fellow officers in the Malay stream as odd or too specialized; this was certainly what Purcell had been warned to avoid.[14] Heussler, whose many studies were informed by voluminous correspondence with former MCS officers, agrees that there were morale problems, because protectorate officers found that promotion came slower than they had expected and that senior positions—as Residents, for instance—were not open to them.[15] Bored by the work, some officers left for other branches of the service as soon as they could. The degree to which MCS officers who specialized in Chinese affairs found their careers disadvantaged has been exaggerated, however. Many obtained senior secretariat jobs or other desirable positions.[16] A number of them were promoted to the highest level, including Wilfred Blythe, who ended his career as Colonial Secretary in Singapore (1950–53).[17]

Wolters had not had much time to settle into his first appointment when the Japanese imperial army swept down the Malay Peninsula and captured Singapore in early 1942. He spent most of the war interned at Changi Prison (1942–44), followed by a period of incarceration in another detention center at the Sime Road Golf Course until the Japanese surrender in August 1945. At Changi, he shared a cell with Carl Gibson-Hill, later to become director of the Raffles Museum. He spent his days keeping up with his written Chinese and reading about Asia, especially about central Asia, and about late nineteenth-century Chinese history and Buddhism.[18]

---

[12] Heussler, *British Rule in Malaya*, pp. 162, 166.

[13] Victor Purcell, *The Memoirs of a Malayan Official* (London: Cassell & Company Ltd., 1965), p. 96.

[14] J. de Vere Allen, "Malayan Civil Service, 1874–1941: Colonial Bureaucracy / Malayan Elite," *Comparative Studies in Society and History* 12,2 (April 1970): 174.

[15] As a result of the 1874 Pangkor Treaty with Perak, the British assigned a Resident to "advise" the ruler in each of the Federated Malay States: Perak, Selangor, Negeri Sembilan, and, later, Pahang. In 1910, the Unfederated Malay States—Kedah, Perlis, Kelantan, and Terengganu—were assigned British advisers who had less authority than residents. See Virginia Hooker, *A Short History of Malaysia* (Crows Nest, NSW: Allen & Unwin, 2003), pp. 135–37. See also J. M. Gullick, *Rulers and Residents: Influence and Power in the Malay States, 1870–1920* (Singapore: Oxford University Press, 1992).

[16] Heussler, *British Rule in Malaya*, p. 161.

[17] J. M. Gullick, personal communication, August 8, 2005.

[18] Wolters, *Some Memories*, p. 3.

While there was a shortage at Changi of food and amenities, books were plentiful. A general library was assembled with books from the supplies internees had brought with them and from libraries in Singapore.[19] Chinese history and philosophy were available, as well as the full gamut of English literature, everything from John Bunyan's *The Pilgrim's Progress* to Pepys's *Diary* to D. H. Lawrence's *Women in Love* to various works by Conrad, Kipling, and Maugham. Literature on Malaya was also reading fare for the internees, who had access to Swettenham's *British Malaya*; Rupert Emerson's *Malaysia: A Study in Direct and Indirect Rule*; Hugh Clifford's *Studies in Brown Humanity*; and Winstedt's *Malay Grammar* and his *Malay–English Dictionary*, which the Changi diarist T. P. M. Lewis used to brush up his Malay.

Wolters almost never talked about his internment, beyond declaring in his memoir that he had little interest in the books written by former internees about their incarceration. He kept his own counsel on the topic and said almost nothing, even to his family.[20] Perhaps he had even actively pushed the memory from his mind. Once, when I was a student, fumbling for a topic of conversation with this reserved Englishman nearly thirty years my senior, and curious about his internment, I brought up the topic of David Lean's 1957 film, *Bridge on the River Kwai*. Alec Guinness, an actor whom Wolters much admired and with whom Wolters shared the same birth year, played an English colonel who inspires the POWs under his command to build a sturdy railway bridge in the face of Japanese brutality and the ravages of tropical disease that decimate the British troops. At the end of the film, British commandos blow up the bridge as Guinness and the POWs, who had labored mightily to put it in place, watch in confounded despair. Wolters listened patiently until I finished, and said, "it was just like that—we hated our liberators." This was almost certainly adroit social conversation rather than an authentic voice from his past. In a letter written home to England shortly after his release, he expressed not regret but elation, gratitude for his good health, and concern for those who had suffered during the war.[21]

When Wolters returned to Malaya from home leave in early 1946, his first appointment was as Assistant Commissioner of Labor for Selangor, an assignment similar to the one he had before the war. Soon afterward, the Chinese Protectorate was abolished. Even before the 1939–45 war, official opinion had come to recognize that, in the interests of a united Malaya, the practice of treating the Chinese as a separate community was anachronistic and divisive.[22] Chinese immigrants required less "protection" from lawless groups, such as the secret societies and exploitative

---

[19] Mary Thomas, *In the Shadow of the Rising Sun* (Singapore: Maruzen Asia, 1983), pp. 108–109; and T. P. M. Lewis, *Changi, The Lost Years: A Malayan Diary, 1941–1945* (Kuala Lumpur: The Malaysian Historical Society, 1984), p. 100; on p. 112 Lewis reports that the Salvation Army brought into the prison a thousand books donated by Singaporean Chinese.

[20] Interviews with Euteen Wolters, November 2–3, 2005, Ithaca, New York.

[21] Letter from Wolters to his family, September 8, 1945. The David Lean film was not historical reenactment but a tale based on a novel by Pierre Boulle. The bridge was actually destroyed by B-24 Liberators flying long missions from eastern India. The film was misleading in many ways, transforming the railway episode "into a piece of Western folklore"; Clifford Kinvig, *River Kwai Railway: The Story of the Burma–Siam Railroad* (London: Brassey's UK, 1992), pp. xii–xiii.

[22] Leon Comber, personal communication, June 3, 2005; Purcell, *The Chinese in Malaya*, p. 153.

labor brokers, than they had in previous eras. The very name "protectorate" sounded condescending in the changed circumstances, so the decision was made to replace the Chinese Protectorate with the Chinese Secretariat.[23]

While some long-serving MCS officers, such as Victor Purcell, whose MCS career ended more or less with the Japanese surrender, supported the abolition of the Protectorate, others were critical of the change. For Wilfred Blythe, for example, the failure of the colonial office to understand the complexity of Chinese affairs and the Malayan Communist Party's (MCP) successes were directly attributable to the abolition of the Chinese Protectorate. Blythe, himself a detainee in Changi, became the Secretary for Chinese Affairs after the war and was in a position to compare the decline in staffing and budget for Chinese affairs with what he had experienced before the war. With the protectorate dismantled, its officers and functions were scattered among many departments with no overall coordination.[24]

The governing of the Chinese by a specialist department was central to the way the British had chosen to govern Malaya. Throughout British rule, the official theory was that Malaya was the land of the Malays. The legitimacy of colonial rule was based on treaties with the Malay sultans, while other peoples such as the Chinese and Indians were regarded as outsiders, even if their families had been on the peninsula for generations.[25] Before the war, the British had stressed that the Malay States were Malayo–Muslim monarchies: "political power in Malaya was the prerogative of the British administrators and the traditional Malay establishments alone."[26] When Victor Purcell joined the MCS in 1921, 80 percent of the cadets in the colonial service studied Malay, while about 10 percent studied Chinese. But by the early 1940s, the demographics in Malaya had changed. With the Chinese population in the majority if Singapore were included, the case for giving more attention to officer training for Chinese specialists was even more compelling. Although understaffed, the newly established Chinese Secretariat was one of the most important departments—indeed an elite department—of the MCS. Among its many duties, the Chinese Secretariat provided officers to help administer the Labor Department, and it shared intelligence with Special Branch.[27]

The British returned after the Japanese surrender to a very different Malaya from the one they had ruled before the war. An identifiable government authority was lacking, and for a time power was vested in the British Military Administration. British officers in Force 136 emerged from the jungle with the communist Malayan Peoples Anti-Japanese Army (MPAJA), which had been an ally during the Japanese Occupation, but there were tensions which soon turned to hostilities.[28] With food in short supply, epidemics threatening, and the economy in chaos, security was a priority. Wolters on a few occasions accompanied soldiers on military patrols at this

---

[23] Gullick, personal communication, August 8, 2005; Robert Heussler, *British Rule in Malaya, 1942–1957* (Singapore: Heinemann Asia, 1985), pp. 154–55.

[24] Robert Heussler, *British Rule in Malaya*, pp. 156–57.

[25] Purcell, *The Memoirs of a Malayan Official*, p. 97.

[26] Allen, "Malayan Civil Service," p. 153.

[27] Comber, personal communication, June 3, 2005.

[28] J. M. Gullick, "My Time in Malaya" (from unpublished memoirs, 1969) in *They Came to Malaya: A Travellers' Anthology*, compiled and introduced by J. M. Gullick (Singapore: Oxford University Press, 1993), p. 313.

time as the communist insurgency intensified.[29] It is melodramatic to say that MCS officers were now "in permanent fear of their lives" and that as an elite group the MCS "were already dead" simply because the police and army were given greater powers to control the insurgency.[30] Personal memoirs by such people as E. K. Fisk, an Australian who served in the British army and later in the MCS, do not convey a sense that MCS officers feared for their personal safety every minute of the day.[31] But there is no question that the communist insurrection forced the British to change the way they ruled Malaya.

His 1946 appointment as Assistant Commissioner of Labor for Selangor embroiled Wolters in intense, bitter, and occasionally violent labor disputes organized by the MCP. The negotiations involved endless meetings and bargaining, and he dealt with the strikers' demands seriously and patiently in the knowledge that "there were plenty of genuine grievances in a country whose economy had been disrupted by the Japanese occupation."[32] His reputation as a negotiator had brought him to the attention of the Governor General, who sent him to Brunei in 1946 to help settle a labor dispute organized by the Chinese Engineering Mechanics Association in the oilfields, which were the most productive in the British Commonwealth and vital to Britain's postwar economy.[33] By the middle of 1948, the MCP decided to take a harder line and declared armed revolution.[34] The British responded by declaring rule by martial law that gave the government sweeping counterinsurgency powers.

From 1948 until 1950, Wolters was heavily involved with the initial planning for the Taiping Rehabilitation Camp.[35] The actual plan for the camp was adapted from recent Greek experience, when the Greek government dispatched 21,800 communists to Macronissos Island for rehabilitation.[36] In Malaya, the Taiping camp was a pilot project for the establishment of Resettlement Areas, though this "dreary-sounding" term was eventually replaced by the more appealing "New Villages" when General Templer arrived on the scene in early 1952.[37] The story of the attempt to deny the MCP recruits to its cause by resettling Chinese cultivators and plantation workers in

---

[29] Wolters, *Some Memories*, p. 13.

[30] Allen, "Malayan Civil Service," p. 154.

[31] E. K. Fisk, *Hardly Ever a Dull Moment* (Canberra: National Centre for Development Studies, Australian National University, 1995).

[32] Wolters, *Some Memories*, pp. 7–8.

[33] Wolters suggested in his report that it was time to approve the formation of trade unions; see Greg Poulgrain, *The Genesis of Konfrontasi: Malaysia, Brunei, Indonesia, 1945–1965* (Bathhurst, NSW: Crawford House Publishing; London: C. Hurst & Co. Publishers Ltd., 1998), p. 74.

[34] In his memoir, Chin Peng, the leader of the MCP, takes credit for organizing and supporting the strikes in Malaya and gives an account of the decision to declare armed revolution; Chin Peng, *My Side of History* (Singapore: Media Masters, 2003), chapter 13.

[35] At some point—the date is uncertain—Wolters went to Africa to see how the colonial authorities were handling the rebellion of the Kikuyu, the Mau Mau movement; the government in Kenya declared a state of emergency in 1952. In Wolters's personal library are two books by L. S. B. Leakey, *Mau Mau and the Kikuyu* (London: Methuen & Co., 1952) and *Defeating Mau Mau* (London: Methuen & Co., 1952). Interviews with Euteen Wolters, November 3–4, 2004, and November 1–2, 2005, Ithaca, New York.

[36] Kumar Ramakrishna, *Emergency Propaganda: The Winning of Malayan Hearts and Minds, 1948–1958* (Richmond, Surrey: Curzon Press, 2002), p. 67.

[37] Kumar Ramakrishna, "'Transmogrifying' Malaya: The Impact of Sir Gerald Templer (1952–54)," *JSEAS* 32,1 (February 2001): 87.

camps, part of the Briggs Plan that had placed Malaya on a war footing, has been told many times.[38] By 1954, upward of half a million people had been forcibly relocated to New Villages; the number is close to a million if those moved to towns and workplaces are counted.[39] The Taiping camp, whose trademark was rehabilitation rather than detention or deportation, was an expensive early experiment in social engineering that aimed to retrain rural Chinese in their new environment. Subsequently, most of the funds for the New Villages were spent on acquisition of land, building, and subsistence allowances rather than on educational, medical, health, and other social services.[40]

On the basis of his work in Taiping, Wolters published a report in the *Community Development Bulletin*, a periodical that carried articles on development throughout the British empire. In it he acknowledged MCP successes in recruiting rural Chinese, especially youth, and he saw that family links between communist party members and rural dwellers on the jungle fringe strengthened the appeal of the MCP. The so-called "outlaws" who had joined the party in the jungle were fathers, sons, daughters, and neighbors of farming families, conditions that enabled "an ancient social habit"—Chinese kin networks—to reinforce the influence of communist campaigns. British rule meant little in these communities because "Chinese self-help and endurance could dispense" with government. In Wolters's opinion, the British had under-governed the rural Chinese population. The casual attitudes of the rural Chinese toward British rule that had flourished before the Emergency were "therefore discarded in favour of grateful submission to the discipline of government."[41] Through rehabilitation, the British would instill obligations of citizenship and civic virtue in a population accustomed to a much lighter governing hand. For his work in establishing the camp, Wolters was awarded an OBE (Order of the British Empire), which Templer personally conferred in January 1952.

In the Second Indochina War the government in southern Vietnam experimented with similar camps or, as they were called in that conflict, "strategic hamlets," to counter the communist insurgency in the south. Sir Robert Thompson, a former Secretary for Defense in Malaya from 1957 to 1961 who had advised on the resettlement camps in Malaya, visited the southern Vietnamese government under President Ngo Dinh Diem to share his expertise in the building of strategic hamlets.[42]

---

[38] T. N. Harper, *The End of Empire and the Making of Malaya* (Cambridge: Cambridge University Press, 1999), chapter 4; Anthony Short, *The Communist Insurrection in Malaya, 1948-1960* (London: Frederick Muller Limited, 1975), chapter 9; Richard Stubbs, *Hearts and Minds in Guerrilla Warfare: The Malayan Emergency, 1948–1960* (Singapore: Oxford University Press, 1989). While it cannot have pleased many MCS officers, including Wolters, Han Suyin's novel, *...And the Rain My Drink* (London: Jonathan Cape, 1956), which deals with events in 1952–1953, contains many insights into the conflict and the dilemmas faced by the British.

[39] The figures in Harper, *The End of Empire*, p. 176, are based on Kernial Sandhu, "The Saga of the Malayan Squatter," *JSEAH* 5,1 (March 1964): 143–77. Using the papers of Tan Cheng Lok, Karl Hack gives a combined figure that approaches one million people affected by the end of 1951, including 600,000 plantation and mine workers who were "regrouped"; "'Iron Claws on Malaya': The Historiography of the Malayan Emergency," *JSEAS* 30,1 (March 1999), p. 102.

[40] Francis Loh Kok Wah, *Beyond the Tin Mines: Coolies, Squatters, and New Villagers in the Kinta Valley, Malaysia, c. 1880–1980* (Singapore: Oxford University Press, 1988), p. 136.

[41] O. W. Wolters, "Emergency Resettlement and Community Development in Malaya," *Community Development Bulletin* 3,1 (December 1951): 3.

[42] Stubbs, *Hearts and Minds*, p. 3.

O. W. Wolters receiving medal from Sultan of Perak, Taiping, early 1950s

O. W. Wolters attending banquet, 1950s

Milton Osborne, one of Wolters's first doctoral students at Cornell University, undertook a comparative study evaluating the two cases of resettlement and argued that the resettlement program in southern Vietnam failed because the socio-economic conditions there were quite different from those in Malaya.[43] New research, however, has shown that the strategic hamlet program in southern Vietnam owed much more to the Ngo regime's own ideas than to the Malayan stratagems advocated by Thompson.[44]

In 1951, Wolters became District Officer (DO) in Tapah, southern Perak, and later in the year moved to Larut and Matang as DO, where he was to spend the next three years. A plaque with Chinese characters donated by "O. W. Wolters MCS OBE" to the local Kwangtung Association in 1954 became the center of attention when it was covered over during a rally of the Parti Keadilan Nasional in 1999, thus causing offence to local Chinese leaders.[45] About these three years in northern Perak, where the Emergency was under control and he could "relax," Wolters later wrote:

> I discovered that I liked nothing better than hopping from one place to another...from *kampongs* of Patani immigrants to *kampongs* of Kelantan immigrants, to Chinese New Villages at different stages in their growth, to tin mines and rubber estates, and out into the mangrove swamps and pirate lairs. Each of these centers clung to its own sense of identity. At the same time, I came to realize how quickly—almost breathlessly—situations could change.[46]

This is romantic language for what was still a tense and fluid situation. In the tin-mining areas of Perak, life was tough for those resettled in New Villages.[47]

From about March 1955 until November 1956, Wolters was head of the Psychological Warfare Section, a position that involved supervising the translation of anti-communist propaganda. In this task he worked closely with C. C. Too, a Malayan Chinese who has been described as "the brains" behind the British strategies in psychological warfare against the communists.[48] Bilingual in Chinese and English, Too was a forceful personality who held grudges and did not always get along with his superiors. He had resigned from the Operations Section of Information Services in late November 1952 in a dispute with the Director-General of Information Services, A. D. C. Peterson.[49] Now, as head of the reorganized psychological warfare unit, Wolters induced Too to return to this important work. His understanding of communist psychology and skills in psychological warfare were second to none, and he ultimately succeeded Wolters as head of the unit in

---

[43] Milton E. Osborne, *Strategic Hamlets in Vietnam: A Survey and Comparison*, Data Paper no. 55 (Ithaca, NY: Cornell Southeast Asia Program Publications, 1965).

[44] Philip E. Catton, *Diem's Final Failure: Prelude to America's War in Vietnam* (Lawrence, KS: University Press of Kansas, 2002), chapter 4, "Origins of the Strategic Hamlet Program," especially p. 96.

[45] *New Straits Times*, June 25, 1999.

[46] *1989–90 Bulletin* (Ithaca, NY: Cornell Southeast Asia Program, Cornell University, 1990), p. 6.

[47] Loh, *Beyond the Tin Mines*, chapter 4.

[48] Kumar Ramakrishna, "The Making of a Malayan Propagandist: the Communists, the British, and C. C. Too," *JMBRAS* 73,1 (2000): 69.

[49] Ramakrishna, "The Making," pp. 79–80.

1956.[50] With the assistance of translators such as Too, Chinese-language works such as *The Danger and Where it Lies* were issued by the Federation of Malaya's Information Services in September 1957 as part of the propaganda war. Another program of the psychological warfare unit, for which Wolters was commended by the high commissioner upon his retirement, involved the preparation of propaganda to be broadcast from airplanes equipped with loudspeakers—so-called Voice Aircraft. The technique had been found effective by the Americans during the Korean War, and Templer, the Director of Operations, immediately saw its value for the conditions faced by the British in Malaya.[51]

In 1955 Wolters married Euteen Khoo, whom he had first met in the late 1940s, when he visited the home of her maternal grandparents in connection with his official duties. Euteen belonged to the class of affluent Chinese at the apex of the socio-economic pyramid who socialized with the British administrators. Her father, Khoo Wee Tat, had business interests in rubber estates and tin mines; her father's brother was a banker. On her mother's side, Euteen was related to Loke Yew, who, in the late nineteenth century, was one of half a dozen Chinese leaders whom the British regarded as their social equals.[52] She had received an English medium education at a Church of England school in Kuala Lumpur and, in 1949, went to England, where she spent five years at Westhill College, which was later to be absorbed into the University of Birmingham, and studied to be a Froebel teacher. She met Wolters again there when he drove up to her Birmingham school in his Riley, a smart car in those days. Shortly after she returned to Malaya, they married in Malacca, where Euteen was working as Inspector of Schools. Their elder child, Pamela, was born in England in 1958, and the younger, Nigel, was born in the United States after Wolters took up his appointment at Cornell in the mid-1960s.

In graduate school, gossiping about our teacher in an ill-informed way, we presumed that Euteen was able to help Wolters with his Chinese, but we should have surmised that, unless schooled, she would have been unable to read Chinese from the Sui-Tang, Song, and Yuan dynastic histories that he was using in his research. While she spoke some Chinese at home, English was her mother tongue.[53]

In chapter five of a novel about Malaya in 1952–53, Han Suyin describes a dinner party given by Quo Boon, "the banker, the rubber king, the millionaire, the company director, one of the men whose life, dedicated to create wealth, had created Malaya."[54] Quo Boon is fictional, yet his portrait represents one sort of Chinese businessman who joined clubs, entertained in the Western style, gambled at the track, and played tennis with British officers. From the first days of the Chinese Protectorate, the British ruled through the affluent Chinese business community. If they did not speak English themselves, these prosperous Chinese spoke to guests in Malay and employed an English-speaking secretary to make social arrangements. Some of the "Chinese Members" of the Kuala Lumpur Golf Club took an early

---

[50] Ibid., pp. 83, 86; Ramakrishna, *Emergency Propaganda*, pp. 187–88.

[51] Ramakrishna, *Emergency Propaganda*, pp. 158–59, 188–89.

[52] John G. Butcher, *The British in Malaya, 1880-1941: The Social History of a European Community in Colonial South-East Asia* (Kuala Lumpur: Oxford University Press, 1979), p. 67.

[53] In fact, Wolters consulted Harold Shadick, professor of Chinese at Cornell University, about language matters. See *Remembering Harold and Lydia Shadick* (Ithaca, NY: East Asia Program, Cornell University, 1994), p. 10.

[54] Han Suyin, *...And the Rain My Drink*, p. 73.

interest in horse racing and entertained in a European style that relaxed their British guests, who could remark, "the cooking, the wines and the service were always perfect."[55]

The socializing between British and Chinese involved business as much as recreation, as these functions provided opportunities for rulers and ruled to mix informally and smooth relationships, as at Quo Boon's dinner, where Chinese *towkays* sit down with the police from whom they need to obtain licenses, permits, and police protection. In order to track the activities of the Malayan communist party, the British relied on this rapport with Chinese business leaders, from whom it was difficult to hide the communist party's activities.[56]

By the middle of the twentieth century, the daughters of some of these Chinese merchants had married British officers. Admittedly, the number of upper-class Chinese women married to British men was small, and for some of those women, such as Euteen, there were adverse consequences. Relaxed relations between Chinese and British depended on class and context. Chinese families could be hostile to marriages between their daughters and British men, and the British clubs continued to enforce exclusionary membership policies, which hardened racial attitudes. A Chinese physician, called to attend an emergency at the Penang Club in 1954, appeared at the front entrance only to be told to enter the building through the kitchen.[57] In Euteen's case, there were sufficient numbers of Chinese women married to British men to form a cohort, and it was in this cohort that she socialized.[58] The academic studies and fiction of the period are consumed with the Emergency—its military urgency, its undercurrent of violence, the displacement of hundreds of thousands of rural squatters—and the history of social relations during the last years of British rule in Malaya are insufficiently studied.[59]

Although the Emergency was a violent time, there were few actual MCS fatalities during the period.[60] Communist violence was focused on the rubber plantations, and in the last months of 1951, forty-nine European planters were killed. These harsher aspects of the Emergency Wolters left to others to document. He sometimes traveled at great personal risk, and he would have known about the tough measures employed by the army and police in "a world turned upside down."[61] In his memoir, Wolters downplayed the physical dangers, discounting what was happening to him as of "passing importance" and saying that his most serious injury was knocking his head on the car's gear lever as he jumped into a ditch during an ambush.

---

[55] Butcher, *The British in Malaya*, p. 68.

[56] Heussler, *British Rule in Malaya*, p. 166.

[57] Interview with Patricia Lim, May 30, 2004, Singapore. For a "period" view on clubs, see Leslie H. Palmier, "Changing Outposts: The Western Communities in Southeast Asia," *Yale Review*, 47 (March 1958), especially pp. 410–11.

[58] Interview with Euteen Wolters, November 3–4, 2004, Ithaca, NY.

[59] This can be said notwithstanding Margaret Shennan's book, *Out in the Midday Sun: The British in Malaya, 1880–1960* (London: John Murray, 2000). There is nothing for the period comparable to Butcher's social history, *The British in Malaya, 1880–1941*.

[60] Three MCS officers and the wife of a fourth were killed during the Emergency. See Robert Heussler, *Completing a Stewardship: The Malayan Civil Service, 1942–1957*, Contributions in Comparative Colonial Studies, no. 15 (Westport, CT, and London: Greenwood Press, 1983), p. 185, n. 65.

LONDON AND ITHACA, 1957–2000

When the time came for Wolters and Euteen to leave Malaya, he was already preparing himself for university research and teaching. From the end of the Japanese Occupation, he had contemplated an academic career as a sinologist, telling his parents in his first letter home after the war ended that he hoped to study late Ch'ing Chinese history at Oxford. During his internment, the nineteenth-century reformist Liang Ch'i-ch'ao had been his "faithful friend."[62] There were no lectureships at the time in Chinese history, however, so friends at the University of London advised him about opportunities in Southeast Asian history. By late 1956, even before he left Malaya, he confided slyly to a correspondent that he had a "sporting chance" of an appointment as a lecturer at the School of Oriental and African Studies (SOAS).[63] D. G. E. Hall, head of the SOAS Department of South East Asia and the Islands from 1949 to 1959, was building a new generation of academic specialists in Southeast Asia across the disciplines, and history would be one of the strengths at SOAS.[64]

Having concentrated on colonial and mercantile history as well as Anglo–Burmese relations in his early work, Hall's histories at first had a distinctly Anglo–centric orientation, though he later became a champion of a Southeast Asian–centered perspective.[65] By contrast, Wolters from the outset decided to confine himself to the earlier history before European contact. It was ancient, not modern, Southeast Asia that he chose to study exclusively.[66] He would strictly heed D. G. E. Hall's dictum that the history of Southeast Asian peoples had been overwhelmed, "thrust into the background," by the wealth of writings on European activities in the region.[67] He also agreed with the sentiment, which Hall would later endorse, that authors of works on Southeast Asia tended to treat the first fifteen centuries "as only a preamble to the five succeeding ones."[68] To redress this imbalance Wolters directed his first research efforts on the early commercial history of Śrīvijaya in the fourth and fifth centuries CE.

He was entering the field at a formative moment. In 1948, George Coedès had written a synthesis of early Southeast Asian history in French, and D. G. E. Hall had in 1955 published the first of many editions of his own history of the region.[69] To prepare himself for his research, Wolters, accompanied by Euteen, took a grand tour

---

[61] The phrase is Harper's in *The End of Empire*; see pp. 153-64.

[62] Letter from Wolters to his parents and relatives, September 8, 1945.

[63] National Library of Australia, Papers of Gordon Luce, MS 6574, letter from Wolters to Luce, December 5, 1956.

[64] Vladimir Braginsky, comp. and introd., *Classical Civilizations in South East Asia: An Anthology of Articles Published in the Bulletin of SOAS* (London, New York: Routledge Curzon, 2002), pp. 16–17.

[65] C. D. Cowan, "D. G. E. Hall: A Biographical Sketch," in *Southeast Asian History and Historiography: Essays Presented to D. G. E. Hall*, ed. C. D. Cowan and O. W. Wolters (Ithaca, NY, and London: Cornell University Press, 1976), pp. 16–17.

[66] Benedict Anderson, *The Spectre of Comparisons: Nationalism, Southeast Asia, and the World* (London and New York: Verso, 1998), p. 13, n. 24.

[67] D. G. E. Hall, "Looking at Southeast Asian History," *JAS* 19,3 (1960): 243.

[68] D. G. E. Hall, "Recent Tendencies in the Study of the Early History of South-East Asia," *Pacific Affairs* 39, 3–4 (Fall and Winter, 1966–67): 347.

[69] G. Coedès, *Les états hindouisés d'Indochine et d'Indonésie* (Paris: E. de Boccard, 1948); D. G. E. Hall, *A History of South-East Asia* (London: Macmillan, 1955).

of the ancient sites of early Southeast Asia—the Borobudur in Java, Ayudhyā in Siam, Angkor in Cambodia, and Pagan in Burma—after leaving Malaya. The purpose of the visit, as he explained to Gordon Luce, whom he visited in Rangoon in late March and early April 1957, was "to acquire some personal feeling" for the Asian countries whose histories he would be studying.[70]

On his return to England, he and Euteen built a house in Reigate, Surrey, where he expected to settle down and stay. In 1958, a little over a year after he left the MCS, he published his first academic article on Tāmbralinga, an ancient place-name on the Malay Peninsula. He published two more studies in 1960, one of which brought him into contact with George Coedès, whom he visited for the first time in Paris in 1960.[71] Wolters received his doctorate from SOAS in 1962, but he was not to enjoy his rose garden in Surrey for very long. Cornell University was looking for a historian of Southeast Asia, and D. G. E. Hall, who had been lecturing there occasionally, recommended Wolters for the position. After a visit in 1962 to look over the university, Wolters and Euteen moved to Ithaca permanently in 1964.

About his many experiences during the Emergency, or even about Malaya more generally, Wolters said almost nothing publicly. An exception was a lecture he delivered in England after he left Malaya concerning rural resettlement during the Emergency, the subject he had written about in *Community Development Bulletin*. In private conversation, his recollections were just as scarce. This reticence in discussion about the Emergency was not unusual for MCS officers. Even high officials were inclined to keep their memories to themselves. One Secretary of Defense, Watherston, "refused to say or write anything at all, and his successor as Secretary for Defense, Hugh Humphrey, gave one lecture at Oxford and thereafter kept silent."[72] This professional reticence eventually gave way to wounded pride when many MCS officers took offence at a critical analysis of the Service and stepped forward to defend their stewardship.[73]

Later, when Wolters was teaching at Cornell University, in Ithaca, New York, decolonization was still underway in Indochina, West Irian, Brunei, and Timor. Wolters's experience in Malaya seemed particularly relevant at a time when the Americans were seeking to contain and defeat communism in Asia. In August 1964, the American congress passed the Tonkin Gulf Resolution, legislation that led to air strikes against northern Vietnam and the build-up of American troops in the south. In response to the mobilization of troops, the anti-war movement swiftly gathered momentum, and within a year university teach-ins against the war became a feature of American campuses. Prominent among the speakers at Cornell were faculty members of the Southeast Asia Program such as George Kahin and Benedict Anderson, who were fierce critics of the American war. What was at stake in these campus discussions and in the more informed media was the very nature of the conflict. Was it a manifestation of Vietnamese nationalism, the final stage of a

---

[70] National Library of Australia, Papers of Gordon Luce, MS 6574, letter from Wolters to Luce, December 5, 1956.

[71] National Library of Australia, The Coedès Collection, MS 2986, letters from Wolters to Coedès, July 18, 1960, and October 3, 1960.

[72] Gullick, personal communication, August 8, 2005.

[73] Allen, "Malayan Civil Service." With the cooperation of surviving MCS officers who filled out questionnaires and otherwise shared their experiences, Heussler's two histories of 1983 and 1985 were written largely to counter Allen's essay.

lengthy struggle that had begun early in the twentieth century for the unification of the country? Or was the conflict instigated by northern insurgents interfering in the sovereignty of an autonomous nation-state, as the American government and the Republic of Vietnam's elites portrayed the southern part of the country? The American and southern Vietnamese efforts to win the "the hearts and minds" of the rural population were often compared to the British campaign in Malaya.[74] Indeed, invention of the phrase "hearts and minds" had often been attributed to Sir Gerald Templer, the Director of Operations and High Commissioner in Malaya from 1952 to 1954.

On numerous occasions during the Second Indochina War, Wolters was invited to speak about his time in Malaya at the midday Thursday gathering of Cornell University faculty and graduate students. The graduate students who organized the program were always on the look-out for speakers to fill the bill, and Wolters was a particularly intriguing prospect. Here was someone who had actually been involved in the Malayan Emergency, which was being compared to the American-led war in Vietnam. Although there was no public record of his appointments in the MCS, idle rumor hinted that he had done this or that, including a story that he had been involved in psychological warfare against the Malayan Communist Party. Wolters repeatedly declined these invitations by suggesting other, "more interesting" speakers. His charming, firm deflections of these invitations only made his graduate students more curious to learn what he had done in Malaya. As it happened, while he declined to talk publicly about the final tremors of decolonization he had lived through, the debate in America over the Second Indochina War helped to "nudge" him toward serious study of Vietnam's earlier history.[75]

In retrospect, it seems foolish to have expected Wolters in these tumultuous times to stand up in public, even the limited public of a Cornell seminar, and talk about the last stage of British colonialism in Malaya. The American military intervention in Vietnam had aroused passionate feelings about neo-imperialism and interference in the nationalist movement of a Southeast Asian nation. At the same time, the US civil rights movement was politicizing American campuses. In April 1969, students at Cornell belonging to the Afro-American Society (AAS) occupied Willard Straight Hall, a student center of the university. Initially unarmed, some of those students subsequently took up arms in response to threats, which led other groups and individuals to arm themselves. A Cornell judicial board had issued sanctions against five AAS students for disruptive demonstrations the previous December, and the immediate objective of the occupation of the student center was to get the sanctions nullified. But there were larger issues as well, such as what the AAS deemed to be the university administration's inadequate progress toward establishing an independent Black Studies program. The faculty became deeply divided over how to handle the use of force by student militants, with several professors from the departments of government and history submitting their resignations to protest the university's acquiescence to the students' demands.

In solidarity with those faculty members who disagreed with the university's position, George Kahin, who had been a member of the Southeast Asia Program from the early 1950s and who had steadfastly opposed American involvement in Vietnam, gave a stirring speech on April 15, 1969, defending academic freedom as a

---

[74] Stubbs, *Hearts and Minds*, p. 3.

[75] Wolters, *Some Memories*, pp. 21–22.

supreme value of the American university, to an assembly of seven thousand students and teachers.[76] Wolters was extremely disturbed by these events, especially by the threat to academic freedom resulting from the university's capitulation to student demands, and he wrote to C. D. Cowan in London asking about the possibility of a position at the University of London or somewhere else. He seriously considered leaving Cornell.[77]

It is thus unsurprising that Wolters hardly ever broke his silence on his time in Malaya. Even when approached by scholars to be a witness to his times, he was only slightly more forthcoming. The authors of standard works on Malaya occasionally acknowledge his correspondence, but he was not as active a contributor to the MCS archive as many of his peers.[78] Perhaps he was just being discreet, or perhaps he felt that writing the history of the MCS was too much about the British, and his focus was now elsewhere. On one occasion, Wolters said as much as he would ever say about his time in Malaya. When he received the Distinguished Scholarship Award from the Association for Asian Studies in 1990, he made it clear that he recognized very well his vulnerability as a former member of the MCS. To an audience of academic colleagues, he spoke with unaccustomed candor:

> From 1937 to 1957 I was a member of the Malayan Civil Service. Yes, indeed, I was a "colonial imperialist" and, perhaps in that respect, an unusual recipient of the award. Unlike you during the corresponding two decades in your own lives, I would occasionally scribble minutes on government files but hardly ever read a book except when I was a prisoner for three and a half years. More often than not, I was out and about. That was the time known to historians as "the Emergency" in Malaya, but for me it was a time of unbridled adventure and among the happiest years of my life. Perhaps the reason was simply that I was still young.[79]

Wolters's use of quotation marks around "colonial imperialist" spoke volumes. Others might call him one, but he was not. The statement also hints strongly at the anti-colonial bias he observed among members of the American academy, though it is impossible to be more precise about his views. He was always reserved about the political opinions of others.

There is also candor here about a matter that had affected his professional standing. Wolters began his academic career late in life. He took up his permanent appointment at Cornell University when he was nearly fifty years of age. He arrived in 1964 with the generous and forceful patronage of D. G. E. Hall but without academic networks in America. While his contemporaries were rising through the academic ranks, Wolters had been "out and about" in the *kampongs*, the New Villages, the rubber estates, and the mangrove swamps. When he left the MCS in

---

[76] For a detailed account of the Straight takeover and the political struggles at Cornell that followed, see Donald Alexander Downs, *Cornell '69: Liberalism and the Crisis of the American University* (Ithaca, NY, and London: Cornell University Press, 1999). Kahin's role in the incident is discussed on pp. 272ff. His speech defending academic freedom is reprinted in *Divided We Stand: Reflections on the Crisis at Cornell*, ed. Cushing Strout and David I. Grossvogel (Garden City, NY: Doubleday & Company, Anchor Books, 1971), pp. 30–36.

[77] Interviews with Euteen Wolters, November 2–3, 2005, Ithaca.

[78] See, for example, Short, *Communist Insurrection*, and Heussler, *British Rule in Malaya*.

[79] *1989–90 Bulletin*, p. 6.

1957, he was fifteen or twenty years behind contemporaries who had been "reared from the cradle to be university teachers," whereas he was "a bumped-up outsider."[80] The sense that he had to work hard to catch up to his contemporaries contributed to his intellectual restlessness and willingness to venture into the thickets of highly theoretical and rarified literary criticism at a stage in life when many scholars begin to slow down. For this reason, as much as because of temperament, his work ethic was legendary.

In February 1998, two years before he died, he went on record again about Malaya, this time to praise Sir Gerald Templer, High Commissioner and Director of Operations in Malaya from 1952 to 1954. Templer has been the subject of a lively historiographical controversy, which began shortly after he left Malaya and Victor Purcell launched a series of criticisms against him. Up to this time, Templer had been lauded as a great leader instrumental in shaping an effective response to the MCP, but now critics asked whether, in his efforts to bring the insurgency under control, the Director of Operations had created a police state. At stake for Purcell and other critics was not only whether Templer's methods had helped win or lose the war against the communist insurgency but also whether his policies had stifled the emergence of national Malayan leadership.[81] Also under scrutiny were Templer's manner and style of leadership. He could be autocratic, his language was violent, and he levied punishment collectively on villages deemed to be harboring insurgents. Wolters met Templer for the first time when he was District Officer in Tapah, where Templer's "reputation for ruthlessness had preceded him." The commanding officer of the regiment there had encountered Templer during the war, when he was known as "Satan"; the officer in Tapah "expected to be fired as soon as Templer identified his presence."[82] Templer's reputation as a pivotal leader has continued to be challenged in recent years, as scholars have asked whether he really made that much of a difference, and at what cost.[83] A later episode in the controversy occurred toward the end of Wolters's life. In one of the rare occasions when he produced something publicly quotable on the subject of Malaya, he declared that he had "never met a more effective and admirable leader than Templer."[84] Did the qualities he first saw in Templer prefigure the charismatic authority he later identified in early Southeast Asian leadership, or does such a suggestion extract too much significance from the morsels of personal information he left behind?[85] In his

---

[80] Wolters, *Some Memories*, p. 18. He confided to the historian Tony Reid his sense of being disadvantaged in beginning his academic career so late in life; Tony Reid, personal communication, May 31, 2004.

[81] See Short, *Communist Insurrection*, pp. 379–87, for an assessment of Purcell's views.

[82] Wolters, *Some Memories*, pp. 10–11.

[83] Karl Hack, "'Iron Claws on Malaya': The Historiography of the Malayan Emergency," *JSEAS* 30,1 (March 1999): 99-125; Ramakrishna, "'Transmogrifying' Malaya"; Simon C. Smith, "General Templer and Counter-Insurgency in Malaya: Hearts and Minds, Intelligence, and Propaganda," *Intelligence and National Security* 16,3 (Autumn 2001): 60–78. For an uncritical assessment of Templer, see Shennan, *Out in the Midday Sun*, chapter 16.

[84] As quoted in Ramakrishna, *Emergency Propaganda*, p. 124; and Ramakrishna, "'Transmogrifying' Malaya," p. 85. Benedict Anderson, in *The Spectre of Comparisons: Nationalism, Southeast Asia, and the World* (London and New York: Verso, 1998), p. 13 n. 24, chides Wolters for his admiration of Templer. Wolters later excused Anderson "for his incomprehension"; *Some Memories*, p. 7.

[85] O'Connor, "Oliver W. Wolters," p. 3.

historical writing, Wolters often discussed personal achievement. He had witnessed it firsthand.

PART 2: EARLY SOUTHEAST ASIAN HISTORY

When Wolters decided to train himself as a historian of Southeast Asia before the coming of Europeans, he put to one side the urgent concerns of Malaya in the 1940s and 1950s. One moment he was an MCS officer with specialized Chinese-language skills "out and about" in the *kampongs*, the rubber estates, and the pirate lairs; the next, he was in the library reading the Tang and Ming dynastic histories. Accident and circumstance drew him away from earlier plans to study reform movements in late nineteenth-century China. But he was still a sinologist, and he would now use his knowledge of Chinese to study Southeast Asia.

The essays reprinted in this volume are grouped by geographic area, with attention to the date of original publication. They have been selected to illustrate Wolters's interest in different parts of the region and the development of his historical thinking. The first group concerns Southeast Asia as a culture, region, and field of study. The second covers early Indonesian commerce and the ancient maritime kingdom of Śrīvijaya, Wolters's first research project and one of his abiding interests throughout his academic career. The last-dated publication on Śrīvijaya appeared in 1996, nearly fifty years after he first began studying it. The third group contains a selection of his studies on mainland history, mostly early Khmer history, and is prefaced by an early study of leadership in late sixteenth-century Siam that was the genesis of his *maṇḍala* model of ancient Southeast Asian statecraft. The last group contains a sample of his work on premodern Vietnamese history—the entirety of which could easily fill a volume of its own. By the end of his career, he had completed thirteen studies of Vietnam, and he was working on a historical novel about Trần Vietnam at the time of his death.

The topics and methodologies that thread their way through the essays range over many parts of Southeast Asia. Wolters's ideas about leadership and royal power, the respectability of public service, and the significance of kin relations and religion recur again and again. My discussion, which follows the headings under which the essays are grouped, highlights intellectual preoccupations and habits of mind that gave shape to a particular historical sensibility. A final section addresses historical methodology as well as strategies for reading that Wolters developed in his studies of fourteenth-century Vietnam.

SOUTHEAST ASIA AS A REGION

Wolters determinedly wrote about many parts of early Southeast Asia, as witnessed by the selection of essays in the following pages. As previously noted, an early mentor who had set an example for a regional perspective was D. G. E. Hall, his PhD supervisor, whose monumental *History of Southeast Asia* went through four editions, the first in 1955 and the last in 1981. Wolters also had an abiding respect for the foundational work of George Coedès, who brought together the early histories of the region in *Les états hindouisés d'Indochine et d'Indonésie*, first published in 1944.[86] Wolters himself had little interest in synthesizing the early history. The closest he came to synthesis—a term he did not care for, possibly because it sounded like dull scholarship—was in his book, *History, Culture, and Region in Southeast Asian Perspectives*, first published in 1982.[87] The merit of this book is not to be found so much in its coverage of the region, generous though that is, but in the questions it poses and the case it makes, almost casually, for deep continuities between the ancient Southeast Asian past and the world of today.

In the era of the sound bite and the keyword, what propels academic knowledge are turns of phrases and snappy concepts, what Robert Cribb has called "euphoric couplets," that catch the imagination and lodge themselves in the mind to embody the spirit of an age or a historical process.[88] Wolters contributed his share of academic "sound bites" to Southeast Asian studies, and not just for the early period. He was associated with the terms *maṇḍala*, "man of prowess," and "localization," although he would be the last to claim that he had a special purchase on their use. *Maṇḍala* has an anthropological pedigree that can be traced back to the segmentary state in the study of African and Indian social systems. Wolters also would not have claimed a monopoly on the term "localization," which stands in dialectical relationship to "globalization" and is to be found in cultural studies, critical theory, and just about every other humanities and social science field. Under the themes of autonomous history and agency, localization has long been a feature of studies of cultural borrowing in Southeast Asia.[89] The concept expressed by the phrase "man of prowess," adapted from "the big man" and the notion of "soul stuff" in anthropological writing on Eastern Indonesia and the Pacific, derived from conversations Wolters had with Cornell anthropologists such as James Boon and Tom Kirsch, who happened to be around as he was considering these matters.[90] There is something improvised about Wolters's methods here. He freely acknowledged that he was a practicing *bricoleur*, throwing together things that seemed to work in the manner of "a restless experimentalist" and not fretting if he had not read every last word on the subject.[91]

What these concepts have in common is that Wolters used them to inquire into what he called "the cultural features" of early Southeast Asia, a concept explained in "Southeast Asia as a Southeast Asian Field of Study" and in "Early Southeast Asian Political Systems," the excerpt from *History, Culture, and Region* reproduced here. The cultural features comprise the "widespread cultural traits" that together make up a "cultural matrix." No society had all of these traits, but taken together they

---

[86] The book became available to English readers as George Coedès, *The Indianized States of Southeast Asia*, ed. Walter F. Vella, trans. Susan Brown Cowing (Honolulu, HI: East–West Center Press, 1968).

[87] O. W. Wolters, *History, Culture, and Region in Southeast Asian Perspectives*, rev. ed. (Ithaca, NY: Cornell Southeast Asia Program Publications, in cooperation with the Institute of Southeast Asian Studies, Singapore, 1999).

[88] For a recent assessment of the production of knowledge in Indonesian studies by this means, see Robert Cribb, "Circles of Esteem, Standard Words, and Euphoric Couplets: Dynamics of Academic Life in Indonesian Studies," *Critical Asian Studies* 37,2 (2005): 289–304.

[89] See Craig J. Reynolds, *Seditious Histories: Contesting Thai and Southeast Asian Pasts* (Seattle, WA: University of Washington Press, 2006), pp. 17–23.

[90] Wolters, *History, Culture, and Region*, pp. 18–19.

[91] Correspondence with John D. Legge, June 27, 1989.

constituted the matrix. One of the most important of the cultural features was cognatic kinship, which included bilateral kinship. Another feature, related to cognatic kinship, was the downgrading of lineage in claims to status, a factor that paved the way for personal initiative and achievement and thus accounted for the rise to power of local chiefs, provincial lords, and, above all, monarchs. To oversimplify, family inheritance had not that much to do with why a particular individual rose to power. Rather, the successful leader accumulated followers, Wolters suggested, by demonstrating evidence of "soul stuff" and by rewarding loyalty. By identifying and articulating these cultural features, Wolters sought to endow a measure of coherence to the region of Southeast Asia up to about the fourteenth century. His model of a cultural matrix that could absorb foreign elements and rearticulate them with local material was an implicit attack on the notion— common in the literature on Southeast Asia—that these societies were composed from "layers" of foreign influence deposited over centuries. Wolters did not suggest the region was bounded—that would be an absurd notion for the premodern period—but it was set apart, imperceptibly, from other regions by the cultural matrix. In such an analysis, early Southeast Asian history was fundamental in accounting for what makes the region distinctive.[92]

These formulations about the "cultural matrix" and Southeast Asia as a "culture area," first published in 1982, were informed by his earlier research on the archipelago. What led Wolters naturally to consider Southeast Asia as a comprehensible entity was his reading of the Chinese dynastic histories, where information had been recorded from tribute missions sent by rulers of Southeast Asian port polities and kingdoms both small and large. The Chinese sources were a window through which he could see Malay, Burmese, Siamese, Khmer, Vietnamese, and Lao polities, enabling him to configure Southeast Asia as a distinct culture area.

In "China Irredenta: The South," published in 1963, the year after he finished his dissertation, Wolters made a series of simple observations. Here, in what might be termed the theoretical background for his work on early Indonesian commerce, Wolters asserted that the Chinese had come to understand the "southern ocean" of Southeast Asia as formed by "a single stretch of ocean, united by a single system of communications," a vast, watery internet. Rulers of Southeast Asian states, including the smallest harbor kingdoms, entered the Chinese record because they sent tribute missions to the Chinese court requesting investiture by the emperor. For the Chinese court, the appearance of the missions, as if attracted by the magnet of the Mandate of Heaven, confirmed the belief that the emperor ruled through his superior *virtus* (*tê*), by means of which harmony among human beings was achieved.

The Chinese viewed the peoples of Southeast Asia as primitive, and their states as weak, politically immature, and inherently unstable. As the history of the Sui dynasty (581–618) expressed it, "They have no chiefs...They love to fight among themselves. Therefore they are weak countries and from time to time acknowledge the supremacy of China." Given this view, it appears the Chinese valued Southeast Asia not for its own sake, but as a pathway to the West, where rare and precious things were to be found. Only by maintaining a series of reliable maritime exchanges

---

[92] For a critique of Wolters's notion of Southeast Asia as a culture area from an anthropologist, who argues that cultural areas have fallen into abeyance, see Grant Evans, "Between the Global and the Local there are Regions, Culture Areas, and National States: A Review Article," *JSEAS* 33,1 (2002): 147–62.

could the Middle Kingdom reach the Mediterranean and the Roman Orient. When a new Chinese dynasty established itself, envoys would be dispatched to reestablish relations with the "immature" Southeast Asian port polities, and thereby bring peace to the southern ocean. Since China had no naval power until Song times (960–1279 CE), the Chinese emperor had to rely on methods of indirect control to keep the squabbling maritime Southeast Asian kingdoms from interfering in the trans-Asian trade.

"China Irredenta: The South" has another value for students of China–Southeast Asian relations. Wolters wrote it at a time when China was showing a strategic interest in lands to its west, particularly Africa, where the People's Republic of China had been lending support to African insurrections since the communist triumph in 1949. He argued that the Chinese view of fledging African nations was imbued with the very same impulse that had motivated the dispatch of huge ocean-going vessels captained by Zheng He during Ming times, or of the Tang envoys sent out to establish communications with lands to the west—namely, that the local peoples would benefit from "the transforming power" of Chinese concern.[93] It was by means of these early contacts that African exotica—the "auspicious deer" (zebra) and giraffe—had found their way into the Chinese imagination via Ming painting and textual sources. The redoubtable Zhou En-lai, Chinese Minister of Foreign Affairs, was himself aware of the People's Republic's historic mission inherited from the earlier centuries of Chinese maritime contact with the West. Both Sun Yat-sen and Chiang Kai-shek had understood the historic mission to be one of "re-establishing interrupted dynasties and reviving dismembered states." It is as if Wolters's vantage point was from "whatever might have served as a conference room in the Tang dynasty Foreign Office."[94] Indeed, the analysis in "China Irredenta" is more present-minded than almost any other piece Wolters wrote.

When Wolters began to contemplate his career in Southeast Asian history, Afro–Asian solidarity was very much in the news because of the Bandung conference in 1955, and he instinctively gave the modern Chinese imperial aspirations historical depth. In this analysis, Southeast Asia was contrived as a region by the watery internet made possible by Chinese commercial and strategic objectives farther afield. This particular delimiting of the region—for it is hardly a definition—predates the later formulations of *maṇḍala*, "soul stuff," and the cultural matrix for which Wolters is better known.[95]

THE LONG *DURÉE* OF MALAY HISTORY

Wolters spent the first decade of his academic life studying the origins of the Malay kingdom of Śrīvijaya, which dominated the commerce of maritime Southeast Asia from the seventh century until its collapse in the late fourteenth century.

---

[93] The classic study of China's proprietary interest in Africa, which accumulated over the ages and which in modern times has shifted priorities, so that China is now more concerned with commercial interests than with the earlier strategic ones, is Philip Snow, *The Star Raft: China's Encounter with Africa* (New York, NY: Weidenfeld & Nicholson, 1988).

[94] O'Connor, "Oliver W. Wolters," p. 4.

[95] Evans, "Between the Global and the Local," for example, does not mention this earlier attempt to talk about Southeast Asia as a region defined by the maritime exchanges that took place.

Śrīvijaya's strategic position around Palembang on the southeastern coast of Sumatra gave it a stranglehold over the vast trade in exotic commodities between India and China through the Straits of Malacca. This early maritime empire was a sea power, a polity knit together by the tide where, as he once put it, no implement was more important than the paddle. Śrīvijaya's successors, including the European trading companies, inherited this strategic advantage and drew from it their fortunes in the international spice trade. Tomé Pires, the Portuguese apothecary and envoy who lived in Malacca from 1512 to 1515 after the European conquest, declared that "Whoever is lord of Malacca has his hand on the throat of Venice." Wolters was fond of quoting this memorable statement and gave it pride of place at the beginning of his first book, *Early Indonesian Commerce.*[96]

Wolters had been led to this research, the focus of his 1962 doctoral thesis, by an article written in 1918 by George Coedès, who identified the empire as Śrīvijaya and located it on Sumatra. Whenever he wrote on Śrīvijaya, Wolters always cited this article by Coedès, returning to it for insights and treating it as a foundation statement of the field. On the basis of Wolters's reputation as a scholar of all of Southeast Asia and the author of the book for which he is best known, *History, Culture, and Region*, it is tempting to think that his ability to envisage Southeast Asia as a geo-political unit, which deserved a scholarship of its own, was a cumulative achievement. In fact, it is evident from "China Irredenta: The South," as well as his early studies of toponyms such as Tāmbralinga on the Malay Peninsula and Chên-li-fu on the Gulf of Siam, that he had always thought of Southeast Asian in terms of international relations, trade between China and India, and cultural and commercial contacts between the mainland states and the archipelago.[97] It was a region of exchanges and networks. He brought this regional perspective to Cornell University in 1964, where it dovetailed with the Southeast Asia Program's own mission as a center devoted to studying the languages, cultures, histories, economies, and political systems of the entire region. Wolters's regional proclivities were particularly welcome to the Cornell program, because in the United States, Southeast Asian studies was always a younger and weaker sibling of the studies of Japan, China, and South Asia.

Wolters's first projects reconstructed the economic history of apparently insignificant harbor kingdoms, tiny port-polities that manifested a genius for seizing the opportunities they enjoyed because of their fortuitous location along the coasts of the southern ocean. His work followed closely in the wake of an important study of the historical geographer Paul Wheatley, whose *The Golden Khersonese* provided Wolters with a meticulously documented and reliable account of toponyms on the Malay Peninsula.[98] The vitality and enterprise shown by these port polities contrasted with the Chinese view of maritime Southeast Asian polities as politically immature, weak, and inherently unstable. Wolters's history of these tributary states of the Chinese emperor allowed them to "write back" against the imperious Chinese view that they were mere stepping stones on the way to richer lands farther to the west. The title of *Early Indonesian Commerce* emphasized the modern, twentieth-

---

[96] O. W. Wolters, *Early Indonesian Commerce: A Study of the Origins of Śrīvijaya* (Ithaca, NY, and London: Cornell University Press, 1967), p. 31.

[97] O. W. Wolters, "Tāmbralinga," *BSOAS* 21,3 (1958): 587–607; "Chên-li-fu, a State on the Gulf of Siam at the Beginning of the Thirteenth Century," *JSS* 48,2 (1960): 1–35.

[98] Paul Wheatley, *The Golden Khersonese: Studies in the Historical Geography of the Malay Peninsula before AD 1500* (Kuala Lumpur: University of Malaya Press, 1961).

century name for this part of the archipelago, but "Indonesia/Indonesian," however effective as a marketing tool for the volume, was anachronistic, to say the least, for the early centuries. There was no "Indonesia" in the sixth and seventh centuries, or in the nineteenth and first half of the twentieth, for that matter. In any case, by the end of the book the true heroes had appeared. The shippers who fed natural products of aromatic woods, resins, and camphor from the hinterland into the international trade that passed through the Straits of Malacca were Malays, not "Indonesians."[99]

In reconstructing the history of an early Malay maritime empire, Wolters went beyond the work of British colonial administrator-historians such as Graham, Linehan, Sheppard, Wilkinson, and Winstedt who had written biographies and dynastic and local histories of the peninsular Malay states. These pre-1950 historians had provided "the historiographical equivalent of the pro-Malay traditions of the MCS."[100] Wolters lengthened that historiography. When Euteen Wolters asked her husband why he did not study Malay history, he replied that there were no sources in Chinese.[101] But in fact, he was writing that history, pushing it deeper into the past and establishing a longer *durée* for the Malays even before they had populated the peninsula.

From the early twentieth century, the Malays had been known in the British colonial world as the "gentlemen of the East," a pro-Malay perspective that corrected an earlier bias against the Malays that regarded them as treacherous and piratical. Allen uses the term "Malayophilia" for this pro-Malay phenomenon and traces it to the time of Raffles.[102] While "Malayophilia" is an overstatement in Wolters's case, *Early Indonesian Commerce* can be read as an argument that control of the Straits of the Malacca by the Malays in ancient times was *not* piratical. Piracy occurred when the vassals of Śrīvijaya managed to evade the "well-established and efficient monopoly over which the rulers of Śrīvijaya presided," and by the fourteenth century Śrīvijaya found the monopoly harder and harder to maintain.[103]

Nor was the Malay social formation piratical in its later stages, as demonstrated in doctoral dissertations on the premodern period and early decades of European colonialism by Wolters's students. Studies by Barbara Andaya, Leonard Andaya, Tony Milner, and Carl Trocki enriched the legacy of the Malay maritime empire by tracing its fortunes and its political culture from the fall of Malacca in 1511 until the founding of Singapore in the early nineteenth century.[104] These were not centuries of decay but of enterprise, if not quite on the regional scale of the Śrīvijayan monopoly.

---

[99] Wolters, *Early Indonesian Commerce*, p. 222.

[100] W. David McIntyre, "Malaya from the 1850s to the 1870s, and Its Historians, 1950–1970: From Strategy to Sociology," in *Southeast Asian History and Historiography*, ed. Cowan and Wolters, p. 265, especially note 20, which lists the historical studies of the "scholar–administrators."

[101] Interviews with Euteen Wolters, November 1–2, 2005, Ithaca, NY.

[102] Allen, "Malayan Civil Service," p. 172.

[103] Wolters, *Early Indonesian Commerce*, p. 249.

[104] Barbara Watson Andaya, *Perak, the Abode of Grace: A Study of an Eighteenth-Century Malay State* (Kuala Lumpur: Oxford University Press, 1979); Leonard Andaya, *The Kingdom of Johor, 1641–1728* (Kuala Lumpur: Oxford University Press, 1975); A. C. Milner, *Kerajaan: Malay Political Culture on the Eve of Colonial Rule* (Tucson, AZ: University of Arizona Press for the Association for Asian Studies, 1982); Carl Trocki, *Prince of Pirates: The Temenggongs and the Development of Johor and Singapore, 1784–1885* (Singapore: Singapore University Press, 1979).

In Trocki's book, which carried the story well into the European period and analyzed the breakdown of the Malay political system under colonialism, piracy returned as a major theme.[105] Trocki used *perintah*, a Malay word that might have also described the ancient polity, to evoke the discontinuous domain—a ring of islands here, a bit of coastline there—over which the raja's authority held sway. Almost three centuries after the Portuguese conquest of Malacca, the eighteenth-century entrepôt of Riau was but the last in a succession of Malay sultanates that could trace their ancestry back to Śrīvijaya in the long afterglow of its hegemony. At the best of times, these Malay rulers were masters of political intelligence who could exploit changes in their environment in order to meet successive crises promptly and resourcefully, as Wolters would have put it.

Just as Wolters had vaulted over the colonial period and used epigraphy and Chinese records to document the pre-European political and economic dynamics, so his students used vernacular historical materials, supplemented wherever possible by Dutch and British records, to establish an indigenous history of the Malay world before Western imperialism changed that world forever. These multiple histories of the Malay social formation broadened and revised the work of the pre-1950 historians mentioned above.

Wolters had set the stage for these studies of the post-1511 Malay world in *The Fall of Śrīvijaya in Malay History*.[106] This sequel to *Early Indonesian Commerce* was greeted with a stinging review by Andries Teeuw, a Dutch scholar of Malay literature. Teeuw criticized Wolters for relying heavily in the second part of the book on the *Malay Annals* (*Sejarah Melayu*), faulting him for using a literary text as an historical source and finding the method "factual precariousness to the fullest" and "fundamentally wrong." By blurring the distinction between historical source and literary artifact, he had made "a sad mistake—and a dangerous one at that."[107] What is interesting about the criticism is that Wolters largely ignored it. He refined his method of studying motifs and patterns and made even more of their significance in his later work. He had ventured into Malay materials and written the book because he "needed to get out of a Chinese slot" and "wanted to become a 'Southeast Asian' historian."[108]

The fact that the historical records for Śrīvijaya, even for the later period, were few and ambiguous forced Wolters to venture into related fields such as archaeology, prehistory, and art history, as well as textual analysis. His friendship with Cornell's art historian of Southeast Asia, Stanley J. O'Connor, was professional

---

[105] Trocki, *Prince of Pirates*, pp. 26–29 and 56–57, defines piracy by distinguishing between trading activity under recognized chiefs as opposed to down-on-their-luck rajas and foreign adventurers. In a study of the same period, Jim Warren, not a student of Wolters's, took up the issue of piracy in his *The Sulu Zone, 1768–1898: The Dynamics of External Trade, Slavery, and Ethnicity in the Transformation of a Southeast Asian Maritime State* (Singapore: Singapore University Press, 1981). Sulu ships plied the maritime trade routes in pursuit of slaves for the Sulu Sultanate. Anne Lindsey Reber, "The Sulu World in the Eighteenth and Early Nineteenth Centuries: A Historiographical Problem in British Writings on Malay Piracy" (MA thesis, Cornell University, 1966), a study supervised by Wolters, addressed piracy as a problem in British historiography.

[106] O. W. Wolters, *The Fall of Śrīvijaya in Malay History* (Ithaca, NY: Cornell University Press, 1970).

[107] A. Teeuw, Review of *The Fall of Śrīvijaya in Malay History*, *JAS* 32,1 (November 1972): 208.

[108] Wolters, *Some Memories*, p. 20.

as well as personal. The Viṣṇu images that O'Connor analyzed in his doctoral thesis were discovered on one of the trans-pensinular trade routes that competed with Śrīvijaya. Along these routes, artistic styles and miniature models of religious shrines traveled with the trading winds as swiftly as Roman oil lamps, Chinese porcelain, glass beads from the Middle East, or Indic scripts. Nowhere were material remains of the past more crucial in solving problems than in efforts to locate the "capital" of Śrīvijaya on Sumatra. The inconclusiveness of the search for material remains led to such adjectives as "fragile," "elusive," "shadowy," and "evanescent" to describe Śrīvijaya. In a particularly dismissive comment that seemed directed at Wolters, Bennet Bronson, wondering about the discrepancy between archaeological and documentary evidence, declared that one possibility was "to conclude that the ancient sources are misleading and that their recent interpreters have been building castles in air."[109] Contrary to what Bronson had said, for Wolters the physical environment itself was "the master-text of Śrīvijayan studies," and he took archaeological evidence seriously enough to persist in locating a probable site for Śrīvijaya when others failed to find it.

Chapters 4 and 5 illustrate Wolters's historical methods for studying Śrīvijaya. In these essays, he returned to familiar source material and discussed new discoveries. These are self-clarifying statements in which the historian is willing to revise his views, admit error, and rethink what needed to be taken into account to identify the location of Śrīvijaya. The article "Studying Śrīvijaya" reviewed the evidence as of March 1979 following an Indonesian and American excavation in 1974 and a visit in 1978 by Wolters himself to Palembang, where he had long thought the Śrīvijayan ruler had resided. Consultative workshops and field surveys organized in Southeast Asia, the results of which were published by E. E. McKinnon, confirmed what Wolters had outlined: traces of a riverine, trade-oriented harbor city with a settlement pattern distinctive to the locality.[110] "Studying Śrīvijaya" puts forward a semiological method for positing the location of the capital, a method that Wolters used to refute the negative findings of the Indonesian–American expedition of 1974. "Restudying Some Chinese Writings on Sriwijaya" (1986) reports new evidence for the empire's location on the basis of observations he made in July 1984. After revisiting the accounts of the seventh-century pilgrim I-ching and other Chinese sources, Wolters concluded that the Śrīvijayan entrepôt was located at Bukit Seguntang on the lower reaches of the Musi River. Wolters's work on Śrīvijaya, which presented it as a kind of paradigmatic harbor polity with a distinctive trade-generated settlement pattern, provided a longer pedigree, *mutatis mutandis*, for the harbor polities of Islamic, insular Southeast Asia in more modern times.[111]

---

[109] Bennet Bronson, "The Archaeology of Sumatra and the Problem of Śrīvijaya," in *Early South East Asia: Essays in Archaeology, History, and Historical Geography*, ed. R. B. Smith and W. Watson (New York and Kuala Lumpur: Oxford University Press, 1979), p. 403.

[110] On the material evidence and surrounding controversy, see the comprehensive summary by Pierre-Yves Manguin that has not been superseded: "Palembang and Sriwijaya: An Early Malay Harbour-City Rediscovered," *JMBRAS* 66,1 (1993): 23–46 and especially p. 24.

[111] Ibid., p. 34.

Mainland Maṇḍalas

Because of Wolters's two books on Śrīvijaya, the studies in historical geography that preceded them, and his follow-up essays on the location of Śrīvijaya's capital, many readers know him only as a historian of the archipelago. In fact, his research on the Malay maritime empire had already brought him to the mainland in his efforts to gauge the extent of the Śrīvijayan empire on the Malayan Peninsula. Later, in a little-known essay published in 1966 in Thailand's *Social Science Review*, he puzzled over how the early Mon center of Lavo (later, Lopburi), which had been a province of Cambodia in the early eleventh century, became the cosmopolitan center of Ayudhyā in old Siam.[112] In 1115 CE, and again in 1155, when dynastic strength at Angkor faltered, Lavo quickly asserted itself and sent tributary missions to the Chinese court instead of to Angkor. Further testimony to Lavo's importance was the appointment at the end of the twelfth century of a son of the powerful Cambodian King Jayavarman VII to rule over Lavo. Wolters attributed the success of Ayudhyā, located on the fringe of the Thai-speaking world, in part to its role as custodian of Lavo's Brahmanical and Buddhist traditions. This essay, described by Wolters as "unambitious," was influential in arguing that the first rulers of Ayudhyā pursued two distinct expansionist policies: one, rooted in Mon experience in the lower Menam basin, that perpetuated an ancient struggle with the Khmer empire over the lands between them; and the other, initiated by the Suphanburi line of the ruling family, which waged war in northern Siam.[113]

Chapter 6, "Ayudhyā and the Rearward Part of the World," is also little known, and is arguably his first essay concerned solely with the mainland. It is the locus of Wolters's first detailed statement on the *maṇḍala* system of interstate relations in Indic Southeast Asia, which he later popularized in *History, Culture, and Region*. The pretext for expounding on Southeast Asian statecraft was what seemed to be a quixotic comment in the Chinese sources. In the late sixteenth century, the expansionist Japanese Emperor Hideyoshi had been menacing Korea, the Ryu-kyu islands, and China. In response, in 1592 the Siamese King Naresuan, who himself saw the world in hostile terms, offered to send troops to attack Japan "in order to embarrass Japan's rear." Wolters seized on this enigmatic passage and, taking into account the *Arthaśāstra*, a treatise in ancient Indian political theory and a textbook of unscrupulous policies for cunning rulers, elaborated the idea of the *maṇḍala* system as the organization of all relevant space. Later, after the Opium War of 1839–1842, the Chinese remembered this gallant Siamese offer of 1592 and suggested that Siam and Vietnam could send troops to take Malacca and Singapore from British hands.

The term *maṇḍala* has a tangled pedigree in historical and anthropological scholarship, a pedigree that Wolters in this essay did not pursue beyond his immediate concerns. As with *negara* (state or realm; court; town), the etymology of *maṇḍala* endows it with a cultural "feel" that has helped it become a favored term for

---

[112] O. W. Wolters, "A Western Teacher and the History of Early Ayudhyā," *Sangkhomsat parithat chabap phiset 3 wa duai prawattisat thai tam thatsanakhati samai patjuban* [*Social Science Review, Special Issue no. 3: Contemporary Perspectives on Thai History*] (June 1966): 88–97.

[113] The argument about the dual expansionist polices was taken up in Charnvit Kasetsiri, *The Rise of Ayutthaya: A History of Siam in the Fourteenth and Fifteenth Centuries* (Kuala Lumpur: Oxford University Press, 1976), and thereby made its way into Thai-language historical studies.

describing the political field in premodern, Indic Southeast Asia.[114] With its roots in Sanskrit, where it means "centered, sacred space," *maṇḍala* has powerful iconic representations in Tibetan, Chinese, and Japanese Buddhist art. For Wolters, *maṇḍala* was not merely a model for understanding early kingdoms—or "state formation," a term he never used—but also a point of departure for discussing the distinctive outlook of Southeast Asian elites. This view of the world, which derived from a common fund of sacred Sanskrit texts (*śāstra*), had "universal and eternal relevance" to a Southeast Asian ruler's understanding of his place in the geopolitics in the known world both locally and afar. It was a perspective, inherited from earlier times when Brahmans and monks traveled along the trade routes on pilgrimages to and from India. It was also outward-looking and flexible.

Wolters wrote three essays on Cambodia, two of which are republished here. They concern political power, religion, and success on the battlefield in the seventh and eighth centuries, a period Wolters termed "protohistorical."[115] For source material he read French translations of Cambodian inscriptions as well as the Chinese records, with which he was familiar from his studies of early Malay commerce. "Jayavarman II's Military Power" traces the path by which Jayavarman II, the putative founder of the Cambodian royal base at Angkor on the northeast edge of the Tonle Sap, acquired the power and prestige that enabled him to be consecrated king on Mount Mahendra. This ceremony of 802 inaugurated the so-called *devarāja* cult that announced Cambodian autonomy from "Java" and established Khmer sovereignty forever after, but owing to the discrepancy between reputation and evidence, Jayavarman II has long been a controversial figure for students of early Southeast Asia. This "first" Cambodian king at Angkor left no inscriptions and no temples in stone to testify to his achievements, and he came from outside the established line of succession. The land grants, honors, and privileges to which his family and officials were entitled are detailed in the Sdok Kak Thom inscription of 1052, two and a half centuries after the Mount Mahendra ceremony. Because of the scarcity of evidence, Jayavarman's reputation as the founder of the Cambodian dynasty at Angkor has often been called into question. Hovering over Jayavarman II's reign is the nagging thought that his achievement as the founder of Khmer sovereignty might be a mid-eleventh-century invention.[116]

At the beginning of the essay, Wolters says rather disarmingly that he will discuss only one aspect of Jayavarman's reign—his military power—and, indeed, he follows the peripatetic king-to-be in his military campaigns for control over local chiefs. In fact, Jayavarman's marriages to seven women helped account for his political success as much as military conquest, and it is the means by which

---

[114] See, for example, Martin Stuart-Fox, "Political Patterns in Southeast Asia," in *Eastern Asia: An Introductory History*, ed. Colin Mackerras, 3rd edition (Frenchs Forest, NSW: Longman, 2000), chapter 8; and Reynolds, *Seditious Histories*, chapter 2, "Paradigms of the Premodern State."

[115] A third essay, "Northwestern Cambodia in the Seventh Century," published originally in 1974, was reprinted in Braginsky, *Classical Civilizations*, pp. 120–49.

[116] See Ian Mabbett and David Chandler, *The Khmers* (Oxford and Cambridge, MA: Blackwell, 1995), pp. 87–92; and Michael Vickery, *Society, Economics, and Politics in Pre-Angkor Cambodia: The Seventh–Eighth Centuries* (Tokyo: the Centre for East Asian Cultural Studies for Unesco, The Toyo Bunko, 1998), pp. 387–402, for an assessment of Jayavarman II's reputation and the historiographical problems involved in studying his reign, including the significance of independence from "Java" signaled by the Mount Mahendra ceremony.

Jayavarman acquired and rewarded his entourage that interested Wolters, rather than military power. Families who supported Jayavarman's cause also provided him with wives, thus extending his network of alliances. In the case of Dharanīndradevī, an influential wife, the union cemented a key alliance and produced Jayavarman's heir. The purpose of the essay was to argue that the ceremony on Mount Mahendra, however important in symbolizing Khmer kingship for future rulers in the centuries to come, capped a period of intense military and political activity that gave substance to the boons listed in the Sdok Kak Thom inscription.

In "Khmer 'Hinduism' in the Seventh Century," Wolters pursued the relationship between entourage and leadership in a slightly different way. In the Khmer world of these early centuries, overlordship never endured for long. "Kingdom" meant no more than the territory over which the ruler held sway at any given moment. Its extent fluctuated from reign to reign, and even within each reign. Coalitions of chiefs endowed the "king" with extraordinary qualities that Wolters called "prowess," personal attributes that were earned by the individual and could not be passed from one generation to the next. Thus dynastic succession, an issue he pursued in the essays on Vietnam, counted for very little. The king's special qualities were recognized in his practice of Śivaite devotionalism, which involved *linga* worship, austerities (*tapas*), and other ascetic practices. Early Cambodian rulers rose above their chieftain peers by seeing themselves inside the Hindu world rather than in its extension overseas. Their capacity to do this stemmed from relevant pre-Hindu beliefs, including the procreative powers of stone with which the *liṅga*s were endowed, as well as religious meanings attached to gifts. The "man of prowess"— "king," ruler, or, in this essay, "hegemon"—attracted followers because he enabled those of lesser prowess to achieve within their own capacities. Wolters presented ample evidence with telling detail in support of his insights, but first-time readers may balk at the sometimes back-handed way he expressed himself. Verbal constructions in the conditional tense such as "would have," "likely to," and "could be seen" made the arguments sound tentative and provisional. This prose style was a matter of professional unwillingness to venture beyond what his sources stated explicitly, and it makes the historian sound speculative and under-confident.

VIETNAMESE HISTORIOGRAPHY AND LITERATURE

Wolters published the first of his thirteen studies of the kingdom of Đại Việt in 1976, the last in 1996. The research interests of one of his students, John Whitmore, whose doctoral thesis concerned fifteenth-century Vietnam, helped to draw Wolters to Southeast Asia's only Sinicized state.[117] Whitmore was unique among Wolters's students in writing on early Southeast Asia; all the other PhD students chose more modern thesis topics. Keith W. Taylor, who succeeded Wolters as Cornell's early Southeast Asian historian, completed his PhD at the University of Michigan, and although he shared many of Wolters's intellectual interests and enthusiasms, particularly when it came to Vietnam, he had been trained elsewhere.

"Historians and Emperors in Vietnam and China," reprinted here, is a companion of the 1976 essay in that it concerns the history of Đại Việt by Lê Văn Hưu, who submitted his edited version of the Vietnamese annals to the throne in

---

[117] John K. Whitmore, "The Development of Lê Government in Fifteenth-Century Vietnam" (PhD thesis, Cornell University, 1968).

1272 during the Trần dynasty (1226–1400). The Trần rulers, destined to be famous in Vietnamese memory for thrice defeating the armies of Kublai Khan, were Buddhist, yet they appointed examination graduates who had studied Chinese classical texts to subordinate government posts. In the earlier part of his history, Lī Văn Hưu spelt out his criticisms of the Lý dynasty (1009–1225), the first indigenous dynasty of reasonable duration after the Vietnamese had wrested free of Chinese overlordship in the tenth century. Lý dynastic structure was flawed, in Lī Văn Hưu's eyes, because of an unsatisfactory succession procedure exacerbated by the emperor's polygamy. Plural wives meant plural heirs who might contest the throne, and in fact the machinations of three wives had placed a two-year-old, Lý Anh Tôn, on the throne in 1137 CE. In judging the early Lý rulers, Lī Văn Hưu found their performance wanting. The Lý had not laid the foundations for strong dynastic government in spite of the veneer of Chinese forms. They had made innovations, but Vietnam was very different from China, and it was not clear that the Chinese dynastic pattern would prove durable.

Responding to the theme of *Perceptions of the Past in Southeast Asia*, the volume in which "Historians and Emperors in Vietnam and China" first appeared, Wolters compared the perceptions of Chinese literati who wrote histories with the perceptions of Lī Văn Hưu in his edition of the Vietnamese annals.[118] As an examination graduate of 1247, Lī Văn Hưu was steeped in the Chinese classics and the historical records, but in important respects he departed from Chinese norms and values in writing about the past. Wolters posed the question: what was the significance of the differences between the way Lī Văn Hưu judged Vietnamese dynastic performance as against what a Chinese imperial historian in the Middle Kingdom would have said? Lê Văn Hưu, who was writing when meditational Buddhism had a strong influence on the emperor, was interested in the "learning of antiquity," which was extracted from the Chinese classics by non-Buddhist scholars called *nho*. This "learning of antiquity" was valuable because it was used to inform the emperor about court style in a way that enabled his court to match the Chinese court style, and also because it could be used to safeguard Vietnamese independence. Lī Văn Hưu began his version of the Vietnamese annals with the reign of Triệu Đà in the third and second centuries BCE. A Chinese adventurer from Hopei, Triệu Đà was credited with inaugurating the Vietnamese imperial institution, and his achievement is the measure against which all subsequent heroic diplomat-rulers were to be judged. Lê Văn Hưu's evaluation of previous rulers mainly serves to highlight the qualities and achievements of Trần Thái-tôn, the emperor ruling at the time Lê Văn Hưu compiled his history. Throughout, Lê Văn Hưu was concerned to show that the Vietnamese court was the peer of the Chinese imperial court, and that the tributary relationship was compatible with Vietnamese independence.

The second essay on Vietnam examines the poetry of Phạm Sư Mạnh, a Vietnamese official who understood the implications of peasant unrest as the Trần dynasty weakened in the second half of the fourteenth century. Departing from their accustomed roles as the emperor's obedient subordinates, officials such as Mạnh began to express their opinions about the norms of good government. Many of them also wrote Tang-style verse, thus confirming their status as *nho*, the lettered members of society in possession of the "learning from antiquity." In Phạm Sư Mạnh's case,

---

[118] Anthony Reid and David Marr, eds., *Perceptions of the Past in Southeast Asia* (Singapore: Heinemann Educational Books for the Asian Studies Association of Southeast Asia, 1979).

the poems were written about the border region between Vietnam and China. In a way, it is surprising that Wolters took up the study of these poems, because, as he admits, they lack the historical references that historians normally treasure for documentary purposes, although in an earlier article he had used one of Mạnh's poems to reconstruct developments of the fourteenth century.[119] In Wolters's phrase, "a timeless atmosphere pervades" the poems. His essay "Phạm Sư Mạnh's Poems" is a study of the poems as poetry by a historian who bears in mind the Vietnamese preoccupations of the age. It is an experimental essay that, employing the reading strategies of structuralist poetics, interprets the poem as a text rather than as a document.

"On Telling a Story of Vietnam in the Thirteenth and Fourteenth Centuries" is probably the most accessible of Wolters's essays on Vietnam, and it usefully concludes the entire volume. It appeared in 1995 in the twenty-fifth-anniversary issue of the *Journal of Southeast Asian Studies*, entitled "Perspectives on Southeast Asian Studies." In it, Wolters outlined a book on Vietnam under the Trần dynasty in the thirteenth and fourteenth centuries, a book that was never published. Later, searching for a form to fit the content of the Vietnamese historical record, Wolters abandoned the conventional academic format of a history and embarked on a historical novel that occupied him until he died. In "On Telling a Story of Vietnam," he declared that he would attend to the narrative history of Vietnam as well as to his sources' "textual properties," which he defined as "patterned literary features and structures" that endowed the sources with meaning over and above the information they might convey.

It is also clear from this late essay what Wolters had hinted at in the earlier essays, namely, that he did not see Vietnam as a predominantly Confucian state. There is now an abundant literature on "Confucianism" in Vietnam, with no fewer than three chapters in a recent volume on rethinking Confucianism in East Asia devoted to Vietnam, studies that build on a debate under way for more than two decades.[120] In Vietnam itself, debates about the relevance of Confucianism fueled the

---

[119] O. W. Wolters, "Assertions of Cultural Well-Being in Fourteenth-Century Vietnam: Part Two," *JSEAS* 11,1 (March 1980): 74–90.

[120] See K. W. Taylor, "Vietnamese Confucian Narratives," and Alexander Woodside, "Classical Primordialism and Historical Agendas of Vietnamese Confucianism," in *Rethinking Confucianism: Past and Present in China, Japan, Korea, and Vietnam*, ed. Benjamin A. Elman, John B. Duncan, and Herman Ooms, UCLA Asian Pacific Monograph Series (Los Angeles, CA: University of California, 2002), pp. 337–69 and pp. 116–43, respectively. Also in the same volume is Shawn Frederick McHale, "Mapping a Vietnamese Confucian Past and Its Transition to Modernity," pp. 397–430; see also McHale, *Print and Power: Confucianism, Communism, and Buddhism in the Making of Modern Vietnam* (Honolulu, HI: University of Hawai'i Press, 2004), chapter 3. Earlier studies argued for and against the relevance of the "Confucian" or "Neo-Confucian" labels in different periods, circumstances, and regions; see Nola Cooke, "Nineteenth-Century Vietnamese Confucianization in Historical Perspective: Evidence from the Palace Examinations (1463–1883)," *JSEAS* 25,2 (September 1994): 270–312; K. W. Taylor, "The Literati Revival in Seventeenth-Century Vietnam," *JSEAS* 28,1 (March 1987): 1–23; and John K. Whitmore, "Social Organization and Confucian Thought in Vietnam," *JSEAS* 15,1 (March 1984): 296–306, as well as his "From Classical Scholarship to Confucian Belief in Vietnam," *The Vietnam Forum* 9 (Winter-Spring 1987): 49–65. An early statement by the late British scholar, Ralph Smith, on Confucianization in Vietnam is now virtually unread by historians of Vietnam because it exaggerates the significance of Confucianism in Vietnamese history. See R. B. Smith, "The Cycle of Confucianization in Vietnam," *Aspects of Vietnamese History*, ed. Walter Vella (Honolulu, HI: Asian Studies at Hawai'i, University of Hawai'i, 1973), pp. 2–20. The pioneering book by Alexander Woodside sparked off much of

nationalist struggle against the French, and essays written in Vietnamese in the 1990s show the sharp divisions in Vietnamese opinion about whether Confucianism bequeathed a positive or a negative legacy. Clearly, "Confucianism," whatever it is, is not dead in Vietnam today. Yet even a cursory reading of Wolters's writing on Vietnam discloses that he rarely used the word "Confucian" to describe the ideological preoccupations of the Vietnamese court. He is on record as imploring scholars "to think twice before they invoke the term 'Confucianism' in Vietnamese history."[121] He was familiar with Chinese dynastic history, with the bureaucratic workings of the Chinese court that produced that history, and with Chinese views of Vietnam. But he had little interest in the mandarinate examination system as it functioned in Vietnam, and in each of the historiographic exercises represented by the essays in this volume, as well as in the others that he wrote on Vietnam, he is at pains to distinguish the habits of mind of Vietnamese historians from those of the Chinese literati-historians. He did not really see that Confucianism was important for the Vietnamese, despite the fact that the Vietnamese kingdom put in place the bureaucratic apparatus, embraced generous parts of the value system, and availed itself of the ancient learning of the Chinese Confucian state. Part of the explanation for his reluctance to accept Confucian influence was that he thought the Chinese dynastic concept as it was adopted in Vietnam prevented the Vietnamese from fashioning their own form of government on their own terms.[122] It is almost as if he thought the Chinese dynastic concept obstructed the Vietnamese, and, on this point, one is reminded of the many occasions in his writing on the region where Wolters discusses—indeed, praises—Southeast Asian flexibility. It is as if the rigid demands of the dynastic concept had kept the Vietnamese from being truly Southeast Asian.

In *Beyond the Bronze Pillars: Envoy Poetry and the Sino–Vietnamese Relationship*, Liam Kelley has boldly set out a sequence of interpretive paradigms that shows the twisting path taken by European-language historiography in its attempt to configure the relationship between Vietnam and China.[123] The "Little China" interpretation had its origins in the work of French Sinologist Henri Maspero. According to this theory, Vietnam became a miniature replica of China during the millennium of Chinese overlordship until the Vietnamese court asserted its autonomy in the tenth century. The reaction to the Little China theory came from the "autonomous history" perspective of scholars trained in the 1950s and 1960s, among whom Wolters was one. In the case of Vietnam, nationalist history was to buttress this scholarly characterization of Vietnam as an autonomous entity from the 1970s by supplying a grand narrative of resistance to foreign (or earlier, Chinese) aggression reinforced by the Second Indochina War fought against the United States and its allies. A second phase of this autonomous history, suggests Kelley, emerged in the work of Keith Taylor, who argued that Vietnamese "spirit and intelligence" was "rooted in a conviction held by Vietnamese that they were not, and did not want to be,

---

this scholarship. See Alexander Woodside, *Vietnam and the Chinese Model: A Comparative Study of Vietnamese and Chinese Government in the First Half of the Nineteenth Century* (Cambridge, MA: Harvard University Press, 1971).

[121] Quoted in Whitmore, "From Classical Scholarship to Confucian Belief," p. 49.

[122] On this and other points about Wolters's views of the relationship between Vietnam and China, I am indebted to discussions with Keith Taylor; personal communication, April 30, 2002.

[123] Liam C. Kelley, *Beyond the Bronze Pillars: Envoy Poetry and the Sino–Vietnamese Relationship* (Honolulu, HI: Association for Asian Studies and University of Hawai'i Press, 2005), pp. 9–17.

Chinese."[124] Taylor once crisply characterized the poles around which the debate has swung as "the Confucian colony" versus the "anti-Confucian nation," a typology that he himself believes has now exhausted its usefulness.[125]

It has been suggested that the terms we use in English—Confucianism, Neo-Confucianism—must now be seen as anachronistic neologisms, obscuring more than they illuminate.[126] Although Wolters for the most part kept his own counsel in this debate, his preference for "*nho* scholars" and "learning from antiquity" circumvented the terminological quagmires, and directed attention to the concerns of Vietnamese literati living at the time. Since the Han dynasty, when the general Ma Yuan reputedly erected bronze pillars to mark the southernmost extent of Chiense paramountcy, Vietnam had always been in China's "borderlands." It therefore seems fitting that Wolters subjected Phạm Sư Mạnh's "border" poems to such intense scrutiny. Phạm Sư Mạnh knew the border, had lived and worked on the border, and his poetry is concerned with what occurs on the Vietnamese side of the border, which resembles a "screen." In Wolters's reading of these verses, China is always, in his phrase, "blocked out." It is tempting to interpret this reading as yet another warning against making too much of China in the Vietnamese past. The adjectives "Chinese" and "Vietnamese" should not be projected into a past Vietnam that was a frontier region, a zone of cultural interaction. "Confronted with ubiquitous signs of Sinitic cultural influence in the Vietnamese writings that he examined," observes Liam Kelley, "all Wolters saw was 'Vietnam' and 'Vietnamese.'"[127]

INTELLECTUAL PREOCCUPATIONS

As a final comment, it might be helpful to discuss Wolters's approach to studying the past. He would have recoiled from being tied to anything that might be called historical method, but he was always conscious of his vocation as a historian—he was intensely proud of it, in fact—and he spoke frequently about the historian's duty and the historian's perspective. He was not, however, a philosopher of history, and while one looks in vain for clues to a historiographical tradition with which he identified, certain intellectual preoccupations are evident in his work.

Wolters had an abiding concern for the historian's accountability to source material. He relished the discovery of new materials and the reworking of familiar ones. He was at pains to establish the provenance and authenticity of texts, to identify gaps in the evidence, to determine the limits of what could be reasonably known, and to extract whatever inferences that could be drawn from grudging documents. He was relatively cautious in *Early Indonesian Commerce*. In later work he took greater risks, but always within these guidelines. The historian's statements about the past, he believed, needed to be grounded in evidence that had passed the tests of accountability. Primary materials were a particular vexed pleasure. In his weekly tutorial, he pressed graduate students to rake over the sources—inscriptions, chronicles, the translated accounts of foreign envoys to Southeast Asia—and unearth

---

[124] As quoted in Kelley, *Beyond the Bronze Pillars*, p. 11.

[125] Taylor, "Vietnamese Confucian Narratives," p. 364.

[126] Elman, *Rethinking Confucianism*, p. 524.

[127] Kelley, *Beyond the Bronze Pillars*, pp. 11–13. Kelley has now extended this critique to other historians of Vietnam before the French; see his "'Confucianism' in Vietnam: A State of the Field Essay," *Journal of Vietnamese Studies* 1,1–2 (Feb.–Aug. 2006), pp. 314–70.

nuggets of new information that had escaped previous readers. Such were the methods of the philologist in a tradition of classicists that stretched back to Theodor Mommsen (1817–1903) and John Bury (1861–1927). Wolters had been schooled in this tradition, and it was second nature for him to advocate its principles long after his time at Oxford. In his last years, to remember colleagues who had retired or passed away, he used his craft to master the genre of the memoir.[128] It is evident from these pieces how anthropology, art history, and literature had enriched his study of history.

Another preoccupation, evident in his early work on Śrīvijaya, was the enduring power and reputation of localities. A tiny kingdom, forced to bow to more powerful suzerains, might be temporarily subjugated, but it could rise up later and assert itself when circumstances changed. Entrepreneurial skill and deft maneuvering by local leaders sustained small polities through lean times, and spirit cults protected them from their enemies in the terrestrial and thanatological worlds. Wolters's first publications on Tāmbralinga (1958) and Chên-li-fu (1960) and *Early Indonesian Commerce* (1967) exhibit the strategies and tactics of the historical geographer marshalling evidence from a variety of grudging sources to draw conclusions about the political and economic dynamics of times when maps did not yet exist.

By the 1930s, historical geography had become a highly developed field through the exhaustive studies of the *Domesday Book* by historians such as H. C. Darby of the University of Cambridge. Having grown up in England, Wolters knew that Roman roads threaded their way across the English countryside. By the time of the Norman Conquest, hundreds of Christian churches dotted the landscape. Nearly every English village known in modern times had appeared on the scene by the late eleventh century. The history of place was inscribed in family names. Such continuities—a favorite Wolters word—were vivid manifestations of ancient events, leaving to the historian the task of excavating the sedimentary deposits of the past and subjecting them to historical inquiry. There was something very English about Wolters's preoccupation with the enduring power of place, which was reinforced by the life he led in provincial Malaya.

Still another preoccupation for Wolters was the historian's duty to see the past on its own terms. How did a society understand the world it inhabited? How did it look to itself? Wolters always respected the evidence, but he also believed in the powers of imagination required to understand the worlds of the past. On his bookshelf in his university office he kept a copy of *The Idea of History*, by R. G. Collingwood, based on lectures Collingwood had given at Oxford during the 1930s.[129] Wolters was studying there at the time, and he attended some Collingwood lectures. For Collingwood, the historian needed to enter into the minds of people in the past, because *"all* history, including that of action, is constituted as the history of thought."[130] History was present knowledge, "what the historian makes of it in the

---

[128] O. W. Wolters, "John M. Echols: March 25, 1913–June 16, 1982," *Indonesia* 34 (October 1982): 1–12; "Anthony Thomas Kirsch (1930–1999)," *JSS* 88,1–2 (2000): xv–xxiii; *Remembering Harold and Lydia Shadick* (Ithaca, NY: East Asia Program, Cornell University, 1994); and in a felicitation volume on his retirement, "Stanley J. O'Connor," in *Studies in Southeast Asian Art: Essays in Honor of Stanley J. O'Connor*, ed. Nora A. Taylor (Ithaca, NY: Southeast Asia Program, Cornell University, 2000), pp. 15–31.

[129] I am grateful to Tony Milner for his recollection of this detail.

[130] Elizabeth A. Clark, *History, Theory, Text: Historians and the Linguistic Turn* (Cambridge: Harvard University Press, 2004), p. 109.

present."[131] The historian's picture of the past involved building a "web of imaginative construction" that tied together "nodal points" of historical facts, however provisionally established.[132] The inferences the historian drew about what happened between the nodes were necessarily implied by the established facts.

Collingwood called the process of linking the nodes "the *a priori* imagination" and likened it to the mental processes of the detective novelist. His study of Hadrian's Wall using archaeological evidence from Roman Britain was the work of the detective-historian. In one of the lectures, delivered in 1935 and reprinted many times since as *The Historical Imagination*, Collingwood spoke about the shared aims of the novelist and the historian in terms of incidents "determined by a necessity internal to themselves":

> The story, if it is a good story, cannot develop otherwise than as it does; the novelist in imagining it cannot imagine it developing except as it does develop. Here, and equally in all other kinds of art, the *a priori* imagination is at work. Its other familiar function is what may be called the perceptual imagination, supplementing and consolidating the data of perception in the way so well analysed by Kant, by presenting to us objects of possible perception which are not actually perceived: the underside of this table, the inside of an unopened egg, the back of the moon.[133]

Here Collingwood makes a case for the alterity of the past, its strangeness and difference, the past as a foreign country.

In view of Wolters's unfinished attempt to write a historical novel, the comparison of novelistic and historical narrative is illuminating, as is Collingwood's metaphor of the historian as detective.[134] *The Fall of Śrīvijaya in Malay History* was, among other things, a series of solutions to puzzles as Wolters tried to decipher the Malay Annals and use them for modern historical analysis.[135] Research on the origins of Śrīvijaya required special methods, Wolters wrote in 1960, owing to the "exceedingly ambiguous data about the historical geography of the region." It was necessary to interpret the evidence indirectly by reading clues and decoding signs, because "except for the seventh century, Śrīvijaya is rather like a stone which has been thrown into a pond: the stone has disappeared and all that is left are the ripples in the form of notices in foreign literatures."[136]

A hint of Wolters's later interest in semiotics and structuralism may be found in "all that is left are the ripples," words echoed by Carlo Ginzburg on the importance

---

[131] Ann Curthoys and John Docker, *Is History Fiction?* (Sydney: UNSW Press, 2006), p. 132.

[132] G. S. Couse, "Collingwood's Detective Image of the Historian and the Study of Hadrian's Wall," *History and Theory*, Beiheft 29 (1990), *Reassessing Collingwood*, p. 59.

[133] Hans Meyerhoff, ed., *The Philosophy of History in Our Time: An Anthology* (Garden City, NY: Doubleday Anchor Books, 1959), p. 77.

[134] Curthoys and Docker, *Is History Fiction?*, pp. 104–5, who find in some of Collingwood's writing a "rationalist megalomania," agree that *The Historical Imagination* is more congenial to the contemporary, skeptical mind, and they argue strongly for the resemblance between historian and novelist.

[135] For a good example of Wolters's puzzle-solving, see his study of feet as symbols of divine and royal power in *The Fall of Śrīvijaya in Malay History*, chapter 6.

[136] National Library of Australia, The Coedès Collection, MS 2986, letter from Wolters to Coedès, July 18, 1960.

of the semiotic method to psychoanalysis as well as to science and history: "reality is opaque, but there are certain points—clues, signs—which allow us to decipher it."[137] To write about the inside of the egg, the back of the moon, or the anklets of sovereignty in fourteenth-century Śrīvijaya, an author must be prepared to take imaginative leaps in order to weave the web of historical interpretation. Wolters did not parade his historical method, and in fact might not have been able to articulate one even if pressed to do so. Having begun his academic career late in life, he felt he was always improvising his methods and striving to catch up with what some of his younger colleagues were doing. But it is not difficult to find a place for Collingwood in his intellectual ancestry.

Late in his career, Wolters discovered the importance of literary studies for the historian's labors. Two Cornell colleagues, James Siegel and Jonathan Culler, were the main intellectual guides leading him on these expeditions: Siegel through conversation and reading he recommended; and Culler through the example of his scholarship and comments on Wolters's studies of Vietnamese poetry. Wolters described this intellectual journey as follows:

> During the decade between 1978 and 1988 I have interested myself in an approach to the past guided by attempts at critical "reading" of the sources as "texts." By this I mean that attention is given to an almost endless number of textual features that help to elucidate "how" a text is "manufactured" so that one can make better sense of it as a specimen of writing: signifying systems and linguistic usage in general; structured presentation of contents and the structures' functions; linguistic combinations and equivalences; figures of speech such as metaphor and synecdoche; literary conventions and writing devices; repetitive language; especially ways in which parts of a text relate to the whole. ... I believe the historian can see himself or herself as doing something *with* the past (dare I say discovering the past?) by following directions and messages provided by the linguistic and structural systems that generate the sources' meaning when they are read as "texts."[138]

By the late 1970s, structuralism and post-structuralism were making a big impact on the humanities in American universities. Jacques Derrida was all the rage in many departments of English and comparative literature; by 1978, the paperback edition of his *Of Grammatology*, translated by Gayatri Spivak, had been reprinted three times. Moving quickly with this intellectual current, in December 1979 Wolters whispered mischievously into the ear of a conference visitor to Cornell, "have you ever heard of Derrida?" The untutored visitor had not.

When asked to discuss Siegel's influence on him, Wolters replied that Siegel had introduced him to the work of Saussure,

> ... and to an awareness of how language works, and this, in turn, encouraged me to observe linguistic usage. ... Over and above these contributions, [Jim] has

---

[137] Carlo Ginzburg, "Morelli, Freud, and Sherlock Holmes: Clues and Scientific Method," *History Workshop* 9 (Spring 1980): 27. See also Robin W. Winks, ed., *The Historian as Detective: Essays on Evidence* (New York and London: Harper & Row, 1969).

[138] O. W. Wolters, *Two Essays on Dai-Viet in the Fourteenth Century* (New Haven, CT: Yale Center For International and Area Studies, Yale Southeast Asia Studies, 1988), pp. viii–ix.

always helped in a way that I find impossible to describe and explain. The closest I can get on the spur of the moment is to declare that he has set me an example of what can be achieved simply by intense thought that enables one to become aware that what seems to be obvious and straightforward conceals much else. He has the kind of mind that can immediately grasp the hidden significance of something and often spot the strange in ordinary situations. He is intensely observant and interested in everything.[139]

Wolters referred playfully to his "conversion" to this new way of thinking about historical materials and was teased about it. At a symposium in Canberra in 1984, a friendly participant suggested that he was invoking literary theory gratuitously and treating it as some kind of black magic that could "do things to documents to make them talk." Wolters wheeled around in mock fury to answer his critic. "I've always thought like this," he said, "I can't help it."

In 1987, his colleague in Australia, John Legge, wrote an essay, "Clio and Her Neighbours" and, subsequently, an expanded version, "Historians and the Semioticians," which was never published.[140] In the expanded version, Legge had referred to Wolters and some of Wolters's students as examples of historians working as "structuralist investigators" to decode texts. When Legge sent him the unpublished draft, Wolters responded vigorously in thirteen pages and an accompanying letter in which he debated Legge's version of how thinking had changed. He did not recognize any of the so-called "semioticians" described by Legge, and even less did he recognize himself in the description. He denied ever using the word semiotics, though he admitted being a structuralist, "probably by instinct," even if structuralists themselves were at their weakest when writing about historians. Textual criticism was highly disciplined, as well as "time-consuming and headache-producing, but it is valuable all the same." He vigorously defended his practice.

> The structuralist processes the document by seeking to establish its facts about itself, and the documentary historian (who may well be the structuralist under a different cap) may then wish to include these facts in his or her discussion of this or that. The structuralist actually enlarges a document's documentary interest by textualizing it. The enlargement is in terms of what I would like to call the "documentariness" of the document. Critics used the term "literariness," so why should we not also speak of "documentariness" in the sense of document-worthy features of a text?[141]

Wolters also denied any interest in matters of epistemology and declared that he had "no bent for philosophical speculation." In reply, Legge argued that Wolters's work contained much important theoretical discussion and that, anyway, Wolters's

---

[139] Personal communication, April 1999.

[140] J. D. Legge, "Clio and Her Neighbours: Reflections on History's Relations with the Surrounding Disciplines," in *Dari Babad Dan Hikayat Sampai Sejarah Kritis Kumpulan karangan dipersembahkan kepada Prof. Dr. Sartono Kartodirdjo*, ed. T. Ibrahim Alfian et al. (Yogyakarta: Gadjah Mada University Press, 1987), pp. 331–350. Legge's essay is in English.

[141] O. W. Wolters, "A Few Comments on 'Historians and the Semioticians'" and accompanying letter to John Legge, June 27, 1989.

historical practice did "not depend on, or follow from, the arguments of the structuralists." Legge was reacting not so much to Wolters, but to structuralist and poststructuralist nostrums that seemed to deny that there was a past "out there" to be studied.[142]

The critical strategies to which Wolters alludes in this correspondence were put to use in "Phạm Sư Mạnh's Poems," which was followed soon after by another essay on the Vietnamese annals that sought to understand "some of the conspicuous textual features and their effects which belong to the text's properties."[143] Devices such as reiteration, repetition, and pauses assisted texts in conveying meaning.[144] For the most part, Wolters applied this critical theory to Vietnamese materials, but in the Postscript to the revised edition of *History, Culture, and Region* he discussed at length the qualities of good government in the Malay and Vietnamese courts by comparing syntagms, or chains of writing elements, in the Malay as well as the Vietnamese historical records.[145] He was exploring Jonathan Culler's conviction that the literary was not a marginal phenomenon but "a logic of signification that generates human meanings of many sorts."[146] Using such reading strategies, Wolters delighted in wringing every drop of meaning from a word, a phrase, or body of text.

As an example of where his reading strategies were leading him, Wolters left behind an unpublished work, *Monologue, Dialogue, and Trần Vietnam*. The study of Trần Vietnam, on which he had been working for over fifteen years, had modulated into a historical novel of more than three hundred pages in various states of completion.[147] In what can only be described as an experimental work informed by his reading of the Vietnamese source material, Wolters was engaged in inventing conversations between fourteenth-, fifteenth-, and sixteenth-century Vietnamese protagonists using the polyphonic narrative techniques of Mikhail Bakhtin. After six chapters, the novel concluded with an authorial self-critique in which Wolters conceded that "the process of contriving confrontation—the essence of the dialogue—is difficult to explain convincingly."[148]

In conclusion, I do not believe it would be a reductive reading of Wolters's historical writing to note the high regard for public service evident in it. He wrote about early Southeast Asian leadership in the way he did because the world of governing was the world with which he was familiar. In his teaching, he nourished the study of what he called the science of government, which had developed in early times and entailed "the cultivation of suitable moral and practical qualities in the

---

[142] John Legge to Oliver Wolters, October 14, 1989.

[143] O. W. Wolters, "Possibilities for a Reading of the 1293-1357 Period in the Vietnamese Annals" in *Southeast Asia in the Ninth to Fourteenth Centuries*, ed. David G. Marr and A. C. Milner (Singapore: Institute of Southeast Asian Studies; Canberra: Research School of Pacific Studies, Australian National University, 1986), p. 398.

[144] At the end of her obituary for Wolters, Virginia Hooker illustrated how pauses functioned as a literary device. See Virginia Hooker, "O. W. Wolters (June 8, 1915–December 5, 2000): An Obituary and Appreciation," *JMBRAS* 74,1 (2001): 1–18.

[145] Wolters, *History, Culture, and Region*, pp. 199–204.

[146] Jonathan Culler in Derek Attridge, Geoff Bennington and Robert Young, eds., *Post-Structuralism and the Question of History* (Cambridge: Cambridge University Press, 1989), p. 88.

[147] Wolters had outlined the book on Trần Vietnam at least by 1989; letter to Virginia Hooker, June 13, 1989. See also her "O. W. Wolters," p. 17, for details of what he was planning.

[148] O. W. Wolters, *Monologue, Dialogue, and Trần Vietnam*, unpublished manuscript, p. 301.

service of the king."[149] In Southeast Asia, the prestige and dignity of public service survived into the modern period, a process Wolters himself had witnessed and to which he contributed. He understood that circumstances could require a ruler to be ruthless—he accepted that even his hero General Templer had to be ruthless at times—but loyalty was always the supreme virtue, even if that loyalty had been secured with tribute or bounty. Court historians could criticize their rulers within the conventions dictated by the historiographical genres in which they wrote, but they were loyal to their ruler-patrons.

Wolters was at ease analyzing the motivations and mental habits of officials who served Southeast Asian rulers, be they Malay sultans, Cambodian and Thai kings, or Vietnamese emperors, for he himself had been such an official, even if it was in the contrived setting where the British residents ruled and the Malay rulers advised. The fact that he had worked in a regime that had compromised Southeast Asian sovereignty is something a reader of his histories might bear in mind.

---

[149] O. W. Wolters, "Foreword," in Soemarsaid Moertono, *State and Statecraft in Old Java: A Study of the Later Mataram Period, Sixteenth to Nineteenth Century*, Monograph Series Publication no. 43, rev. ed. (Ithaca, NY: Cornell Modern Indonesia Project, Cornell Southeast Asia Program, 1981), pp. v–vi.

PART I

SOUTHEAST ASIA AS A REGION

CHAPTER ONE

SOUTHEAST ASIA AS A SOUTHEAST ASIAN FIELD OF STUDY

My first reaction to your kind invitation was a nervous one.[1] I do not like to throw my weight around and did not feel that it was really my business to give advice to Lembaga Ilmu Pengetahuan Indonesia (LIPI). But I had to admit to myself that I wanted to visit Indonesia again, and here I am—but mourning the absence of two friends: my old traveling partner of Sriwijayan days, Yati Suleiman, and my old sparring partner, also of Sriwijayan days, Boechari. Yet, when I began to ask myself questions about the meaning of the field of Southeast Asian studies as something more than the personal excitement of studying this or that about this or that part of the region, I once more became nervous.

The field, and area studies in general, emerged in the United States in 1948 with the explicit purpose of teaching Americans, many of whom were returning from Southeast Asia to civilian life, what they should know about a region of new nations whose affairs were beginning to impinge on their own at a time when the Cold War was getting under way. But recently, and more than forty years later, the report of a conference on Southeast Asian studies in the United States, the Wingspread Conference, was published under the disturbing title of *Southeast Asian Studies in the Balance: Reflections from America.*[2] Does the title mean that these scholars were unsure of the identity of the field or was it simply a particular American reflection on how the field had developed in America? Indeed, one can go further and wonder for how much longer Southeast Asia will be regarded as an identifiable object for study. Perhaps the region we have been accustomed to refer to as "Southeast Asia" is

---

[1] The article is an address, slightly modified, given on November 3, 1993, to a conference, held in Jakarta, of Southeast Asian historians from the region itself and jointly organized by the Indonesian Institute of Sciences (Lembaga Ilmu Pengetahuan Indonesia, LIPI) and the Toyota Foundation. The conference's theme was "The Promotion of Southeast Asia Studies in Southeast Asia." I am grateful to Taufik Abdullah, chairman of the Steering Committee, for permitting me to publish the address in *Indonesia.* I would also like to thank A. Thomas Kirsch (anthropologist), Stanley J. O'Connor (art historian), and the late Lauriston Sharp (anthropologist) for their valuable advice.

[2] I am referring to the Wingspread Conference held at Racine, Wisconsin, in 1990. See *Southeast Asian Studies in the Balance: Reflections from America,* ed. Charles Hirschman, Charles F. Keyes, and Karl Hutterer (Ann Arbor, MI: Association for Asian Studies, 1992).

already dissolving into other kinds of alignments such as the Asia Pacific Economic Cooperation Forum. Indeed, we have been given to understand that transnational influences are likely to transform the focus and issues of global and national affairs.[3]

Obviously, Southeast Asians are unlikely to feel the compelling need to learn about the societies and governments of Southeast Asia which Americans felt. Similarly, they are hardly likely to be seized by the sense of urgency with which Australians are approaching the field, a mood expressed in a recent report as a need to become "at ease with our geographical place in the world." How, then, can one attempt to state the case for Southeast Asian studies in Indonesia or, for that matter, elsewhere in Southeast Asia?

I suggest, for the purpose of discussion, that the major contribution of Southeast Asian studies within the region itself could be the enhancement of one's self-awareness in order to assist one in reaching a better understanding of the present. Perhaps, in an age of great change, there is more than ever a need for self-awareness: "Whence do we come? What are we? Where are we going?" Paul Gauguin exclaimed in 1897, though his intention, alas, was suicide.[4] I shall go further and suggest, and again for the purpose of discussion, that LIPI might wish to involve itself in an informed critique of the present by undertaking what I shall refer to as a "watchdog" role by way of calling attention to history-oriented aspects of the field of Southeast Asian studies that may tend to be ignored. In this way LIPI could argue that the past, and therefore its study, might have a distinct and valuable bearing on what is happening today.

To this end I shall try to make a case for the relevance of Southeast Asian studies by calling attention to what I believe are some prominent cultural features or patterns associated with the region's past that, in my opinion, should not be neglected, and my listeners may then wish to ask themselves whether any of these features or patterns tend to be mirrored in the contemporary scene and, if so, with what consequences.[5]

What I shall say cannot help being only the views of one outsider, but I defend the salience of these features because I believe that they help to explain how people behaved in the past and how things happened. They would be influences that helped to shape the direction of Southeast Asian historical experience. My listeners may also ask themselves whether anything I shall say sheds light on the substance of "Southeast Asian civilization," something that those who contributed to the report of the Wingspread Conference found to be elusive.

These features or patterns—eight of them—were, I believe, widely shared throughout Southeast Asia. They were communalities, and the elite in this or that

---

[3] David L. Featherman, "What Does Society Need from Higher Education?" *Items* (Social Science Research Council), 47,2/3 [1993]: 38. The author is responding to Paul Kennedy's *Preparing for the Twenty-First Century* (New York, NY: Random House, 1993).

[4] *"D'où venons nous? Qui sommes nous? Où allons nous?"* is the title of a Gauguin painting in the Museum of Fine Arts, Boston.

[5] For example, an Englishman, familiar with the history of nineteenth-century England and observing the contemporary scene in his own country, could be sensitive to signs of persisting class distinctions and anti-foreign sentiment. He might, too, have reservations concerning the long-term consequences of the Enlightenment, with its overweeningly self-confident rationalism and its legacy of fascism and communism. He might also recognize more clearly the club-like atmosphere of party politics in the House of Commons. An American friend tells me that Americans today can recognize themselves in the pages of de Tocqueville.

country could, if the occasion arose, understand each other.[6] Today, too, perhaps they may help those living in one part of the region go some way in understanding those living in another part of the region. I am not claiming that Southeast Asia had the monopoly on these features, and I am not identifying them with cultural values or attitudes of mind, though, of course, they would have generated values, a point to which I shall return. Above all, I am not proposing these common cultural features to the exclusion of cultural differences within the region, the study of which should surely be given the highest priority in any definition of Southeast Asian studies, provided that the case for the field in Southeast Asia itself has been made. The following eight cultural features represent my case for the field.

Cultural Feature 1—The first feature is that the only time that mattered was "now," the karma-fraught moment, for example, or the moment of spiritual enlightenment, or when an opportunity for earning worldly merit could occur. The past was pertinent only when it was believed to be clearly relevant to specific contemporary needs. The possibility of gradual progress was denied; instead, time was measured in terms of recurring cycles. The future held out no new possibilities.

And so it was that, during a conference a number of years ago, historians concluded that in the Southeast Asian tradition there was no interest in the past for its own sake.[7] As one participant, a specialist on Thailand, put it, "the contemporaneity of the distant past is a hallmark of (indigenous) Southeast Asian historiography."[8] In the same tradition, a thirteenth-century Vietnamese historian could artfully quote ancient Chinese texts to counter Kublai Khan's claims to suzerainty, and in the fourteenth century a golden age in antiquity was invented to express nostalgia for a recent Vietnamese past. The past was the receptacle for myths and imagined times of prosperity. There would have been no sense of a linear past or notion that one should plan further ahead than, say, for the next campaigning season or for the next harvest. I hasten to observe that this should not be understood to mean cultural stagnation but, instead, a sense of achievement and even exultation when one could live at peace with oneself and one's environment.

Cultural Feature 2—Because "now" was the time that mattered, importance was attached to being up-to-date or "contemporary": one should maximize one's opportunities for appropriating what were known to be useful skills appearing over the horizon by way of international trade routes or from within Southeast Asia itself.

The consequence of this opportunist and pragmatic attitude toward the present is seen in what historians used to refer to as "waves" of foreign influences which reached Southeast Asia first from India and later from the Middle East. New developments in India, for example, were soon registered in Southeast Asia. The great Indian philosopher, Śankara, who died about 750 CE, is mentioned in a ninth-century Cambodian inscription. The signs of prompt movement of ideas across the Indian Ocean are manifold: successive Indian scripts and art styles, new texts— among which were the revised Theravada texts of Sri Lanka from the eleventh

---

[6] Tom Kirsch suggests that it is not improbable that Jayavarman II, coming, according to a Cambodian inscription, from "Java" to Cambodia, felt at home in either country. At least, the author of the inscription may have thought so.

[7] Wang Gungwu in *Perceptions of the Past in Southeast Asia*, ed. Anthony Reid and David Marr (Singapore: Heinemann Educational Books [Asia]) Ltd, 1979), p. 4.

[8] Craig J. Reynolds, "Religious Historical Writing and the Legitimation of the First Bangkok Reign," in Reid and Marr, *Perceptions of the Past*, p. 103.

century onward—and religious systems such as Tantricism or schools of Islamic mysticism and, later, calls for modernization from Islamic centers in the Middle East. Special means to special ends lie at the heart of Tantricism and would have been irresistible to empirically minded Southeast Asian rulers and their religious advisers.

The Southeast Asian elite's propensity to be *au courant* is to the historian's advantage because it encourages reflection on the conjuncture of events responsible for introducing new possibilities and enquiry about the nature and process of the changes which could then take place. In this way, the past can be rendered in diachronic as well as in the synchronic terms suggested by the expression "cultural patterns."

Here is an illustration. The earliest known instance of what were once regarded as "waves" of foreign influence was the arrival in Southeast Asia of recently emerging schools of Hindu devotionalism in the first centuries of the Christian era. Cambodian inscriptions, which provide the earliest and reasonably ample materials on the subject, reveal that flamboyant Indian religious teachers, surely recognized by Khmers as exciting versions of their local "shamans" or whatever, were now becoming available to proclaim that supreme spiritual power could be attained here and now by means of simple and unbookish ascetic and meditative techniques that gave access to Śiva's cosmic power (*śakti*) so that one could be hailed as Śiva-like. Attaining something desirable here and now would be expected of any efficacious religious rite. The techniques—probably seen as of heroic proportions—were aimed at strengthening one's will-power and self-control, and the teachers' pupils were, first and foremost, the local chiefs. Thus, devotionalism and not Brahmanical rituals hit the epigraphic headlines, but it was not the popular devotionalism of southern India but a Southeast Asian elitist construction of its meaning and benefit to themselves.[9]

This episode, the details of which we owe to Cambodian epigraphy, suggests a paradigm applicable to the region as a whole in the form of a statement concerning what the present could offer and therefore why it was the present that mattered: the present could offer *up-to-date* skills and techniques that, if appropriated and mastered, would lead *here and now* to spiritual *success* and, no doubt, to all kinds of success.

Cultural Feature 3—The possibility of being "up-to-date" was often linked to and sustained by the sense of being an integral part of the whole of the known "world" rather than merely belonging to one's own patch of territory. The origin of this urbane, outward-looking, and global perspective, nourishing the elite's self-esteem, is, in my opinion, attributable to an ancient awareness among the elite that there was a "Hindu world," not an Indian one, which was an ever-to-be-updated world of Sanskrit books of canonical status in a sacred language which assumed that there were universally acceptable norms of behavior and shared symbols, images, and ideals, no matter what the local languages were. Here was a "cultural" community that spanned the whole region. To ignore it would be to remove perhaps a crucial element in early Southeast Asian historical experience. References to the great epic, the *Mahābhārata*—the window on the "Hindu world" and a limitless

---

[9] Indigenous texts could also be updated and to the historian's advantage. For example, the so-called Vietnamese folktales (the *Việt-điện u-linh tập*) were adapted and therefore updated in the late fourteenth or in the fifteenth century to teach the need to discipline villagers. In this instance, the updating process reinforces what is already known about the elite's changing attitude toward the countryside.

source of metaphors for the Southeast Asian elite—begin to appear in fifth-century inscriptions as far apart as southern Laos and eastern Kalimantan and are eloquent testimony to the "Hindu world's" span of scriptural authority.

The "Hindu world" was what we could now regard as an "imagined community."[10] It was no more than a selective appropriation and localization of materials, usually recorded in Sanskrit texts, to make local sense of and therefore familiar and valuable what was originally "foreign." Southeast Asians had the capacity to construe their own milieu and circumstances in terms of what they knew was recorded in Sanskrit literature as universal phenomena, and they would then proceed by a process of self-Hinduization to give "Hindu" names to themselves and to what they saw around them: for example, their mountains, rivers, sacred bathing pools, caves, stones, chiefs, overlords, and also those who did not belong to the elite groups in society. There was no limit to what could be described in "Hindu" language. Indeed, this world view required diversity. As my colleague Professor Kirsch has put it, in this process nature spirits could be "upgraded" to become part of the "Hindu" hierarchy and Siva "parochialized" to become the Creator of this or that region in Southeast Asia.

Indonesia was firmly in this universalist "Hindu world." As you know, Agastya is honored in the Prambanan. He is the sage of Tamil Nadu; to him Śiva dictated the twenty-eight *agama*. And not far from the Prambanan in distance and time stands the Borobudur, a Mahāyāna Buddhist monument but assuredly of the "Hindu world," where Hinduism and the Mahāyāna never made exclusive claims on their followers but rather fed into each other. You will recall that the bas-relief of three of its galleries was identified by means of a Japanese recension as depicting passages from the *Gaṇḍavyūha*, a Mahāyāna text from perhaps southern India, translated into Chinese at the beginning of the fifth century and acclaimed in seventh-century China and eighth-century Japan. Here is further convincing evidence of the wide world within which a Southeast Asian people could effortlessly belong.[11]

The Vietnamese, too, belonged to the wide world or, rather, overlapping worlds. A thirteenth-century emperor, anxious to preach to his subjects the benefits of the meditation school of Buddhism, known in Japan as Zen, could extol without embarrassment the debt China and Vietnam owed the Indians who first propagated the Buddha's teachings across the deserts of Central Asia. But, again in Vietnam, Chinese classical writing about antiquity was held to reflect universal norms of experience and could be rhetorically invoked to ratify Vietnamese behavior.[12] In the same mood, elsewhere in Southeast Asia the name of Kauṭilya, the Hindu master of statecraft, or of Manu, the lawgiver, could be invoked to validate local behavior as reflecting universal norms. And educated Vietnamese, familiar with and using such

---

[10] Benedict Anderson, *Imagined Communities*, rev. ed. (London: Verso, 1992), pp. 12–19, on "The Religious Community." The "Hindu World" is not included among communities defined in terms of a sacred language and written script.

[11] I am puzzled by the Cornell University Press's advertisement of the recently published *Southeast Asia in the Early Modern Era: Trade, Power, and Belief,* ed. Anthony Reid (Ithaca, NY: Cornell University Press, 1993): "This book is the first to document ... the shift from experimental spirit worship to the universalist scriptural religions of Islam, Christianity, and Theravada Buddhism." I would think that nothing had been more magnificently "universalist" than "Hinduism."

[12] Occasionally, but only rarely, Vietnamese rulers were urged by their advisers to be guided by ancient Chinese wisdom.

Chinese cultural artifacts as poetic forms or Chinese-style coinage or reign-periods, could enjoy the sensation of participating in the "civilized" world on equal terms with the Chinese.

In this "world" the center could be anywhere according to where one claimed it to be, which would be where one lived. There were innumerable centers. Professor Hendrik Maier observes that the Malay words for the compass points "tend to conceive the world from the perspective of their own community and plotted space relative to their ruler's (and their own) compound."[13] Here is another instance of a genuine "world view," a basic element in the Southeast Asian cultural heritage. Part of the same heritage was hospitality toward those from elsewhere in that world and especially their bookish knowledge. Useful information and also foreigners with expert religious lore at their disposal traveled regularly over the trade routes from the most distant places.

Cultural Feature 4—What gave distinctive shape to public life within Southeast Asia itself was a cultural emphasis on "person" and "'achievement" rather than on "group" and "hereditary" status. At the same time—and in contrast with South and East Asia, with their emphasis on ascribed status and collective units such as family, lineage, and caste—there was a downgrading of the importance of lineage based on claims to status through descent. Society had to be continuously monitored to spot potential leaders in a particular generation, and this outlook encouraged the habit of "present-mindedness." "Government" was not a matter of elaborate institutions but of a relaxed unbureaucratic style of public life, where importance was attached to man-management and ceremony and where personal qualities of leadership and example played the major role. I like the expression "relaxed" because it absolves one from having to beg the question of what is "strong" or "weak" government. Similarly, I prefer the neutral expression "polity" to "State." A relaxed style of public life did not mean that every polity was usually on the brink of collapse. One reason is the tradition that rulers and ruled depended on each other; the ruled could migrate if government suddenly became more severe. Interdependence would also be expressed when the villagers' shrines were protected by the ruler and, of course, when the ruler kept the peace in the countryside or repelled invaders.

In Vietnamese sources, too, mention is sometimes made of "extraordinarily" endowed persons who attracted followers. Vietnamese rulers, though believed to be protected by the spiritual authority of their family, were also attributed with possessing such special qualities as discernment in managing officials.

The crucial importance of the individual qua ruler could and usually was infinitely enhanced by the identification of his personal prowess with the divine attributes of a cosmic god of the "Hindu" pantheon or of a local spirit or, indeed, of both. "Hinduization" had been a process of making sense of what was "foreign" in terms of what was already familiar, and so it was that the attributes of Śiva could be construed as those of the local man of prowess. Thus, the ruler was "god-like" and associated with the sources of fertility and therefore of life itself. There was a pervasive apprehension of the supernatural forces of the land and water. According to Vietnamese popular belief, he who deserved to rule would apprehend the presence of a local spirit and thereby win its allegiance and invincible support. The

---

[13] H. M. J. Maier, "The Malays, the Waves, and the Java Sea," in *Looking in Odd Mirrors: The Java Sea*, ed. V. J. H. Houben et al. (Leiden: Vakgroep Talen en Culturen van Zuidoost-Asië en Oceanie, 1992), p. 12.

spirits were always at hand to be summoned, and this perception, too, reinforced the conviction that "now," the time of apprehending, was the time that mattered.

There was bound to be competition between contending men of prowess; there was no room at the top for more than one person. While the amount of prowess in the world was limitless and could be shared, authority and power were limited in amount. When a person's prowess had been satisfactorily tested, the successful competitor's authority and power would be absolute and could not be shared or transmitted.

A leader with discernibly superior prowess was associated with the capacity to attract followers, who were anxious to earn a meritorious reputation, personal advancement in the leader's service, and a share of the leader's wealth, though the same followers would switch their allegiance when their leader could no longer protect them. Rulers would provide impressive public occasions when their followers could advertise their relative status. Earning merit by serving a leader with divine attributes in order to stand oneself in good stead after death could also be a significant motive in public life. Relations with one's peers within an entourage could be uneasy. This, at least, was Vietnamese experience, where a ruler's followers tended to compete against each other for his favors.

Apart from the prestige of the hermitage and the priesthood, nothing rivaled that of public life.[14] Response to an established leader would be automatic, and processes of social mobilization would be set in train. Leadership could be exercised in various ways; a recent study of the Minangkabau polity in the seventeenth century indicates that receipt of the ruler's written word could be expected to transform the situation even in distant places.[15]

The leader-led relationship may have put a brake on the extension of wider human collectivities. There were cults of kingship rather than "kingdoms"; a "kingdom" was the geographical projection of a leader's prowess. The institutions of entourage, dependency—in various forms—and alliance thrived in the shadow of this kind of leadership because these institutions contributed to what a leader most needed, which was ample manpower resources. The experience of belonging to entourages might have helped to foster a tendency to seek consensus, a cultural feature reflected in the context of current ASEAN diplomacy.[16] But this is unlikely. "Consensus" is associated with the composing of ideological differences. An "entourage" can be more properly described as a set of personal loyalties animating a group of followers, each of whose loyalty was directed to his leader. In general, ties were personal rather than based on an abstract notion of "loyalty." Behavior would

---

[14] In a major study of early Southeast Asian coinage, Robert Wicks has established the validity of Philip Grierson's model: "It was only after a physical money, such as a standardized coinage, came to be accepted for use in making administrative payments that money was able to be utilized in commercial (marketized) exchange." See Robert S. Wicks, *Money, Markets, and Trade in Early Southeast Asia* (Ithaca, NY: Cornell Southeast Asia Program, 1992), p. 312. In other words, public administration and not private trade first brought this facility into being.

[15] Jane Drakard, "A Kingdom of Words: Minangkabau Sovereignty in Sumatran History" (PhD thesis, The Australian National University, 1993). A captured letter from Amangkurat II, Susuhunan of Mataram, in connection with his receipt of Raja Sakti's letter, states that he bowed "reverently before the great Sultan of Minangkabau since we share the Islamic faith"; Drakard, "A Kingdom of Words," p. 242.

[16] On ASEAN (Association of Southeast Asian Nations) diplomacy, see Pushpa Thambipillai, "Negotiating Styles," *The ASEAN Reader*, comp. K. S. Sandhu et al. (Singapore: Institute of Southeast Asian Studies, 1992), pp. 72–75.

be informal except during ceremonial occasions; the followers' roles could change when circumstances required. The entourage had, of course, to be rallied before an adventure could be undertaken. "Rallying" was one of the dynamic happenings in the region. An entourage need not have been large. With about 600 men whom he had rallied in a small river valley, Datu Uto in the nineteenth century turned Magindanao upside down.

Here is a famous example of an entourage in Javanese history. After the "disaster" (the *pralaya*) in the eleventh century, Erlangga escaped with "the best of his servants," his faithful entourage. His cause gradually snowballed. He was always victorious, but he distributed the booty among his "servants" and "took away only the glory for himself" (meaning, I take it, the verification of his prowess).

There was no widespread "corruption" in the sense of hoarding wealth for personal ends. Instead, there was an imaginative redistribution of wealth in the form of gracious favors. There were patrons and clients. Generosity, creating a sense of obligation, was a required royal virtue. Loyalties had to be continually replenished by rewards in bad as well as good times.

Successful warfare was, of course, a sign of a proven leader, even though military campaigns rarely led to permanent political solutions and never to large-scale colonization. Leaders needed the maximum space in which to flex their muscles. Warfare did not change the map except at the expense of Vietnam's southern neighbors during the few short-lived intervals of strong dynastic government in Vietnam. One did not have to belong to a ruler's ethnic group to be his subject. The ethnic patchwork of Southeast Asia was sometimes accentuated by the movement of captives and their resettlement in a conqueror's heartland.

The institutions of entourage and alliance, nourished by largesse available from trading treasure, were probably especially important influences among those societies, such as the Javanese, which practiced bilateral kinship and where extensive followings could be readily built up on both sides of one's family.

What Anthony Reid has referred to as the high degree of "autonomy of women" should be regarded as a cultural feature in its own right, but in my present context of entourage and alliance I shall do no more than endorse, if I may, what he has to say about "descent," which "was (usually) reckoned bilaterally in terms of the status of both father and mother, which provided one element of uncertainty about succession."[17] I doubt whether sufficient emphasis can be given to the institution of bilateral kinship, especially when one takes the practice of multiple marriages into account. Here we are in the presence of a veritable reservoir of potential claimants to kingship and of a source of political instability; there were few more dangerous persons in Southeast Asia than half-brothers or brothers-in-law. Such was the entrenched social status of Southeast Asian women that in Vietnam before the nineteenth century, and in spite of the authority of Chinese legal codes, protection was guaranteed to "the right of daughters to equal inheritance of the portion of family estate remaining after disposition of the worship property."[18] Furthermore,

---

[17] Anthony Reid, *Southeast Asia in the Age of Commerce, 1450–1680* √ol. 1: *The Lands below the Winds* (New Haven, CT: Yale University Press, 1988), p. 120.

[18] Nguyễn Ngọc Huy and Tạ Văn Tài ..., *The Lê Code. Law in Traditional Vietnam*, vol. 1 (Athens, OH: Ohio University Press, 1989), p. 80.

women enjoyed the legal protection of some personal rights such as the right to sue husbands for neglect.[19]

Cultural Feature 5—In this achievement-oriented culture, manpower was a leader's chief economic resource and was especially necessary for providing a surplus agricultural product to support the Court, public works, military adventures, and overseas trade. Rulers would be expected to prevent disasters, protect religious works, and be accessible to the people by providing mediators when disputes arose. One may suppose that nowhere should authority have been more valued than in village communities, where the inhabitants could pursue their agricultural activities without interference from powerful families in the neighborhood, though I have been given to understand that Thai and Burman villagers would view their rulers as one of the intrinsic "disasters" they faced and comparable with natural disasters such as flood and drought.

An uninterrupted arrival of trading treasure, regarded as the ruler's right, was assumed. A contributor to *Southeast Asia in the Early Modern Era* has rightly stated that "the importance of appropriating a commercial resource base for establishing political power cannot be overestimated in the Southeast Asian context."[20] Another historian has remarked that "Malays, it would seem, sought wealth not for its own sake but as a means of gaining political influence in the form of a sizeable personal following."[21] There has always been an age of commerce in Southeast Asia even if the levels, conditions of exchange, and sources of economic stimulus were not the same over the centuries. A notable feature of a recent conference on the Java Sea is that Malay and Javanese literature, though referring to the sea, was found to be virtually silent on matters of trade; overseas trade could be taken for granted.[22]

I have referred to an "outward-lookingness" in earlier Southeast Asia which promoted the sense of belonging to a wide world. The same trait could serve local concerns. The structure of Indonesian written and oral sources has suggested to a maritime historian that the origins of "kingdoms" on the coasts of the Java Sea were associated with the success of local heroes in manipulating the arrival of foreign trading treasure to their advantage.[23]

Cultural Feature 6—Not surprising in this cultural context, leaders were idealized and even venerated as teachers of good behavior, usually conceptualized as good religious behavior. The qualities expected of worthy rulers could comprise all or some of the following according to the degree with which the qualities were respected in a particular society: courage, ascetic self-control, physical strength,

---

[19] Ibid., pp. 81–82.

[20] Jeyamalar Kathirithamby-Wells, "Restraints on the Development of Merchant Capitalism in Southeast Asia before c. 1800," in Reid, *Southeast Asia in the Early Modern Era*, p. 129.

[21] A. C. Milner, *Kerajaan: Malay Political Culture on the Eve of Colonial Rule* (Tucson, AZ: University of Arizona Press, 1982), p. 27. Robert Wicks observes that "in early Southeast Asia internal trading activities were frequently supervised in order to limit the amount of surplus that could be accumulated by traders and merchants" (*Money, Markets, and Trade*, p. 310). Or again, "foreign goods more often appear in the context of status enhancement, supporting an argument that intercultural trade was most often carried on, not to accumulate surplus for its own sake, but for the political, social, and religious benefits that could accrue from control over exotic and unusual goods" (see Wicks, *Money, Markets, and Trade*, pp. 312–13).

[22] Houben et al., *Looking in Odd Mirrors: The Java Sea.*

[23] Pierre-Yves Manguin, "The Merchant and the King: Political Myths of Southeast Asian Coastal Polities," *Indonesia* 52 (October 1991): 41–54.

resourcefulness, rhetorical skill, discernment, accessibility, compassion, willingness to protect the rights of others, an ability to mediate, generosity, and especially skill in managing and mobilizing networks of personal relationships. The ruler, partaking of divinity, was expected to be the exemplar of all that was deemed good, beautiful, and true.

Monuments, visual aids to worship and reminders of the rulers' ubiquitous presence, bore witness to the rulers' stature as well as to their successful control and manipulation of resources. The inscriptions relayed religious messages, and art made the great Hindu epics and the Buddhist canon visible and therefore accessible. These are the texts, to which the shadow puppet plays belonged, that shaped behavior and taught Southeast Asian societies what could and should be the quality of an individual's life. These were the texts which defined the ideal ruler.[24]

Cultural Feature 7—But in spite of the high expectations of kingship, there were no prolonged or, probably, any periods of strong "centralized" government. Although a ruler's authority could be seen as absolute, this was on account of his God-like attributes and not his administrative powers. Śiva could be the Creator of the Universe without having to supervise it in every detail. The ruler's day-to-day power was based on the norms in his society. A political system cohered only in the sense that it was a projection of a leader's personal influence, backed by the personal loyalty and ubiquity of the leader's representatives. Only short-term goals were plausible.

And so it was that regimes were not long-lasting, a circumstance consistent with the principle of cyclical time.[25] Even in Vietnam effective "dynastic" government was always short-lived, though the Chinese-style imperial institution had been localized in the tenth century to suit Vietnamese needs.[26] Ngô Sĩ Liên, a Vietnamese historian of the later fifteenth century, reviewed what had happened under the previous dynasty in the thirteenth and fourteenth centuries and deplored what he regarded as signs of instability such as dependence on entourages, obsessive merit-seeking, and personal and informal relations at Court. We would recognize these features as being "Southeast Asian" without judging them to be defects.[27] Only Vietnamese historians made a fetish of the need for strong government because they knew that it rarely existed. Their "imperial'" institution should have offered the promise of strong

---

[24] I am grateful for Stanley J. O'Connor's guidance.

[25] According to Claude Jacques, "From the inscriptions it emerges clearly enough that regional rebellions were seldom absent in the Angkorian period, and the Royal Chronicles, not to speak of some present-day reports, tell of many such rebellions against the central power. I am sure it would not be going too far to say that they have been endemic in the Khmer land from the very beginning of history"; see "Sources on Economic Activities in Khmer and Cham Lands," in *Southeast Asia in the 9th to 14th Centuries*, ed. David G. Marr and A. C. Milner (Singapore: Institute of Southeast Asian Studies, Singapore, 1986), pp. 229–30.

[26] Primarily to protect the succession to the throne within a particular family. One consequence of the weakness of the Vietnamese dynastic institution was its frequent dependence on right-hand men, usually known as *thái-úy*, instead of on an entrenched bureaucracy to assist young or weak rulers. These "protectors," as they were called, were liable to usurp when the chance occurred, and, for this reason, the Trần dynasty in the thirteenth and fourteenth centuries appointed their closest kinsmen as *thái-úy*.

[27] I discussed this matter in my article "What Else May Ngô Sĩ Liên, a Fifteenth-Century Vietnamese Historian, Mean? A Matter of Distinctions," in *Sojourners and Other Settlers: Histories of Southeast Asia and the Chinese, in Honor of Jennifer Cushman*, ed. Anthony Reid (Sydney: Allen and Unwin, 1996), pp. 94–114.

government in what they imagined was China's style, yet they knew that it was always being corroded. The fifteenth-century historian, Ngô Sĩ Liên, was, in my opinion, nervous about the future because of what he regarded as endemic institutional and cultural weaknesses revealed in the recent past.

Cultural Feature 8—Because of relaxed governmental institutions, ethnic identities on the edges of the major polities were left undisturbed and often represented by contiguous ecological layers on the physical map. There were no "borders" in the modern sense but only porous peripheries. The region was "Balkanized" but without ethnic-grounded "Balkan" wrath. Populations might be transferred after a war or there might be raiding for slaves. Otherwise, ecological factors kept ethnic groups in habitation zones where they could live comfortably. There were, of course, vital economic interdependencies such as upstream and downstream, forest and agricultural peoples, forest collectors, and port polities. In some areas there was a considerable degree of bilingualism and opportunities for manipulating one's identity. Bilingualism signifies that people with different origins had learnt to live together.[28]

Yet peripheries were indispensable to the center's status. A ruler's prestige depended on his claim to be the overlord of a multi-ethnic polity.[29] Moreover, overlordship, though often no more than ceremonial, was a form of self-defense because the rival overlord would be deprived of the services of those who lived in the porous borderland. What lay beyond the porous borders was always a matter of concern to an overlord, and one consequence would be the importance attached to up-to-date and accurate political intelligence in order to monitor developments in neighboring territories. I suggest that the skills of diplomacy are part of the Southeast Asian tradition.

An exception to this situation is provided by the Vietnamese, who were able gradually to extend their southern borders at the expense of the Chams. Yet as late as the fourteenth century, discontented Vietnamese were prepared to seek refuge over the southern border in Champa, and an edict was issued to forbid Vietnamese from adopting foreign speech and clothes. And in the nineteenth century the Húê emperors complained that some Vietnamese villagers in the south were becoming "Khmer" in speech and clothing.

So much for some proposed "cultural features."[30] The first three are associated with the notion of "now": "now" is the time that matters in all fields of useful knowledge; the sense of belonging to a wide world would multiply the opportunities for being up-to-date. The other five features are similarly related to the notion of "now": "now" is when one identifies among one's generation an up-and-coming man of prowess, who will need and attract manpower and trading revenue and will be venerated, though his political influence will be no more than a projection of his personal prowess and will not be territorially defined.

---

[28] During the conference in Jakarta, considerable attention was given to the need to study how those living in pluralistic societies managed to fit in together. Here could be a further cultural feature of the region.

[29] For example, in the Lao and Perak courts, leaders of the hill peoples were accorded status and titles.

[30] For a succinct formulation of prehistoric and persisting Southeast Asian "cultural inlays," see Lauriston Sharp, "Cultural Continuities and Discontinuities in Southeast Asia," *JAS* 22, 1 (1962): 9, n. 9.

Few, if any, of these features are peculiar to Southeast Asia.[31] Perhaps the importance of "person" and "achievement," a relaxed exercise of power, extreme multicentricism, and unusual geographical access to the outside world, though no doubt non-Southeast Asian examples can be adduced, are more pronounced in the region than in many other parts of the world. On the other hand, the combination of these features—their configuration—may be distinctively Southeast Asian, with the effect that each feature would reinforce the others. For example, I noted that the habit of spotting potential leaders in a particular generation would encourage the habit of "present-mindedness."

The conclusion would therefore seem to be that Southeast Asian experience in the past had always been a matter of endless "nows." I have, in effect, made a case for Southeast Asia's remarkable propensity for being "modern." Furthermore, the benefits to be gained from being "modern" are today obviously overwhelming. For example, in April 1993 *The Economist* had a supplement on Indonesia, and its title was "Wealth in its Grasp."[32] It would not be surprising if some should suppose that the influence of the past was a retarding one and that tradition was a drag on progress and the benefits of modernity.

I must now remind you that I have proposed these cultural features with the hope that they may stimulate self-awareness among a Southeast Asian audience. It is not my purpose to impose my views on you. You may reject what I have suggested as being historically implausible. Or you may acknowledge some of these features in a modified form but suggest additional and more important ones. But, whatever the case, I hope that the question will be whether today any feature of the past is still visible on a significant scale or, at least, whether tendencies or even inclinations can be detected that resemble what I have been trying to describe. Has there been a fundamental change in form or is it only a matter of paraphernalia or technology? Alternatively, have entirely new patterns of life and new types of public figures come to occupy the stage? Above all, is there anything in the past—features or merely tendencies—that can be regarded as a resource or impediment in this present age?

I can at last return to the notion of LIPI as a "watchdog." If a lively sense of the past does not happen to be a Southeast Asian cultural feature and if, as I have suggested, such a sense would stimulate self-awareness and therefore a critique of the cultural background to what is happening at the present time, LIPI could respond by taking the initiative and arguing that an indifference to past experience could compromise the way one manages the present on behalf of the future. LIPI would demonstrate how historians possess their own insights into the contemporary situation.

LIPI could first examine and criticize the assumptions and perspectives reflected in my sketch of the past and, where necessary, come up with different sketches of what may be salient in the sense of explaining how people behaved and how things happened. LIPI could then make the essential point that these cultural features could

---

[31] For example, as Benedict Anderson puts it on page 23 in *Imagined Communities*, "...the mediaeval Christian mind had no conception of history as an endless chain of cause and effect or of radical separations between past and present." He goes on to quote Auerbach: "The here and now is no longer a mere link in an earthly chain of events, it is *simultaneously* something which has always been, and will be fulfilled in the future." See footnote 8, above, for a comment on a similar Southeast Asian approach to time.

[32] "A Survey of Indonesia. Wealth in its Grasp," *The Economist*, April 17, 1993.

have generated a core of shared values or attitudes of mind, prejudices against as well as for certain modes of behavior, which persist even today. For example, a present-focused attitude toward time and a tradition of hospitality toward ideas and individuals from the outside world are still surely forces to be taken into account. The Southeast Asian experience of a widely open world suggests that multinational corporations and anything else that can be labeled "cosmopolitan" readily fits into this aspect of the cultural tradition. And what about the notion that wealth is less valuable for its own sake than as a source of political power? And would a tendency to think in terms of what the present has to offer engender consumer habits?

LIPI might then choose to insist that persisting values need not be repudiated wholesale in a frenzy of self-modernization. Instead, they should be scrutinized, judged, asserted, or kept under tight control in the light of priorities created by the extraordinary circumstances of the modern world and by future goals. Instead of a frenzy of modernization, one could calmly and critically assess the strengths and weaknesses of the cultural heritage still visible in its traces today, and consider which values would be a resource and which would be otherwise. Here might be a means of mobilizing the past to guide or even manipulate one's response to changed conditions in the world.[33]

If, however, there were to be no such scrutiny and reordering of inherited values, what would the future be? Would there be an endlessly recurrent influence of the same cultural features or tendencies? Would there be a state of involution that would not give enlightened modernism its chance? To take the worst prospect, perhaps the configuration of Southeast Asia in the past would have already prefigured the postmodern condition, in which progress would be neither thinkable nor achievable.

But only Southeast Asian historians would be able to pounce on those inherited values that could contribute to goals set for the future or hinder the management of necessary changes. Only they may know whether a traditional focus on the present may encourage improvidence in respect of the future. Only they may know whether more prestige still accrues to those in government service than to those, for example, who work in the private sector and whether it matters. Only they may know whether the traditional respect paid to the individual who achieves and attracts an entourage represents an appropriate standard of leadership in the modern age. Is the institution of the entourage more or less prominent today? And only they may be able to evaluate the influences that work in favor of a less relaxed style of government.[34]

---

[33] Here are two examples of a positive approach to the past, present, and future. A Cambodian teacher, able only recently to resume her vocation, states that she has decided that her calling is "to help my country, the future of my country" by dancing and teaching. She is an educator but of a special kind: she is concerned to "re-educate" her fellow countrymen so that they may recover what in the past had been smothered by the Khmer Rouge; see Toni Shapiro, "Dancing in Cambodia," *Southeast Asia Program Bulletin* (Ithaca, NY: Cornell University, Spring 1993), pp. 2–3. A Javanese artist provides an example of how one can emulate behavior patterns of earlier times to replenish contemporary life. She has in mind the practice of meditation and everything associated with it, such as the sensation of being in harmony with nature. "People forget where they come from," she says. "There is a need for self-awareness in the present age of endless competition so that one may overcome a sense of inferiority. One needs to ask oneself what are the achievements of the past—always cultural ones—in order to challenge and maybe bring order to the present." From a personal communication with Hilda Soemantri Siddhartha.

[34] I have read *Southeast Asian Capitalists*, ed. Ruth McVey (Ithaca, NY: Cornell Southeast Asia Program, 1992). Dr. McVey's introductory essay, "The Materialization of the Southeast Asian Entrepreneur," covers a great deal of ground I had ignored and especially the shifting

I am not qualified to comment on such matters. They are for the scholars of the areas, as also are three more questions. Is there anything in the modern world which seems to make particular sense and is therefore familiar in terms of what was already there, and, if so, what confidence can this provide? "Hinduization," I suggested, should be understood as a "Hinduizing" process that depended essentially on a Southeast Asian capacity for making sense of what was "foreign" and unfamiliar in terms of what was already familiar.[35] Is modernization being construed in a similar way and, if not, why not? The second matter is whether an intensive study of the past would encourage regional centricisms at the expense of a supra-regional nation and, at the same time, demolish pleasing historical myths.

Finally, LIPI may wish to examine from the perspective of cultural history a recent World Bank report, *The East Asian Miracle*. How much in the report, when read between the lines and freed from the language of economists, is predictable to a cultural historian? How far does its description of contemporary economic developments mirror cultural features in the region's past? Indonesia, Thailand, Malaysia, and Singapore comprise the report's four Southeast Asian "superstars." To what extent are value systems inherited from the past responsible for this economic situation?

I am sure that many more questions can be raised on these lines. All I have tried to do is to suggest that, within Southeast Asia itself, there may be practical as well as academic reasons for studying the Southeast Asian past and reviewing its legacy in

---

relationship of bureaucrats and businessmen. She evinces a measured optimism about the prospects awaiting Southeast Asian capitalists. Yet much of what she writes makes sense to a historian of earlier Southeast Asia and, above all, what she has to say about the attraction of "modern" skills and the influence of the international environment, though I wonder whether an MBA would be sufficient to smother one's traditional cultural attitudes when reaching middle age. Can one identify a man of prowess in the business world? He might be someone adept at man-management as distinct from technical skills and one who was entirely at home in the international business and professional society in general. I believe that Ruth McVey has this kind of society in mind when she refers, on page 32, to "the interplay of complex interests ... which will be expressed more and more through agencies, associations, and lobbies rather than through the dyadic relationships of patron–client networks." The modern man of prowess would build up his entourage by developing relationships with potential partners, by organizing mergers—maybe by marriages—and by acquiring subsidiaries. Here would be contemporary scope for the traditional aptitude for building alliances.

[35] Ruth McVey's second option, below, is obviously congenial to me. Studying the Taman Siswa, she supposes: "Some, conscious of lost time and fearful the country might never catch up to modernity's receding image, might urge that the most modem ideas and methods must be imposed; others might feel that anything that was itself very modem in style was less likely to have a modernizing effect on the society than something less radically different from the society's own experience." See Ruth T. McVey, "Taman Siswa and the Indonesian National Awakening," *Indonesia* 4 (October 1967): 135. It would be interesting to bring together discussions of the meaning of modernity. According to Jurgen Habermas, "Modernity revolts against the normalizing functions of tradition; modernity lives on the experience of rebelling against all that is normative. This revolt is one way to neutralize the standards of both morality and utility." See his "Modernity Versus Post Modernity," in *Postmodern Perspectives: Issues in Contemporary Art*, ed. Howard Risatti (Eaglewood Cliffs, NJ: Prentice Hall, 1990), p. 56. I am grateful to Stanley O'Connor for the reference. Habermas also points out that modernity is something that is itself always doomed to be outmoded. Rudolf Mrázek has suggested to me that being self-consciously or even fashionably "modern" could reflect personal insecurity, a sense of being uprooted to the extent that one felt obliged to denounce the past.

terms of appropriate attitudes of mind in the context of confronting the modern world. LIPI may wish to foster a public opinion favorable to this proposition.[36]

May I suggest one further responsibility for LIPI, which is to consider how the Southeast Asian past may be profitably studied to make it intellectually exciting as well as relevant?

In my opening remarks I referred to the Wingspread report on Southeast Asian studies in the United States. LIPI might wish to respond to certain passages in it. For example, the author of the epilogue referred to "the perception that Southeast Asian studies may lack both a coherent intellectual foundation and a compelling practical rationale for mobilizing the public and private resources needed to sustain and expand its academic practice."[37] He also stated that "we must define the core of our field by seeking to understand the essence of Southeast Asian civilization. This means that we must refocus our efforts on the study of the literatures, religions, and the arts of the region in their historical development and contemporary contexts.... I have no doubt," he went on to say, "that such studies will find common themes underlying the Southeast Asian social and cultural mosaic, themes that define the essence of Southeast Asian civilization."[38] I wonder whether one explanation of the Wingspread Conference's hand-wringing mood may be that participants looked wistfully backward rather than forward. Surely the civilizations of Southeast Asia are being created today and tomorrow; the contribution of the past is to enable us to establish valuable continuities or needed breaks.

I suggest, therefore, and I hope not mischievously, that LIPI may wish to respond to Wingspread's impression of the impoverished state of the field and the phantom-like nature of Southeast Asian "civilization."

The effectiveness of LIPI's response to these reservations of their colleagues overseas would be closely connected with the question of "how" to study the past: the disciplines involved and their relationships. There is always a need to create an interest in the field by innovative and challenging research. Southeast Asian studies must be lively; after all, they are an arena for interdisciplinary work and, for this reason, the field may have enviable prospects. The experience of interdisciplinary activity can foster a tendency to build bridges with additional disciplines in order, if I may quote something I have read recently, "to expand the technical repertoire and conceptual boundaries."[39] As a result, entirely new problems can be identified and the educational merits of the field thereby safeguarded. Ideally speaking, the field should be perpetually renewing itself, and part of LIPI's role could be to call attention to what is exciting about the region and methodologies deployed in its study.

The "watchdog" may also wish to argue the case for the purposes and contributions of certain disciplines in the humanities. Which are the particularly

---

[36] On page 13 of *Culture and Society in New Order Indonesia*, ed. Virginia Matheson Hooker (Kuala Lumpur: Oxford University Press, 1993), Hooker notes that one "theme which runs through the essays is that traditions which survive have done so in new contexts." The cultural features explored in the present essay are behavioral patterns rather than artistic forms. Moreover, the question is less whether they are capable of surviving than whether they should.

[37] Hirschman et al., eds., *Southeast Asian Studies*, p. 135.

[38] Ibid., p. 141.

[39] Featherman, "What Does Society Need ... ?," p. 40.

creative disciplines at the moment?[40] I wish to make a special plea for anthropology, the study of the arts and archaeology, and literary studies, because I believe that these are disciplines likely to bring one close to the heartbeat of "Southeast Asian civilization" or, more accurately, the heartbeats of the various civilizations of Southeast Asia, for regional communality in respect of certain cultural patterns cannot possibly mean that cultural differences did not and do not exist among these societies.

The case for anthropology and the study of the arts and archaeology hardly needs to be made here. Both fields are well established in Southeast Asia. Anthropology studies how things in societies happen, whereas historians may sometimes tend to be content with what happened and why. One way of stating the contribution of art history is that it concerns itself with the realm of appearance, where people once lived and where they could define and recognize themselves. Art history deals with self-awareness in the past, and self-awareness is the central theme of my remarks today. Art history, in the words of an art historian, "offers ways of reconnecting perception and imagination, the circuit of cognitions, which these works once ignited and through which their meanings were established.[41]

I would, however, like to say a few words on behalf of literary studies within the context of Southeast Asian regional studies. Several Wingspread participants stressed the importance of studying literature.

What I have in mind by "literary studies" is the study of literature for its own sake: "how" a piece of writing is "made" in the sense that its "text" is an artifact comprising structures and the linguistic usages conventional in a particular culture. Here we can get closer to a text's "voice," and here is an opportunity for exploring the notion that Southeast Asia comprises numerous cultures, each leaving its special mark on a local literature.[42] Exposure to the discipline of textual study, the essence of this approach to literary studies, can sharpen curiosity and alertness when one is investigating the presence of connections, relationships, differences, disruptures, and instabilities mirrored in literature and also in the web of social and political

---

[40] One contributor to the Wingspread report, the only historian, made a powerful case for the history of religions in order "to establish an effective humanistic beachhead within Southeast Asian studies." See Hirschman et al., eds., *Southeast Asian Studies*, p. 64, n. 11.

[41] I am again grateful to Professor O'Connor.

[42] I tried to fly this kite in my *History, Culture, and Region in Southeast Asian Perspectives* (Singapore: Institute of Southeast Asian Studies, 1982 [1999 rev. ed.]). My intention was not to preclude the study of "early regionalized networking as the basis for the more meaningful study of administrative structure and for political, religious, and commercial development...," though Kenneth Hall, in a review of Robert Wicks's *Money, Markets, and Trade*, regrets that my influence has discouraged such a study (see *JAS* 52,3 [1993]: 803–4). I am sufficiently familiar with art history to realize that this would be foolish. My point was simply that one should not take it for granted that the unit we recognize as "Southeast Asia" was always conveniently intact and familiar so that historians could go ahead and explore with confidence "the cultural and economic integration" to which Hall refers and evidently prefers to study. As I put it in 1982, "Until more is known in historical terms of this singular feature of Southeast Asia [its cultural diversity], the search for an overarching shape to the region's history will lack a satisfactory basis" (see *History, Culture, and Region*, pp. 45–46). Needless to say, I accept Keith Taylor's article of faith which Hall sorrowfully quotes in his review. But I did not box myself in. I was aware of the phenomenon of cultural relocalization within the region, and this prevents too restricted a sense of locality. I also conceded that there was a wide span of peoples with concurrent modes of behavior and with communalities of outlook. My paper today is an extended discussion of such communalities.

happenings. Textual study can enlarge a scholar's sensitivity and especially to the use of language within a culture.[43]

I am sure that literary studies, anthropology, and the study of the arts would go some way in responding to the Wingspread Conference's perplexity about the nature of Southeast Asian civilization and therefore about the substance of "Southeast Asian studies." One participant referred to "our efforts to convince our humanities-oriented colleagues in other fields that Southeast Asian civilizations and cultures are, in fact, worthy of focused attention."[44] I prefer to consider one's expectations of literary studies by referring again to what I suggested were pronounced cultural features in Southeast Asia. If what I have said has any validity, it would be to an important extent because it is reflected in literary sources, defined in the widest meaning of the term. But the special contribution of literature and also of the arts and anthropology must be to bring to light so much more that is interesting about the region's independent cultural heritage and without the needless obligation of having to make the case for "Southeast Asian civilizations."

The influence of LIPI's role as I have presumed to define it would not be limited to Indonesia or Southeast Asia. LIPI would have the obligation of communicating westwards scholarly perspectives gathered from within Southeast Asia. My final point, therefore, is that LIPI might wish to respond to the Wingspread Conference's hope that a greater exchange of ideas between Western and Southeast Asian scholars would invigorate the field. Few developments would be more enlivening than the beaming of Southeast Asian scholarly perspectives beyond the region. We, at the Western end of the academic spectrum, would learn from having our concerns scrutinized and evaluated from a vantage point we could never occupy.

In the past I have unsuccessfully urged that Southeast Asian historians of Southeast Asia should hold a modestly priced conference somewhere in Southeast Asia, be locked up in order, undisturbed, to discuss matters of concern to each of them, and then consider, among other things, whether they could produce their own joint History of Southeast Asia.[45] The possibility would now arise of a seminar to prepare a new history of Southeast Asia and one that was not simply a stringing together of National Histories but would be informed by regional self-awareness and values as well as being professionally acceptable. And perhaps the same seminar could explore the possibility of a comparative study of modernizing Southeast Asian countries in historical perspective.

This morning I have suggested that a sense of the past should stimulate self-awareness and that historians could possess their own and valuable critical insights in respect of what they saw happening around them. With these suggestions in mind, I would like to conclude by recalling the words of a famous nineteenth-century Englishman, the future Cardinal Newman, who, in *The Idea of a University*, ascribes many noble qualities to the educated intellect. Among these qualities is one which Javanese historians not too long ago and, I am confident, LIPI's historians

---

[43] For example, Rudolf Mrázek's regret that a recent and valuable translation of Tan Malaka's *From Jail to Jail* suppressed the "strangeness" of his language, which played a crucial role in his appeal; see Rudolf Mrázek, "Tan Malaka: Just as Artisans, When Gathered Together," *Indonesia* 53 (April 1992): 67.

[44] Hirschman et al., eds., *Southeast Asian Studies*, p. 62.

[45] A comparative study of how Southeast Asian scholars have rendered Southeast Asian national histories and cultural identities would be a singular contribution to the field.

today and surely all in this room would affirm. Such an intellect, writes Newman, "is almost prophetic from its knowledge of history."[46]

Thank you.

3 November 1993

---

[46] Owen Chadwick, *Newman* (Oxford: Oxford University Press, 1990), p. 55; Nancy K. Florida, "Writing the Past, Inscribing the Future: Exile and Prophecy in an Historical Text of Nineteenth-Century Java," vol. 2 (PhD dissertation, Cornell University, 1990), chap. 8 (Conclusion: History and Prophecy).

CHAPTER TWO

EARLY SOUTHEAST ASIAN POLITICAL SYSTEMS

A remarkable development in Southeast Asian studies since the second World War has been the steadily improving knowledge of the region's prehistory.[1] The best-known discoveries, made possible by scientifically conducted excavations and the tools of carbon dating, thermo-luminescence, and palaeobotany, are signs of bronze-working and domesticated agriculture at certain sites in northeastern Thailand attributable to the fourth millennium BCE. Iron-working, too, seems to have been underway at one of these sites by about 1500 BCE. Moreover, by the second half of the second millennium BCE at the latest, metallurgy had become the most recent stage in a local cultural process over a sufficiently wide area in northern Vietnam to permit Vietnamese archaeologists to broach sophisticated sociological enquiries.

For my purpose, the important consequence of current prehistoric research is that an outline of the ancient settlement map is beginning to be disclosed. The map seems to comprise numerous networks of relatively isolated but continuously occupied dwelling sites, where residential stability was achieved by exploiting local environmental resources to sustain what is sometimes called continually expanding "broad spectrum" subsistence economies. The inhabitants' original skills were those of "forest efficiency," or horticulture, although during the second millennium BCE domesticated modes of wet-rice agriculture were probably appearing in the mainland alluvial plain."[2]

---

[1] For recent surveys of current prehistoric research, see I. W. Mabbett, "The 'Indianization' of Southeast Asia: Reflections on Prehistoric Sources," *JSEAS* 8,1 (1977): 1–14; the "Introduction" in *Early South East Asia: Essays in Archaeology, History and Historical Geography*, ed. R. B. Smith and W. Watson (New York, NY: Oxford University Press, 1979), pp. 3–14; Donn Bayard, "The Roots of Indochinese Civilisation," *Pacific Affairs* 51,1 (1980): 89–114; Nguyễn Phúc Long, "Les nouvelles recherches archéologiques au Vietnam," *Arts Asiatiques*, Numéro special, 31 (1975); Jeremy H. C. S. Davidson, "Archaeology in Northern Viet-Nam since 1954," in Smith and Watson, *Early South East Asia*, pp. 98–124; and Hà Văn Tấn, "Nouvelles recherches préhistoriques et protohistoriques au Vietnam," *BEFEO* 68 (1980): 113–54.

[2] See Donn Bayard, "The Roots of Indochinese Civilisation," p. 105, for an evaluation of the evidence of rice-cultivation techniques.

These tendencies in prehistoric research provide helpful perspectives for historians of the early Southeast Asian political systems, for they are now being encouraged to suppose that by the beginning of the Christian era a patchwork of small settlement networks of great antiquity stretched across the map of Southeast Asia. For example, no less than about three hundred settlements, datable by their artefacts as belonging to the seventh and eighth centuries CE, have been identified in Thailand alone by means of aerial photography.[3] Seen from the air, they remind one of craters scattered across the moon's surface. The seventh-century inscriptions of Cambodia mention as many as thirteen toponyms sufficiently prominent to be known by Sanskritic names. The multiplicity of Khmer centres, for there were surely more than thirteen, contradicts the impression provided by Chinese records of protohistoric Cambodia that there was only a single and enduring "kingdom of Funan."[4] "Funan" should not, I shall suggest below, be invoked as the earliest model of an "Indianized state" in Southeast Asia.

The historian, studying the dawn of recorded Southeast Asian history, can now suppose with reasonable confidence that the region was demographically fragmented. The ethnic identity and remotest origins of these peoples are questions that I shall eschew. Before the Second World War, prehistorians framed hypotheses based on tool typology to argue that culturally significant migrations into the region took place from the second half of the second millennium BCE. These hypotheses have now been overtaken by the disclosing chronology of much earlier technological innovation established by means of prehistoric archaeology. Rather than assuming migrations from outside the region, we can be guided by Don Bayard's view that prehistoric Southeast Asia was a "continually shifting mosaic of small cultural groups, resembling in its complexity the distribution of the modern hill tribes."[5] The focus of attention must be on what some of these groups could do inside the region and what they became.

The ancient inhabitants of Southeast Asia were living in fairly isolated groups, separated by thick forests, and would have had powerful attachments to their respective localities. I shall have occasion later to discuss the continuation of the prehistoric settlement pattern in historical times, and I shall content myself here by noting that in Java, for example, local scripts[6] and local sung poems[7] survived through the centuries. Or again, Malyāng, a small principality in north-western

[3] I am grateful to Srisakra Vallibhotama for this information.

[4] Claude Jacques, "'Funan.' 'Zhenla.' The Reality Concealed by these Chinese Views of Indochina," in Smith and Watson, *Early South East Asia*, p. 378; O. W. Wolters, "North-western Cambodia in the Seventh Century," *BSOAS* 37,2 (1974): 355–84 [reprinted in *Classical Civilizations of South East Asia: An Anthology of Articles Published in the Bulletin of SOAS*, ed. Vladimir Braginsky (London and New York: RoutledgeCurzon, 2002).—Ed.]; and "Khmer 'Hinduism' in the Seventh Century," in the present volume, chapter 8.

[5] Bayard, "The Roots of Indochinese Civilisation," p. 92. Recent excavations at Ban Chiang in northeastern Thailand have suggested a movement of people into the alluvial plains in the millennium after the transition to wet-rice cultivation at Ban Chiang (p. 105).

[6] J. G. de Casparis, *Indonesian Palaeography: A History of Writing in Indonesia from the beginning to c. A.D. 1500* (Leiden: E. J. Brill, 1975), p. 72.

[7] Martin E. Hatch, "Lagu, Laras, Layang. Rethinking Melody in Javanese Music" (PhD thesis, Cornell University, 1980), pp. 38–50. Old Javanese inscriptions show that those who called themselves "Mahārāja" retained the words "Raka of..." in their titles to indicate their home territory; see F. H. van Naerssen, *The Economic and Administrative History of Early Indonesia* (Leiden: E. J. Brill, 1977), pp. 46–55.

Cambodia during the seventh century, disappears from the records after the late eighth century but reappears in the late twelfth century as a rebellious area when Angkor was sacked by the Chams in 1177.[8] The modern names of villages and subregions are also often identifiable in early written records.

The multiplicity of settlement areas, each of which could go its own way, means that the historian should be cautious before he decides that any part of the region once occupied only a peripheral status in the general picture. Everything depends on what the historian is looking at in particular times in the past. For example, one still knows very little of the early history of the Philippines, but one should not conclude that these islands remained on the fringe of early Southeast Asia. Their inhabitants did not perceive their map in such a way. They are more likely to have looked outward to what is the Vietnamese coast today or to southern China for the more distant world that mattered to them. Every centre was a centre in its own right as far as its inhabitants were concerned, and it was surrounded by its own group of neighbours.

The ancient pattern of scattered and isolated settlements at the beginning of the Christian era would seem to suggest little prospect that the settlements would generate more extensive contact between themselves. The tempo of communication was probably slow even though linguists have been able to delineate major and overarching language families. The languages of the archipelago can be conveniently defined as belonging to the "Austronesian" language family. The language map of mainland Southeast Asia is much more complicated. In early times, the Mon-Khmer, or "Austroasiatic," family of languages stretched from Burma to northern Vietnam and southern China. The Tai and Burman languages were wedges thrust into the Mon-Khmer language zone. But the reality everywhere in Southeast Asia is likely to have been that the major language families were represented by numerous local and isolated speech variations. Only in later times did some variations take on the characteristics of neighbouring speeches, a development that gradually led to a more widely used standardized speech. Linguistic similarities were not in themselves cultural bridges. When, therefore, we enquire how these scattered settlements were able to reduce their isolation, we have to consider other cultural features with greater possibilities for creating more extensive relationships within the region.

There are, in fact, several such features, though we must bear in mind that not all societies can be attributed with identical features. Exceptions can always be found. Moreover, similar cultural features did not in themselves guarantee that extensive relationships would develop across localities as a matter of course, even if their inhabitants came to recognize that they had something in common.

One well-represented feature of social organization within the lowlands in the region today is what anthropologists refer to as "cognatic kinship,"[9] and we can

---

[8] Wolters, "North-western Cambodia in the Seventh Century," p. 358.

[9] This generalization does not include important groups such as the Chams and Minangkabau. I am referring, for example, to the Burmans, Thai, Khmers, Malays, Javanese, and Tagalogs. I follow Keesing's definition of "cognatic" as meaning (a) a mode of descent reckoning where all descendants of an apical ancestor/ancestress through any combinations of male or female links are included; and (b) bilateral kinship, where kinship is traced to relations through both father and mother. See Roger M. Keesing, *Kin Groups and Social Structure* (New York, NY: Holt, Rinehart and Winston, Inc., 1975), chapter 6 and the glossary. Sometimes examples are found of nuclear families and neolocal residence. The *Sui-shu*, referring to Cambodia in about 600 CE, states: "When a man's marriage ceremonies are completed, he takes a share of his parents' property and leaves them in order to live elsewhere." See O. W. Wolters, "Khmer 'Hinduism'

suppose that this feature was present throughout historical times. In simple terms, the expression means that descent is reckoned equally through males and females and that both males and females are able to enjoy equal inheritance rights.[10] The comparable status of the sexes in Southeast Asia may explain why an Indonesian art historian has noted the unisex appearance of gods and goddesses in Javanese iconography, whereas sexual differences are unambiguously portrayed in Indian iconography.[11]

A notable feature of cognatic kinship is the downgrading of the importance of lineage based on claims to status through descent from a particular male or female. This does not mean that early settlements were egalitarian societies; prehistoric graves with sumptuary goods and status symbols reveal hierarchical distinctions evolving from before the beginning of the Christian era. Moreover, the principle of cognatic kinship by no means implies that kinship ties are unimportant. The contrary is the case. Kinship ties are the idiom of social organization in the region and part of its history. For example, when the Khmers founded or endowed religious cult centres, their commemorative inscriptions mention a variety of male and female kinship relationships over several generations. Nevertheless, the forebears, members of the devotees' kin (*kula*), are not presented as a lineage. Certain forebears are signalled out for their personal accomplishments, but the focus of the inscriptions is always on those who are performing and commemorating their own acts of devotion. One inscription explicitly excludes the devotee's parents from enjoying the fruits of his devotion.[12]

The relative unimportance of lineage means that we have to look elsewhere for cultural factors that promote leadership and initiative beyond a particular locality, and I suggest that leadership in interpersonal relations was associated with what anthropologists sometimes refer to in other parts of the world as the phenomenon of "big men." Here is a cultural trait in early Southeast Asia that seems to offer a helpful perspective for understanding much of what lay behind intraregional relations in later times.

The leadership of "big men," or, to use the term I prefer, "men of prowess," would depend on their being attributed with an abnormal amount of personal and innate "soul stuff," which explained and distinguished their performance from that of others in their generation and especially among their own kinsmen. In the Southeast Asian languages, the terms for "soul stuff" vary from society to society, and the belief is always associated with other beliefs. The distinctions between "soul

in the Seventh Century" in this volume, chapter 8. Excavations in Bali indicate burials of nuclear families; see R. P. Soejono, "The Significance of the Excavation at Gilimanuk (Bali)" in Smith and Watson, *Early South East Asia*, p. 195.

[10] The nuclear family was the typical family in the Lê legal code, and both husbands and wives enjoyed property rights; see Insun Yu, "Law and Family in Seventeenth and Eighteenth Century Vietnam" (PhD thesis, University of Michigan, 1978). The Chinese census statistics in Vietnam during the early centuries of the Christian era purport to reveal an increase in the number of households rather than in the total population, and one would expect this evidence in a society practising bilateral kinship. I am grateful to Keith Taylor for the information.

[11] I owe this observation to Satyawati Suleiman. For a discussion of female property rights and the appearance of women in negotiations with royal representatives, see J. G. de Casparis, "Pour une histoire sociale de l'ancienne Java principalement au Xème s," *Archipel* 21 (1981): 147.

[12] A. Barth and A. Bergaigne, *Inscriptions sanscrites du Cambodge et Champa* (Paris: Impr. Nationale, 1885) p. 20, v. 34.

stuff" and the associated beliefs are so precise and essential that they can be defined only in the language of each society.[13] Nevertheless, a person's spiritual identity and capacity for leadership were established when his fellows could recognize his superior endowment and knew that being close to him was to their advantage—not only because his entourage could expect to enjoy material rewards but also, I believe, because their own spiritual substance, for everyone possessed it in some measure, would participate in his, thereby leading to *rapport* and personal satisfaction. We are dealing with the led as well as the leaders.

Difficulties are bound to arise in studying continuities in early Southeast Asian experiences when one thinks of "states," as I have done for too long.[14] Even prehistorians, when they are correcting earlier misapprehensions about what happened during the several millennia before the beginning of the Christian era, may tend to reinforce earlier dogma about the appearance of "states" during protohistory. Prehistorians are interested in "incipient state formation and political centralization" prior to Indian influence, but, while they can now show that Indian influence did not move into a vacuum when it brought a "state" like "Funan" into being,[15] they still cannot rid themselves of an awareness of discontinuity between prehistory and protohistory. The reason is that they take "Funan" as their model of the first fully fledged state and attribute to it such features as the ruler's strategy of monumental self-validation" and "time-tested Indian strategies of temple-founding, inscription-raising, and support for brahmanical royal cults."[16] A state, according to this line of thought, which owes much to Van Leur's ideas in the 1930s, must be distinguished from anything else in prehistory. The effect is that a new lease on life is given to the significance of Indian influence.

I suggest that a gap persists between prehistory and protohistory represented by "Funan" because different terminologies are used when discussing each period. An outline of "incipient state formation" depends on such Western terms as "fairly extensive trade relations," wet-rice, iron technology, and "probably increasing population density and political centralization in some of the alluvial plains of the mainland."[17] These terms, taken by themselves, signify economic developments that would be accompanied by the appearance of more complex political systems.

---

[13] Anthropological studies about "soul stuff" in a regional context do not seem available at the present time. Indeed, James Boon remarks with respect to Indonesia that "the ultimate comparativist accomplishment would be to plot the various soul-power terms—*semangat, roh,* and so on—against each other across Indonesian and Malay societies"; James A. Boon, *The Anthropological Romance of Bali 1597–1972* (Cambridge and New York: Cambridge University Press, 1977), p. 240, n. 7. See Appendix A: Miscellaneous notes on "soul stuff" and "prowess."

[14] Virginia Matheson, writing about the inhabitants of the Riau-Lingga archipelago as they are described in the *Tuhfat al-Nafis*, addresses this matter of terminology: "...I can find in the *Tuhfat* no evidence for the existence of the state as a concept, an abstract ideal above and beyond the ruler, which was to be sustained and protected. What does seem to have existed was a complex system of personal loyalties, which it was in the ruler's interest to maintain"; see Virginia Matheson, "Concepts of State in the *Tuhfal al-Nafis* [The Precious Gift]," in *Pre-Colonial State Systems in Southeast Asia: The Malay Peninsula, Sumatra, Bali-Lombok, South Celebes,* ed. Anthony Reid and Lance Castles (Kuala Lumpur: Monographs of the Malaysian Branch of the Royal Asiatic Society, no. 6, 1975), p. 21.

[15] Bayard, "The Roots of Indochinese Civilisation," p. 106.

[16] Bennet Bronson, "The Late Prehistory and Early History of Central Thailand with Special Reference to Chansen," in Smith and Watson, *Early South East Asia,* p. 316.

[17] Bayard, "The Roots of Indochinese Civilisation," p. 106.

Nevertheless, prehistorians have to deny prehistory the achievement of "statehood" by indigenous processes because of what they believe is known of the fully fledged "state of Funan." The elaboration of the features of a "Funanese" typology, however, depends on an altogether different set of signifiers that owe their origin to Chinese documents and are therefore influenced by Chinese preconceptions of a "state." The Chinese supposed, for example, that any state should be associated with rules of dynastic succession and be described by fixed boundaries. No such polity existed anywhere in earlier Southeast Asian history except, as we shall see below, in Vietnam. Yet the Chinese were unable to conceptualize "Funan" as being anything other than a "state," albeit an unstable one, and, because of this Chinese perspective, "Funan" has become the earliest Southeast Asian example of what sociologists refer to as a "patrimonial bureaucracy," a model that does not seem to fit the prehistoric evidence.[18]

The two sets of signifiers—Western and Chinese—have precise meaning only in cultural contexts outside Southeast Asia, and the result of linguistic confusion is that the passage of the region from prehistory to protohistory reads in language that is bound to give the impression that the Southeast Asian peoples could graduate to statehood only with the assistance of Indian influence. The same reading may even lead scholars to postulate a lag in the process of state formation in some parts of the region, exemplified by the "impermanence" of certain polities,[19] or to assume that particular geographical circumstances influenced the pace of the graduation to statehood.

In other words, the criteria for incipient and fully fledged states are established by an arbitrary vocabulary drawn from an archaeology with an economic bias and from Chinese conventions transferred to a part of the world that was virtually unknown to them. The result is that one is in danger of looking for what could never be there in either prehistoric or protohistoric times. If, however, we think simply of "political systems"—a neutral expression—the way is open for considering other cultural phenomena, such as religious and social behaviour, that can be expected to affect political and economic activities in both prehistory and protohistory. No evidence at present exists for supposing that unprecedented religious and social changes were underway in the protohistoric period that sharply distinguish it from late prehistory. For example, there is no evidence to suppose that a chief's small-scale entourage in late prehistory was different in kind from the large-scale entourages of the historical period that supplied rulers with practical means of exercising political influence. In both periods, services are likely to have been rewarded with gifts of

[18] Bayard, "The Roots of Indochinese Civilisation," p. 107. Karl Hutterer, studying how far the lowland societies of the Philippines had reached urban and state formation on the eve of the Spanish intervention, observes that "there is no evidence whatsoever for the formation of bureaucratic structure that would have been interjected between the chief and the daily affairs of politics, commerce, and religion, as is usually found in state societies"; see Karl L. Hutterer, "Prehistoric Trade and the Evolution of Philippine Societies: A Reconsideration," in *Economic and Social Interaction in Southeast Asia: Perspectives from Prehistory, History, and Ethnology,* ed. Karl L. Hutterer, Michigan Papers on South and Southeast Asia, no. 13 (Ann Arbor, MI: Center for South and Southeast Asian Studies, University of Michigan, 1977, c. 1978), p. 191.

[19] See, for example, B. Bronson, "Exchange at the Upstream and Downstream Ends: Notes toward a Functional Model of the Coastal State in Southeast Asia," in Hutterer, *Economic and Social Interaction in Southeast Asia,* p. 51; and Bennet Bronson and Jan Wisseman, "Palembang as Srivijaya: The Lateness of Early Cities in Southern Southeast Asia," *Asian Perspectives* 19, 2 (1978): 234.

honor, posts of responsibility, and produce from the land.[20] All these gifts would be valued because the recipients knew that they participated in the donor's spiritual authority.

The territorial scale of a political system is certainly not the correct measurement for describing and defining it. Instead, we should think of sets of socially definable loyalties that could be mobilized for common enterprises. This was the case in protohistoric times, and it would be surprising if these loyalties did not have their origin in prehistory. In late Balinese prehistory, for example, persons were buried according to their rank on earth,[21] which indicates some kind of hierarchy, with one person in the neighbourhood perceived as the point of reference for distinguishing ranks. This prehistoric background may be reflected in a Sanskrit inscription from western Java in the fifth or sixth century. The inscription has been translated as referring to a ruler's "allies,"[22] but the term used is *bhakta* ("worshippers" or "princes devoted [to him]"). Khmer chiefs in the seventh century also frequently referred to themselves as *bhaktas* and venerated their overlord because of his spiritual relationship with Śiva, which brought spiritual rewards to those who served him. The Javanese inscription may refer to a chief's entourage with "prehistoric" features but described in the Sanskrit language.

The peoples of protohistoric Southeast Asia retained, I suggest, much more than vestiges of earlier behaviour, though their behaviour would not have been identical in every locality. But their cultures are unlikely to be entirely illuminated by artefacts recovered from graves or by Chinese evidence of commercial exchanges in the protohistoric period. Tools and trade represent only fractions of a social system.

I have dwelt on definitions partly because I believe that the time is now promising for a reexamination of the passage of Southeast Asia from prehistory to protohistory in terms of continuities rather than of discontinuities. But I am especially anxious to indicate the origins of the early political systems that furnish the appropriate background to later tendencies in Southeast Asian intra-regional relations.

---

[20] Van Naerssen suggests that the origin of the Javanese *raka* can be explained in ecological terms. The *raka* was responsible for the equitable distribution of water over a number of agrarian communities (*wanua*), and he therefore had the right to dispose of the produce and labour of his subjects; see F. H. van Naerssen, *The Economic and Administrative History of Early Indonesia*, pp. 37–38.

[21] R. P. Soejono, "The Significance of the Excavation at Gilimanuk," p. 198.

[22] B. Ch. Chhabra, *Expansion of the Indo-Aryan Culture* (Delhi: Munshi Ram Monhar Lal, 1965), p. 94.

CHAPTER THREE

CHINA IRREDENTA: THE SOUTH

The term "irredenta" contained in the title of this essay should be understood to imply "claims" that need not be territorial in character. The term "south" is more helpfully vague. Professor Lattimore has argued that, from the traditional Chinese point of view, the northern and north-western frontiers of China had to be sealed.[1] The situation on the southern frontier at the shores of the South China Sea was very different; here was an open frontier, with distant and congenial horizons.

This article will not be concerned with the countries of mainland Southeast Asia, lying immediately beyond the south-western provinces of China. It is likely that the Chinese have always recognized problems of internal security created by the tribal peoples living astride the porous frontiers of Vietnam, Laos, Thailand, and Burma. The need to protect outlying areas in China herself would have involved the Chinese from time to time in special measures, sometimes requiring military action and always justifying the assertion of the tributary principle. Sino–Viet relations in particular were probably very different from other forms of Sino–Southeast Asian relationship. If, again according to Professor Lattimore, Chinese slipping over the northern borders into the competitive steppe society were liable to become dangerously different people, the Chinese, who in the early centuries of the Christian era slipped into Tonkin, helped to create a dangerously similar Sino–Viet society. Viet dynasties in their prime had a Chinese-like self-consciousness in seeking to recover what they believed to be the Viet sphere of influence over the porous frontier.[2]

The scope of this essay is limited to some first impressions growing in the writer's mind on the subject of the relations between China and "maritime" Southeast Asia and especially on the Sino–Indonesian relationship as it developed over the centuries. "Maritime" Southeast Asia is a legitimate term, corresponding not to the region as a whole but to those parts in maritime communication with China. The Chinese expression has been "the countries of the southern ocean," the countries of the *Nan-hai* or *Nan-yang*,[3] and it is possible that, as a result of long experience, the

---

[1] Owen Lattimore, *Inner Asian Frontiers of China*, 2nd ed. (New York, NY: American Geographical Society, 1951), pp. 469 ff.

[2] E. Gaspardone, "Annamites et Thai au XVe siècle," *JA* 231 (1939): 405–6.

[3] Wang Gungwu, "The Chinese in Search of a Base in the Nanyang," *Journal of the South Seas Society* 14,1–2 (1958): 88.

Chinese developed attitudes towards the *Nan-yang* that in the end became habitual. One may be tempted to inquire whether these attitudes have been completely abandoned even today. Are there historical overtones in Chinese policies during the twentieth century?

HISTORICAL BACKGROUND

No study of the subject is satisfactory that ignores the long stretch of time from about the beginning of the Christian era to the fifteenth century. It is likely that, as a result of their experiences during these centuries, Chinese Governments formulated a practical policy towards the south. In historical perspective the period from the decline of the Ming dynasty to the end of the nineteenth century would have been for the Chinese a time of unhappy reflection and comment on what they regarded as a deteriorating situation in maritime Southeast Asia. Writers such as Hsü Chi-yü were aware not only of the humiliations of the nineteenth century but also of the golden age of Chinese influence in maritime Southeast Asia, culminating in Chêng Ho's famous voyages in the first half of the fifteenth century.

But, in the writer's opinion, it is difficult to analyse Chinese attitudes towards the *Nan-yang* without also taking into account their attitudes towards other parts of Asia accessible by sea and especially their objectives in Asia when they sought to develop their maritime communications. Analogies are often misleading, but it may be fair to adapt a recent statement by Dr. J. H. Parry as a description of the Chinese experience during the early centuries of the Christian era. According to Dr. Parry, Europeans between the middle of the fifteenth and the latter part of the seventeenth centuries "learned to think of the world as a whole and of all seas as one."[4] The Chinese long ago came to a similar conclusion, and one consequence was that they began to realize that maritime Southeast Asia played a strategically important role in promoting their interests much farther afield. Their awareness of this role was probably the chief political factor in moulding the historical relationship between China and the *Nan-yang*.

Before the T'ang period (618–906) certain prejudices had taken shape in the minds of the Chinese, which were never discarded. In the first place, the Chinese realized that the Indian Ocean and the "southern ocean" of Southeast Asia formed a single stretch of water, united by a single system of communications. They did not hear of the Indian Ocean long after they knew of the *Nan-yang*. They began to learn something of the "southern ocean" as a result of their conquests in Tonkin towards the end of the third century BCE, and it was no more than a century later that they heard of the western Indian Ocean as a result of their penetration of central Asia. It was during the reign of the Han emperor Wu Ti (141–87 BCE) that a mission was sent by means of "barbarian" ships through Southeast Asia to India, and the information available to the Chinese in the following few centuries convinced them that this vast ocean, stretching from southern China to the Mediterranean world, possessed a series of maritime exchanges across it which gave it a genuine unity.

Secondly, the Chinese never freed themselves from their first impression that, of all the many countries on the shores of this single ocean, those in the Indian Ocean were, in terms of cultural development, trading goods, and access to the relatively

---

[4] J. H. Parry, *The Age of Reconnaissance: Discovery, Exploration, and Settlement, 1450 to 1650* (London: Weidenfeld & Nicholson, 1963), p. 1.

civilized parts of the known world, immeasurably more important than those of the *Nan-yang*. Buddhism came from India, and farther west lay the wonderland of the "western regions." The nomenclature of the most desirable portion of the Chinese foreign trade reflected in particular the reputation of western Asia as the source of wealth. In Later Han times *Ta-ch'in*, the "Roman Orient," produced "the rare and precious things." Later this trade was known as the "Persian" trade, and finally as the "Arab" trade. Beginning as a trade in exotic goods, by Sung times (960–1279) it had become very valuable. The importance of the maritime countries of Southeast Asia, on the other hand, lay primarily in the geographical circumstance that they lay astride the shipping routes to and from the countries on the shores of the Indian Ocean. In themselves the countries of the *Nan-yang* were regarded as being relatively backward and weak, a judgment conveyed, for example, in the *Hsin T'ang shu* (the *New T'ang History*): "The various *Man* barbarians on the shores of the sea have no broad lands or strong cities which they can defend."[5] It is true that from T'ang times onwards these countries were known to be wealthy, but their wealth was the gift of nature rather than the handicraft of men; the factories were in India and the Middle East. Never did the *Nan-yang* countries acquire the prestige of those in the Indian Ocean.

In the third place, however, these weak peoples of maritime Southeast Asia constituted a threat to China in a special way. Their "primitive" polities were regarded as inherently unstable. Thus, the *Sui shu*, the history of the dynasty ruling from 581 to 618, states: "They have no chiefs ... They love to fight among themselves. Therefore they are weak countries and from time to time acknowledge the supremacy of China."[6] As a result of their political immaturity, they were liable to disrupt China's valuable lines of communication with the west, and the symptoms of political weakness that would have disturbed Chinese governments were piracy on the high seas and rivalries among the maritime kingdoms, situations provoking general unrest and causing embarrassment to merchant ships. Because the narrow waters of western Indonesia and the Straits of Malacca represented for the Chinese the important part of the *Nan-yang* in terms of the movement of international trade, we may get closest to the instinctive response of the Chinese to the south by studying Sino–Indonesian, and especially Sino–Malay, relations.

Although documentary evidence is scanty, there are hints that Chinese governments from about 400 to 1450 CE formulated, under cover of the conventional tributary system, a practical relationship first with rulers in western Indonesia and later with those on the Malay peninsula with the purpose of keeping open the shipping routes between China and the whole of the Asian maritime world.[7] As part of the background it has to be borne in mind that it was not until Sung times that the Chinese developed naval power; thus, in the earlier and formative period of the relationship, they had to rely on methods of indirect control over this region.

---

[5] *Hsin T'ang shu*, 222 C, p. 4162 (*Êrh shih wu shih*, K'ai ming edition).

[6] *Sui shu*, 82, Ia (Po-na edition).

[7] It is the writer's view that, chiefly because of the growth of markets in southern China, the sea route from western Asia to China was becoming important from about 400 CE. By then the Malays of western Indonesia were probably providing most of the shipping facilities, at least between Indonesia and China. The fifth century coincides with the first Chinese accounts of western Indonesian kingdoms.

It would not be surprising, therefore, if the emperors came to realize the value to them of a strong maritime kingdom not too far from the Straits of Malacca, whose rulers could absorb in their fleets the Malay pirate potential[8] and maintain well-stocked entrepôts and good harbour facilities, and whose general stability ensured it a dominating position in the network of Asian maritime communications converging on China.[9] A kingdom with these pretensions flourished in southeastern Sumatra from the seventh to the thirteenth centuries, and since 1918 its name has been revealed as Śrīvijaya.[10] By the thirteenth century, however, it is probable that the rulers of Śrīvijaya could no longer contain the enormous expansion in foreign shipping, including Chinese shipping; her vassal harbour princes were able to defy their overlord and cultivate their own trading relations with foreigners,[11] and when Marco Polo sailed through Southeast Asia at the end of the thirteenth century his companions from China had no occasion to visit the ports of southern Sumatra, the base of the former empire of Śrīvijaya. But the temporary absence of a maritime overlord was then making itself felt in piracy, which endangered Chinese ships returning from the Indian Ocean. Peace on the seas was restored only with the rise of the Malacca Sultanate in the early fifteenth century, when her navy controlled the waters of western Indonesia.

The relationship between the emperors and the rulers of Śrīvijaya and later of Malacca was, concealed in the formal emperor–vassal system, probably that of patron and client. The emperors would have regarded the Malay rulers as their agents, who undertook on their behalf the task of maintaining conditions for successful trade. To these rulers the emperors would have extended favors, which would have impressed traders and encouraged them to sail to China from the clients' ports. One naturally inquires to what extent imperial prestige would have been sufficient to help the clients hold their own against their enemies. The Chinese certainly believed that the civilization of the Middle Kingdom was a weighty political factor, and it is unlikely that this was merely a matter of cultural conceit. The rulers of Śrīvijaya and Malacca were undoubtedly "loyal vassals" when they were in trouble with their enemies; their envoys then came persistently to China, and one imagines that marks of imperial favor were flaunted for all to see. There is clear evidence of the help Malacca sought from the Ming emperors against her enemies. For Śrīvijaya, an inadequately documented kingdom, the evidence is not so specific, but it is significant that, in spite of the attacks by Javanese and Tamils in the 992–1025

---

[8] Tomé Pires describes how the Cellates, "the Malay for sea robbers," flocked to Malacca in the fifteenth century and were brought from their island bases to serve in the Sultans' fleets; see *Suma Oriental*, vol. 2 (London: Hakluyt Society, 1944), pp. 235 and 264. Pires states that Cellates followed the founder of Malacca from Palembang, where, in Śrīvijaya's day, they would certainly have supplied the naval manpower.

[9] The Chinese assessment of the situation would have been similar to that of Sir Stamford Raffles, who wrote: "Nothing can tend so effectually to the suppression of piracy, the encouragement and extension of lawful commerce, and to the civilization of the inhabitants of the Eastern islands, as affording a steady support to the established native sovereigns, as assisting them in the maintenance of their just rights and authority over their several chiefs...," John Bastin, *Essays on Indonesian and Malayan History* (Singapore: Eastern Universities Press, 1961), p. 120.

[10] G. Coedès, "Le royaume de Çrīvijaya," in *BEFEO* 18,6 (1918): 1–36.

[11] By 1178 ships from Canton were wintering in Lamuri, in northern Sumatra. Haru, on the northeastern coast of Sumatra, had by 1225 recovered its independence from Śrīvijaya, and many ships were anchoring there.

period, the Chinese continued to show goodwill to this still powerful trading kingdom. Śrīvijayan missions were never so numerous as during and after this troubled period, suggesting that the client had special reasons for wishing to retain the patron's interest, while the emperors seem to have gone out of their way in evincing friendliness towards the client's envoys at the imperial court. Moreover, for an understanding of the motives of the Malay rulers it should be borne in mind that their access to the Chinese ports and the enormous shipping and entrepôt profits from the Asian trade, shared out among the chiefs composing the aristocracy of Śrīvijaya and Malacca, were in themselves powerful inducements for making the dominant maritime kingdom ruthless in protecting its trading monopoly. At the beginning of her career in the seventh century, Śrīvijaya annexed rival trading harbours on the Straits of Malacca, while late accounts of this kingdom testify to the rulers' determination to compel traders to use her ports.

There was a further factor that supported the illusion of Chinese influence. For reasons which are still not clear, the accession of a new and powerful Chinese dynasty always seemed to coincide with a period of temporary political upheaval in maritime Southeast Asia, when the overlord was either under attack or had disappeared.[12] In the event, the established overlord held his own or was succeeded by a new one, and this meant that peace in the southern ocean was restored at a time when there was a new Chinese dynasty, deliberately recovering the traditional frontiers of China and, by means of special envoys, announcing its accession overseas in order to revive China's foreign trade.[13] Thus, it would not have been difficult for the Chinese to persuade themselves that the maritime rulers of Southeast Asia were responsive to imperial initiative in taking action to restore stability in the south.[14]

In other words, it is likely that there was a convergence of interests between the emperors and the maritime rulers. No doubt there was plenty of wishful thinking among the Chinese concerning the extent of their authority overseas, but one should not underestimate the tendency among Indonesian naval princes to cultivate the emperors in order to persuade them that their kingdoms were the foci of Asian maritime trade and dependable suppliers for the Chinese market. It need not be

---

[12] The early T'ang period saw Śrīvijaya emerge as the mistress of the Straits of Malacca; see this writer's "Śrīvijayan Expansion in the Seventh Century," *Artibus Asiae* 24, 3–4 (1961): 417–24. The early Sung period saw the survival of Śrīvijaya in spite of Javanese and Tamil retaliation. The Mongol period coincided with a time when there was no naval overlord in western Indonesia, unless the Javanese kingdom of Majapahit can be regarded as such. The early Ming period coincided with the rise of Malacca.

[13] The Sui, Sung, Mongol, and Ming dynasties sent envoys overseas soon after they were established, and there are two references to T'ang envoys in Southeast Asia during the seventh century. The stated purpose of the Sui envoy Ch'ang Chün (607–10) is particularly significant; it was "to open up communications."

[14] These prejudices would have been reinforced by the ancient Chinese belief that foreign relations were only a subsidiary function of domestic administration; war or peace abroad depended on conditions within China herself; see Ssu-yu Teng and John K. Fairbank, *China's Response to the West* (Cambridge, MA: Harvard University Press, 1961), p. 125. Part of the Chinese experience in the formative period of Sino–Malay relations before 600 CE was a tendency among Southeast Asian rulers to appeal to China for help against enemies. Help was not given, because the southern dynasties of China were too weak, but no doubt the records of these appeals, preserved in the imperial histories, helped to create the dogma of the salutary influence of China on the political life of the region.

surprising if the dogma grew in China that the emperors had a special role in maintaining peace in the *Nan-yang*, a role that could be effectively discharged by means of political manipulation.

The appearance of Chêng Ho's fleets in Asian waters during the first half of the fifteenth century was, in Chinese eyes, the culmination of the policy of imperial pacification. The Sultans of Malacca were now the clients, and they could rely on more than the distant prestige of the patrons. Chêng Ho was responsible for the engraving of an inscription as an act of thanksgiving for protection in a storm, and, in spite of its old-fashioned expressions, a passage in the inscription may take us some way in understanding the essentials in the relationship between maritime Southeast Asia and China as it was understood by the Chinese:

> On arriving in the outlying countries, those among the barbarian kings who were obstructing the "transforming influence" [of Chinese culture] and were disrespectful we captured alive, and brigands who gave themselves over to violence and plunder we exterminated. Consequently, the sea route was purified and tranquillized and the natives, owing to this, were enabled quietly to pursue their avocations...[15]

ARRIVAL OF THE EUROPEANS

For the Chinese, the Portuguese capture of Malacca in 1511 was the first event in a long process of political deterioration in the *Nan-yang*,[16] and by the nineteenth century Chinese writers were well aware that the geopolitical situation in Asian waters had become unfavorable. Trading centres in maritime Southeast Asia still linked China with the Indian Ocean, but the Europeans, and especially the British, had gained control of the Indian Ocean and, under pretext of trading, were now dominating the *Nan-yang*. The Indian Ocean and the seas of Southeast Asia, always known by the Chinese to be served by a single system of communications, now provided bases from which Europeans were able to demand more and more privileges at the expense of China. In these circumstances it was natural for writers to recall that the Malay kingdoms had always been weak. According to the author of the *Hai lu*, Palembang (a former capital of Śrīvijaya), a pirate centre, did not respect China but instead feared the Dutch and the English, whose extortionate demands the Malays dared not refuse.[17] Wei Yüan noted that there were many islands in the *Nan-yang*, all ready to submit to the strongest island, and he implied that this situation was the explanation of the ever-changing nomenclature of the most powerful

---

[15] J. J. L. Duyvendak, "The True Dates of the Chinese Maritime Expeditions in the Early Fifteenth Century," in *T'oung Pao* 34 (1938), pp. 345–46. Among the events of this period, attributable to the Ming fleets, were the protection of Malacca from the Thai, the expulsion of Chinese pirates from Palembang, and the restoration of the ruler of Pasai, in northern Sumatra, to his throne.

[16] The Chinese Government quickly realized the disturbance in trading conditions, affecting even the security of the Chinese coast, created by the arrival of the Portuguese. In comparison with the Sultans of Malacca, the Portuguese were fierce pirates, unworthy of immediate investiture as vassals.

[17] *Hai lu chu*, p. 42 (Fêng Ch'êng-chün's edition, 1955).

kingdom in the region as recorded in the imperial histories.[18] Now the Dutch were the overlords. The persistent political weakness of the Malay kingdoms had long been known, but in the nineteenth century the consequences were serious. Hsü Chi-yü wrote in 1848: "In former times the *Nan-yang* was the den of the southern barbarians. Today it is a lodging house for the Europeans. How can we regard this as only a recent situation? In fact, the Europeans have been building up their power there for more than 300 years."[19]

Nevertheless, by the end of the nineteenth century it was also becoming clear that there was at least one living token of China's former influence in maritime Southeast Asia, a token offering promise of the future revival of that influence. Chinese writers were now becoming aware of the achievements of the overseas Chinese, a reflection that stirred Liang Ch'i-ch'ao to think of the contribution of the heroic Chêng Ho who did most to lay the foundation for the power of the overseas Chinese in Southeast Asia.[20] At the end of the nineteenth century, "colonies" were being regarded as the mark of a successful Great Power, and Liang was convinced that the Chinese, because of their ancient culture and remarkable powers of endurance, were destined to become a Great Power in the twentieth century.[21] In the meantime he could admire the overseas Chinese, because of whom the economy of Southeast Asia was largely under Chinese control, and he no doubt believed that they were in the vanguard of the forces that would one day reestablish the *Nan-yang* as China's chief sphere of influence.[22] He was writing at a time when the Darwinian concept of "the survival of the fittest" was being construed to prove the eventual victory of "the yellow race." These sophisticated and not pronouncedly pro-Asian sentiments would have strengthened the traditional Chinese contempt for the peoples of Southeast Asia.[23] The intellectual climate in China at the beginning of the twentieth century was hardly congenial for the sponsoring of an Asian liberation movement in the wake of revolutionary successes in China.

POLICY OF THE KUOMINTANG

In their racial arrogance, their concern for the prestige of China among the Asian countries, and their manipulation of the overseas Chinese, the leaders of the Kuomintang revealed themselves, within the narrow limits of activity available to

---

[18] *Hai kuo t'u chih* (1842); 9, 13a–14a (1844 edition).

[19] *Ying huan chih lüeh*, 2, 33a (title page dated 1848). See Teng and Fairbank, *China's Response to the West*, p. 41, for information about Hsü Chi-yü. The mid-nineteenth-century view in China seems to have been that the mainland kingdoms of Southeast Asia were stronger than any ever known in the archipelago.

[20] "Chêng Ho chuan," *Yin ping shih wên chi*, 41, 43a.

[21] "Lun Chung kuo jên chung chih chiang lai," *Yin ping shih wên chi*, 16, 9a.

[22] "Chêng Ho chuan," 42b. Liang noted with admiration that the overseas Chinese were never assimilated; "Lun Chung kuo jên chung…," 10b. To the end of his life, Liang held chauvinistic views concerning the overseas Chinese; see Teng and Fairbank, *China's Response to the West*, p. 269.

[23] Liang regarded the black and brown peoples as lazy and stupid; "Lun Chung kuo jên chung…", 12a. In K'ang Yu-wei's *Ta t'ung* the peoples of India and Southeast Asia were thought to have no future as long as they remained in their present environment; see *Ta T'ung shu: The One-World Philosophy of K'ang Yu-wei*, tr. Laurence G. Thompson (London: Allen & Unwin, 1958), pp. 142–46.

them, as the heirs of the emperors. The greatest concentration of overseas Chinese was in maritime Southeast Asia, but now the whole of the region attracted the interest of the Kuomintang. Both Sun Yat-sen and Chiang Kai-shek understood China's traditional role to have been one of maintaining stability there. Chiang's view was that "in the conflicts among her neighbours China always adhered to the principle of 'reestablishing interrupted dynasties and reviving dismembered states,' and never adopted the policy of taking advantage of the precarious position of other countries to seize their territory."[24] A Taiwan writer has recently written in similar terms on the policy of the Ming emperors, and he regrets that China subsequently surrendered her responsibilities in the region to the Europeans.[25]

From 1942 and especially from 1945, when Chinese leaders could begin to think more hopefully of the post-war situation, there were glimpses of China's pretensions. Kuomintang publicists made it clear that she would need an honorable status among the nations and would not be without her "vanities." One means of enhancing her dignity in the eyes of the smaller Asian nations would be by giving her a share in guaranteeing the independence of Indochina and Burma.[26] The impending recovery of independence by the Southeast Asian countries was probably regarded, partly at least, as the end of a disgraceful interlude in Sino–Southeast Asian relations, when China had been unable to fulfil her historic function of protecting a politically weak region within her sphere of influence.[27] In 1947 Indian observers at the Asian Relations Conference in New Delhi observed with distress that the Chinese there seemed concerned to counter Indian influence in Asian affairs.

THE PEKING GOVERNMENT

From the second half of the fifteenth century up to 1949, the internal situation in China was such that her links with Asian maritime countries had, with the exception of the overseas Chinese, gradually disappeared. With the establishment of the communist regime, however, there has been a dramatically extended range of Chinese overseas contacts, and one may inquire whether there is anything in the communist approach to the south which suggests that, perhaps unconsciously, ancient habits of mind have not been entirely discarded during the initial and probing period of Chinese expansion. Does the present contribution of Southeast Asia in the promotion of Chinese international relations resemble in any way the contribution that maritime Southeast Asia was once believed to make?

There have, of course, been breaks with the past. In particular, there has been a break with that part of the past which the Kuomintang sought to emphasize, for the

---

[24] Chiang Kai-shek, with notes and commentary by Philip Jaffe, *China's Destiny* (New York: Roy Publishers, 1947), p. 36. The expression "precarious," reflecting the Chinese sense of the political weakness of the region, is reminiscent of the passages from the *Sui shu* and the *Hsin T'ang shu*, translated above, and also of nineteenth-century opinions about maritime Southeast Asia. Sun Yat-sen's interpretation of history is in *San min chu i* (The Three Principles of the People), tr. F. W. Price (Shanghai, 1927), pp. 146–47.

[25] Hsü Yü-hu, Chêng *Ho p'ing chuan* (Taipei, 1958), p. 119.

[26] T. S. Chien, "New China's Demands," *Foreign Affairs* 21,4 (1943): 696.

[27] Su-ching Chen, in *China and Southeastern Asia* (Chungking: China Institute of Pacific Relations, 1945), p. 21, wrote, "China came into contact with the Western people first through her own people in Southeastern Asia, and it was there the conflict began between the Chinese and Westerners."

Peking regime advises the overseas Chinese to be obedient to their local governments, provided the latter have recognized the Peking government. The antiquity of the overseas Chinese presence in Southeast Asia is not suppressed; their history "dates back over 1,000 years."[28] They are, however, represented as having contributed to the development of the Southeast Asian economy as well as having participated in the Indonesian independence movement.[29] Yet it is likely that the overseas Chinese are often an embarrassment to Peking; they are, as it is said, "a problem left over by history," a problem that the Kuomintang did much to exacerbate.

There are also features of the historical record that are suppressed by the communists. "Tribute" is not mentioned, and the same term is used for the exchange of envoys in imperial times as for present-day exchanges. It is stressed that the Southeast Asian countries were independent before the Europeans came. Their communications with China were merely trading ones, from which they and the Chinese equally benefited. History is the record of "friendship" and "peace." An honored place remains, however, for Chêng Ho. Liang Ch'i-ch'ao had conceived an admiration for the great navigator, and, consistently with the view proposed earlier in this essay that the Chinese always looked far beyond Southeast Asia when they thought about their maritime communications, Liang considered that the motive of Chêng Ho's voyages was to get in touch with Western Europe and not with the *Nan-yang*.[30] A communist historian has honored the admiral for similar reasons; Chêng Ho's great work was in opening up the sea route for Chinese shipping as far as the Red Sea and east Africa, making possible economic and cultural exchange on a greater scale than ever before,[31] and Peking's propaganda handling of its present relations with the Somali and Yemeni Republics has provided the opportunity of stressing the point that the Europeans subsequently placed artificial barriers between China and these countries.[32] Thus, Chêng Ho has become the pretext for recalling earlier times when China had Asian-wide contacts by way of the south.

But it is possible that the records of history are available for more than sentimental purposes. It has been suggested in this essay that the traditional Chinese view, supported by their experience over many centuries, was that the seas of the Indian Ocean and of Southeast Asia possessed a genuine unity and a single system of communications, and therefore it is not surprising that Peking spokesmen should be irritated when this geopolitical situation is interpreted in favor of another country. In Peking's reactions to "Greater India" conceptions we may be getting closer to a field where there is some continuity between past and present Chinese attitudes towards

---

[28] Professor Chu Hsieh notes that the overseas Chinese preceded Chêng Ho, whose exploits greatly stimulated their migration; *Chêng Ho* (Peking: Hsin chih san lien shu tien, 1956), p. 111. Sun Yat-sen had taken the view that Chêng Ho's deeds caused "the barbarian tribes" to admire the Chinese to the present time; Sun Yat-sen, *Memoirs of a Chinese Revolutionary: A Programme of National Reconstruction for China* (London: Hutchinson & Co. Ltd., 1927), p. 79.

[29] Chu Hsieh, *Chung kuo ho Yin-tu-ni-his-ya jên min ti yu i kuan hsi...* (Peking: Chung kuo piao nien ch'u pan shê, 1956), pp. 18–21.

[30] "Chêng Ho chuan," *Yin ping shih wên chi*, 43b.

[31] Chu Hsieh, *Chêng Ho*, pp. 104–11.

[32] Professor Hsia Nai has written an article on seventeen centuries of Sino–African relations, published in *Renmin Ribao* (People's Daily) and summarized in the *Survey of the China Mainland Press*, 2824, September 24, 1962 (US Consulate-General, Hong Kong).

Southeast Asia. A year ago the Peking press unearthed the following passage in Mr. Nehru's *The Discovery of India*:

> India will also develop as the centre of economic and political activity in the Indian Ocean area, in Southeast Asia and right up to the Middle East. Her position gives an economic and strategic importance in a part of the world which is going to develop rapidly in the future... The small national state is doomed. It may survive as a culturally autonomous area but not as an independent political unit.[33]

These sentiments, owing much to evidence of earlier Indian cultural influences in Southeast Asia, have not been uncommon in India since the war, and the rendering of maritime Asian history and prospects that is implied is naturally repugnant to Peking.[34] Peking's comment on this passage in *The Discovery of India* was that Indian reactionaries had taken over the British imperialist concept of India as "the centre of Asia" and that Mr. Nehru was aiming at a great empire from the Middle East to Southeast Asia, in which there would be no small nations but only Mr. Nehru's vassals. Peking's counterattack, which was part of the propaganda campaign against India in 1962, may, however, rest on something more than the rejection of India's claim to lead uncommitted Asia. In historical terms, India's claim may also be seen as another threatened usurpation of influence in the area of the single ocean which, according to Chinese tradition, has always known only two dominant powers, first the Chinese and then the intruding European imperialists.[35]

There may be a further carryover from history, providing an instinctive element in Chinese communist tactics. In former times the "patron–client" relationship, a technique devised for promoting the indirect authority of the emperors, was cultivated in maritime Southeast Asia to safeguard Chinese interests lying far beyond that region, when the client guaranteed the passage of trading ships to and from the Indian Ocean. The purpose of Chinese policy was then, so the Chinese probably believed, to manipulate the political situation in the *Nan-yang* by lending moral support to the strongest Indonesian naval power in order to achieve stability in a notoriously restless region. Today the single ocean of Chinese tradition is encompassed by the Afro–Asian world where, as far as the Chinese are concerned, it is the passage of ideas that is important. In this world the Southeast Asian countries may continue to make a helpful contribution, from the Chinese point of view, in the form of protecting Chinese international relations, and it is probable that the Afro–

---

[33] Quoted in *Peking Review*, November 2, 1962 (a translation of *Renmin Ribao*, October 27, 1962). Mr. Nehru's book first appeared in 1946 (New York: The John Day Company, 1946). It was written in jail, where the author met imprisoned scholars who apparently introduced him to the "Greater India" school of history.

[34] And also to Taiwan Chinese. See Nehru's *Illusions* (Taipei: Asian Peoples' Anti-Communist League, 1955), pp. 10 ff.

[35] Mr. K. M. Panikkar has provided a "historical" background to Indian naval power in Southeast Asia. According to him Śrīvijaya was "a great Indian naval power ... Only Śrīvijaya prevented the Chinese from establishing authority in the Indonesian Archipelago"; see his *India and the Indian Ocean: An Essay on the Influence of Sea Power on Indian History* (London: Allen & Unwin, 1945), p. 84. Mr. Girilal Jain has recently observed that Chêng Ho's voyages marked the end of Hindu power, which had dominated the Malayan archipelago for nearly one thousand years; see Girilal Jain, *Panchsheela and After* (London: Asia Publishing House, 1961), p. 147.

Asian contacts of such countries as Indonesia are being deliberately encouraged and manipulated to carry a favorable image of communist China at least as far as Africa. One of the themes stressed during Liu Shao-chi's visit to Southeast Asia earlier this year was the importance of Sino–Southeast Asian relations as an outstanding example to Afro–Asian countries of the policy of coexistence. On the occasion of the visit of Prince Sihanouk of Cambodia to Peking in February this year [1963], Liu Shao-chi said that "it should be noted that the significance of the close friendship between China and Cambodia goes far beyond the borders of the two countries. It will have a positive and far-reaching influence throughout the world."[36] Chinese spokesmen have expressed the hope that India would be influenced by the countries that met at Colombo in December 1962 to discuss the Sino–Indian border dispute, and it may be significant that the Chinese, anxious to begin direct negotiations with the Indians, have succeeded in persuading the three Southeast Asian Governments represented at the Colombo conference to issue statements to the effect that the Colombo proposals were a basis for Sino–Indian negotiations. The Indian government, on the other hand, has insisted that these proposals were intended to contain specific conditions that had to be fulfilled before negotiations could begin.[37]

There could, in fact, be few more eloquent spokesmen for China's good intentions than her closest neighbours, whose apprehensions have been well known, and it would not be surprising if the Peking Government should do everything possible to enlist their support on current issues.[38] On the other hand, a clumsy and aggressive handling of the Southeast Asian countries would certainly do much to discredit the Peking Government among the "emerging nations."

In this way one begins to see a historical background to the Chinese version of "neutralism" in Southeast Asia. Chinese propagandists frequently defend Southeast Asian neutralism as a means of "stabilizing" peace in Southeast Asia and of "strengthening Afro–Asian solidarity." It need not be argued that these conceptions reflect deeply rooted Chinese folk-memories, but it may be that, reduced to their geopolitical essentials, they would be comprehensible to earlier generations of Chinese. The expression "stabilizing peace" takes us back to the problems of the pre-European period in maritime Southeast Asia, when "stability" in the *Nan-yang* was sought as the precondition of fruitful Chinese links with western Asia. Nor would the geographical dimensions of the notion of "Afro–Asian solidarity" have taxed the Chinese imagination when, many centuries ago, they were already looking hopefully beyond the shores of the South China Sea.

---

[36] *Peking Review*, February 22, 1963. On October 19 the *Renmin Ribao* quoted a speech by Prince Sihanouk to prove that, in spite of the slanders of the imperialists, the Chinese were regarded by the peoples of all countries as trustworthy friends.

[37] The statements were included in the joint communiqués issued when Liu Shao-chi visited Burma, Cambodia, and Indonesia. The *Hindu* (April 23, 1963) regretted that President Sukarno had allowed himself to be "manoeuvred" by the Chinese into signing a statement that ignored the Colombo proposals.

[38] The Cambodian Government has recently sponsored the transfer to the Peking Government of China's seat at the United Nations.

PART II

THE LONG DURÉE OF MALAY HISTORY

CHAPTER FOUR

STUDYING ŚRĪVIJAYA

A workshop was convened in Jakarta in March 1979 to prepare an international and multidisciplinary research proposal for studying Śrīvijaya during the next five years. The workshop was sponsored by SPAFA and attended by delegates from Indonesia, Malaysia, the Philippines, and Thailand.[1]

The delegates met almost two and a half centuries after the Abbé Renaudot, anxious to refute what he deplored as misleadingly favorable statements about Chinese civilization circulated in France by Jesuits, published the earliest translations in a European language of two Arab travelogues of 851 CE and the beginning of the tenth century, respectively.[2] The texts provided him with ample polemical ammunition, but the second text also happens to mention an important trading kingdom situated somewhere between India and China, which the Abbé transcribed as "Serbeza." In 1918, exactly two centuries later, Coedès revealed that the kingdom's name was "Śrīvijaya."[3] Today historians of Southeast Asia unanimously agree that a substantial span of Indonesian, Southeast Asian, and Asian maritime history in general during the second half of the seventh century and for a long time thereafter is subsumed under its august name, in spite of the circumstance that its own records, unlike those of its fame, Buddhist as well as commercial, in regions as far apart as the Persian Gulf, India, Tibet, and China, are few and ambiguous. Even its capital's location is still unknown.

The Jakarta workshop makes it certain that 1979 will be remembered as an *annus mirabilis* in Śrīvijayan studies. In this essay, offered as a personal tribute to those who organized the workshop and formulated the research proposal, I shall sketch and

---

[1] SPAFA represents "The Southeast Asian Ministers of Education Organization's Project in Archaeology and Fine Arts." I am grateful to Dra. Satyawati Suleiman for inviting me as an observer and to Cornell University for enabling me to accept the invitation.

[2] Eusèbe Renaudot, *Anciennes relations des Indes et de la Chine de deux voyageurs mahometans* ... (Paris: chez Jean-Baptiste Coignard, 1718).

[3] G. Coedès, "Le royaume de Çrīvijaya," *BEFEO* 18, 6 (1918): 1–36. Reinaud, who called the kingdom "Sarbaza," was the first to draw attention to its importance. He considered it to be part of a great Javanese empire of "Zabedj"; Joseph Toussaint Reinaud, *Relation des voyages par les Arabes et les Persans dans l'Inde et à la Chine dans le ixe siècle de l'ère chrétienne*, vol. I (Paris: Imprimerie royale, 1845), pp. lxxiii–lxxv.

discuss the state of the subject up to the eve of the workshop,[4] and I shall begin with Coedès's article of 1918.

Noting Chinese records of the Cham center mentioned in several inscriptions as "Vijaya" and known to the Chinese as *Fo-shih*, Coedès was able to restore the Arab toponym of Sribuza and the T'ang Chinese toponym of *Shih-li-fo-shih* as "Śrīvijaya,"[5] which he identified as a kingdom mentioned in a Bangka island inscription of 686, in an inscription of 775 from Ligor on the isthmus of the Malay Peninsula, and in Cōḷa inscriptions of the eleventh century. Scholars instantly hailed Śrīvijaya as a major and enduring kingdom in early Indonesian history, for Coedès, influenced by Groeneveldt's study of 1876,[6] at first diffidently and then ever more confidently believed that the kingdom was Malay and that its capital was at Palembang in southeastern Sumatra. But in 1918 Palembang was an impoverished region as far as monuments were concerned, and the discrepancy between Śrīvijaya's fame in foreign sources and what was on the ground in Palembang was so egregious that Coedès felt compelled to suppose that the rulers were preoccupied with superintending the traffic in the Straits of Malacca and seemed to have "neglected the spiritual values" that inspired Javanese rulers to cover their island with religious buildings. Coedès never revised his judgment.[7] I shall return to it.

Only a meager amount of Śrīvijayan literary and artistic evidence has been recovered anywhere since 1918, and for many years Śrīvijayan studies remained a somewhat fitfully pursued branch of early Southeast Asian historical research. Nevertheless, from time to time scholars left their chosen fields to pay attention to Śrīvijaya, and two contexts for its study gradually evolved: the international context of medieval Asian trade and the Southeast Asian context of Śrīvijaya's neighborhood relations.

The earliest impressions of Śrīvijaya were derived from Arab and Chinese descriptions of an important trading kingdom, and this was the context I explored in 1967 and 1970.[8] I mention my work first only because it lies on the periphery of Śrīvijayan studies and I want to put it comfortably behind me before I consider the study of Śrīvijaya's neighborhood relations, the *élan vital* of Śrīvijayan research.

I suggested that the economic background that brought Śrīvijaya to the fore in the seventh century had its origins in an earlier export trade in Middle Eastern resins to China, which eventually stimulated a subsidiary trade in comparable Sumatran resins. I emphasized the initiative of Malay "shippers," by whom I meant those who

---

[4] Considerations of length have required me to ignore several important studies. I hope that I have not discriminated too arbitrarily. The literature up to the mid-1960s can be consulted in George Coedès, *The Indianized States of Southeast Asia*, ed. Walter F. Vella, trans. Susan Brown Cowing (Honolulu: East–West Center Press, 1968).

[5] In 1883–1886 Van der Lith transcribed the Arab name as "Serboza" and Ferrand in 1913 as "Sribuza." Eventually Sauvaget restored the transcription as "Srvja," or "Śrīvijaya"; Coedès, *The Indianized States*, p. 320, n. 173.

[6] Coedès, on page 3, note 5, of "Le royaume," cited W. P. Groeneveldt, *Notes on the Malay Peninsula and Malacca, Compiled from Chinese Sources* (Batavia, 1876), pp. 67 ff. Groeneveldt's famous study, still consulted, was reprinted in 1887 for the Straits Branch of the Royal Asiatic Society.

[7] Coedès, "Le royaume," p. 25; *Indianized States*, p. 131.

[8] O. W. Wolters, *Early Indonesian Commerce. A Study of the Origins of Śrīvijaya* (Ithaca: Cornell University Press, 1967); *The Fall of Śrīvijaya in Malay History* (London: Lund Humphries Publishers Limited, 1970).

improvised the exports as well as those who manned the ships. I also emphasized the Śrīvijayan Mahārājas' influence in the offshore islands to the south of the Malacca Straits and their successful policing of the western Indonesian seas, which earned the Chinese emperors' respect in the centuries before the twelfth; only by the twelfth century were Chinese merchant ships sailing regularly to Southeast Asian centers of production.[9] I then proposed a broad chronological framework for Śrīvijayan history based on what I called the "tributary trade" traveling from so-called "vassal" harbors and especially from Śrīvijaya. When China enjoyed political stability and the tributary trade was brisk, Malay chiefs could be expected to be attracted to the Mahārājas' court by prospects of material advancement, motives of self-esteem, and above all, I am now convinced, by the sensation of spiritual well-being inspired by serving rulers attributed with supernatural qualities. Malay maritime society, which I took to be the substance of Śrīvijayan history, would therefore exemplify centripetal and centrifugal social tendencies according to the waxing and waning of the tributary trade at any point in time.

Today I realize that my work needs revision. I have been criticized for unenterprising reconstructions of Chinese transcriptions of Indonesian toponyms, and I have also been criticized for paying insufficient attention to Śrīvijayan hinterland relations.[10] To these criticisms I can add my own. As I shall explain at the end of this essay, I now have reservations whether *A Study of the Origins of Śrīvijaya* was a suitable subtitle for *Early Indonesian Commerce*. Again, I should have given more thought to the Indian Ocean trade, prospering independently of the fortunes of the China trade, and also to the movement of trade within Southeast Asia itself.[11] Political unrest in China should have been more carefully taken into account to explain interruptions in tributary missions. The origins of Chinese shipping in Southeast Asian waters required more precise chronological definition. I was indifferent to the phenomenon of geomorphic changes in the lands I studied, and my map of ancient shipping routes was naively drawn, for Dr. Manguin has shown that what I casually assumed was the direct and quickest passage across the South China Sea was avoided because of navigational hazards associated with the Paracel reefs. Ships from the south headed for the Cham coast to make a safe passage to China.[12]

---

[9] *The Straits Times* of May 10, 1979, reported the discovery of a Chinese junk about a mile inland on Bintan island in the Riau archipelago. The pottery was said to be of early Ming times.

[10] See Kenneth R. Hall, "State and Statecraft in Early Śrīvijaya," in *Explorations in Early Southeast Asian History: The Origins of Southeast Asian Statecraft*, ed. Kenneth R. Hall and John K. Whitmore, Michigan Papers on South and Southeast Asia, No. 11 (Ann Arbor, MI: Center for Southeast Asian Studies, 1976), pp. 61–105.

[11] An item of Persian origin has been found at the Kota Cina site near Medan in northeastern Sumatra; E. P. Edwards McKinnon, *Oriental Ceramics Excavated in North Sumatra, Transactions of the Oriental Ceramic Society* 41 (1975–1977): 75. Dr. Colless has studied a Syriac text that suggests that Syrian Christian monks and no doubt their mercantile compatriots were visiting the Malay Peninsula before 650 CE. He has not discovered evidence of Persian shipping to China before the seventh century; see Brian E. Colless, "Persian Merchants and Missionaries in Medieval Malaya," *JMBRAS* 42,2 (1969): 10–47.

[12] P. Y. Manguin, "La traversée de la mer de Chine méridionale, des détroits à Canton, jusqu'au 17e siècle (La question des iles Paracels)," *Actes du XXIXe Congrès international des Orientalistes* (Paris, 1976), vol. 2, pp. 110–15. Dr. Manguin is studying Indonesian maritime technology.

But I suspect that the chief consequence of my work was to fan the controversy about the site of the Śrīvijayan capital, which I identified with Palembang from 671 until the second half of the eleventh century. By doing so, I incautiously embroiled myself in the second and much more lively context of Śrīvijayan studies, which is the kingdom's geographical location and neighborhood relations. I propose to introduce the topic, the most familiar one in this field, by referring to Pelliot's 1904 article.[13]

When Pelliot, a distinguished sinologist, interested himself in what we call "Śrīvijaya," the Chinese transcription was still rendered as "Śrībhoja."[14] He was writing fourteen years before Coedès's seminal study and lacked epigraphic materials for confronting his interpretation of the already closely scrutinized foreign sources and especially the evidence of the seventh-century Chinese pilgrim, I-ching, who visited Śrīvijaya three times. In 1904 Pelliot's first responsibility was to establish whether Śrīvijaya was in Java or Sumatra. He was convinced that references to Java were recognizable in Chinese sources, and he could give his attention to Sumatran historical geography in the seventh and subsequent centuries.

Pelliot believed, as Beal had done in 1886, that the Śrīvijayan capital was at Palembang. He was influenced by Groeneveldt, as Coedès was in 1918. Groeneveldt noted that early Ming sources stated that, after a Javanese attack about 1377, the king of *San-fo-chi*, a toponym that Pelliot was prepared to accept as the Sung and Ming rendering of "Śrīvijaya," lived at Jambi and that Palembang then became known as "the Old Harbour."[15] But Groeneveldt's analysis of the Ming evidence is not entirely lucid, and Pelliot himself many years later came to doubt whether the Śrīvijayan capital in the fourteenth century was ever at Palembang. In 1933 he accepted the suggestions of Rockhill and Fujita that the capital had been at Jambi since the second half of the eleventh century,[16] though he did not change his mind with respect to earlier centuries. An irony of Śrīvijayan studies is that the earliest and frequently reiterated identification of the capital, sponsored by both Pelliot and Coedès, was influenced by misunderstood fourteenth-century Chinese evidence.

Pelliot's contribution to Śrīvijayan studies is not, however, because of where he identified the capital, but rather in the scrupulously careful way in which he laid down provisional guidelines for examining the historical geography of Sumatra in the seventh century on the basis of the Chinese sources. He discerned three fixed points: northern Sumatra, known to I-ching as "Barus"; Śrīvijaya; and also Malayu, whose capital was somewhere between "Barus" and Śrīvijaya, and therefore north of Śrīvijaya. Malayu was a fixed point because its ruler sent a mission to China in 644–645 and because I-ching stayed there two months in 672, though it was also a *dvīpa*, or a sizeable stretch of territory. Śrīvijaya was a fixed point because, although I-ching visited it no less than three times between 671 and 695, he never suggests in what he wrote there in 691–692 that events when he himself was overseas involved a displacement of the Śrīvijayan capital.[17] Instead, he continued to enjoy there the same

---

[13] P. Pelliot, "Deux itinéraires de Chine en Inde à la fin du VIIIe siècle," *BEFEO* 4 (1904): 321–48.

[14] In 1861 Julien had recognized this name in the writings of I-ching, the seventh-century pilgrim.

[15] Pelliot, "Deux itinéraires," pp. 346–47.

[16] Pelliot, "Les grands voyages maritimes chinois maritimes chinois au début du XVe siècle," *T'oung Pao* 30 (1933): 376–77.

[17] I-ching states that Kedah is a "dependency" of Śrīvijaya and the "Malayu kingdom is now changed to Śrīvijaya."

facilities for studying Buddhism that he first experienced in 671, when he probably made his way to what was already known in Chinese Buddhist circles as a seat of learning. Unfortunately, the only hint of the geographical relationship between Śrīvijaya and Malayu from 672 until after 685[18] is provided by I-ching's information that Wu-hsing, whom I-ching met in India some time before he returned to Śrīvijaya after 685, had sailed for fifteen days from Śrīvijaya to Malayu and for a further fifteen days from Malayu to Kedah. I-ching made the same voyage in 672 and stayed two months in Malayu. Pelliot was satisfied that Śrīvijaya was at Palembang, but he did not know where the Malayu capital, north of Palembang, was, and he was content to suggest that it could have been, for example, in the Siak area.

Pelliot is the pioneer of the study of early Sumatran neighborhood relations. His article continues to remind us that a location for seventh-century Śrīvijaya cannot be satisfactorily proposed if its geographical relationship with its contemporary, Malayu, is not considered.

Coedès, however, and not Pelliot introduced Śrīvijaya to the scholarly world,[19] and the consequence was a sudden interest in Palembang, where Coedès tentatively identified the capital. In 1920 Westenenk, the Dutch Resident at Palembang for less than a year, had read Coedès's article and instigated a search for antiquities.[20] His interest in Malay legend took him to Bukit Seguntang, about five miles west of the modern city of Palembang on the Musi's northern shore. There, on the southern slopes of the hill, fortuitously disturbed by roadbuilding operations, he found a stone lotus-cushion and the fragment of a granite statue, later to be known as the Buddha statue of Bukit Seguntang. The many bricks on the surface in this area caught his eye. He also discovered the Old Malay Talang Tua inscription of 684, about four miles northwest of the hill. In 1920, too, Batenburg found the Old Malay Kedukan Bukit inscription in a Malay house in the village of that name, just below the southern slopes of the hill. These were the first inscriptions found in the Palembang area.[21] The damaged Kedukan Bukit inscription, dated 682, commemorates a major military expedition and is probably the most important inscription so far found in Sumatra. Westenenk performed another service by compiling a catalogue of surface archaeological sites in the Musi river basin, and he recorded a local tradition that in ancient times there were four rajas in the area, one of whom on the Sungei Leko had easy access to the Batang Hari river to the north.

No one maintained Westenenk's initiative, however, though Rouffaer reaffirmed in 1921 what he wrote in 1909 in support of locating I-ching's Malayu, at Jambi on the Batang Hari.[22] Coedès reedited the Old Malay Śrīvijayan inscriptions in 1930 and called attention to the religious status of the ruler mentioned in the Talang Tua

---

[18] For the uncertainty of the exact year when I-ching returned from India to Śrīvijaya, see J. Takakusu, trans., *A Record of the Buddhist Religion as Practised in India and the Malay Archipelago (AD 671–695) by I-Tsing* (Oxford: Clarendon Press, 1896), p. liii.

[19] Notice was first taken of Śrīvijaya in C. O. Blagden, "The Empire of the Mahārāja, King of the Mountain and Lord of the Isles," *JSBRAS* 81 (1920): 23–28.

[20] L. C. Westenenk, "Uit het land van Bittertong (Zuid-Soematra)," *Djawa* 1,1 (1921): 5–11; "Boekit Segoentang en Goenoeng Mahaméroe uit de Sedjarah Melajoe," *Tijdschrift voor Indische taal-, land- en volkenkunde* 63 (1923): 212–26. Hereafter, *TBG*.

[21] Śrīvijayan Old-Malay inscriptions had been found in 1892 and 1904 at Kota Kapur on Bangka and at Karang Brahi in the upper reaches of the Batang Hari.

[22] G. P. Rouffaer, "Was Malaka emporium vóór 1400 A.D, genaamd Malajoer?," *Bijdragen tot de Taal-, Land- en Volkenkunde van Nederlandsch-Indie* 77 (1921): 359–569.

inscription of 684. The ruler appeared to be exhibiting the bodhisattva's compassion by dispensing spiritual gifts defined according to the terminology of the emerging school of Vajrayana Buddhism in Northeast India.[23] The Buddhist associations of Palembang now seemed assured, although in Palembang itself few cultural remains were visible. Road works at Bukit Seguntang in the 1920s brought new debris to light,[24] and Perquin, who in 1928 was the first archaeologist to visit Palembang, found dispersed brick building remains at Bukit Seguntang, a stone image, and a few bricks with spiral ornaments, one of which had a hole where a small golden plate with a Buddhist formula was recovered.[25] Yet Perquin's visit led to one important result, which was the discovery of further fragments of what could be partly reconstructed as a great granite Buddha, the first fragment of which Westenenk found in 1920. Perquin believed that the statue had been hacked to pieces. The statue, still headless in 1928, became known as the standing Buddha of Bukit Seguntang and is a valuable cultural document. Yet Bosch was discouraged when he visited Palembang in 1930 and recovered very few additional remains.[26]

The early phase of Śrīvijayan studies was to move in a very different and seemingly more promising direction. Even before Westenenk searched for evidence, another and apparently tractable possibility was being broached for studying Śrīvijaya's neighborhood relations, and I shall now disengage a riddle that engrossed scholars' attention for a long time, took them away from Pelliot's modestly conceived perspective for Sumatran historical geography, and led to startling attempts to revise and downgrade Śrīvijaya's place in early Southeast Asian history.

The origins of this development were innocent enough. In 1919 Krom, having read Coedès's article, suggested that the Ligor inscription, with a reference to Śrīvijaya on its dated face of 775 and a reference to the Śailendra family on its undated face, indicated a connection between Sumatra and Java in 775, for he knew that an inscription of 778 showed that a Śailendra prince was ruling in central Java. He therefore proposed a "Sumatran period" in Javanese history, characterized by Śrīvijaya's Mahāyāna influence in central Java in the eighth and ninth centuries. Krom introduced Śrīvijayan studies to the riddle of the relationship of the two faces of the Ligor inscription with each other. Ten years later Stutterheim reversed Krom's view. He noted that a recently edited inscription at the Nālandā Mahāyāna monastery in Bihar mentioned a Javanese prince who sponsored a religious foundation there. The prince claims to be descended from the Śailendra, family of "Yavabhūmi" and to be ruling in "Suvarṇadvīpa," and Stutterheim was persuaded that the central Javanese rulers of the Śailendra family exercised authority in Sumatra. The Nālandā inscription does not mention Śrīvijaya, but we can suppose that its author chose to extol the two famous islands in the archipelago.

---

[23] Coedès, "Les inscriptions malaises de Çrīvijaya," *BEFEO* 30 (1930): 27–80.

[24] The finds were a fragment of an inscribed stone, fragments of a stone image, and a bronze Buddha head.

[25] P. J. Perquin, "Oudheidkundig onderzoek te Palembang," *Oudheidkundig Verslag,* uitgegeven door het Koninklijk Bataviaasch Genootschap van Kunsten en Wetenschappen, Bijlage J, 1929, pp. 123–28. Hereafter, *OV.*

[26] F. D. K. Bosch, "Verslag van een reis door Sumatra," *OV,* 1930, Bijlage C, pp. 152–57. His inspection resulted in the discovery of irregular piles of brickwork at Bukit Seguntang and two stones with symbolic triangular holes at Angsoka, just behind Palembang city. He noted that three bronze Buddhist statues had recently been dredged from near the confluence of the Komering and Musi.

Interest in the Śailendra riddle grew in the 1930s. In 1933 the Indian scholar, Professor Majumdar, contradicted the earlier view that the two faces of the Ligor inscription comprised a single inscription of 775 and insisted that face "B" was written later than 775. His reasoning was accepted. But he went further and introduced a theory whose influence has not entirely disappeared. He argued that, although the ruler of Sumatran Śrīvijaya established himself on the Malay Peninsula by 775, his authority there was soon superseded by that of the Śailendra rulers, who, according to Professor Majumdar, might have recently come from northeastern India. Nakhorn Si Thammarat on the peninsula became the center of an empire that in the late eighth century and for a long time afterwards extended to Sumatra and, though he did not make it clear, to Java as well. In support of his view, he noted that the Cōḷa inscriptions of the eleventh century usually referred to the ruler of "Kaṭāha" or "Kaḍāram," a center associated with the west coast of the Malay Peninsula, rather than to the ruler of Śrīvijaya. The Arab sources seemed to provide an even more cogent reason for his theory. In the ninth century these sources begin to refer to "Zābag" as a great archipelago power and later give longitudes and latitudes that could be interpreted as meaning that Zābag's center was in the Chaiya area of the Peninsula, near the site of the Ligor inscription. And in the tenth century the Arab sources begin to refer to "Sribuza," or Sumatran Śrīvijaya, as Zābag's dependency. In support of his view that Zābag, concealing the word "Java," was on the peninsula, Professor Majumdar noted that the *Cūlavaṃsa* of Sri Lanka referred to a "Jāvaka" king on the isthmus of the peninsula in the early thirteenth century.[27]

A Chinese text of about 800 prevented Professor Majumdar from denying that Sribuza in the Arab texts was the Sumatran kingdom of Śrīvijaya,[28] but he could argue that its overlord from the end of the eighth century reigned on the peninsula. The famous maritime empire of early Southeast Asia could now be seen as a peninsular one.

Not all of Professor Majumdar's contemporaries were convinced by his revision of Śrīvijayan history, and they continued to recognize in "Zābag" a Sumatran empire, controlling both sides of the Malacca Straits.[29] On the other hand, the Śailendra riddle had become complicated by the possibility that the family came from mainland Southeast Asia, and the immediate response was Coedès's hypothesis in 1934 that the origin of the Śailendras in Java could be explained by a connection they claimed with the Funanese, or Cambodian, "kings of the mountain," who were overthrown in Cambodia in the seventh century. Coedès was among those who were beginning to suspect that the inter-states situation was more complex than was supposed in the 1920s. In this period of early Southeast Asian historical research, scholars may have been eager to establish a broad outline for the early history of the whole of Southeast Asia, and the far-flung distribution of Śrīvijayan evidence would have lent itself admirably to such a purpose.

---

[27] R. C. Majumdar, "Le rois Śailendra de Suvarṇadvīpa," *BEFEO* 33, 1 (1933): 121–41. Dr. Tibbetts attributes the longitudes and latitudes in the later Arab texts to the authors' confusing efforts to embody Ptolemaic material; G. R. Tibbetts, "The Malay Peninsula as Known to the Arab Geographers," *The Malayan Journal of Tropical Geography* 8 (1956): 22–23.

[28] Chia Tan's information in about 800 CE shows unmistakably that Śrīvijaya occupied the east coast of Sumatra from approximately the latitude of the Singapore Strait.

[29] I make a plea for a study by a Tamil philologist of the toponyms in the Tanjore inscription of 1030–31, mentioned in Coedès, *Indianized States*, pp. 142–43. I wonder what is the meaning of "Mēviḷimbaṇgam."

Professor Majumdar had disclosed a possibility for exploring a Malay Peninsula front in Śrīvijayan studies, and in 1935 Dr. Quaritch Wales wondered whether the archaeological remains in the Chaiya region argued in favor of locating the Śrīvijayan center there.[30] In 1926 Coedès already suggested that some Buddhist images of peninsular provenance in the Bangkok Museum were specimens of Sumatran Śrīvijayan art. The study of Indonesian art influences among the heterogeneous art styles of the Malay Peninsula continues to be a valuable aid for disentangling inter-regional cultural relations within the so-called "Śrīvijayan" world.[31]

But the 1930s saw an even more ambitious revision of Śrīvijayan historical geography. I am referring to Moens's long article in 1937.[32] Moens, who was not a sinologist, launched the first major challenge to Pelliot's guidelines of 1904. I shall not recapitulate his involved plotting of the fortunes of the Śailendra family, a family that he believed came from eastern India and ruled in Sumatra, Java, and eventually in the southern part of the Malay Peninsula, but I shall observe how he tried to demolish Pelliot's treatment of seventh-century Śrīvijayan history.

Disregarding Pelliot's judgment, Moens reinterpreted a sundial reading in the New T'ang History's paragraph on Śrīvijaya to prove that the capital which I-ching visited in 671 was in Kelantan in the southern Malay Peninsula. Moreover, in Moens's opinion, at about the time when the Kedukan Bukit inscription was written later in the same century, the capital was transferred to Sumatra in the vicinity of the equator near Muara Takus in the neighborhood of the junction of the Kampar Kanan and Batang Mahat rivers, a neighborhood with archaeological remains and access to the highlands in the interior. At the same time Malayu, whose capital, according to Moens, was at Palembang, was conquered by the Śrīvijayan ruler. I-ching, returning from India, went to the Muara Takus site.

Moens was able to propose Muara Takus as the capital's second site because he noted I-ching's statement in the *Record of the Buddhist Religion* that "in the country of *Shih-li-fo-shih* [Śrīvijaya]" the shadow at noon disappeared about the time of the spring and autumn equinoxes. Moens construed this to mean that the location in question was close to the equator. But he arbitrarily and inaccurately rendered "country" as "capital" (*hoofdstadt*). He also took I-ching's statement out of its context, for the pilgrim was not interested in Śrīvijaya *per se* but in demonstrating how shadow readings differed in various parts of the world, a circumstance that required monks to be careful in reckoning the canonically prescribed time for taking their meals at noon. I-ching wrote this passage in 691–692 after he knew that Śrīvijaya was an extensive "country." He may have recalled his voyage down the Sumatran coast when he returned from India after 685 and took his noon meal on board ship near the equator; alternatively, he may have found himself somewhere near the equator when he spent two months at Malayu on his way to India in 672, for he tells us that Malayu-dvīpa is now the kingdom of Śrīvijaya. What is certain is that he uses the

---

[30] He later withdrew this view.

[31] The concept of "Śrīvijayan" art is now under fire. "Javanese" art influence in the peninsula is considered instead, and there is by no means agreement on the scale of its presence there. For a recent critical study of "Śrīvijayan art," see H. G. Quaritch Wales, "The Extent of Sri Vijaya's Influence Abroad," *JMBRAS* 51,1 (1978): 5–11. See also Satyawati Suleiman, *A Few Observations on the Use of Ceramics in Indonesia, Aspek-aspek arkeologi Indonesia*, no. 7 (1980).

[32] J. L. Moens, "Śrīvijaya, Yāva en Kaṭāha, *TBG* 77,3 (1937): 317–486. Abridged English translation by R. J. de Touché, *JMBRAS* 17, 2 (1939): 1–108.

Chinese character for "country" (*kuo*) and not for "capital." His statement does not in itself prove where the capital was. Moreover, if archaeological evidence were to suggest that the seventh-century capital was close to the equator, I-ching must have visited it three times, for he does not give us reasons for supposing that the center he knew as "Śrīvijaya" was ever anywhere other than where it was in 671.

Neither Professor Majumdar nor Moens influenced all their contemporaries, but the revisionism they set in train has not come to an end. The expectation that the heartland of a great maritime empire was on the Malay Peninsula survives, and M. C. Chand Chirayu Rajani's recent studies are its best-known rejuvenation in the English language.[33]

I respect M. C. Chand's enthusiasm, and I shall limit myself to two comments.[34] I would like to know more of how the Śrīvijayan theme has been localized in the Chaiya area during the twentieth century. Were there, for example, local traditions concerning the island world of Southeast Asia before Coedès resurrected Śrīvijaya in 1918? Secondly, I am perplexed that M. C. Chand should suppose that "some of Paranavitana's sources of interlinear writing [on Sri Lanka inscriptions] will have to be used as plaster to cement the whole of the [Śrīvijaya] story together."[35] He is referring to interlinear inscriptions that only Paranavitana has claimed to decipher. One of them is said to refer to "Palambanpura" in the ninth century, a detail that enables M. C. Chand to elaborate his revision of early Southeast Asian history.[36] Until I am encouraged by epigraphers in Sri Lanka to believe that the interlinear inscriptions actually exist I shall continue to disregard historical reconstructions that depend on Paranavitana's evidence.[37] My reason for suspicion is that his evidence purports to supply unexpected answers to specific and troublesome problems that defied Paranavitana's generation of scholars.

I have lingered on the Śailendra riddle because in the 1930s it became a substantial and bewildering episode in Śrīvijayan studies. The riddle throve on two aspects of Śrīvijaya's neighborhood relations, reflected in the inscriptions and foreign records. The first of these concerned the Śailendra presence in Java, Sumatra, and the Malay Peninsula, and the second was evidence of Śrīvijaya's authority on both shores of the Malacca Straits, attested especially in the Cōḷa inscriptions concerning Kaṭāha or Kaḍāram. By hopping from one piece of isolated evidence to another Professor Majumdar sought to identify the original Śailendra base of the late eighth century with the Malay Peninsula, and Moens sought to identify a branch of the Javanese Śailendras on the Johore river from the second half of the ninth century. In these ways both of them could represent "Śrīvijayan" history as an extension of the history of the Malay Peninsula. Their details varied, but each reconstruction had a

---

[33] M. C. Chand Chirayu Rajani, "Background to the Sri Vijaya Story—Part I," *JSS* 62,1 (1974): 174–211; "Part II," *JSS* 62,2 (1974): 285–324; "Part III,"*JSS* 63,1 (1975): 208–56; "Part IV," *JSS* 64,1 (1976): 275–325; "Part V," *JSS* 64,2 (1976): 237–310.

[34] He writes not without flashes of ribaldry. He tells us, for example, that "Professor Coedès's Empire of Śrīvijaya is now off the menu." He plays with me so often that I feel that I resemble the immortal windmill.

[35] *JSS* 64,2 (1976): 306.

[36] He discusses this and other interlinear inscriptions in *JSS* 63,1 (1975): 208–56.

[37] See the discouraging comments by R. A. L. H. Gunawardhana, *Ceylon and Malaysia: A Study of Professor S. Paranavitana's Research on the Relations Between the Two Regions*, reprinted from the *University of Ceylon Review* 25,1–2 (1967); W. M. Sirisena, *Sri Lanka and South-East Asia. Political, Religious, and Cultural Relations from A.D. c. 1000 to c. 1500* (Leiden, 1978), pp. 4–5.

particular consequence: the Chinese toponym *San-fo-ch'i* of the tenth and subsequent centuries was dissociated from Sumatra. As a result, the time span of Sumatra's role as a major maritime center was truncated.

The Śailendra riddle has not yet disappeared, but it is reduced to sensible proportions. In 1962 an Old-Malay inscription, containing the name "Selendra," was discovered in north-central Java and is written in a script that Professor Boechari identifies as being of the seventh century. Details of the Śailendra connection with Sumatra remain to be clarified, but one need no longer doubt that the Śailendras were an Indonesian family.[38] As for the undated and later face of the Ligor inscription, perhaps it flaunts the fame of the same Śailendra prince of Javanese ancestry whose fame is flaunted in the Nālandā inscription of the mid-ninth century and who is described as ruling in Suvarṇadvīpa, or Sumatra.[39] The prince's Javanese ancestry may even explain why ninth-century Arabs refer to the maritime empire as Zābag, or Java. With respect to the political relationship between the two coasts of the Malacca Straits, no new material has come to light to contradict the generally held belief that the overlord was in Sumatra. Towards the end of the tenth century the overlord was at war with a Javanese ruler, and Dra. Satyawati Suleiman, noting Professor Boechari's suggestion that the transfer of the central Javanese ruling family to eastern Java in the early tenth century was connected with a disastrous eruption of Mount Merapi,[40] has recently proposed that the eruption severed road communications between central Java and the northern coast. Here, she believes, was a state of affairs that enabled the harbor princes to develop close relations with the Śrīvijayan rulers and their trading network, a situation that helps to account for the Chinese ceramics near the northern Javanese coast in the tenth century.[41]

I shall now leave the mainland front of Śrīvijayan neighborhood relations and return to Sumatra. The long archaeological haul was resumed in the 1930s. Yet in Sumatra, too, the liveliest issue centered on an epigraphic problem. The contents of the Kedukan Bukit inscription of 682, discovered in 1920, seemed to be the single tractable piece of Sumatran evidence. Two toponyms are mentioned in the context of a military expedition, led by the Ḍapunta Hiyaṃ. One is Mināna Tāmwan, and the other was restored by Coedès in 1930 as *mata jap* and by Krom in 1938 as Malayu. Some thought that the inscription celebrated the conclusion of a Palembang ruler's

---

[38] Boechari, "Preliminary Report on the Discovery of an Old-Malay Inscription at Sodjomerta," *Madjalah Ilmu-Ilmu Sastra Indonesia* 2–3 (1966): 241–51. Professor Jacques believes that the name "Funan" should be removed from the history of early Cambodia; C. Jacques, "'Funan,' 'Zhenla.' The Reality Concealed by these Chinese Views of Indochina," *Early South East Asia: Essays in Archaeology, History, and Historical Geography*, ed. R. B. Smith and W. Watson (Oxford: Oxford University Press, 1979), pp. 371–79. I agree; see Wolters, "Khmer 'Hinduism' in the Seventh Century" in this volume, chapter 8, especially note 5.

[39] Professor Boechari's personal communication at the Jakarta workshop. Professor Jacques's revised chronology for Jayavarman II of Cambodia (770–834) may have a bearing on mysterious references to Java connected with this king. Jayavarman II began to reign not long before the year of the dated face of the Ligor inscription. Could he have been a vassal of the Śrīvijayan overlord on the peninsula?

[40] Boechari, "Some Observations on the Problem of the Shift of Mataram's Center of Government from Central to East Java in the 10th Century AD," *Bulletin of the Research Center of Archaeology of Indonesia*, no. 10 (Jakarta, 1976): 16.

[41] Satyawati Suleiman, *A Few Observations on the Use of Ceramics in Indonesia*, Aspek-aspek Arkeologi Indonesia, no. 7 (1980).

successful victory, but others thought that Palembang itself was conquered.[42] The discussion was not assisted by the discovery in September 1934 of a new inscription at Sabokingking to the northeast of the modern city of Palembang, for its contents were not translated until Dr. de Casparis studied it after the war.[43]

Archaeological research, always focused on monuments, had low priority in Sumatra before the war. Nevertheless, Schnitger established a museum at Palembang and busied himself in the quest of the "forgotten kingdoms in Sumatra," though not exclusively in search of Śrīvijaya.[44] The results were further catalogues of archaeological sites in the Musi and Batang Hari river basins and elsewhere in Sumatra.[45] Schnitger's published reports lacked detailed site descriptions; he was more interested in commenting on the stylistic affinities of the remains he catalogued. Yet his activities were noticed by Krom. Krom, of all the Dutch scholars, was the one who took most interest in Śrīvijaya. He made a broad distinction between Javanese and un-Javanese art in Sumatra. The Śailendra connection seemed to explain the presence of central Javanese art influence in Buddhist and Śaivite statuary and monumental art in the Musi and Batang Hari river basins and also as far afield as South Tapanuli, but Krom was especially interested in un-Javanese remains. No specimen of the latter category interested him more than the partly reconstructed granite Buddha of Bukit Seguntang, whose head Schnitger discovered in Batavia in 1935. Schnitger suggested that the granite came from nearby Bangka island. Several scholars in the 1930s analyzed the statue's style; Krom's view was that it was made before the seventh century and under the influence of a workshop in the Vengi area of southeastern India.[46]

Śrīvijayan studies on the Sumatran front were leisurely in the 1930s, but the next two decades saw the beginning of a gradual but none the less remarkable transformation. Even during World War II a new and sharper focus was introduced by Obdeyn, a geographer, who raised questions of the shape of the ancient coastline of eastern Sumatra, and not long afterwards Van Bemmelen, a geologist, argued that

---

[42] Coedès summarizes the debate in "A Possible Interpretation of the Inscription at Kedukan Bukit (Palembang)," *Malayan and Indonesian Studies: Essays Presented to Sir Richard Winstedt on his Eighty-Fifth Birthday*, ed. John Bastin and R. Roolvink (Oxford: Clarendon Press, 1964), pp. 25–26.

[43] J. G. de Casparis, *Selected Inscriptions from the 7th to the 9th Century AD*, II (Bandung: Masa Baru, 1956), pp. 15–46. Dr. de Casparis provides in this volume a valuable study of every epigraphic fragment found in the Palembang area. The site of the Sabokingking inscription was kindly supplied to me by Raden Haji Mohamad Akip, who discovered it.

[44] F. M. Schnitger, *Forgotten Kingdoms in Sumatra* (Leiden: Brill, 1939).

[45] Schnitger, *Oudheidkundige vondsten in Palembang* (Leiden 1936); *Hindoe-Oudheden aan de Batang Hari* (Leiden 1936); *The Archaeology of Hindoo Sumatra* (Leiden 1937). See Louis-Charles Damais, "Bibliographie indonésienne," *BEFEO* 51,2 (1963): 555, for a note on remains found at Kayu Agung up the Komering. Remains have been reported at Tanjung Raja up the Ogan river; *OV*, 1921, p. 5. I am grateful to Mr. Wisnu Widjaya for telling me about ceramic remains in the Belani area about sixty miles up the Musi from Palembang.

[46] N. J. Krom, "Antiquities of Palembang," *Annual Bibliography of Indian Archaeology for 1931* (Leiden 1933), pp. 29–33; "De Heiligdomen van Palembang," *Mededelingen der Koninklijke Nederlandsche Akademie van Wetenschappen* 7 (1938): 397–423. Also see K. A. Nilakanta Sastri, *History of Śrī Vijaya* (Madras: University of Madras, 1949), chapter 7 on "Śrī Vijaya Art." This book gives a detailed survey of Śrīvijaya studies up to the beginning of the war. Nik Hassan Shuhaimi returns to the subject of the Palembang Buddha in "The Bukit Seguntang Buddha," *JMRAS* 52,2 (1979): 33–40.

the coastline in early times lay at a significant distance behind the alluvial plains that form the modern coastline. Moreover, a more realistic perception of early Sumatran topography coincided with the recovery of Indonesian independence and the Indonesians' conviction that Śrīvijaya was the symbol of their country's maritime achievements in medieval times. A new generation of Indonesian scholars now began to interest itself in Śrīvijayan studies; for them, the study of the past was more than collecting and publishing of source materials that Coedès saw his generation as undertaking in the tradition of the Renaissance philologists and humanists in Europe.[47] And so pride in the past and an awareness of the relevance of geological phenomena combined to give a new impulse and direction to languishing Śrīvijayan studies,[48] and no one urged action more than the late Muhammad Yamin, a historian and member of the government. In 1954, at his instigation, a team of historians and geologists organized a field survey of southern Sumatra, and a modern study aid was employed in the form of aerial surveys.

New ground was now broken by Professor Soekmono,[49] who was a member of the expedition and invoked up-to-date geological information. He knew that the art remains at Palembang were sparse, and he also knew that the earliest remains in the Jambi region up the coast were at Solok Sipin, west of the modern town of Jambi, while the remains at Muara Jambi, later in time, were about twenty miles northeast of Jambi town. The distribution of remains in this area seemed consistent with the geologists' view that in early times a deep inland gulf reached forty miles or so from Jambi town to Muara Tembesi. Professor Soekmono therefore suggested that the gulf occupied a strategic position in respect of shipping from the Malacca Straits, and he proposed that Śrīvijaya should be sought on its shores. He found support from the Sabokingking inscription northeast of Palembang city, recently edited by Dr. de Casparis and perhaps attributable to the same scribe who wrote the Kota Kapur inscription of Bangka in 686.[50] The inscription records an oath of obedience that could more reasonably be expected to be administered in a conquered land than at the ruler's capital.

In 1963 Professor Slametmuljana reviewed the epigraphic evidence and argued forcefully on behalf of Palembang as the capital.[51] The capital's site continued to be discussed, and Indonesian scholars became convinced that the problem would be settled only by archaeological research. In 1973 another ground survey of Sumatra was undertaken,[52] and the conclusion was reached that Palembang justified intensive field study. Sumatran archaeology was now concerned with what could be found beneath as well as above the ground.

---

[47] George Coedès, *The Making of South East Asia* (Berkeley: University of California Press, 1966), p. vii.

[48] Poerbatjaraka published the first volume of his *History of Indonesia* in 1952; *Riwajat Indonesia* (Djakarta: Pembangunan, 1952).

[49] R. Soekmono, "Geomorphology and the Location of Śrīwijaya," *Madjalah Ilmu-Ilmu Sastra Indonesia* I,I (1963): 79–92.

[50] J. G. de Casparis, *Prasasti Indonesia* (Bandung: Masa Baru, 1956), p. 16.

[51] Slametmuljana, *Kerajaan Sriwijaya* (Singapore: Dewan Bahasa dan Kebudayaan Kebangsaan, 1963).

[52] B. Bronson, Basoeki, Machi Suhardi, and J. Wisseman, *Laporan Penelitian Arkeologi di Sumatera* (Jakarta: Lembaga Purbakala dan Peninggalan Nasional); B. Bronson and J. Wisseman, "An Archaeological Survey in Sumatra, 1973," *Berita Kajian Sumatera* 4,1 (1974): 87–94.

And so a team of Indonesian and American archaeologists worked in the Palembang area from July 13 to August 28, 1974.[53] A detailed survey was made and trial pits dug to the east of Palembang city and in the Bukit Seguntang area in the hope that traces of an "urban settlement" would be found. The results were wholly unexpected. In the words of two members of the team, "the entire vicinity of Palembang does not contain enough pre-fourteenth-century domestic artifacts to make one small village." Their inference was inevitable: "we feel forced to conclude that Śrīvijaya in all except perhaps the very last stages of its existence was not in or near Palembang and probably not anywhere in the area drained by the Musi River."[54] The results were so negative that these scholars even suggested that the inscriptions and statues at Palembang were redeposited there in later times, a practice known in Thailand. The first full-scale archaeological research undertaken at Palembang seemed to remove Palembang from Śrīvijayan space. If I may be permitted a crude expression, the capital was more than ever "up for grabs." On the other hand, Dr. Bronson's reflections on his experience, which I shall note later, are a catalytic influence on Śrīvijayan studies that I, for one, gladly acknowledge.

Surveys in the Lampungs, Western Sumatra, and Muara Takus followed shortly afterwards. Professor Boechari was now becoming interested in the possibility that the Śrīvijayan capital was somewhere in central Sumatra, and he developed his thesis in a paper for the Indonesian delegates' pro-seminar in preparation for the workshop. He asked whether the expedition whose victory was commemorated in the Kedukan Bukit inscription of 682 had been launched from the Batang Kuantan, the upper part of the Indragiri river.[55]

We are now approaching the Jakarta workshop, on the eve of which Professor Boechari made what I believe is the most exciting advance in Śrīvijayan studies since Coedès's article in 1918. He reexamined the Kedukan Bukit inscription and succeeded in retrieving the toponym that Coedès had read as *mata jap* and Krom as Malayu.[56] The toponym is "Upang" and appears in the inscription just before a mutilated passage that ends with "...Śrīvijaya, victorious, successful in his expedition, endowed with plenty...."[57] Upang is the name of a village about twenty-five miles downstream from Palembang and about halfway between Palembang city and the Musi estuary; it is also the name of a river that flows to the sea from its confluence with the Musi at Upang village. Professor Boechari's discovery

---

[53] For reports on this expedition, see Bennet Bronson, "A Lost Kingdom Mislaid: A Short Report on the Search for Śrīvijaya," *Field Museum of Natural History Bulletin* 46,4 (1975): 16–20; Bennet Bronson and Jan Wisseman, "Palembang as Śrīvijaya: The Lateness of Early Cities in Southern Southeast Asia," *Asian Perspectives* 19,2 (1978): 220–39.

[54] Bronson and Wisseman, "Palembang as Śrīvijaya," p. 233. An interesting find behind Palembang city was an ancient pit filled almost entirely with small unbaked clay models of stupas; Bronson and Wisseman, "Palembang as Śrīvijaya," pp. 229–30. I commented on the find in "Landfall on the Palembang Coast in Medieval Times," *Indonesia* 20 (October 1975): 45.

[55] Professor Boechari communicated his view to the workshop. The Indonesian delegates held a "pra-seminar" in December 1978. The papers, an important contribution to Śrīvijayan studies, will be published in English.

[56] Communicated to the workshop by Professor Boechari.

[57] I reproduce Coedès's translation in "A Possible Interpretation of the Inscription at Kedukan Bukit (Palembang)," p. 25. Dr. de Casparis has shown that a fragmented Palembang inscription supplies a missing date in the Kedukan Bukit inscription; de Casparis, *Prasasti Indonesia*, pp. 12–14.

establishes beyond doubt that the Palembang area belongs to the historical geography of seventh-century Śrīvijaya. Students of Śrīvijaya eagerly await his analysis of the inscription's significance and a clarification of the historical geography of Sumatra for which Pelliot laid down provisional guidelines in 1904 by means of the foreign sources.

I have now sketched some prominent features of the prolonged, though not always sustained, study of Śrīvijaya up to the eve of the Jakarta workshop.[58] Śrīvijaya has established itself as a classic example of an Indonesian coastal state, "basing its might and wealth," in Van Leur's words, "on the stapling of the international trade of Southeast Asia." Yet the discrepancy between the amount of literature devoted to it and the paucity of evidence is, perhaps, the most surprising feature of the subject. What do we know? Its capital in the seventh century and thereafter seems to be near a river mouth on the east coast of central or southeastern Sumatra, though some believe that Śrīvijaya was either under the control of a peninsular state or was itself on the peninsula. The location of its neighbors, and especially of its seventh-century contemporary, Malayu, is still uncertain, though obscurity has now been dispelled to the extent that we know that an expedition in 682 traveled up the Musi to the Bukit Seguntang area. We also know that it sometimes controlled an outpost at Kedah, that its ruler commissioned a Buddhist foundation in the Ligor area in 775, and that in the early thirteenth century Chao Ju-kua indicated that it had exercised power on the northeastern coast of Sumatra. A connection existed between Śrīvijaya and the Śailendras of central Java, but more remains to be known of the circumstances. Śrīvijaya was undoubtedly a famous entrepôt. Missions were sent to China as early as from 670–673 to 742 and from 960 until the second half of the eleventh century, though rarely thereafter. Śrīvijaya was also a Buddhist center, though Buddhist art remains on an impressive scale have been found nowhere in Sumatra. "The art of Śrīvijaya" has become a suspect category. In general, one is almost tempted to conclude that Śrīvijaya has left little more than traces of its illustrious name.

The curious aspect of this record is the extent to which scholars have had to depend on extraneous and often ambiguous sources about Śrīvijaya rather than on evidence unambiguously identifiable as being of Śrīvijaya itself. Only the Sumatran inscriptions of the 680s can be confidently regarded as indigenous evidence. And so the Śailendra riddle led scholars far afield, and the 1974 expedition to Palembang discovered that its expectations, derived from experience of "cities" in mainland Southeast Asia, were disappointed. Chinese and Arab documents supported the belief that Śrīvijaya was an important entrepôt but also entangled scholars in controversial problems of Southeast Asian historical geography. The external archives have been endlessly reshuffled, yet the object of the study continues to be elusive. We have glanced at such strange initiatives as a non-sinologist's revision of I-ching's texts, the suggestion that Palembang's inscriptions and statutory were redeposited, and recourse to Paranavitana's interlinear inscriptions.

A friend recently asked me what there was about Śrīvijaya that made it so difficult to study. The quick answer, of course, is a marked insufficiency of evidence and especially of indigenous evidence. But I am beginning to wonder whether the answer is satisfactory. When we refer to an absence of evidence, we tend to think of

---

[58] Among my omissions are references to Ferrand's work, to the now abandoned effort to find a place for the Philippines within the Śrīvijayan sphere of influence, and especially to Damais's Sumatran studies, published in the *BEFEO*.

an absence of types of evidence familiar to those who have studied the early history of other parts of Southeast Asia and were able to depend on reasonably ample data from local epigraphic and monumental evidence to broach such topics as the territorial range of overlordships, religious systems, vassal relationships, social structure, definitions of authority, shifts in art styles, and, as a bonus, chronological frameworks sufficient to permit at least a provisional linear outline of the past.

Within the next few years these types of familiar evidence may be less conspicuously absent. But let us suppose that this never happens. Should Śrīvijaya then be regarded as unstudiable?

I do not think so. Even if very little additional familiar evidence is recovered, scholars will not be impeded. Instead, the continued absence of such evidence will stimulate thought about the idiosyncratic nature of Śrīvijayan culture responsible for the situation and will also encourage a search for types of fact that provide authentic signs of Śrīvijaya. Absence of evidence is as significant as its presence and can be brought into relationship with new and visible signs in order gradually to reveal an interrelated sequence or environment of differing signs that will enable "Śrīvijaya" to be read as a text, just as linguists read a text by paying equal attention to what is and is not present. If Śrīvijaya is studied in what can be called a semiological way, or through its signs, perspectives will open up for criticizing the Chinese and Arab sources on which we have relied so much for our impressions of Śrīvijaya, and more attention will be paid to their textual framework and cultural background.[59] Foreign sources can never be taken at face value.

My conjecture is that both present and absent signs will be associated with the landscape anywhere in Southeast Asia that, in the light of what is already known, can be reasonably regarded as part of "Śrīvijaya." The signs will come from the physical environment, the master text for Śrīvijayan studies. I shall now take note of Professor Boechari's topographical precision in rendering the Kedukan Bukit inscription of 682, for he has provided us with a new and quite specific fixed point in the Śrīvijayan world such as Pelliot was unable to do in 1904. The establishment of the name "Upang" in the Kedukan Bukit inscription means that we can take it for granted that southern Sumatra, at least, belonged to the Śrīvijayan world at that time. In this area, which, in terms of geographical conditions, can be extended to include central Sumatra, we have an opportunity of considering whether a text-like relationship between invisible and visible signs can assist us in discovering the Sumatran part of the Śrīvijayan polity and the culture that generated it.

We can begin, for example, with the possibility that, unless field research shows otherwise, only patches of wet-rice agriculture were cultivated. The consequence would be very few permanently settled villages in the form and on the scale well-known in early Javanese history. Here, then, may be one invisible sign of Śrīvijaya that can be related to another invisible sign, which is the absence of the land-grant inscriptions helpful in constructing a chronology of Javanese rulers and their spheres of territorial influence. The land and population in this part of Sumatra would not ordinarily be available for the rulers' gifts to the gods. To this extent Coedès's haunting judgment that the rulers "neglected the spiritual values" is contested by

---

[59] Part of the merit of Professors Wang Gungwu's and Wheatley's work is that it focuses on these matters; Wang Gungwu, "The Nanhai Trade: A Study of the Early History of Chinese Trade in the South China Sea," *JMBRAS* 31,2 (1958): 1–135; Paul Wheatley, *The Golden Khersonese: Studies in the Historical Geography of the Malay Peninsula before A.D. 1500* (Oxford: Oxford University Press, 1961).

local geography, even if stone were at hand in quantity. The Sumatran rulers in the plains behind the east coast were prohibited from covering the land with monuments simply because they lacked settled agricultural villages for endowing and maintaining temples. Religious artifacts in this part of the Sumatran environment are usually in the form of small buildings or small statues. Here signs of "spiritual values" need to be discovered in other ways, and I shall suggest a possibility.

The relationship between the ruler and divinity in early Southeast Asia is the aspect of the system of beliefs most visibly signified by inscriptions and monuments. But the complementary aspect was the ruler's relationship with his people; it, too, was a religious one and attracted venerating followers to his person. Professor Soekmono has recently demonstrated that this other relationship helps us to recognize the Javanese *candis* as the heirs of the ancient menhirs, signs of the ties between departed ancestors and their people.[60] Drs. Sukarto has called attention to similar evidence of ties in Bali between ruler and people in the form of the sixty-four stone seats of the king's brave followers that are reminiscent of the megalithic ancestral stone seats.[61] The congregations of little shrines around the royal temples of Prambanan, Plaosan, and Sewu in central Java suggest the same tradition. In all these instances men attributed with divine authority attracted followers.

Sumatra had its menhir-worshipping tradition, and in early times Sumatran chiefs would also be attributed with spiritual prowess that attracted followers. To the landscape of central and southern Sumatra we can again turn for signs of "spiritual values" other than monuments and inscriptions.

Perhaps the most obvious feature of the landscape is its extraordinary access to riverine communications. In such an environment no implement was more important than the paddle, and I suggest that the paddle in tidal and non-tidal waters alike is the key, though no longer visible, sign that can be associated with early riverine culture in Sumatra. In the nineteenth century, local craft manned by paddlers could make the fifty-mile journey from Palembang to the Musi estuary in a few hours when the tide was ebbing,[62] and goods from Palembang sent to the Pasemah region were brought upriver in fourteen days over the three hundred miles or so to Muara Malang, close to the foothills of the Barisan range,[63] and then by land to the Pasemah base in one day. Energetic paddling up and down the long Sumatran rivers meant that the scattered inhabitants of riverine neighborhoods, each of which comprised a number of settlements separated on the map by deceptive distance, belonged to social collectivities in touch with each other and with those whom they acknowledged as their rulers. Signs of the shared values that united a ruler with his people would therefore be visible in the form of stately river traffic and especially in the royal messengers, traveling in boats of appropriate distinction and communicating orders to dispersed settlements. In Java the royal presence was

---

[60] Soekmono, "*Candi,* fungsi dan pengertiannya. Le *candi,* sa fonction et sa conception," *BEFEO* 61 (1975): 455.

[61] M. M. Sukarto K. Atmodjo, *The Charter of Kapal, Aspek-aspek Arkeologi Indonesia,* no. 2 (1977): 9.

[62] J. J. van Sevenhoven, "Beschrijving van de hoofdplaats van Palembang," *Verhandelingen van het Bataviaasch Genootschap van Kunsten en Wetenschappen* 9 (1823): 50.

[63] William Marsden, *The History of Sumatra* (Kuala Lumpur and New York: Oxford University Press, 1966; reprint of third edition, introduced by John Bastin), p. 360.

immanent in the immovable monuments and inscriptions that signified it, but on the Sumatran rivers signs of the royal presence, the messengers, were mobile. The messengers probably flourished portable royal tokens, and we need not discount the possibility that the tokens were sometimes written ones, honored even if they could not be read.[64]

No royal order up and down the rivers would be more urgent than that the people should "assemble" under their chiefs on the ruler's business. A summons to assemble is the conventional mechanism of mobilization in the *Sejarah Melayu*. In connection with the Kedukan Bukit inscription of 682, Coedès suggests that the ruler waited for twenty-five days until preparations for the expedition were complete and then embarked and gave the signal for departure.[65] A feature of the Sabokingking inscription behind the modern city of Palembang is that some of those to whom the oath was administered served at a distance from the ruler's base and had presumably been summoned for the occasion.[66] Abū Zayd in the early tenth century records the tradition that the Śrīvijayan ruler, vexed by a Khmer ruler's impertinence, ordered a thousand ships to be prepared. When the preparations were complete, the ruler embarked. Another glimpse of the same mechanism of mobilization is given by Chao Ju-kua in the early thirteenth century: the people of *San-fo-ch'i* would "assemble" in wartime and each chief would provide his own military equipment and provisions.

These scraps of evidence point to the conclusion that riverine "spiritual values" in the Sumatran part of the Śrīvijayan polity were signified by the responsiveness of loyal networks of dispersed and distant settlements to royal orders, conveyed by fast-paddled messengers. Neighborly obedience in a riverine landscape represented, I suggest, a spatial integration comparable with the congregations of small shrines around the royal temples in central Java.

What happened on the rivers would therefore supply the most visible signs of Śrīvijaya to be expected in a paddle-based culture. These signs have disappeared and have to be supplied. But would other and still visible signs, we may ask ourselves, be found in the royal center set in the same landscape?

The impression given in Arab sources, reflecting what merchants saw, is that nothing was seen on the ground at the Śrīvijayan capital except its natural features and especially water, though some Arab sources refer to numerous villages likely to be riverine settlements in the vicinity. One Arab writer at the beginning of the tenth

---

[64] The Saribas Ibans were convinced that writing was somehow the key to European power; Robert Pringle, *Rajahs and Rebels: The Ibans of Sarawak under Brooke Rule, 1841–1941* (Ithaca and London: Cornell University Press, 1970), p. 201. See de Casparis, *Prasasti Indonesia*, p. 41, note 44, for the interesting suggestion that the expression "samayaṅku" (? "my orders") in the Sabokingking inscription may refer to written *akṣaras* such as those on the royal seal that symbolised the king himself. According to the Sung History, the *San-fo-ch'i* ruler used his ring as a seal. The Palembang Sultans sent their distant subordinates *piagems*, or "decisions," inscribed on copper or silver plates; *Notulen van de Algemeene en Besturs-vergaderingen van het Bataviaasch Genootschap*, 26 (1888): 117–21. In all these cases, writing, even if emptied of meaning, reinforced authority.

[65] Coedès, "A Possible Interpretation of the Inscription at Kedukan Bukit (Palembang)," p. 29. But we must await Professor Boechari's forthcoming study of the inscription and its timetable. [The editors of this current collection were unable to locate the "forthcoming study."—Ed.]

[66] Mr. McKinnon suggests that the higher ground, adjacent to a creek giving direct access to the Musi and near this inscription, lent itself as an excellent place for assembling a large number of people.

century even asserts that "in India there are no towns."[67] The emphasis in these sources is always on the ruler's power and generosity to his entourage and therefore on what happened in the capital rather than on its appearance. The Arab evidence is not contradicted by I-ching in the seventh century, though I am among those who have quoted him as saying that the Śrīvijayan capital was a "fortified city." I-ching merely uses a conventional Chinese term for the protected compound of royal dwellings beyond which the monks, his real concern, lived. His statement should not be construed as meaning that the compound was protected by stone or brick. Similarly, the monks' quarters would not contain permanent materials. Dra. Suleiman has persuasively recaptured the scene known to I-ching when she reminds us that the monks would use bamboo and leaves as eating utensils and coconut husks and gourds for drinking purposes. She also suggests that the monasteries were made of wood and bamboo, with grass or palm roofs such as can be seen today in Bali or at the Purba Baru *pesantren* in South Tapanuli.[68] The monks were part of the local population; their calling required them to disdain privileges of any kind.

The royal compound probably resembled what Malays call a *kota*, with its defense works depending on a river bank and comprising earth, felled trees, and bamboo, a fortification similar to what Anderson saw near Medan in 1823.[69] The river, facilitating reinforcements or temporary evacuation, provided reliable defense. The absence of an elaborately walled city is a predictable morphological sign of a riverine situation, where readily mobilized paddle-power rendered permanent fortifications superfluous.

Again, there is no reason to suppose that the ruler's residence was constructed of anything more permanent than elegantly carved timber.[70] Such was the basic structure of the palace described in the *Sejarah Melayu*. In the Śrīvijayan royal center the only permanent buildings would have been brick stupas, remains of which have been found in different parts of Sumatra. Dra. Suleiman has reminded us that bricks were reserved for the gods and not for men.[71] Ancient Sumatran bricks are so durable that they are often used today for secular purposes such as road construction, for supporting house posts, and even for hearths.

---

[67] G. Ferrand, *Relations de voyages et textes géographiques arabes, persans et turks relatifs à l'Extrême-Orient du VIIIe au XVIIIe siècles* (Paris: E. Leroux, 1913), vol. 1, p. 63. The Arab convention was to regard maritime Southeast Asia as part of "India." The Sung History states that the capital of *San-fo-ch'i* was a fortified city with a wall of piled bricks. I believe that the city in question was in the Jambi region, where the monuments are larger than anywhere else in southern Sumatra. Perhaps here we are in the presence of Javanese notions of how a settlement should be laid out.

[68] S. Suleiman, "A Few Observations on the Use of Ceramics in Indonesia." I-ching's definition of a monastery is worth noting: "what we call a monastery is a general designation for the place of residence (for the Sangha), the whole of which may be regarded as a monastic kitchen"; Takakusu, *Record*, p. 84.

[69] James Anderson, *Mission to the East Coast of Sumatra* (Edinburgh: W. Blackwood, 1826), pp. 23–32. We should remember that in Anderson's day fortifications were designed to give effect to musket fire. On the subject of Malay fortifications, see G. B. Gardner, *Keris and Other Malay Weapons* (Singapore: Progressive Publishing, 1936), pp. 125–27.

[70] On the subject of palaces and wood carving, see Mubin Sheppard, *Taman Indera, A Royal Pleasure Ground: Malay Decorative Arts and Pastimes* (Kuala Lumpur: Oxford University Press, 1972), pp. 28–46.

[71] Personal communication.

The essential distinguishing signs of the ruler's court were those of behavior and rank, expressed by the raiment the ruler bestowed on trusted members of his entourage.[72] One could "read" the situation at court by noting the clothing signs that signified the status of the courtiers. None of this evidence is visible today. Permanent signs of the royal favor such as the magical triangles mentioned in a Palembang inscription[73] may survive but are as likely to be found in the recipients' settlements as in the royal center.

In central and southern Sumatra, therefore, everything was organized in a landscape that provided livelihood, defense, and royal resources. Definitive material signs of a Śrīvijayan ruler's center may always be absent unless an inscription, identifying it beyond all possible doubt, is discovered. The landscape itself is the source of the surviving signs and the opportunity for recuperating absent signs and enabling what is not there to become a significant part of the Śrīvijayan "text." Indeed, Dr. Bronson and Ms. Wisseman, unable in 1974 to find an early "city" in Palembang, contemplated the possibility of a capital with absent signs when they asked themselves what would have been characteristics of a settlement which "(a) might look sufficiently urban to a contemporary observer but (b) could be quite inconspicuous to an archaeologist."[74] They approached the question in terms of the center's location. Such a settlement, they imagined, would exist in comparative isolation from its hinterland but would have to be close to the sea and have access to easy transportation and to major international trade routes in order to accumulate economic resources for keeping a major settlement in operation in spite of the absence of a large exploitable hinterland population. Again, the settlement would be "organized politically in such a way as to dispense with large, durable ceremonial foci" and to be built flimsily and, "if possible, in a location where a proportion of domestic and industrial waste will be disposed of in such a way as to be unnoticeable to later archaeologists." "A settlement that meets all these requirements," they concluded, "does not seem abstractly impossible or implausible."

They foresaw that the inhabitants of such a settlement could throw their waste in the water, and geologists and archaeologists may locate the beds of ancient streams alongside or over which the inhabitants lived. Moreover, in another article, Dr. Bronson admits that a ruler's personal prestige was an element in the riverine situation,[75] which implies that leadership could be exercised in the hinterland from an isolated royal settlement, though I wonder whether leadership was simply a matter of guaranteeing the ferrying of produce to the royal center, the activity that

---

[72] The significance of gifts of raiment is examined in detail by A. C. Milner, "The Malay Raja: A Study of Malay Political Culture in East Sumatra and the Malay Peninsula in the Early Nineteenth Century" (PhD dissertation, Cornell University, 1977). Dr. Milner concludes that royal service, symbolized by these gifts, "offered the opportunity for social and spiritual advancement," p. 217. [Published as *Kerajaan: Malay Political Culture on the Eve of Colonial Rule* (Tucson: University of Arizona Press for the Association for Asian Studies, 1982)—Ed.]

[73] See de Casparis, *Prasasti Indonesia*, pp. 29–31.

[74] Bennet Bronson and Jan Wisseman, "Palembang as Śrīvijaya," p. 235.

[75] Bennet Bronson, "Exchange at the Upstream and Downstream Ends: Notes Towards a Functional Model of the Coastal State in Southeast Asia," *Economic Exchange and Social Interaction in Southeast Asia: Perspectives from Prehistory, History, and Ethnography*, ed. Karl L. Hutterer, Michigan Papers on South and Southeast Asia, no. 13 (Ann Arbor, MI: Center for South and Southeast Asian Studies, University of Michigan, 1977), p. 49.

Dr. Bronson assumes to be the *leit-motif* of riverine life. What we know of Malay literature suggests that the ruler was much more than a hoarder of material wealth. His influence promoted sensations of psychological well-being among his followers, for his person was the effective ceremonial center and he did not have to dispense with monuments *faute de mieux*. I even wonder whether the commercial activity of the hypothetical Sumatran polity, for which Dr. Bronson proposes a model,[76] was ever obsessively concerned with extracting riverine produce for purposes of foreign trade. The foreign accounts of Śrīvijaya indicate that the capital was a major entrepôt, where goods from many parts of the world besides Sumatra were exchanged. The polity's first priority is more likely to be the tapping of riverine manpower to protect the entrepôt's monopoly. Foreign treasures would have enabled the ruler to maintain a glittering court and honor his entourage.

The crucial question posed by Dr. Bronson and Ms. Wisseman, however, is whether the ruler could reside far apart from his neighborhood. I doubt it. The significant spatial unit in Śrīvijayan history, at least in this part of Sumatra, would not have been a lonely "city," distinguished by material "urban" signs and exercising coercive power over a distant hinterland. The unit in question was a network of settlements up and down the river, from which people sallied forth to participate in the ruler's adventures and provided him with key members of his entourage, sometimes bound to him by marriage alliance. The discovery of signs of networks and not of cities will resurrect the Sumatran map in Śrīvijayan times.

I shall hazard a few guesses on what may be signs of networks and their royal centers. I would expect fairly dense clusters of settlements, all close to each other in terms of paddle-speed distances and sometimes at the confluences of tributaries. The clusters would show evidence of cultural homogeneity in the form of earthernware, wooden as well as metal or stone objects of religious and status significance, imported ceramics, and perhaps pieces of paddles scientifically datable and even tokens of the royal messengers.[77] I would also expect evidence to show that the settlements were continuously occupied over long periods of time and tended to become larger. I disagree with Dr. Bronson that these polities were evanescent,[78] though changes in the Sumatran coastline or of river channels may sometimes have required minor shifts of sites. The polities give the illusion of being short-lived simply because their dates are supplied by their missions to China, but mission sequences often depended on political circumstances in China and not in Sumatra. Royal centers may have shifted from one river basin to another, but former royal centers would not be permanently deserted; instead, they would be ruled by vassals. The Śrīvijayan neighborhood networks were almost certainly stable during the many centuries of the tributary trade.

Finally, I would expect that, where a network was closest to the sea, there would be an extensive and sprawling group of settlements that merged into a fringe of nearby upstream settlements. Here would be the royal center: The center need not be invisible. Instead, it awaits recognition within the context of its neighborhood, and the first question is always how far away riverine settlements had to be, paddle-wise, to be beyond the center's influence.

---

[76] Bronson, "Exchange at the Upstream and Downstream Ends."

[77] Dr. Bronson thinks on these lines; "Exchange," p. 49. He also suggests that manufactured goods in a coastal center would be exchanged for upriver goods; "Exchange," pp. 49–50.

[78] Bronson, "Exchange," pp. 49 and 51.

The plotting of networks is a practicable objective. Dispersed settlements can be distinguished by aerial photography and studied on the ground by means of soil and pollen analyses of materials recovered from test pits. One can determine chronologies of soil disturbance as the result of human occupation. Post holes may help to measure the size of a settlement at different times and indicate whether it expanded and had local influence. Disintegrating artifacts, ceramics, and fragments of religious remains may throw light on a settlement's technology and cultural context.

Research on these lines depends above all on modern skills for identifying and dating changes in the landscape and soil. Distances up and down the long rivers can be reduced to realistic proportions in terms of paddle-speed, and villagers will express their sense of the significance in riverine life of the space they occupy. Ethnographic data, venerable place names, and unexpected details of folk memory will contribute to a better-informed map.[79] When individual settlements are intensively studied, questions of their age and maximum size will arise. Eventually a map of related networks will disclose itself, each with its own ecological, chronological, and regional identity. The map may eventually become more than a map of riverine settlements. The distribution of natural resources on the island of Sumatra as well as its oceanic location and geographical access both to the east and west coasts are likely to have encouraged the development of a number of discrete societies, with the result that the early histories of lowland and highland peoples sometimes overlapped. The highlands are nowhere far from the sea or navigable rivers.[80]

An "insular" perspective may help historians when they are considering the role of the upper reaches of the Batang Hari, Indragiri, and Kampar rivers in early Sumatran history. The mountains to the west of these rivers were known to southern Indian traders in the first centuries of the Christian era, and in very early times the toponym "Malayu" seems to have been already associated with the mountains.[81] I-ching knew of a "Malayu *chou*," or Malayu-*dvīpa*. In his day the highlands were probably closer to the east coast; Professor Soekmono took this possibility into account in his discussion of Jambi's claim to be the Śrīvijayan capital. Perhaps a Buddhist center, known to I-ching as Malayu and visited by him because he was interested in its religious teachings, existed in the upper reaches of the Batang Hari, Indragiri, or Kampar rivers or even in the highlands.[82] He may have traveled inland

---

[79] De Sturler mentions a concentration of Kubu settlements on the Leko river, an important tributary of the Musi. Here is an area that produces benzoin and other valuable natural products; W. L. de Sturler, *Proeve eener beschrijving van het gebied van Palembang* (Groningen: J. Oomrens, 1843), p. 203. Westenenk mentions Kubus in the Upang area near the Musi estuary and suggests that Lebar Daun, described in the *Sejarah Melayu* as Sri Tri Buana's faithful follower, was a Kubu chief there. I would like to know something of Pulau Wijaya, not far upstream from Palembang.

[80] Dr. Miksic discusses these possibilities; J. N. Miksic, "Archaeology, Trade, and Society in Northeast Sumatra" (PhD dissertation, Cornell University, 1979), chapter 3.

[81] Jean Filliozat, "L'inscription dite 'de Võ-canh,'" *BEFEO* 55 (1969): 107–16; Filliozat, "Pline et le Malaya," *JA* 262,1–2 (1974): 119–30; Paul Wheatley, "The Mount of Immortals—A Note of Tamil Cultural Influence in Fifth-Century Indochina," *Oriens Extremus* 21, 1 (1974): 97–109; and Louis-Charles Damais, "Bibliographie indonésienne," *BEFEO* 54 (1968): 424.

[82] Sir Roland Braddell suggested that the whole area from the Jambi-Kampar district to Palembang was part of the kingdom of Malayu; Roland Braddell, "Notes on Ancient Times in

to a settlement now in the deep hinterland. Traveling upstream near the equator, where the winds drop, can be slow and would help to explain why Wu-hsing's journey from Śrīvijaya to Malayu took fifteen days.[83] We can also recall I-ching's statement that, after leaving Malayu in 672, he "changed direction," which is Chavannes's rendering of this passage and one that I now accept. I-ching's course would be intelligible if his ship came downstream in an eastern direction and then made an abrupt turn in a northwestern direction towards the Malacca Straits.

The likelihood that "Malayu" always referred to a substantial part of Sumatra, situated in the deep hinterland as well as in the riverine plains, may have a bearing on the situation in later times. Dra. Suleiman has recently revived interest in the Chinese statement of the second half of the fourteenth century that there were three kings of *San-fo-ch'I*, one of whom was the Palembang ruler.[84] The other two, she suggests, were the rulers of Jambi[85] and of the Malayu kingdom in the highlands over which Kĕrtanagara claimed to be the overlord in the second half of the thirteenth century and where Ādityavarman ruled for many years in the fourteenth. She, as Moens did, wonders whether the *San-fo-ch'i* toponym, which careful Chinese officials would never have used to transcribe "Śrīvijaya," means no more than the "Three Vijayas." I agree. Chinese officials sometimes attempted to name foreign countries in ways that took into account what they had been told about them,[86] and a Śrīvijayan ruler as early as 960, the date of the first Śrīvijayan mission to the Sung, probably explained through his envoys that he was the ruler of three neighboring Sumatran states, thereby causing the Chinese to improvise the expression *San-foch'i*, or "the three Vijayas," as an abbreviated device for registering an important kingdom that they never associated with the T'ang toponym of *Shih-li-fo-shih* ("Śrīvijaya").[87] The Yüan History does not mention *San-fo-ch'i* but only "Malayu" and "Palembang," though the conservative Ming court in the second half of the fourteenth century revived the nomenclature of the Sung dynasty. The relations

---

Malaya. 8: Che-Li-Fo-Che, Mo-Lo-Yu and Ho-Ling," *JMBRAS* 24,1 (1951): 14. Braddell, p. 15, accepted Pelliot's location of Śrīvijaya at Palembang.

[83] Marsden quotes an early seventeenth-century Portuguese reference to the twenty-two days required to ascend the Batang Hari to the town of Jambi, in Marsden's day said to be about sixty miles from the sea; Marsden, *The History of Sumatra*, p. 358. A feature of the French maps of the late seventeenth century is the deep gulf that reaches inland up the Indragiri river basin. Map 6 in Wolters, "Landfall on the Palembang Coast in Medieval Times," is one example.

[84] Satyawati Suleiman, *The Archaeology and History of West Sumatra, Bulletin of the Research Center of Archaeology of Indonesia* [Jakarta], no. 12 (1977): 10–11.

[85] The toponym "Jambi" first appears in Chinese records of the ninth century; Wolters, *Early Indonesian Commerce*, p. 144. I no longer assume that the ninth-century Javanese prince was ruling from Palembang.

[86] For example, *Ch'ih-t'u* (the "Red Earth" kingdom), "Land" and "Water" *Chen-la* (in Cambodia), and the "western" and "eastern" kings of Java in the late fourteenth century.

[87] "San" merely means "three." In 1017 the Mahārāja of Śrīvijaya told the Sung court that he was "the king of the ocean lands." In 905 "Vijaya" (*Fo-ch'i / dz'iei* = jay [a]) sent a mission to China. In 960 the Sung scribes also used the *ch'i* character and added the *San*, and their transcription was retained in Sung and early Ming times. Oddly, the Sung transcription of the Cham center of Vijaya, cited by Coedès in 1918 to restore the T'ang transcription of Śrīvijaya, was *Fo-shih.* I suggest that here we have an example of the influence of different Austronesian pronunciations on Chinese transcriptions. The nineteenth-century author, Wei Yüan, who was interested in Sino–Southeast Asian geopolitical relations, introduced Śrīvijaya with the Sung texts. He, and his Sung predecessors, did not recognize the identity of *Fo-shih* and *Fo-ch'i.*

between the constituent parts of Śrīvijaya in early Sung times were probably adjusted by marriage alliances; changes in the site of the overlord's capital need not have been violent episodes, as I once supposed. The Śrīvijayan overlordship certainly did not extinguish the "Malayu" toponym, which reappears in records of the thirteenth and fourteenth centuries. The waning of an entrepôt-based tributary trade by that time would have intensified centrifugal tendencies in the Sumatran world and given particular currency to regional identities and ancient place-names.

My extension of the Sumatran landscape in Śrīvijayan times to include the upper reaches of the rivers and the highlands has led me into the realm of speculation, and speculation will not cease until the landscape everywhere begins to disclose its evidence. As far as Sumatra is concerned, everything depends on the long archaeological haul, and this is precisely the future the Indonesian delegates at the Jakarta workshop, with plenty of survey experience behind them, had already foreseen before they met in March, 1979. The same prospect, adapted to local environments and with particular research objectives in mind, was also envisaged in respect of the peninsula in Thailand and the east coast of Western Malaysia. The landscape of the Philippines is likely to yield valuable comparative data.[88]

The imaginative combination of the methodologies of the natural sciences as well as of the humanities, the combination to which the workshop gave top priority, will assure a range and scale of enquiry that will transform the perspectives of Śrīvijayan studies in ways beyond the reach of earlier generations of scholars. More exact information about distinct regional cultures on both sides of the Straits of Malacca will be an important long-term consequence, and we can also expect well-supported arguments for narrowing down, distinguishing, and evaluating candidates for the site of the Śrīvijayan capital or capitals, though subtle problems of interpretation will arise when similar evidence from two or more neighborhoods close to the Sumatran east coast is compared. Today's distribution of archaeological remains should not be accepted too rigidly as an ipso-facto argument in favor of a particular neighborhood; all kinds of surprises may be in store for us. The size and chronological continuity of several sprawling settlements, disclosed after intensive research, will have to be considered, and, in Sumatra, the importance that Pelliot attached to Malayu as well as to Śrīvijaya will deserve to be remembered.[89] One day, too, the cultural background that enabled the Śrīvijayan rulers to exercise long-distance influence and even sovereignty overseas, so eloquently attested in foreign records, will be better understood. We shall also be able to examine more critically the concept of "coastal" states as something distinct from "inland and agrarian" ones. The possibility that the riverine polities eventually developed maritime outreach may offer a more correct perspective for understanding the substance of Śrīvijayan history.

I have ended my sketch of Śrīvijayan studies with the refreshingly sharp focus proposed by the delegates to the Jakarta workshop. The result will be a culturally oriented conception of Śrīvijayan history that will inform the diffuse lines of enquiry hitherto associated with the subject. One day historians will understand better how

---

[88] The remains of several boats have recently been discovered near Butuan city in northeastern Mindariao. The site, which seems to date from at least the eighth and ninth centuries, is in a low-lying swampy area in a region that today is continuously flooded.

[89] In 1904 Pelliot furnished three theoretical fixed points for seventh-century Sumatra: "Barus," Malayu, and Śrīvijaya. Professor Boechari has now discovered a fourth and actual fixed point in Upang. In a note on *Mo-ho-hsin* at the end of the essay I suggest a fifth one that may be actual as well as theoretical.

things could happen in the Śrīvijayan world, and they will profit from new lines of enquiry set in train by the workshop.[90] 1979 will, I am confident, be remembered as a turning point in Śrīvijayan studies.

One conclusion is self-evident. Śrīvijayan studies in the future will not be so usefully pursued in libraries. I was forced to realize this when I visited Palembang in July 1978.[91] My experience there is why I have become alert to the need for a semiological approach. I shall conclude the essay by indicating how the scene awaiting me in Palembang made me think somewhat differently about Śrīvijaya or, more accurately, about that part of Sumatra which Professor Boechari's discovery of the "Upang" toponym of 682 justifies our regarding as part of the Śrīvijayan landscape, for I would be unfaithful to the relaxed mood of the Jakarta workshop if I were now to argue Palembang's case for being the capital. And so I shall content myself with a few observations on what I saw and required me to criticize the Chinese sources.

I shall begin with what I had to unlearn when I traveled down the lowest reaches of the Musi river. Considerable geomorphic changes in the eastern coastline of Sumatra were taking place over the centuries, but their effect in the Palembang area may be exaggerated.[92] My visit led me to suppose that an early fifteenth-century Chinese map showed that the Musi estuary was where it was today, and the perceptibly higher land in the vicinity of Upang makes it likely that land already existed there at the time of the Kedukan Bukit inscription.[93] The twenty-five miles or so between the modern city of Palembang and the confluence of the Musi and Upang rivers, twenty-five miles from the Bangka Strait, could be as much a riverine as a coastal scene in Śrīvijayan times, when the outline of today's banks of the Musi was slowly taking shape among the many mud islands created by long-shore drift as well as by upstream alluvial deposit. The southern shore of the Musi opposite Palembang city was probably an archipelago of gradually enlarged mud islands.

---

[90] I have not mentioned linguistic studies or the study of riverine experiences in Malay literature. Both these matters are obviously important. In connection with the former, see Louis-Charles Damais, "Études soumatranaises. III. La Langue B des inscriptions de Sri Wijaya," *BEFEO* 54 (1968): 523–66.

[91] I am grateful for the opportunity of accompanying Dra. Suleiman, of the National Research Center of Archaeology, Indonesia, and her colleagues, Dra. Sopjatmi Satari and Dra. Rumbi Mulia. Dr. Milton Osborne was with us. An informative and lively account of our visit, written by Mr. E. P. Edwards McKinnon and Dr. A. C. Milner, is available in their "A Letter from Sumatra: A Visit to Some Early Sumatran Historical Sites," *Indonesia Circle* (London) 18 (March, 1979): 3–21.

[92] For an account of our visit to the lower reaches of the Musi, see Wolters, "A Note on Sungsang Village at the Estuary of the Musi River in Southeastern Sumatra: A Reconsideration of the Historical Geography of the Palembang Region," *Indonesia* 27 (April 1979): 33–50. The extent of the enlightenment I gained by visiting Sungsang can be estimated by comparing this essay with what I wrote in "Landfall on the Palembang Coast in Medieval Times." For rivers in south Sumatra, see Figure 1. For toponyms, see also Figure 2 in chapter 5.

[93] There are graves behind the northern bank of the confluence, and Westenenk reported that one of them is still honored as the grave of Lebar Daun, described in the *Sejarah Melayu* as Sri Tri Buana's faithful follower when the prince was ruling at Bukit Seguntang; L. C. Westenenk, "Uit het land van Bittertong," p. 6.

Figure 1: Rivers in Southern Sumatra

Nevertheless, the Palembang terrain was never entirely swampy. An elevated laterite peninsula behind the city on the alluvial northern shore of the Musi stretches from west to east to disappear where the river begins to sweep northwards to the sea. The airport, palm oil plantations, and the University of Sriwijaya are on the peninsula. But Bukit Seguntang, also on the northern side of the river, approximately five miles west of Palembang and reached from Palembang in the nineteenth century in about an hour's paddling,[94] is not part of the peninsula. This illustrious site in Southeast Asian history because of its association with the Malacca rulers is often demeaningly described as a little hill, for it is only about ninety feet high. The hill is certainly not a towering landmark, but in early times, when it was not yet separated from the Musi by extensive alluvial deposits,[95] the riverine people beheld its graceful tree-clad slopes as the last impressive feature on the river bank before they reached the sea.

The beauty of the slopes blends with the surrounding scene. The alluvial soil around the hill is cultivated as paddy fields, interspersed with patches of slightly higher land (*talang*) and houses, fruit trees, and tapioca gardens. The whole area is riddled with creeks, and a nineteenth-century visitor remarked that one could approach the fields and gardens by land and water.[96] The remains of a boat and cargo of ceramics are said to have been found not far from the hill; the rudder, about four meters long, is in the Palembang museum. The scene we saw may resemble what the *Sejarah Melayu*'s annalist imagined when he describes how the *padi* of the Bukit Seguntang widows turned into gold and gleamed in the night to herald the approach of Sri Tri Buana, the ancestor of the Malacca kings. In the nineteenth century the scene was so choice that it excited the imagination of Dutch visitors. Olivier described it as "very enchanting and even romantic," and de Sturler was impressed by the frangipanni trees on the slopes.[97]

Bukit Seguntang is now rather more than a mile behind the Musi's northern shore. The shoreline is indented by the estuaries of small creeks. The creeks, with the exception of the Lami Daro at the western end of the Bukit Seguntang area, are empty at low tide. One creek is known as the Sungei Tatang and its upper course as the Kedukan Bukit, whose source is in the southern slopes of the hill. The *Sejarah Melayu* states that the river of Palembang was "the Muara Tatang." In the seventeenth century "Tatang" was the name of the lower reaches of the Musi,[98] and what is today the Tatang creek may once upon a time have been sufficiently prestigious a tributary to give its name to the main river in the neighborhood of Palembang. The Kedukan Bukit creek, as its name and present appearance imply,

---

[94] W. L. de Sturler, *Proeve eener beschrijving*, p. 190. Visitors rowed to Bukit Seguntang to pay their respects to the grave of Raja Iskandar Dzu'l-Karnain.

[95] A Palembang explanation of the word "Guntang" is that it means "floating"; Louis-Charles Damais, "Bibliographie indonésienne," *BEFEO* 51, 2 (1963): 557.

[96] Anonymous, "Schetsen van Palembang," *Tijdschrift voor Neêrland's Indië* 8,3 (1846): p. 291. Europeans spent a day's enjoyment there.

[97] Johannes Olivier, *Land- en zeetogten in Nederland's Indië en eenige Britsche etablissementen, gedaan in de jaren 1817 tot 1826* (Amsterdam: Bij C. G. Sulpke, 1828), p. 347; W. L. de Sturler, *Proeve eener beschrijving*, p. 190.

[98] M. Leidekker (1645–1701) knew "Tatoeng" as the name of the Palembang river, called the Musi only in its upper reaches. He is the author of the *Maleisch-Hollandsch Woordenboek*. See H. von der Wall, *Maleisch-Nederlandsch Woordenboek* (uitgegeven door H. N. van der Tuuk), vol. 1 (Batavia: Landsdrukkerij, 1880), p. 322, where Leidekker is quoted.

may be a fairly recent rectification of the upper course of the Tatang. Geologists will be able to assist archaeologists in distinguishing recent from early mud deposits behind the Bukit Seguntang creeks. Their research will also establish the antiquity of the land now cultivated as rice fields to the north and northwest of the hill. I am convinced that somewhere in this creekland was part of the center of a neighborhood network in Śrīvijayan times.

Miscellaneous metal and stone antiquities have been recovered over the years from the southern slopes of Bukit Seguntang, and even now visitors will notice, as Westenenk did, numerous wafer-shaped bricks strewn on the ground or embedded in roots of fallen trees. The Bukit Seguntang area still enjoys the reputation of possessing valuable objects; farmers told us of two recent accidental finds.[99] We, for our part, observed surface shards on the southeastern slopes that we believe are specimens of a Yüeh-type ware of the tenth century or somewhat earlier or later.[100] These shards seem to be the oldest imported ceramics found in verifiable contexts anywhere behind the east coast of Sumatra. We also noticed plenty of surface ceramics to the north and northwest of Bukit Seguntang in the area of Talang Kikim, through which a tributary of the Lami Daro flows and is navigable by small prahus at low tide. Many of them were of middle Sung or later times, but a handful resembled the shards of the so-called "dusun-jar" type, first exported from China in T'ang times.[101]

Indonesian ceramic studies, pioneered by Orsoy de Flines in the late 1920s and 1930s, will undoubtedly play an increasingly important role in identifying early settlement sites.[102] Hitherto trading centers in the Middle East have provided the best dated sites for studying pre-Sung export trade, though central Java and the Lubo Tua site in the Barus area on the Sumatran west coast have also yielded T'ang ware.[103] A particular problem in connection with the Chinese export trade with Southeast Asia is the circumstances and scale of the earliest ceramic exports. Mrs. Grace Wong, having examined the historical records of Chinese gifts to Southeast Asian rulers in Sung times, found only one instance when porcelain was given. This was in 963, when the Chinese emperor gave "white porcelain" to the Śrīvijayan ruler.[104] By late Sung times Chinese merchants were themselves carrying ceramics to Southeast Asian centers of production, and the evidence today is the numerous shards continuously being discovered in many parts of Southeast Asia. Economic, political, and social changes can be expected in the wake of more convenient access to world markets, and I am tempted to wonder whether the twelfth century was a turning point in the history of certain regions in Southeast Asia. One consequence may be that a proliferation of local prosperities in what had once been the Śrīvijayan sphere

---

[99] They told us that a small gold image and a golden headgear were recently found in the fields. According to a Palembang art dealer, not long ago Bukit Seguntang enjoyed the reputation of containing treasures.

[100] See Mr. McKinnon, "Spur-marked Yüeh Type Shards at Bukit Seguntang," *JMBRAS* 52,2 (1979), for a discussion of the shards. The shards are now in Jakarta.

[101] McKinnon, "Spur-marked Yüeh Type Shards."

[102] Mr. McKinnon mentions Orsoy de Flines in his essay.

[103] We were told of the Lubo Tua finds when we were in Medan on the eve of our departure for Palembang.

[104] Grace Wong, *A Comment on the Tributary Trade between China and Southeast Asia, and the Place of Porcelain in this Trade, During the Period of the Song Dynasty in China*, Transaction No. 7 (Singapore: Southeast Asian Ceramic Society, 1979).

of influence tended to obliterate memories of the earlier entrepôt that flourished during the period of the Chinese tributary trade.[105]

The Bukit Seguntang Yüeh-type ware closes a typological gap in the material evidence from this site; hitherto, only inscriptions and religious art had been found. I do not, however, wish to suggest that a similarly comprehensive range of remains will be recovered only in the Palembang area.

So much for a brief impression of the creek-riddled landscape that awaited me in Palembang and alerted me to the possibility of thinking of visible and absent signs in a riverine cultural environment and its center. No "city" in any conventional sense of the term ever existed there. But something else happened to me, a library-tied historian, when I visited the creeks. In 1967 I had studied Śrīvijayan history within the context of Sumatra's pre-Śrīvijayan maritime commerce. In Palembang I was asking myself questions that did not occur to me in 1967 and especially questions about what first brought the riverine people into contact with the maritime world.

I began to recall the evidence of very early southern Indian trade with Southeast Asia, and I took into account recent discoveries of rouletted pottery at the Buni sites near Jakarta that indicate a trading connection with southern India early in the Christian era.[106] We are now surely justified in identifying Ptolemy's "Argyre," the "city" at the western extremity of Iabadiou, as further testimony to ancient trading activities in western Java.[107] Ptolemy's information would have come secondhand from Indian merchants. Again, the Buni remains, considered in relationship with the fifth-century Taruma ruler's inscriptions in the same part of Java, help us to identify two Javanese place-names mentioned in Chinese records up to the seventh century. I believe that *To-lo-mo*, mentioned in the New T'ang History as a geographical feature, is an exact rendering of Tārūmǎ or Tārūmǎ[108] and that *Ho-lo-tan*, whose rulers sent missions in the fifth century, can be confidently restored as Ciruton, a river in the same area.[109] The Ciruton ruler's letter to the Liu Sung emperor in 430 has survived and shows that he ruled an important trading kingdom but was under attack from his neighbors.[110]

These considerations came to mind in Palembang when I was asking myself how this part of Sumatra was originally introduced to the world of international trade. In 1967 I proposed, with reservations, that *Ko-ying*, a toponym in Chinese sources of the

---

[105] Marsden was familiar with Renaudot's translations in 1718 but attached no significance to "Serbeza"; Marsden, *History of Sumatra*, p. 4.

[106] Michael J. Walker and S. Santoso, "Romano–Indian Rouletted Pottery in Indonesia," *Mankind* 11,1 (1977): 39–45.

[107] I accept the conclusions of Drs. Walker and Santoso.

[108] I have discussed the *Ta-lo-ma (Tâ-lâ-muâ)* toponym with Professor John McCoy, and he comments that the *lo* sound has often retained a feature of a rounded back vowel (i.e. *u* or *o*). This feature encourages us to believe that fifth-century Chinese were responding to the *u* in the Indonesian word "Taruma" and chose the character pronounced in modern Mandarin as *lo*. Taruma was adjacent to *Tan-tan*, and the latter place is bound to be in Java.

[109] We are again in the presence of the *lo* character, and the second and third characters can be safely restored as *-ruton*. The important Ciruton river flows in the same part of western Java (Ci = "river"). The early Chinese sound of the consonant in the first character is x â (the sound of the x is close to the *ch* in the German *machen*), and it is difficult to derive *ci* from it. But *-ruton* is convincing, and Indonesian linguists may be able to throw light on how the name of this river was heard in the fifth century.

[110] Wolters, *Early Indonesian Commerce*, p. 151. I take *Ho-lo-t'o* to be a variant of *Ho-lo-tan*.

third-century CE, should be located in southeastern Sumatra.[111] I did not attempt to restore its Indonesian name. I now believe that *Ko-ying* means "Kawang" and is likely to be the center of international trade in western Java known to Ptolemy as Argyre.[112]

If I am right, an early glimpse of the east coast of Sumatra is provided by the Chinese records of the third-century CE about the *Wên* bay and the inhabitants of the *P'u-lei* region, who sailed out to sea to intercept passing ships and exchange food supplies for metal objects.[113] The *Wên* bay is described as being "south" of Kawang, but we are not obliged to accept literally every Chinese geographical detail of the third century CE; the Chinese writers at that time had to depend on foreign merchants for their information, and all kinds of errors could have crept into their texts. But I continue to believe that the *Wên* (*mįuzn*) toponym refers to the Menumbing range of hills at the northwestern end of Bangka island and an important landmark for the Tamils' pilots at the beginning of the eleventh century and for the Chinese pilots at the beginning of the fifteenth.[114] The inhabitants of the *Wên* region sailed out to sea, I suggest, from the estuaries of central and southern Sumatra and knew that the Bangka Strait was the passage habitually taken by ships from the Indian Ocean on their way to Kawang in western Java in the early centuries of the Christian era.[115]

And so, in Palembang, I asked myself whether the spectacle of trading ships sailing to and from western Java and India gave the riverine people their introduction to the opportunity for wealth within their grasp beyond their estuaries. What I called in 1967 "the favored coast" may originally have been "favored" not because it faced Canton but because it faced western Java in the sense of being on or close to the Bangka Strait and enabled its inhabitants to learn of exciting happenings in western Java.[116] This possibility is one reason why I am now dissatisfied with the subtitle to my study of early Indonesian commerce: *A Study of the Origins of Śrīvijaya*. The other reason, as this essay shows, is that I am coming to believe that ancient

---

[111] Wolters, *Early Indonesian Commerce*, pp. 55–58 and note 53 on p. 277.

[112] I have discussed the Koying (*Kâ-iwäng*) toponym with Professor McCoy, who agrees that Kawang is an accurate third-century CE reconstruction of the sounds of the two characters. I am tempted to see a connection between Kawang and the Krawang peninsula not far from the Buni remains. Indonesian linguists may wish to comment on this possibility. Sinologists are sometimes said to play "the names' game." Indonesian linguists can join the game by suggesting how Indonesian words sounded when they were heard by Chinese ears.

[113] See page 53 of *Early Indonesian Commerce*. I have improved the translation. The *P'u-lei* people lived in a *chou*, which I take to be a sizeable stretch of coastal territory rather than an island. We can note for what it is worth that the Sung History states that many of the inhabitants of San-fo-ch'i were called *P'u*.

[114] See Wolters, "Landfall on the Palembang Coast in Medieval Times," pp. 50–51, in respect of a Tamil voyage in 1015. See my "Landfall on the Palembang Coast," p. 53, for the possibility that a T'ang text refers to the "Palembang" river.

[115] Early European travellers from the Malacca Straits to Java sailed through the Bangka Strait, and the Arabs may have done likewise; G. R. Tibbetts, *Arab Navigation in the Indian Ocean before the Coming of the Portuguese* (London: Royal Asiatic Society, 1971), p. 495. The Chinese pilots, sailing from the Malacca Straits in Ming times, used the Bangka Strait to make Tuban in eastern Java as well as western Java.

[116] Perhaps the threats against "Java" in the seventh-century inscriptions are connected with an episode in the relationship between the rival trading coasts of central-southern Sumatra and western Java. The Kota Kapur inscription of the west coast of Bangka faces the route to Java.

riverine experience in mobilizing neighborhoods, the substance of Śrīvijayan history, rather than maritime or commercial acumen first stood the rulers in good stead when they began to participate in foreign trading enterprise and developed entrepôt pretensions. It would have been only a matter of time before they began to assert their "spiritual values" by exercising long-distance influence overseas and absorbing the offshore islanders south of the Malacca Straits, expert oarsmen, into their networks.

MO-HO-HSIN

I-ching's list of Indonesian *dvīpa*, enumerated "from the west," begins with Barus, Malayu "which is now Śrīvijaya," *Mo-ho-hsin*, and *Ho-ling*.[117] *Ho-ling* is in Java, Malayu is in Sumatra, and scholars have located *Mo-ho-hsin* in Java, Borneo, Billiton, or on the Malay Peninsula.[118]

I believe that the indigenous name represented by *Mo-ho-hsin* is "Mukha Asin," or "Briny Face."[119] I propose to translate the name as "Briny Surface." Present-day place-names are often historians' lifelines with the past; examples of enduring Indonesian place-names are increasing. I am therefore influenced by the fact that the river Banju Asin, or "briny water," flows to the sea immediately north of the Musi estuary.[120] The Banju Asin's estuary is much broader than the Musi's but is shallow and does not lead to long rivers in the interior. Instead, the river resembles a vestige of an ancient and wide gulf, a trace of which can be seen on the early fifteenth-century Mao K'un map.[121] Another map, prepared with the cooperation of geologists and supplied by Professor Soekmono in his study of "Geomorphology and the Location of Crīwijaya," shows that much of the present coastline between the Banju Asin and the Batang Hari estuary was under the sea in early times.

The ancient configuration of this part of the Sumatran coast probably explains why *Mo-ho-hsin*, or "Briny Surface," appears immediately south of Malayu-*dvīpa* in I-ching's list. The coast here and south through the Bangka Strait was known to be associated with saline mud flats behind an indeterminate coastline and without

---

[117] Wolters, *Early Indonesian Commerce*, p. 199.

[118] For a discussion of *Mo-ho-hsin*, see L. -C. Damais, "Bibliographie," *BEFEO* 48,2 (1957): 614–19; Slametmuljana, *Kerajaan Sriwijaya*, pp. 36–40; W. J. van der Meulen, "In Search of 'Ho-ling,'" *Indonesia* 23 (April 1977): 105; Slamet Muljana, "A New Interpretation of I-tsing's statement," *Majalah Arkeologi* 11,2 (1978): 50–60. Moens ignored this place-name. To the best of my knowledge only Schlegel, restoring the name to Bĕkasin or Bogas, believed that it was in Sumatra, though he could find no such names on the map; G. Schlegel, "Geographical Notes XVI," *T'oung Pao* 11 (1901): 115–16.

[119] I have discussed *Mo-ho-hsin* with Professor McCoy. The early T'ang sounds were *Muok-* x *â-siĕn*. The first two sounds exactly render *mukha*, or "face." *Siĕn* or "Sin" could be a truncated version of a place-name, but I doubt it. *Mo-ho-hsin* appears in two seventh-century Chinese texts and is an established word; on this point see Pelliot, "Deux itinéraries," p. 325, note 2. I follow Professor McCoy's suggestion that an elision has occurred; the "a" in "*mukha*" has merged with the "a" in "*asin*," or brine. I am very grateful to Professor McCoy for spending time on these matters.

[120] "Banju" is Javanese Ngoko for "water," and the name may have come into use during the Sultanate period in Palembang history.

[121] See my "Landfall on the Palembang Coast in Medieval Times," Map 1. Also see Map 10, dated 1708. According to the *Eastern Archipelago Pilot*, the Banju Asin has a course of only about thirty-five miles; it is formed by the junction of several small rivers and streams; *Eastern Archipelago Pilot*, IV (London: Hydrographic Office of Great Britain, 1890–), p. 67.

freshwater rivers. *Mo-ho-hsin*'s waterways were merely ever-shifting tidal creeks. The landscape in this part of Sumatra was signified by impenetrable salt marshes and distinguished itself from the estuary-punctured coastline further north on the same coast that signified communications with the interior. The *Mo-ho-hsin* coast was inhospitable, and it was appropriately known as the "Briny Surface"-*dvīpa* because during many centuries salt deposits had been left in the mud by the advancing coastline.[122] The Menumbing hills on northwestern Bangka were bound to be an indispensable landmark for those who made the voyage off Mukha Asin through the Bangka Strait to Palembang and western Java. Somewhere south of the Bangka Strait was the region known to the Chinese in the fifth century as Tulang Bawang, a mission-sending state that is also mentioned in a seventh-century Chinese source.[123] I-ching does not refer to Tulang Bawang, and the reason is that he was only interested in the *dvīpa*s on the route from the Indian Ocean to famous Buddhist centers in Sumatra and Java. The pilgrims' ships sailed through the Bangka Strait and took the direct route southeast from the southern entrance to the Strait in order to reach western Java. Thus, Ho-ling is the next *dvīpa* in I-ching's list after Mukha Asin.

My reconstruction of the toponym Mukha Asin, or "Briny Surface," is, I believe, acceptable from the geomorphic point of view, and the obvious implication of I-ching's distinction between Malayu-*dvīpa* and Mukha Asin-*dvīpa* is that the Palembang area was regarded in the seventh century as part of the latter. Malayu-*dvīpa*'s southern border would have been approximately at the Batang Hari estuary at the head of the gulf on Professor Soekmono's map, and my surmise is that its northern border was the most northern river basin that can be shown to have provided the Minangkabau highlands with access to the east coast. The river-basins were not, of course, political frontiers in the modern sense. They comprised territory whose inhabitants were accustomed to thinking of themselves as living in "Malayu."

If I-ching never visited Palembang,[124] both Śrīvijaya and the royal center known to him as Malayu *kuo* may have been in Malayu-*dvīpa* and probably in the Batang

---

[122] The Upang section of this coast is "Briny Surface"-*dvīpa*'s single access to the interior. Such a matter-of-fact place-name as "Briny Surface" need not surprise us. I believe that the Medan coast was known as "Mollusc-*dvīpa*"; Wolters, "Molluscs and the Historical Geography of Northeastern Sumatra in the Eighth Century AD," *Indonesia* 22 (October 1976): 9–17.

[123] Wolters, *Early Indonesian Commerce*, p. 202.

[124] I have recently wondered whether I-ching used the name "Śrīvijaya" retrospectively to identify his destination in 671. The only other evidence of a place identified by that name before the inscriptions of the 680s is in the New T'ang History's statement that Śrīvijaya sent missions "from the 670–673 to the 713–742 reign-periods." No Chinese text known to me supplies the date of a mission in the 670–673 reign-period. Nevertheless, the compilers of the New T'ang History may have noted a record of this mission, now lost, when they were preparing the paragraph on Śrīvijaya that the compilers of the Old T'ang History neglected to write, and one possibility for identifying it occurs to me. At the end of 671 I-ching sailed to Śrīvijaya in a *Po-ssŭ* ship. The official Fung Hsiao-ch'üan had introduced him to the person in charge of the ship, who must have been known in official circles in southern China and may have been returning to Śrīvijaya after bringing tribute earlier in the same year. I-ching sailed across the Bay of Bengal in the Śrīvijaya ruler's ship, and the ship that took him from Canton may have belonged to the same ruler. At all events, I-ching's Sumatran port in 671 was already in commercial communication with China, and its Buddhist learning would be respected. I-ching was not sailing to an unknown destination. I see no reason for doubting that his destination was already known as "Śrīvijaya." In 695 Śrīvijayan envoys were among those who were granted provisions by the Chinese court, even though the first mission

Hari, Indragiri, or Kampar river basins. The events that resulted in Malayu-*dvīpa*'s becoming known as "Śrīvijaya" would have occurred some distance north of Palembang, while what happened in Palembang at the time of the Bukit Kedukan inscription in 682 would have been connected with Śrīvijaya's expansion from Malayu-*dvīpa* into southern Sumatra. On the other hand, if Palembang in the "Briny Surface"-*dvīpa* were the original seat of Śrīvijaya, Malayu-*dvipa*'s change of name would have been the result of a successful attack from the south, though the possibility exists that a northern conqueror of Śrīvijaya-Palembang chose to retain the prestigious name of his victim's settlement. I-ching's statement that Wu-hsing sailed in the ruler's ship from Śrīvijaya "country" (*kuo*) to Malayu-*dvīpa* in fifteen days[125] is the closest he gets to excluding Śrīvijaya from Malayu-*dvīpa* and may reflect his knowledge that Śrīvijaya was in the "Briny Surface"-*dvīpa* and therefore in the Palembang area. If this were the correct interpretation, I-ching would be providing guidance on the location of the Śrīvijayan capital between 671 and 695 with a precision unparalleled in any text on Śrīvijayan historical geography written at any time.

In 1904 Pelliot believed that only two Sumatran centers were involved in the events of the seventh century; they were Śrīvijaya at Palembang and Malayu to the north. But when we take into account Professor Boechari's Upang evidence and the Mukha Asin evidence, another possibility has arisen. Three centers could have been involved: Śrīvijaya, Malayu, and Palembang. Archaeological research will one day supply empirical data about important neighborhood centers on the Musi, Batang Hari, Indragiri, and Kampar rivers, and we need not discount the possibility that in one of these river basins were two centers. The number of protagonists in the events of the seventh century will then be disclosed by extensive clusters of settlements, and one of them in 682, according to the Kedukan Bukit inscription, was able to mobilize a naval force of more than 20,000 men and a land force of 1,312. The Kedukan Bukit inscription, so important for studying Śrīvijaya, reminds us that shifts in political power took place on I-ching's map of Sumatra.

---

unambiguously attributed to Śrīvijaya is as late as 702. A T'ang envoy visited Śrīvijaya in 683. In 689 I-ching returned to China from Śrīvijaya on a merchant ship.

[125] E. Chavannes, *Les religieux éminents qui allèrent chercher la Loi dans les pays d'occident* (Paris, 1894), p. 144; I-ching, *Ta Tang hsi yü ch'iu fa sêng chuan*, Taishō Tripitaka, vol. 51, no. 2066, p. 9b.

CHAPTER FIVE

RESTUDYING SOME CHINESE WRITINGS ON SRIWIJAYA*

THE BUKIT SEGUNTANG AREA

In July 1984 I had the opportunity to visit an early settlement site at Karanganyar behind the northern bank of the Musi river and a few miles upstream from the *kota* of the former Sultanate in the modern city of Palembang.[1] Karanganyar is near and almost due south of the little hill known as Bukit Seguntang. The site in question is an elaborate complex of canals, tanks, and a central quadrangular enclosure of about 310 by 230 meters, known locally as "the Bamboo Fort." The central enclosure is surrounded by a man-made moat, the southern and especially the northern ends of which were once broad sheets of water. The northern end has a small artificial island exactly at its center, and numerous fragments of wafer-shaped bricks on the surface

---

* I wish to take the opportunity of thanking my friends for what they taught me on our visits to Sumatra, and I wish to thank in particular Dra. Satyawati Suleiman, who was always optimistic about the prospects for Sriwijayan research during the dreary years before the SPAFA "Sriwijaya Project" was launched in 1977. Dra. Suleiman is the godmother of Sriwijayan students today as Pelliot and Coedès were the godfathers of earlier generations. Whether as a governor of SPAFA or as an indefatigable research worker on tour in Sumatra, she is responsible more than anyone else for the present promising stage in Sriwijayan studies.

When this essay version of a talk delivered in Jakarta was first published in October 1986 (*Indonesia* 42), "Sriwijaya" was spelled as shown in the title and consistently thereafter throughout the essay (except that footnote references remain true to the original-source spellings). The current volume preserves that Indonesian spelling in this chapter, while elsewhere in this collection Sriwijaya is spelled "Śrīvijaya." —Ed.

[1] I was accompanied by Drs. Bambang Budi Utomo of the Indonesian National Research Centre of Archaeology, Dr. E. Edwards McKinnon, and Nigel Wolters. I am grateful to Dr. McKinnon for his detailed comments on an earlier draft of the article and for communicating additional information discovered by Drs. Budi Utomo. For a detailed and well-informed account of the terrain and archaeological sites of southern Sumatra, see E. Edwards McKinnon, "Early Polities in Southern Sumatra: Some Preliminary Observations Based on Archaeological Evidence," *Indonesia* 40 (October 1985): 1–36. For details about archaeological discoveries in 1984–1985, see Bambang Budi Utomo, "Karanganyar as a Srvijayan Site: New Evidence for the Study of Settlement Patterns of the Śrīvijayan Period" in *SPAFA, Final Report, Consultative Workshop on Archaeological and Environmental Studies in Srivijaya (I-W2b)*, September 16–30, 1985 (Bangkok: SPAFA Coordinating Unit, 1985), pp. 273–289. See Figure 1 for toponyms and rivers.

suggest that the island was originally planned to accommodate a sacral foundation. Unfortunately, farmers have disturbed the soil, and what may have been a foundation base is now irretrievably lost. A square-shaped tank of considerable dimensions lies east of the enclosure and also has an island at its center, and a small tank, with a similar island, is not far southwest of the enclosure. Miscellaneous T'ang sherds were found on the enclosure's surface, in the debris of a well, and in test pits dug subsequently at Karanganyar. We also found wafer-shaped bricks alongside each other in the profile of another well in the enclosure. A test pit nearby later revealed additional bricks.

The enclosure, moat, and tank are today irrigated padi fields, tapioca gardens, houses, roads, and small factories. The landscape is changing all the time and burying the past more deeply.

The Karanganyar site is the latest in a long record of discoveries in and adjacent to the Bukit Segun T'ang area. I need list only the most significant discoveries. An Old-Malay inscription of 682, mentioning Sriwijaya, was found in 1920 in the vicinity of the Sungei Tatang near Karanganyar, and also another Old-Malay inscription of 684 northwest of Bukit Seguntang in the same year. In the 1920s the trunk of a large Buddha image was unearthed not far from the southern slopes of Bukit Seguntang; the image is now attributed to the late seventh or early eighth centuries. Three bronze Buddhist images were dredged up in the 1930s from the confluence of the Musi and Komering rivers at the eastern end of the modern city of Palembang, and a bronze Bodhisattva image and a bronze Śiva image were discovered in the Geding Suro area in the city's eastern suburbs. In the 1930s, too, the Sabokingking inscription, undated but contemporaneous with the Old-Malay inscriptions mentioned above, came to light in the eastern suburbs.[2] In the 1960s a large statue of Avalokiteśvara was found in the same area, and a Gaṇeśa image was discovered in a garden very close to the city center in the early 1980s. Moreover, in 1978, 1980, and 1982 quantities of T'ang and early Sung sherds were recovered in the fields on and around Bukit Seguntang. The Karanganyar settlement site, with sherds of the same vintage, unmistakably belongs to the Bukit Seguntang area not only spatially but also in the sense that every part of the area shares a significant archaeological feature: remains of T'ang and early Sung stoneware and porcelain attributable to the centuries when Sriwijaya was flourishing. Nowhere else in southern southeastern Sumatra has evidence of early ceramic imports been discovered on this scale. The imports are superior in quality to anything produced locally at that time. One is now beginning to be confident that every visit to Palembang will recover more sherds of the same vintage.

I happen to be one of those for whom the question has never been whether or not the center of Sriwijaya was at Palembang but, instead, where in that area it was located. I realize that the antiquity of these princely hydraulic works is at present unknown, though the carbon dating of charcoal and wood at the bottom of the moat would soon throw light on the matter. But even in the unlikely event that these works were constructed in post-Sriwijayan times, it would be unfortunate if this were to distract from the significance of the accumulating evidence that the Bukit Seguntang area, with its seventh-century inscriptions, was receiving quantities of T'ang and early Sung ware from the seventh or eighth centuries to the eleventh or

---

[2] Nik Hassan Shuhaimi, "The Bukit Seguntang Buddha," *JMRAS* 52,2 (1979): 33–40; F. M. Schnitger, *The Archaeology of Hindoo Sumatra* (Leiden: Brill, 1937).

twelfth. Sufficient reason already exists for regarding this area, including Karanganyar, as the focus for a major research project in the field of Sriwijayan studies.

Confluence of the Ogan and Musi (Bukit Seguntang on left).
Photo by Nigel Wolters

Tempora Bridge at Palembang City (seen from Bukit Seguntang).
Photo by Nigel Wolters

Another reason why the Karanganyar site deserves sustained archaeological research also has nothing to do with the waterworks. The settlement is located on a terrain with a particularly favorable combination of topographical advantages, which would not have been ignored in the seventh century. The location is on the tidal waters of the Musi, near the confluences of the Komering, Ogan, and Belidah rivers, and as I discuss below, is one of the two tracts of somewhat higher and drier land close to the Musi in the neighborhood of Palembang. The southern shore is much less stable and has changed its river bed over the centuries. The other higher and drier land is also on the northern Musi shore and east of the modern city of Palembang, but it is not far from where the river suddenly sweeps in a northeastern direction towards the sea and would be less secure than the Karanganyar site upstream from surprise attack by invading fleets. Karanganyar's location possesses strategic advantages, and they would be recognized by riverine Malays long before the waterworks were built.

Rather than presuming, as I did when I visited Karanganyar in 1984, that the settlement was a Sriwijayan creation, I prefer to identify the whole of the Bukit Seguntang area with that part of Sumatra which constituted the Sriwijayan heartland. The identification removes the difficulty of having to propose another and more probable polity to account for what is certainly an important archaeological site. I-ching, who lived in Sriwijaya in 671–672 and in the 680s until 695, knew from personal knowledge only two centers in southeastern Sumatra: Sriwijaya and Malayu. The precise location of Malayu in his day is still problematic, but the Malayu of later times was certainly on the Batang Hari river. If Sriwijaya is identified with the Palembang area, we can explain why I-ching's sailing itinerary from Sriwijaya to the Malacca Strait in 672 reveals that Malayu was north of Sriwijaya. His geographical evidence convinced me more than anything else over the years that Takakusu[3] and Pelliot[4] were justified in arguing that Sriwijaya was in the neighborhood of Palembang. The discoveries in the Bukit Segungtang area are already sufficient to make its identification with Sriwijaya a reasonable presumption, and it is mine in this essay. The locations of the imprecatory inscriptions of Bangka (686) and the contemporaneous ones of Karang Brahi on the Merangin river in the Batang Hari river system, of Palas Pasemah at the southern end of Sumatra, and of another recently discovered one at Jabung in the Lampongs[5] seem to represent an outreach of influence from a major center in southeastern Sumatra.

The reemergence of the Bukit Seguntang area has changed the focus of Sriwijayan research. The future lies fairly and squarely in the archaeologists' hands, and my essay acknowledges the new development. I propose to review or, as I prefer to put it, restudy some Chinese sources in the light of what is being disclosed about the lower reaches of the Musi river and especially the Bukit Seguntang area, and I shall consider whether Chinese details now become more intelligible.

---

[3] J. Takakusu, trans., *A Record of the Buddhist Religion as Practised in India and the Malay Archipelago (A.D. 671–695) by I-Tsing* (Oxford: Clarendon Press, 1896), p. xliv. The Chinese text is known as the *Nan-hai chi-kuei nei-fa chuan*. Tripiṭaka. Chinese version (Ta tsang ching) (Tokyo: Society for the Publication of the Taisho Edition of the Tripiṭaka, 1924–32), No. 2125. I refer to it as the *Nan-hai*.

[4] P. Pelliot, "Deux itinéraires de Chine en Inde à la fin du VIII siècle," *BEFEO* 4 (1904): 348.

[5] Dr. McKinnon, personal communication, July 10, 1985.

The historiographical tradition in Sriwijayan studies over many years has been to consult Chinese sources for useful data about Sriwijaya's location. These sources, in my opinion, can now be read in a more relaxed mood and for more modest purposes. I shall restudy them to consider not only how far they make better sense when read alongside the topography and artifacts of the lower Musi river valley but also to remind archaeologists of what the sources profess to tell us and, more important, what they do not. But the same sources can be approached more curiously and for their own sake, and this is why "restudying" seems an appropriate expression. As specimens of Chinese writing, they possess narrational features such as the conventions of various genres and idiosyncratic linguistic usage. These features are responsible for what can be expected from the sources and should be taken into account in recuperating their meaning. A critical approach on these lines is less concerned with what historical geographers have regarded as ambiguities, gaps, and bias than with ways in which statements on matters of historical geography are formulated. What will interest me may appear to be trivial details, but I hope that sometimes possibilities may suggest themselves to those who study the most important "text" of all, which is the terrain itself. Archaeologists try to read what the terrain is telling them by means of multiple and related signs on the ground, and the Chinese sources should similarly be read as systems of signification before they are read alongside the archaeologists' text. Such, then, are the limits of enquiry I have set myself.

I-CHING, THE PILGRIM

My sketch of the sixty or so miles of the Musi river valley from the Bangka Strait to Bukit Seguntang takes as its point of departure what I-ching knew of "Sriwijaya" in the second half of the seventh century. Though he supplies little information, what he writes is an indispensable contribution to our knowledge. I have already noted that he clarifies the geographical relationship between Sriwijaya and Malayu when he was sailing up the east coast of Sumatra in 672. I shall suggest in this essay that he is probably the most perceptive of all Chinese writers on Sriwijaya whose works have survived, and I shall bear him in mind when I have occasion to mention later Chinese works and make a few discursive comments in the light of what we now know from other sources, chiefly archaeological. But first I wish to introduce I-ching. He was a pilgrim and not a geographer, and our expectations of what he has to offer should be based on who he was.

I-ching (635–713), born in northern China, was thirty-seven years old when he sailed from Canton on December 7, 671, and reached Sriwijaya within twenty days.[6] He proceeded to India via Malayu six months later and returned to Sriwijaya after 685 and before 689; the date of his return to Sumatra is unknown. In 689 he visited China for three months and again visited Sriwijaya, which he finally left in 695.

I-ching is the only Chinese writer known by name who actually lived in Sriwijaya, and he provides snatches of information in three books. His *Record*, written there in 691–692, was intended to correct Chinese misinterpretations of the

---

[6] E. Chavannes, *Mémoire composé à l'époque de la grande dynastie T'ang sur les religieux éminents qui allèrent chercher la loi dans les pays d'occident, par I-tsing* (Paris: Ernest Leroux, 1894), p. 119. The Chinese text is known as the *Ta-T'ang hsi-yü ch'iu-fa kao-sêng chuan*. Tripiṭaka. Chinese version, No. 2066, p. 7. I refer to it as the *Ta-T'ang*.

Buddhist discipline (*vinaya*). His *Memoir*, also written in 691–692, comprises short accounts of contemporary Chinese pilgrims who visited India; some of them studied in Sriwijaya. The third book, written in China between 700 and 703, is a translation of a Sanskrit *vinaya* text, to which he occasionally refers in the *Record*, and it is known as the *Mūlasarvāstivāda-ekaśatakarman*.[7]

The *Memoir*, which mentions Sriwijaya most frequently, is a narrative focusing on the zeal and heroism of Chinese pilgrims who helped propagate Buddhism in China by collecting *sūtra* in India, and it belongs to the genre of Chinese writing represented by the works of the famous pilgrims Fa-hsien and Hsüan-tsang, whom I-ching admired.[8] A Chinese reader's expectations would be hagiographical within the context of the expansion of Buddhism outside India, and he would soon realize that I-ching was edified by knowing that every generation in Buddhist history had produced those who transmitted the doctrine.[9] The *Record* is a detailed description of the *vinaya* as it was practiced in India and the Southern Ocean, and the *Mūlasarvāstivāda-ekaśatakarman* is his translation of a *vinaya* text.

The marginal importance of Sriwijaya in the three texts is indicated by I-ching's habit of relegating items of interest to Southeast Asian historians to the status of notes. The notes sometimes read as if they were intended to update his information. A conspicuous instance is when he notes what is now the relationship between Sriwijaya and Malayu, a matter to which I shall return later. His two longest notes are in the *Record* and the *Mūlasarvāstivāda-ekaśatakarman*, and they read as illustrations of the span of the various schools of Buddhism or the maritime communications within the Buddhist world. The note in the *Record* comes after an account of the schools of Buddhism adopted beyond the boundaries of India and in the Southern Ocean, and the purpose is to enumerate the major geographical areas in the Southern Ocean. He then resumes his narrative with further information about the Buddhist schools there.[10] The long note in his translation of the *Mūlasarvāstivāda-ekaśatakarman* is inserted after the *vinaya* text's description of India's "border countries." The note includes the sailing route from India to the Southern Ocean and China, and he observes that those with good *karma* will not suffer on the journey. He adds that he is informed that many of the Southern Ocean rulers seek to accumulate good *karma*, and he seems to illustrate his point by noting that there are many monks in Sriwijaya and that Chinese monks should study there.[11] Rulers would naturally encourage monks to visit their territories.

---

[7] Tripiṭaka. Chinese version, No. 1453. I refer to it as the *Mūla*. For the date of the translation according to the Sung dynasty *Sung-kao sêng-chuan*, see Chavannes, *Mémoire*, pp. 194–195. For the dating of the *Record* and *Memoir*, see Takakusu, *Record*, pp. liii–lv.

[8] Takakusu, *Record*, p. 207 (referring to Fa-hsien); p. 184 (referring to Hsüan-tsang).

[9] Chavannes, *Mémoire*, p. 153; *Ta-T'ang*, p. 9. On the hagiographical tradition followed by I-ching, see Arthur F. Wright, "Biography and Hagiography: *Hui chiao's Lives of Eminent Monks*," *Silver Jubilee Volume of the Zimbun Kagaku Kenkyo sya* (Kyoto: Kyoto University, 1954). Pt. I, pp. 383–432. This text was written in the first half of the sixth century.

[10] Takakusu, *Record*, pp. 10–11; *Nan-hai*, p. 205. The note begins with "Counting from the west..." and ends with "cannot all be mentioned here." Takakusu does not always indicate the length of I-ching's notes.

[11] Takakusu, *Record*, pp. xxxiii–xxxiv; *Nan-hai*, p. 476. The note begins with "Roughly speaking..." and ends with "then proceed to Central India."

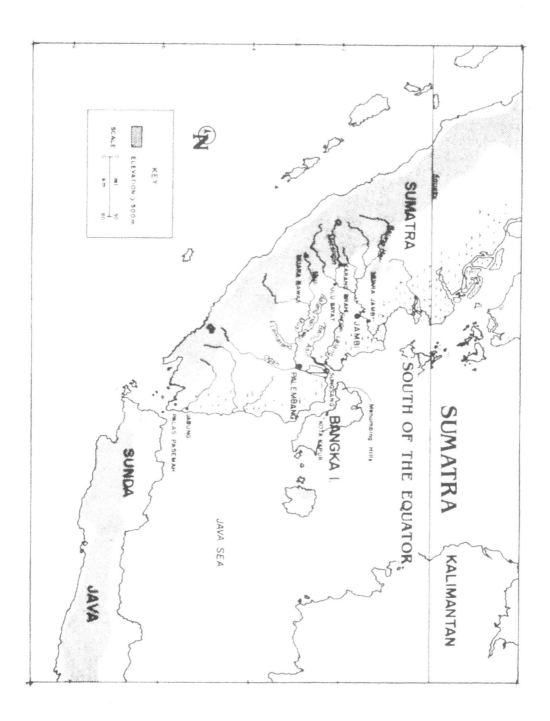

Figure 1: Southern Sumatra

I-ching's texts are pious ones, and those who read them today should not complain that he does not supply densely packed descriptions of the Southeast Asian countries he and his fellow pilgrims visited. His references to India are similarly lacking in descriptive detail unless he is writing about famous monasteries. When we read his *Memoir*, we are reading about the courage, rigorous self-discipline, and scholarly pursuits of those who went overseas. The narrative structure of the passages on Sriwijaya is uniform and terse: the aspirations of the pilgrims, the dangers they faced on their voyages, and their religious preoccupations when they made landfall. Their heroic enterprise was bound to be accompanied by disturbing experiences. I-ching wrote a poem before he sailed in 671, and the language expresses his expectation of unhappiness when traveling long distances:

> When I travel myriads of miles,
>   a hundred layers of unhappy thoughts will weigh me down.
> How shall I compel myself
>   to walk alone within the borders of the Five Indias?[12]

His friends in Canton shared his apprehensions, and he uses Buddhist language to express his debt to Fêng Hsiao-Ch'üan, an official in southern China who helped him obtain a shipping passage to Sriwijaya. Fêng is described as a *dānapati* (檀主), or host and benefactor of monks. I-ching may also be conceptualizing the gifts from Fêng and Fêng's family in Buddhist terms when he says that they "bestowed parting gifts" (資贈) to provide the necessities of life to alleviate his suffering when traveling;[13] "bestowing" something on a departing pilgrim is the equivalent of a pious deed. Monks and laity "bestowed" provisions when he left Canton on December 18, 689, to return to Sriwijaya.[14]

The hazards of foreign travel are emphasized in early Chinese secular writings,[15] but I-ching uses different conventions in describing them. For example, he never says that he is traveling to "pestilential" lands, a favorite Chinese allusion to Southeast Asia. Instead, he writes as a Buddhist. A pilgrim's safety depends on his *karma*.[16] Waves are compared with the back of the sea monster (the *makara*).[17] Of his own swift voyage in 671 he says that he entered a vast abyss of water, with waves like mountains and billows that reached the sky.[18] His *Memoir* mentions storms and shipwrecks.[19] In 689 only one person in a group of prospective pilgrims finally decided to accompany I-ching to Sriwijaya.[20] The courage of those who crossed the sea was sustained by religious intentions; they wished to be ladders for those who suffer and be the ship that crossed the sea of desire for the benefit of mankind.[21]

---

[12] Chavannes, *Mémoire*, p. 115; *Ta-T'ang*, p. 7.

[13] Chavannes, *Mémoire*, pp. 116–117; *Ta-T'ang*, p. 7.

[14] Chavannes, *Mémoire*, p. 179; *Ta-T'ang*, p. 13.

[15] O. W. Wolters, *The Fall of Śrīvijaya in Malay History* (London: Lund Humphries Publishers Limited, 1970), pp. 23–24.

[16] Takakusu, *Record*, p. xxxiv; *Mūla*, p. 477.

[17] Chavannes, *Mémoire*, p. 53.

[18] Ibid., p. 119.

[19] Ibid., pp. 43, 76, 108.

[20] Ibid., p. 159.

[21] Ibid., p. 179.

I-ching writes of himself in the *Record*: "If, as I earnestly hope, one man out of a million improves himself [by my words], I shall not be sorry for the difficulty and bitterness I endured ..."[22]

I-ching was willing to face hardship but did not feel obliged to record profane information about the countries he visited. As soon as he reached Sriwijaya, he began to study Sanskrit texts. His books never distinguish the cultures of India and Sumatra except in respect of a few minor Buddhist practices. When in the *Record* he refers to the countries of "the Southern Ocean," he has in mind the Indonesian lands and probably the only area he knew, which was Sriwijaya.[23] Here he writes of the lavish celebration of the six fasting days each month when an image was carried in procession and music played. This did not happen in India.[24] The closest he gets in the *Record* to recognizing more substantial differences is when he records that in the Southern Ocean those who were ill dieted for only two or three days rather than anything up to a week as in India, and he explains the difference in terms of "territory, customs, and the constitution of the body."[25]

Because I-ching was a zealous Buddhist pilgrim, one need not expect him to provide ample information on matters of historical geography. Nevertheless, as we shall see, his religious preoccupations do not disqualify him from providing some valuable details on this subject; in fact, they contribute to the value that we should attach to his geographical observations.

In the first place, his linguistic usage is likely to have been systematic and exact. He was a distinguished Sino-Sanskrit scholar and therefore concerned with the correct definition of Sanskrit technical terms. In the *Record* he states that one needs an exact knowledge of the Sanskrit texts in order to read them as they should be read: "one has to rely on [them] and give up [lit. "block out"] individual inclinations."[26] Texts, he would insist, should not be interpreted by reading between the lines. I-ching's concern for linguistic accuracy has persuaded Professor Wheatley that he had acquired "a rare expertise in the transcription of foreign words."[27] A concern for accuracy explains why he includes a long and detailed description of the great Nālandā monastery and even draws a model "to avoid error."[28] No Chinese visitor to Sumatra would be better qualified to describe what he knew with a discriminating use of language, and we shall not be disappointed when we come to examine the distinctions he observes when he is defining the outline of Indian and Southern Ocean geography.

---

[22] Takakusu, *Record*, p. 95; *Nan-hai*, p. 219.

[23] He describes Sribhoga (Sriwijaya) as being In the Southern Ocean; Takakusu, *Record*, p. 184. For I-ching's brief reference to countries on mainland Southeast Asia, see *Record*, p. 67, where he distinguishes the twenty *kua* (polities) extending from the Mahābhōdi temple in India to what is today northern Vietnam from the more than ten *kua* in the Southern Ocean; *Nan-hai*, p. 214. Takakusu translates the "*kuo*" in the Southern Ocean as "islands"; the text gives "*kuo*."

[24] Takakusu, *Record*, pp. 45–47.

[25] Ibid., p. 137. I-ching observed brahmans in India but not in the Southern Ocean; *Record*, p. 182.

[26] Ibid., p. 142; *Nan-hai*, p. 225.

[27] Paul Wheatley, *Nāgara and Commandery: Origins of the Southeast Asian Urban Traditions* (Chicago, IL: University of Chicago Department of Geography, 1983), p. 147, n. 2.

[28] Chavannes, *Mémoire*, p. 93; *Ta-T'ang*, p. 5.

In the second place, and of particular concern to historical geographers, he had a special reason for being exact when supplying geographical relations within the Buddhist world. He was an experienced traveler and knew that the patchwork of countries he visited or heard of from fellow pilgrims constituted the map where the four schools (*nikāya*) of Buddhist doctrine were situated, though, as he points out, "the number of votaries in each school is unequal in different places."[29] The location of the various *nikāya* was of great importance to him, for each *nikāya* used its own texts, which Chinese pilgrims had to identify, collect, and translate for the benefit of those who did not leave China. Thus, he had a religious obligation to describe the communications and traveling directions that linked the overseas Buddhist centers with each other and with China.

I-ching's linguistic expertise and preoccupation with pilgrim itineraries encourage us to suppose that his geographical information, though sparse, would be meticulous and systematic.

I shall now follow I-ching on his pilgrimage as far as Sriwijaya and begin with his voyage from Canton.

THE VOYAGE FROM CANTON TO SRIWIJAYA

Two interesting details appear in I-ching's otherwise conventional accounts of the voyage from China to Sumatra. The first concerns the itinerary his ship followed at the end of 689. The voyage's duration is not given; in 671, it had taken less than twenty days, though other voyages could last longer. But the route was always the same and off the Cham coast of what is now southern Vietnam. I-ching identifies this itinerary when he was sailing in 689. He says, according to Chavannes's translation, that the pilgrims on board ship were determined to arrive in Sriwijaya "par une lonque route" (長 驅). He is using figurative speech; the meaning of "a long route" in this passage is "pressing on with" the voyage as an act of Buddhist zeal, and he goes on to say that the pilgrims wanted to be a ship for carrying mankind over "the ocean of desire." The detail is worth noting because I-ching's personal observation of the shipping route off the Cham coast is consistent with Dr. Manguin's conclusion that the direct route out to sea from southern China to the south was never used, and the reason was the dangerous reefs of the Paracels, feared by sailors.[30]

Because I-ching is reliable about this part of the voyage, we can believe the other detail implied in his account of the voyages: the absence of piracy in Indonesian waters as a hazard facing pilgrims. This circumstance may reflect the maritime influence of the Sriwijayan rulers, whose own ships were sailing to Kedah and India in the second half of the seventh century. The situation was otherwise when pilgrims approached Tāmralipti in northeastern India and knew that their ships might be plundered.[31]

Yet I-ching traveled incuriously unless he was interested in Buddhist practices or heroic pilgrims. He takes the voyage to Sumatra for granted and ignores the final lap

---

[29] Takakusu, *Record*, p. 8.

[30] For I-ching's voyage in 689, see Chavannes, *Mémoire*, p. 179; *Ta-T'ang*, p. 11. Pierre-Yves Manguin's study of the route over the South China Sea is in "La traversée de la mer de Chine méridionale, des détroits à Canton jusqu'au 17e siècle (La question des îles Paracels)," *Actes du XXIXe Congrès international des Orientalistes*, vol. 2 (Paris, 1976), pp. 110–115.

[31] Chavannes, *Mémoire*, p. 71.

of his journey to Sriwijaya, when, I am assuming, he entered the Musi estuary. The Musi is south of the Batang Hari river, always associated with Malayu; according to I-ching, Sriwijaya was south of Malayu. When, therefore, he mentions the estuary (口) of "the Vijaya river," he is surely referring to the Musi estuary. He states that in the summer of 689 he boarded (舟+) a merchant vessel in this estuary in order to send a request to China for assistants and writing materials.[32] A strong wind suddenly took him out to sea as an involuntary passenger to Canton, where he arrived on August 10. He may have traveled to the estuary in a small local craft. When still ashore upstream, he could have heard that a merchant ship was about to sail, and thereupon hurried downstream, perhaps on an ebb tide, to deliver his errand.

Today something more, however, can be said of the Musi estuary. Ming sailing directions encourage one to suppose that this part of the Sumatran coastline did not change significantly in historical times, and two Landsat images, taken in 1978, support the view.[33] The images disclose that the Musi watercourse, after it sweeps northeastwards beyond Palembang, has not in the past meandered. The contrast between the lower Musi and the watercourse upstream from Palembang is distinct. When a river meanders, it deposits sediment carried downstream and causes changes in the river banks. The Musi as it approaches the sea has not been affected in this manner. Upstream sediment has not altered the shape of the lower reaches. Minor changes in the coastline are merely the result of sediment deposited by offshore currents very gradually over time. The likelihood is, therefore, that an estuarine settlement existed at the mouth of I-ching's "Vijaya river" in the neighborhood of the present-day fishing village of Sungsang. I-ching's merchant ship could have anchored in the small channel to the southwest of Sungsang and off the northern shore of the river. Perhaps, too, in Sriwijayan times a guard post was maintained at the estuary and also on the other side of the Bangka Strait near the site of the Kota Kapur inscription of 686. The Sultans of Palembang maintained a guard post at Sungsang.[34] The identification of subcenters in the Sriwijayan sphere of influence is one of the archaeologists' targets.

The commercial contacts between Bukit Seguntang and T'ang and Sung China attested by the ceramic remains also permit a more confident reading of a passage in the *Sung-shih*, which records the sailing itinerary of the Cōḷa envoys to China in 1015 and throws light on the same estuary. The envoys left San-fo-ch'i, always the Sung name for the major center in southeastern Sumatra, and "crossed the strait by the *Man* hill." The envoys then sailed in the direction of Pulau Tioman off the Pahang coast on the Malay Peninsula and towards the Cham coast. "The strait by the *Man* hill" suggests that the ship came in sight of the Menumbing hills on northwest

---

[32] Chavannes, *Mémoire*, pp. 176-77.

[33] O. W. Wolters, "A Note on Sungsang Village at the Estuary of the Musi River in Southeastern Sumatra: A Reconsideration of the Historical Geography of the Palembang Region," *Indonesia* 27 (April 1979): 33-50. The Landsat Images are in the possession of Dra. S. Suleiman. I am grateful to Professor Ta Liang for helping me to obtain and interpret the images. Professor Liang is Professor of Civil and Environmental Engineering, Emeritus, Cornell University.

[34] M. O. Woelders, *Het Sultanaat Palembang, 1811-1825,* Verhandlingen van het Koninklijk Instituut voor Taal-, Land- en Volkenkunde, 72 (The Hague: Nijhoff, 1975), passim.

Bangka. The hills are clearly visible from Sungsang.[35] The Bukit Seguntang settlement, with its sherds, unquestionably existed in 1015. My reading of the passage in the *Sung-shih* implies that the Bukit Seguntang polity was already known as "San-fo-ch'i" in early Sung times and therefore before the toponym came to be associated later in the eleventh century with a polity on the Batang Hari river to the north.

Chinese sailors in the first half of the fourteenth century identified the Musi estuary in another way. Wang Ta-yüan, who was overseas in 1330 though he did not necessarily visit Palembang, states in his section on "the Old Harbor" (Palembang area) that ships sailed from the "Fresh Water Channel" into the Bangka Strait.[36] The "Fresh Water Channel" is certainly the equivalence of the Musi, and Wang may be using the nickname for a feature of the estuary that helped Chinese pilots plot the correct approach to Palembang from the sea. This part of the coast has several estuaries very close to each other, and pilots had to be careful in distinguishing the correct one. The toponym "Fresh Water Channel" suggests that they had observed a reduced saline content at the Musi estuary and knew that they were not entering the Banju Asin ("Salt River") estuary a little further north. The contrast in the water content of the two estuaries would have impressed itself on Chinese pilots. The need to identify the correct approach to Palembang is also emphasized in the Ming sailing directions, where pilots were instructed to take care in spotting the entrance to the Musi by means of an "island" on the northern shore. The "island" was probably Sungsang.[37]

I-ching knew of the Banju Asin estuary and refers to it as "Mukha Asin" or "Saline Estuary."[38] He mentions this place in the *Mūlasarvāstivāda-ekaśatakarman*, where, in a note, he enumerates the major geographical regions, or *chou* (州) = *dvīpa*, on the east coast of Sumatra. A *chou* is a land mass that borders on the sea. The *chou* in question were "Barus" in the northern part of Sumatra, "Malayu" north of Sriwijaya, and "Mukha Asin."[39] If he had told us that Sriwijaya was in the region of the Mukha Asin *dvīpa*, he would have saved historians a great deal of speculation about Sriwijaya's location. He did not do so because, in this passage, he was only concerned with delineating large tracts of coastal hinterlands where, according to him, Buddhism flourished. He was not concerned in this passage with locating political centers.

The prominence I-ching gives to Mukha Asin need not be surprising. Portuguese pilot charts in the early sixteenth century reveal "a wider and deeper opening of the Sungei Banyuasin than that represented nowadays on nautical charts."[40] This part of

---

[35] O. W. Wolters, "Landfall on the Palembang Coast in Medieval Times," *Indonesia* 20 (October 1975), p. 47. I have slightly modified my translation. The Cōla envoys sailed from the Sumatran to the Cham coast, and Dr. Manguin has shown that this was bound to be the case.

[36] W. W. Rockhill, "Notes on the Relations and Trade of China with the Eastern Archipelago and the Coast of the Indian Ocean during the Fourteenth Century, Part II," *T'oung Pao* 16 (1915): 135.

[37] Wolters, "Note on Sungsang Village," pp. 36–39.

[38] O. W. Wolters, "Studying Śrīvijaya," *JMBRAS* 52,2 (1979): 30–32. [See also the present volume, chapter 4.—Ed.] I now follow Professor Paul Wheatley's advice and translate "Mukha" to read "Estuary"; Wheatley, *Nāgara and Commandery*, p. 256, n. 45.

[39] Takakusu, *Record*, p.10. "Mo-ho-sin" in this passage is Mukha Asin.

[40] Pierre-Yves Manguin, "Sumatran Coastline in the Straits of Bangka: New Evidence for Its Permanence in Historical Times," *SPAFA Digest* 3,2 (1982): 25.

the coast would be an even more prominent topographical feature when I-ching sailed along it on his way to India.

I-ching gives a glimpse of the Musi estuary in 689 only because he visited it to obtain assistance in continuing his translations in Sriwijaya. In 671 he had sailed upstream from the same estuary, but we do not know where he disembarked from the merchant ship that brought him from Canton. A passage in the *Hsin T'ang-shu*, however, mentions an important shipping center associated with Sriwijaya, and what is now known of the Bukit Seguntang area again invites us to read a Chinese source more confidently.[41] The reference cannot be dated but is likely to be early in the ninth century.

The *Hsin T'ang-shu* mentions *B'ịuət-d'ậi* (佛代).

> This country is on a river whose tributaries number 360. The king's name is [?] Śrī Samitra. There is a stream (川) called *Si-lji-b'ji-ljię-ńźịwäi*. The soil produces many rare aromatics. In the north there is a market, and trading ships of different countries gather there. Java is reached by crossing the sea [from *B'ịuət-d'ậi*].[42]

In 1975 I suggested that *B'ịuət-d'ậi* was an attempt to transcribe *B'ịuət-d'ậi*, or "Vijaya" and that the name of the stream could be restored as "Śrī Palembang."[43]

When I commented on this passage I had not yet rejected Obedijn's hypothesis that the lower reaches of the Musi took their present shape only in late historical times, when an ancient gulf of the sea, reaching as far inland as Palembang, receded as the result of sedimentation from upstream. What is today known about the geomorphology of this part of Sumatra and of the lower reaches of the Batang Hari river makes it certain that Obedijn's hypothesis is a figment of the imagination, and I

---

[41] George Coedès, *The Indianized States of Southeast Asia,* ed. Walter F. Vella, trans. Susan Brown Cowing (Honolulu, HI: East–West Center Press, 1968), p. 106.

[42] Wolters, "Landfall on the Palembang Coast," p. 53. I have modified my translation.

[43] Ibid., pp. 53-54. I have wondered whether the early eighth century Korean pilgrim Hye ch'o (慧超) referred to "Vijaya" in the account of his pilgrimage to "the countries of the Five Indias." (The term "Five Indias" is discussed in the next part of this essay.) Hui-lin's *I-chieh-ching yin-i* (Tripiṭaka. Chinese version [Tokyo] No. 2128, p. 926b) cites Hye ch'o as mentioning *Puât-tiei* (撥帝). In Hui-lin's list of words cited from Hye ch'o's description of his voyage from China to India, *Puât-tiei* appears immediately after the "Khmer" country. The toponym that follows *Puât-tiei* in Hui-lin's list is "*Kât-la* city = Middle *Lâng-kât*," a transcription that suggests Kalāh identified by Professor Wheatley with the Mergui area, though others have identified it with Kedah. Unfortunately, this part of Hye ch'o's text is lost. Could *Puât-tiei* be another rendering of *B'ịuət-d'ậi* in the *Hsin T'ang-shu*, which I have suggested means "Vijaya"? If this were so, Hye ch'o's itinerary, as far as it is available, reproduces I-ching's down the coast of mainland Southeast Asia to Sriwijaya and then northwards to a port on the Indian Ocean, which, in I-ching's case, was Kedah. One can suppose that early in the eighth century ships from China would frequently make their way to Sriwijaya. Sriwijayan missions were being sent to China at that time. I do not know, however, how Koreans in the eighth century sounded Chinese characters; linguists may comment on the plausibility of my identification of *Puât-tiei* with *B'ịuət-d'ậi*. On the other hand, Hye ch'o could have traveled with Chinese pilgrims, heard them pronounce "Vijaya," and then supplied the Chinese characters that he considered would reproduce the sound he heard. On Hye ch'o see Jan Yun-hua, "Hui-Ch'ao and His Works: A Reassessment," *The Indo-Asian Culture,* 12,3 (1964): 177–190. I am grateful to Dr. Insun Yu for introducing me to Hye ch'o.

am more confident that the "stream" could be the "Śrī Palembang" somewhere in the vicinity of Bukit Seguntang. Another reason why *B'ĭuət-d'âi* has every chance of being Sriwijaya is suggested by a conventional structural feature in early Chinese texts about southeastern Sumatra. From I-ching's day into the fourteenth century Chinese writers monotonously describe southeastern Sumatra as being on the route to or close to Java, as *B'ĭuət-d'âi* was.[44] The compilers in question probably heard of the navigational importance of the Bangka Strait, a facility that continued to be used as late as the sixteenth century.[45] Ships sailing from the Malacca Strait and bound for Java did not sail off the Bangka east coast and away from Sumatra. The Chinese writers would naturally stress Sriwijaya's proximity to Java. The *Hsin T'ang-shu* may therefore contain the earliest known mention of the name "Palembang."

The origin of the name is unknown, but we can bear in mind that a creek on the northern bank of the Musi and east of Karanganyar is called "Palembang." Indonesian place-names are often of great antiquity; "Asin" in the present-day Banyuasin is a place-name as old as the seventh century. The Palembang creek may repay investigation by archaeologists. The Tatang creek east of Karanganyar should undoubtedly be investigated, if only because it leads to the artificial tank close to the eastern side of the Karanganyar enclosure. The *Sejarah Melayu* associates "the Muara Tatang" with Demang Lebar Daun, the Palembang ruler who became the faithful ally of the founder of Malacca.

We observed that the *Hsin T'ang-shu* mentions a trading center to "the north" of *B'ĭuət-d'âi*. I suggest that the direction should be corrected to "northeast" to conform with the Chinese geographical convention that one sailed "south" from China and not "southwest" when a ship made its way to western Indonesia. But the harbor's location need not be accepted literally. Only archaeologists will be able to discover possible harbor sites in the Bukit Seguntang area, and much will depend on improved knowledge of early watercourses there. I shall return to this question later.

We have now followed I-ching to Sumatra in 671. The next matter concerns an important feature of his writings on Sumatra: how he signified the organization of Sumatran space and situated Sriwijaya within it.

I-CHING'S DEFINITION OF "SRIWIJAYA"

His Sumatran destination in 671 and 689 was "the *kuo* (國)" of Sriwijaya. What did the term *kuo* mean to him in this particular context? Chavannes, Takakusu, and Pelliot translated it in various ways: "country," "kingdom," and "state."

When the term appears in Chinese writings, it has optional meanings. The term can certainly signify a "kingdom/state" or "a country," and this meaning is usually preferred by the compilers of the Chinese imperial histories when they want to account for as much geographical space as possible in the non-Chinese world. The so-called "kingdom of Funan," in reality only an agglomeration of chieftainships, is an example of the usage.[46] The *Hsin T'ang-shu* follows the same usage in its section

---

[44] Viz.: I-ching, Chia Tan, *Sung-shih*, Chou Ch'ü-fei, Chao Ju-kua, and Wang Ta-yüan. We have to reckon, however, with copied information.

[45] Manguin, "Sumatran Coastline In the Straits of Bangka," pp. 24–28 and p. 49. Manguin's study is based on the Portuguese Roteiros.

[46] C. Jacques, "'Funan,' 'Zhenla.' The Reality Concealed by These Chinese Views of Indochina," *Early South East Asia: Essays in Archaeology, History, and Historical Geography,*

on Sriwijaya, which is depicted as being more or less the equivalence of the island of Sumatra.[47] Sriwijaya is said to have "fourteen cities" and to be divided into two *kuo* for administrative purposes; its "western" unit (= northwest) was "Barus" at the northern end of the island. A remarkable feature of this account is that the breadth and length of Sriwijaya are recorded (1,000 by 4,000 *li* [3 *li* = about 1 English mile, or 1.6 kilometers]). Details such as these resemble the description of a modern state in their exactness. Another passage in the *Hsin T'ang-shu* contains extracts from Chia Tan's geography, compiled about 800. Chia Tan notes that much of the east coast of Sumatra belonged to Vijaya *kuo*.[48]

On the other hand, a *kuo* in the Chinese imperial histories may mean a specific place in the form of a "capital city." Professor Wheatley cites the example of Langkasuka *kuo* in the Singora area on the Thai isthmus and considers the word *kuo* in this instance to mean "capital" or simply "city," and he goes on to define quite precisely the nature of the political unit involved as "a polity in which a focally situated settlement exercised direct control over a restricted peripheral territory and exacted whatever tribute it could from an indefinite region beyond."[49]

Before we consider whether the Sriwijaya *kuo* as I-ching knew it resembles the *Hsin T'ang-shu's* notion of a Sumatran-scale *kuo* or only a Langkasuka-scale one, we have to bear in mind that well-traveled Chinese pilgrims were familiar with Indian geographical conceptions and were able to describe India in language that made sense to those who knew the subcontinent.[50] I-ching's predecessor, Hsüan-tsang (c. 596–664), visited India and, adopting the Indian convention, writes that India comprises "the regions (境) of the Five Indias (五印度)." The "Five Indias" were grouped around Central India in the four directions, and their circumference was more than 90,000 *li*.[51] Moreover, according to him, this vast span of land is "divided into seventy and more *kuo*."[52] He reserves the term *kuo* for smaller territorial units, corresponding with political ones and situated within the large areas signified by "the regions" of the Five Indias.

I-ching follows the same usage when writing about India, though he chooses to refer to "the lands" (地) of the Five Indias. His poem, written just before he left Canton in 671, mentions "the Five Indias," and in the *Record* he writes that "the lands of the Five Indias are wide and remote; roughly speaking, the east, west, south, and north are all four hundred *yojanas* (one *yojana* = 16 to 40 miles, or 25.6 to 64 km) [from Central India]."[53] Unlike Hsüan-tsang, he does not attempt to estimate the number of

---

ed. R. B. Smith and W. Watson (New York, Kuala Lumpur: Oxford University Press, 1979), pp. 371–79.

[47] *Hsin T'ang-shu*, Po-na edition, ch. 222 C, p. 5a.

[48] *Hsin T'ang-shu*, ch. 43 B, p. 18b.

[49] Wheatley, *Nāgara and Commandery*, p. 233.

[50] As long ago as 1871 Cunningham noted Hsüan-tsang's indebtedness to Indian notions of geography; Alexander Cunningham, *The Ancient Geography of India*, new ed. (Varanasi: Bhartiya, 1975), pp. 9–11.

[51] Samuel Beal, *Si-yu-ki. Buddhist Records of the Western World. Translated from the Chinese of Hiuen Tsiang (A.D. 629)*, vol. 1 (London: Kegan Paul, Trench, Trübner, 1906), p. 70; Hsüan-tsang, *Ta-T'ang hsi-yü chi* (Shanghai: Jên-min pan-shê, 1977), p. 32.

[52] Hsüan-tsang, *Ta-T'ang hsi-yü chi*, p. 32.

[53] Takakusu, *Record*, p. 43; *Nan-hai*, p. 210. I-ching uses "lands" elsewhere in the *Record*; for example, *Record*, p. 128 and *Nan-hai*, p. 223.

kuo in the Five Indias, though he visited some of them.[54] Occasionally he states that the rulers of *kuo* provided pilgrims with escorts through their territories.[55] He pinpoints the location of a *kuo* in terms of distance. The Tāmralipti *kuo* was between sixty and seventy *yojana* east of Nālandā.[56] He also mentions the smallest unit of space in India; this was the "city" within a *kuo*. He tells us how far a monastery or temple was from a royal city.[57]

By the seventh century the notion of "the Five Indias" was a familiar one in China. The "Five Indias" represented geographical space, and in each "India" there were smaller and political units, known to the Chinese as *kuo*. A *kuo* was a kingdom or, as I prefer to translate it, a polity. "Polity" is a neutral term and begs no questions about its institutional form. The pilgrims' knowledge of India was sufficiently confident for them to use such terms as "circumference," "divided," measured distances, and "roughly speaking." But a similarly exact knowledge of Indonesian geography was not available in China before I-ching's day; Hsüan-tsang did not visit the archipelago, and geographical details in the imperial histories were limited to indistinct references to *kuo* in the Southern Ocean and vague sailing directions between them. A more systematic map of Indonesia emerges only with I-ching, and its significant feature is that it closely parallels what Hsüan-tsang and he write about India. We can suppose that I-ching had been guided by Indian spatial definitions and transferred them to the Southern Ocean because they made sense to him there.

Thus, I-ching, writing about the Southern Ocean, distinguishes between large geographical areas and small political units and leaves one in no doubt that he sees both India and the Southern Ocean from the same perspective. And so he writes of "the lands [地] of the Five Indias and the *chou* [洲] of the Southern Ocean where the people speak of the four *nikāya*."[58] *Chou* is the Chinese word used to render the Sanskrit term *dvīpa*, or land bordering on the sea and an appropriate term in the setting of maritime Indonesia. *Dvīpa* becomes the Indonesian equivalent of the "lands" of the Five Indias; both terms represent large geographical areas.[59] I-ching also uses "islands" (島) as an equivalence of *chou*. For example, he writes that "in the ten 'islands' of the Southern Ocean and in the Five Indias of the western *kuo* people do not use wooden pillows to raise the head."[60] Elsewhere he writes of "the ten *chou*" in the Southern Ocean.[61] *Chou* and "island" refer to large geographical space.

The parallelism in the description of India and the Southern Ocean is maintained when I-ching refers to the smaller and political units in the Southern Ocean. He mentions only one city, and that by inference in a famous note to which I shall return; he says that the monks in Sriwijaya lived "in the suburbs" (郭下). "Suburbs"

---

[54] The *Sung kao-sêng chuan* states that I-ching visited more than thirty countries; Chavannes, *Mémoire*, p. 193.

[55] For example, Chavannes, *Mémoire*, p. 20. I-ching gives several instances of Indian rulers who honored Chinese pilgrims; *Mémoire*, pp. 15, 24, 31, 39, and 46. Except on p. 39 the Chinese text always refers to a *kuo*, or political unit.

[56] Chavannes, *Mémoire*, p. 97.

[57] Ibid. The royal city is Kouśāgārapura, near Nālandā.

[58] Takakusu, *Record*, p. 205; *Nan-hai*, p. 8.

[59] I-ching was familiar with the rendering of *dvīpa* as *chou*. We shall observe below that he uses the expression "Gold *chou*" to signify "Suvarṇadvīpa."

[60] Takakusu, *Record*, p. 112; *Nan-hai*, p. 221.

[61] Takakusu, *Record*, pp. 45 and 49 (where Takakusu omits "ten"); *Nan-hai*, pp. 210 and 211.

imply a "city."[62] On the other hand, he writes of the "more than ten *kuo* in the *chou* of the Southern Ocean."[63] His statement is the Indonesian equivalent of Hsüan-tsang's that the regions of the Five Indias contained seventy and more *kuo*. I-ching admits that he cannot describe the circumference of the Southern Ocean *kuo*; only those who travel in merchant ships can do so.[64] His observation reflects brisk trade in the archipelago and his assumption that every *kuo* possessed a trading harbor. We have to remember that I-ching knew only southeastern Sumatra and did not travel inland as he did in India. But he traveled up the Sumatran east coast, and this is why one of his notes records the names of the three Sumatran *dvīpa*: the *chou* of Barus, Malayu, and Mukha Asin.[65] He and other pilgrims visited Sriwijaya and Malayu, and one pilgrim visited Barus,[66] and these passages consistently depict pilgrims as sailing out at sea past the *chou* but sailing to the *kuo* at the end of their voyages.

I-ching's systematic use of Indian geographical conventions to structure his account of the geography of the Southern Ocean enables him to conceptualize Sriwijaya's place on the Sumatran map. Sriwijaya would not have been a *dvīpa*-scale polity; instead, it would have been one of a number of *kuo*. To this extent Professor Wheatley's definition of Langkasuka *kuo* ("a polity in which a focally situated settlement exercised direct control over a restricted peripheral territory and exacted whatever tribute it could from an indefinite region beyond") could apply equally well to Sriwijaya *kuo*.

A note in the *Mūlasarvāstivāda-ekaśatakarman* confirms that I-ching knew Sriwijaya as being only one of the Sumatran polities (*kuo*). In the note he describes the sailing route from Tāmralipti in northeastern India to China, and he states that Malayu *chou* (洲) "has now become one of Sriwijaya's many *kuo*," that a change had occurred, and this is why he adds an emphatic sign (矣).[67] Here he happens to refer to Malayu as a *chou* but only because his topic is an itinerary; he is describing a sailing route, and this required him to use language appropriate for geographical description. Landmarks are conveniently indicated by the *dvīpa* coasts skirted by ships.[68] But I-ching knew that Malayu was also the name of a *kuo* as well as of a *chou*; he himself visited it in 672. A passage in his *Memoir*, mentioning his visit to "Malayu *kuo*," has a note which states that "[Malayu *kuo*] has now become Sriwijaya," and the note again ends with an emphatic sign (是). Each of I-ching's three notes on the relationship between Malayu and Sriwijaya contains "now" and an emphatic sign in

---

[62] Takakusu's translation of this note is in *Record*, p. xxxiv. The note is in *Mūla*, p. 477.

[63] Takakusu, *Record*, p. 10; *Nan-hai*, p. 205. Also see *Nan-hai*, p. 214; "more than ten *kuo* in the Southern Ocean," which Takakusu translates on p. 67 as "more than ten countries [islands]." *Nan-hai*, p. 228, states: "there are more than ten *kuo* in the islands of the Southern Ocean," which Takakusu, p. 163, translates as "there are more than ten islands in the Southern Sea."

[64] Takakusu, *Record*, p. 11.

[65] Ibid., p. 10; *Nan-hai*, p. 205. In this note the character for *chou* ("Malayu *chou*") is 州 and not 洲. The two characters are interchangeable. I-ching calls Sri Lanka a 洲 in the *Record* (p. 122; *Nan-hai*, p. 221) but in the *Ta-T'ang*, p. 9, he refers to it as a 州 (Chavannes, *Mémoire*, p. 9)

[66] Chavanness, *Mémoire*, p. 36, in respect of Barus.

[67] Takakusu, *Record*, p. xxxiv; *Mūla*, p. 477. I have modified Takakusu's translation.

[68] A clear instance is in one of his notes in the *Record*. He is enumerating the *dvīpa* in the Southern Ocean in order to indicate areas hospitable to the different schools of Buddhism, and he again states that Malayu *dvīpa* is "now Sriwijaya *kuo*" and ends with an emphatic sign (是); Takakusu, *Record*, p. 10; *Nan-hai*, p. 205.

order to stress the important change in the relationship that occurred when he was overseas.[69]

When he was writing his *Record* and *Mémoire* in the 691–692 period, I-ching was aware that Malayu *kuo* had, in an undisclosed way, been subordinated to Sriwijaya *kuo*. Malayu would not have been a solitary example of a subordinate *kuo*. Kedah *kuo* on the west coast of the Malay Peninsula was, according to I-ching, a "dependent" of Sriwijaya.[70] Historians have often wondered about the significance of his statements concerning the relationship between Malayu and Sriwijaya. There need be no mystery. The explanation is provided in the note in the *Mūlasarvāstivāda-ekaśatakarman*, quoted above: "Malayu *chou* has now become one of Sriwijaya's many *kuo*." The notes in the *Record* and *Memoir* read as abbreviated versions of the same statement.

I-ching knew from his traveling experience that Malayu was north of Sriwijaya. I shall not discuss the problem of Malayu's location, which I am sure was on the Batang Hari.[71] I am concerned with I-ching's definition of Sriwijaya *kuo*, which he knew as the name of one polity on an island with an unknown number of polities, many of which became subordinated to Sriwijaya. His perspective resembles that of students of early Southeast Asia today who emphasize the multiplicity of centers in the region. More interesting, his perspective also resembles that of the Old-Malay inscription of Sabokingking, discovered to the east of Palembang city and written about the time of the Kota Kapur inscription of 686.[72] The inscription is in the name

---

[69] Chavannes, *Mémoire*, p. 119; *Ta-T'ang*, p. 7. See the previous note for the juxtaposition of "now" and an emphatic sign in I-ching's note in the *Record*. Another instance of the use of an emphatic sign (也) to stress an unusual situation is when he observes that teachers from India smile when they see the cloth used for kneeling to perform salutations in the Southern Ocean; Takakusu, *Record*, p. 111; *Nan-hai*, p. 221. Malayu was undoubtedly the name of a *kuo*. In 644 it sent its single mission to T'ang China; *T'ang hui-yao*, Chung-hua shu-chü edition (Shanghai, 1957), ch. 100, p. 1790. The pilgrim Ch'ang-min sailed to Malayu *kuo*, though the date of his voyage is unknown; Chavannes, *Mémoire*, p. 43; *Ta-T'ang*, p. 3.

[70] Takakusu, *Record*, p. xxxiv; *Mūla*, p. 477. I do not accept Takakusu's translation of this passage.

[71] Neither Takakusu nor Pelliot was prepared to identify Malayu. Historians subsequently agreed with Rouffaer's view in 1909 and 1921 that Malayu was on the Batang Hari, though he relied on evidence from later times. Rouffaer proposed Kota Jambi as the location in question. Historians today prefer Muara Jambi, about twenty miles downstream from Kota Jambi. Muara Jambi is the site of a magnificent complex of Buddhist *stūpa*, and one can suppose that this site was associated with Buddhism in I-ching's day. Several pilgrims mentioned in the *Memoir* visited Malayu. Two small rivers at Muara Jambi are known today as the Malayu and the Jambi. Jambi sent missions to China in 852 and 871. Recently a gold plate inscription has come to light at Muara Jambi and been attributed to the so-called "standard" Kawi script of the middle of the ninth to the beginning of the tenth century. See Boechari, "Ritual Deposits of Candi Gumpung (Muara Jambi)," *SPAFA, Final Report: Consultative Workshop on Archaeological and Environmntal Studies on Srivijaya*, September 16–30 (1985), pp. 237–238. On Muara Jambi and the lower reaches of the Batang Hari, see McKinnon, "Early Polities in Southern Sumatra," pp. 28–30.

[72] J. G. de Casparis, *Prasasti Indonesia II: Selected Inscriptions from the Seventh to the Ninth Century AD* (Bandung: Masa Baru, 1956), pp. 15–46. Professor de Casparis notes that the script of this inscription is "virtually similar" with that used in the Kota Kapur stone of 686, and he suggests that the two inscriptions are roughly contemporary; de Casparis, "Some Notes on the Epigraphic Heritage of Sriwijaya," *SPAFA, Final Report: Consultative Workshop on Archaeological and Environmental Studies on Srivijaya* (I-W2A), Indonesia, August 31–September 12, 1982, Appendix 4h.

of the ruler, who refers to himself as "I" (*Aku*) and also refers to his *kadatuan*, which Professor de Casparis renders as "empire."[73] The *kadatuan* is signified in a particular way: *sakalamaṇḍalāña kadatuan-ku*, or "the large number of *mandala* of my *kadatuan*." Professor de Casparis understands the expression to mean that "the empire" was divided into a considerable number of *mandala*, each of which was under the authority of a *dātu*.[74] We can suppose that the Sriwijaya ruler possessed his own *mandala* (regarded by I-ching as a *kuo*) and was also the overlord of the other *mandala* in his *kadatuan*. Each *mandala*, no doubt, comprised its own dependent settlements, which boosted its *dātu*'s power and justified the use of the Sanskrit term *mandala*, or circle. The inscription makes it clear that the ruler of the *kadatuan* feared disaffection; the loyalty of not all the *dātu* could be taken for granted. Some are likely to be *mandala dātu* now in involuntary subordination to the ruler of Sriwijaya.

I-ching probably returned to Sriwijaya from India not long after this Malay inscription was written. He later updated his knowledge of the relationship between Sriwijaya and Malayu by means of footnotes to emphasize that a change had "now" occurred, the result of which was that Malayu had become one of Sriwijaya's "many *kuo*." The new situation seems to correspond with the description of the ruler's *kadatuan* in the Sabokingking inscription as "a large number of *mandala*." I suggest that I-ching's definition of Sriwijaya should be rendered in Malay as a *mandala* in the sense of meaning the ruler's own *mandala* and one of the numerous *mandala* under his control. Malayu and Kedah were examples of subordinate *mandala*. I-ching wrote very little about Sumatra, but what he wrote was perceptive. In 1904 Pelliot considered the relationship between Malayu and Sriwijaya in the late seventh century and could not decide which one "annexed" the other, but he did not take into account I-ching's note that Malayu was "now one of Sriwijaya's many *kuo*." The Sabokingking inscription was unavailable to Pelliot. In the multi-centered context of Sumatra, Malayu would have retained its political identity, albeit a subordinate one, and would not have been amalgamated with Sriwijaya as Pelliot supposed.[75]

I have suggested that I-ching's perception of a *kuo* resembles that of a *mandala* as signified in the Sabokingking inscription. The *kuo* were as numerous as the *mandala*, and this implies that the territories of a *kuo/mandala* need not have been extensive. In the following section of the essay I shall consider how far the Sriwijayan polity, if it is

---

[73] De Casparis, *Prasasti II*, p. 18, n. 10.

[74] Ibid.

[75] Pelliot, "Deux itinéraries," p. 348. Sanskrit inscriptions of seventh century Cambodia describe the ruler as the master of "the *mandala*"; A. Barth and A. Bergaigne, *Inscriptions Sanscrites du Cambodge et de Champa* (Paris: Institut national de France, 1885), pp. 40 and 42 (verses 3); G. Coedès, *Les inscriptions du Cambodge*, vol. 4 (Hanoi and Paris: EFEO Publication, E. de Boccard, 1952), pp. 7 and 9 (verses 2). Here *mandala* means a large unit of space and is a conventional literary expression, drawn from early Indian literature, to eulogize the Khmer ruler's influence. In my *History, Culture, and Region in Southeast Asian Perspectives* (Singapore: Institute of Southeast Asian Studies, 1982), I used the term in this sense as a convenient metaphor for conceptualizing subregional history. On the other hand, *mandala* in Indian writings can also signify a small unit of space; P. V. Kane, *History of Dharmasastra*, vol. 3 (Poona: Bhandarkar Oriental Research Institute, 1973), pp. 138–39. The Javanese Ferry Charter of 1358, an administrative document, uses *mandala* as meaning a small-scale unit, translated by Pigeaud as "district": "all districts of the island of Java (Yawadwīpa)"; T. G. Th. Pigeaud, *Java in the 14th Century: A Study in Cultural History. The Nāgara-kĕrtāgama by Rakawi Prapañca of Majapahit, 1365 A.D.* (The Hague: Nijhoff, 1960), vol. 1, p. 110; vol. 3, p. 158. The Sabokingking Inscription, another administrative document, follows the same usage.

identified with the lower Musi valley, resembles Professor Wheatley's definition of the Langkasuka *kuo*, with its "focally situated settlement,"[76] its "restricted peripheral territory" (which it directly controlled), and its "indefinite region beyond" over which it sought to exact tribute. At this stage we need conclude no more than that, if the subordinated Malayu was on the Batang Hari, as I believe it was, it would belong to the "indefinite region beyond," and that the reach of the "Vijaya" river between the sea and the ruler's residence would be under the latter's direct control.

Before I discuss possibilities for identifying Sriwijaya in terms of a particular terrain, I wish to restudy two more of I-ching's miscellaneous details that bear on his definition of Sriwijaya as a *kuo* and one of many *kuo*.

Though he recognized Sriwijaya as a *kuo*, on three occasions he refers to it as a *dvīpa*, even though the context is that of a specific sailing destination and not a geographical expression appropriate when describing stages in an itinerary or the span of Buddhist-influenced areas in the Southern Ocean. The first of these occasions is in the *Memoir* when he mentions the arrival of a Chinese envoy to "Sriwijaya *chou* (洲)" in 683.[77] Perhaps he wrote this passage carelessly, or he may have chosen to embellish Sriwijaya's size so that it would seem an appropriate destination for the envoy. The other two occasions when he refers to Sriwijaya as a *chou/dvīpa* need not cause any difficulty. He calls Sriwijaya "the Gold *chou/dvīpa*" (金洲) in two passages that record his destination when he returned to Sriwijaya from China in 689 with companions.[78] He is using figurative speech to describe his destination. "The Gold *dvīpa*" is the Chinese equivalent of the Sanskrit expression "Suvarṇadvīpa," an ancient Indian literary allusion to the wealthy Southeast Asian lands awaiting merchants who dared to cross the sea. The expression was already current in Buddhist as well as in Hindu Sanskrit literature before the beginning of the Christian era.[79] In 689 I-ching knew that he was returning to a Sumatran center associated with valuable Buddhist texts, and he wanted to exalt its fame by means of hyperbole. "The illustrious Mahārāja" Bālaputradeva, the Javanese prince who established himself in Sumatra in the middle of the ninth century, had a similar notion of the grandeur of his center when he made himself known to the Pala ruler as "the king of Suvarṇadvīpa."[80]

I-ching's use of the grandiloquent expression "Suvarṇadvīpa" may be noteworthy for a further reason. The year 689 is only somewhat later than the 682–686 period, when the Old-Malay inscriptions in the extreme south of Sumatra reveal Sriwijaya's militancy. There is also a Sriwijayan inscription from Karang Brahi in the upper reaches of the Batang Hari river system. I-ching may therefore be signifying by means of figurative speech the political status acquired by the famous Buddhist center since he first arrived there in 671.

---

[76] Dr. McKinnon has suggested to me that the Kedukan Bukit inscription of 682, discovered near Karanganyar, celebrates the establishment of a settlement at the Karanganyar complex after the submission of Malayu.

[77] Chavannes, *Mémoire*, p. 159.

[78] Ibid., pp. 181 and 186; *Ta-T'ang*, pp. 11 and 12.

[79] The ancient Indian literature on Suvarṇadvīpa, epitomized by Professor Wheatley as "a beckoning eldorado," is summarized in *Nāgara and Commandery*, pp. 264–67.

[80] Coedès, *Indianized States*, p. 108.

I do not think that I-ching's reference to Sriwijaya as "Suvarṇadvīpa" is inconsistent with his otherwise systematic definition of Sriwijaya as a *kuo* and therefore a specific location in Sumatra.

One more miscellaneous detail deserves to be reconsidered. My understanding of this detail is based on my confidence that I-ching always regarded Sriwijaya *kuo* as a specific place and also on my assumption that he was in the Bukit Seguntang area when he was writing his books in 691–692.

According to Takakusu's translation, I-ching states in the *Record* that the sun was immediately overhead in Sriwijaya *kuo*, in "the middle" of the second and eighth lunar months in the Chinese calendar.[81] As usual his context is that of Buddhist practices. He is describing the care Buddhists have to take wherever they live in identifying the exact time for their midday meals according to the rules of the *vinaya*. "If the monk," writes I-ching, "fails in this, how can he carry out other precepts?"[82] He goes on to quote an Indian saying: "he who observes the water and the time is called a Vinaya-teacher."[83] Drinking clean water and eating at midday were a monk's essential obligations.

The first question is whether we should translate the Chinese character for "middle" (中) as meaning literally "in the middle" of the relevant lunar month. I doubt whether this is the correct translation. The lunar calendar is a variable one, and adjustments have to be made periodically by adding an extra, or intercalary, lunar month in certain years. The sun could never be overhead anywhere on the same day in the lunar calendar. Instead of translating "middle" as meaning the exact middle of the lunar months, I prefer to translate it as "during" those months.[84]

Takakusu believed that Sriwijaya was at Palembang, but he was reluctant to use this passage to plot Sriwijaya on the map because he did not know which calendar I-ching used to date the equinoxes in Sumatra.[85] I suggest that a distinction should be made between his use of the Chinese lunar calendar when writing in Chinese to instruct monks in China and how, when he himself was overseas, he chose to identify the exact time for observing Buddhist festivals and especially for breaking his fast at midday. When he was writing for monks in China, he was meticulous in providing Chinese dates.[86] But for his own purposes overseas he is likely sometimes to have adopted local dating systems. In India he would have been guided by the clepsydrae in the monasteries "for the purpose of announcing hours" to the monks.[87] But he had a further means at his disposal for ascertaining when it was midday. He says in the *Record*: "Eminent men ... who preach and carry out the laws, and who are

---

[81] Takakusu, *Record*, p. 143; *Nan-hai*, p. 225.

[82] Takakusu, *Record*, p. 144.

[83] Ibid. I refer to the "water" practices in the next section.

[84] If I-ching had meant "in the middle," he could have written 月之中. See Takakusu, *Record*, p. 143, n. 2, for an instance of this usage for signifying "the center" (? Central India). In the passage on the equinoxes he renders "midday" as 月中, but here [Takakusu, *Record*, p. 143] the context makes it clear that he is referring to "noon."

[85] Takakusu, *Record*, p. 143, n. 3. For Palembang and the area around it, see Figure 2.

[86] He took the trouble to use the reign-period of the "Chou" ruler (690–704), the emperor Kao-tsung's wife and successor. References to the "Chou" ruler in I-ching's narrative as well as in his footnotes persuaded Takakusu that the notes were written by him and not by a monk living under the tenth-century Chou dynasty, as Chavannes had supposed; Takakusu, *Record*, pp. 118 and 214, n. 3.

[87] Ibid., p. 144.

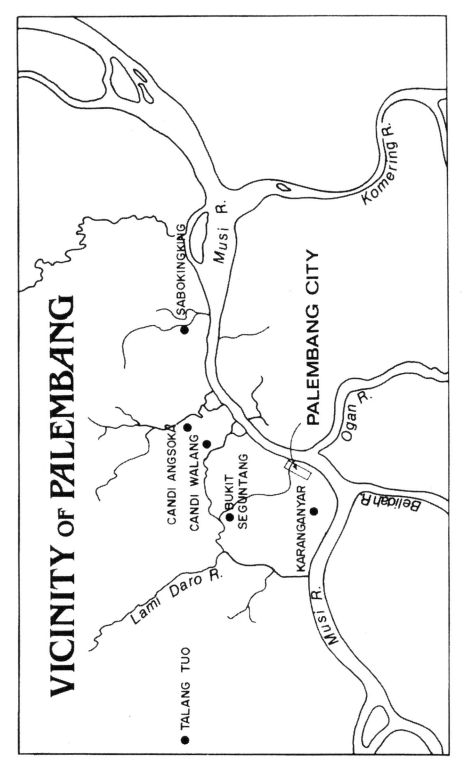

Figure 2: Vicinity of Palembang

not surprised at the minute and complicated rules, should take a dial (土) with them even when traveling by sea, much more so when they are on the land."[88] And he tells us, in fact, that it was by means of a dial (土) that one could observe the position of the sun overhead during the second and eighth months in Sriwijaya *kuo*. He would have done so himself in order to know when he could eat his midday meal on those days and discharge his personal responsibility as a Buddhist. He would have been at a particular place at a particular time, and the place would be among the monks of Sriwijaya and the year, I believe, was in 690 or 691. These are the only years when we know for certain that he was in Sriwijaya during every month of the year. We do not know when, sometime after 685, he returned from India to Sriwijaya, where he was in 689, but we know that he sent his *Record* and *Memoir* to China on June 2, 692.[89] 690 and 691 are likely years when he made his observations and when he was writing or about to write the *Record,* which preserves his information about the position of the sun during the second and eighth months. The information would have been fresh in his mind.

In 690 and 691 I-ching was certainly south of Malayu and about two and a half degrees south of the equator. If he wrote in the Bukit Seguntang area, we can establish the days when he observed the positions of the sun at midday in the second and eighth lunar months. In 690 at the time of the spring equinox the sun was exactly overhead at Bukit Seguntang on the fourteenth day of the second lunar month and a day corresponding to March 29. In 691 the day in question was the twenty-fourth day of the same lunar month. In 690 at the time of the autumn equinox the sun was exactly overhead on the twenty-fourth day of the eighth lunar month and a day corresponding to October 1. In 691, however, October 1 corresponds with the fifth day of the ninth month and is not during the eighth lunar month. In Bukit Seguntang I-ching could have made his observations only in 690, and he would have recalled them to illustrate the *vinaya's* rule that "the hour is determined according to midday at respective places."[90]

Whether or not I-ching was in the Bukit Seguntang area on March 29 and October 1, 690, his statement about the sundial readings was based on the observations he was required to make because he was a monk. When he recorded the sundial readings in "Sriwijaya *kuo,*" he was not thinking about anywhere in Sumatra south of the equator. For him a *kuo* was not a vague *dvīpa*-scale tract of territory but a specific location, which is how he consistently defines the Sriwijaya *kuo.*

I-ching's definition of Sriwijaya supplies no more than a sense of its limited territorial scale; it was only one of the Sumatran polities. I shall now consider the territory with which it was associated and return for this purpose to the Bukit Seguntang area. I am not alone in conjecturing that here was Sriwijaya. Professor de Casparis, reviewing the contents of the Sabokingking inscription found in the eastern side of Palembang city and written when I-ching was overseas, has suggested that the administration of the oath to the *dātu*, commemorated on the inscription, took place in the neighborhood of the ruler's seat of power. The engraved stone, he says, "must have stood at not too far a distance from the capital,"[91] and he goes on to

---

[88] Ibid.

[89] Ibid., pp. liii–lv, for a detailed discussion of the time when I-ching was writing in Sriwijaya.

[90] I am grateful to Professor L. Pearce Williams, John Stambaugh Professor of the History of Science, Cornell University, for guidance in calculating these dates.

[91] De Casparis, "Some Notes on the Epigraphic Heritage," p. 33.

observe that "this inscription strongly indicates that the capital was in the Palembang area during the period when the stone was in use for the oath ceremony."[92]

The Bukit Seguntang area, with its T'ang and Sung artifacts, was unquestionably flourishing in Sriwijayan times, and this circumstance has encouraged me to consider the territorial scale of a Sumatran *maṇḍala*, which had its heartland there. I shall not ignore what I-ching has to say about the Sriwijayan *kuo*, and I shall also be guided by what Professor Wheatley has written about the Langkasuka *kuo*.

The Bukit Seguntang Arrea in Srwijayan Times: Glimpses and Possibilities

I shall begin with Karanganyar's terrain but not on account of its hydraulic works. Landsat images, taken by satellites in 1978, indicate that the distance between Karanganyar and the northern shore of the Musi has always been more or less half a mile (.8 km), though at some unknown and perhaps very remote time in the past a small promontory or cape jutted almost immediately in front of the settlement into what would be a loop of the river.[93] The northern bank of the river near Karanganyar, with the exception of the promontory, has been stable, and the land behind is relatively high and dry and certainly not waterlogged. The advantage of the terrain can be compared with what the Landsat images reveal about the site of the modern city of Palembang, especially its western end, and also about the southern bank of the river. Palembang city is on swampy land and needs drainage canals. Canals were until recently a major means of access to much of the area. As for the southern bank, considerable changes in the rivercourse have occurred. For example, the present lower reaches of the Ogan river are of fairly recent formation; the Ogan's confluence with the Musi was once a few miles further south. Mud, clay, organic materials, and fine silt, deposited in meandering water, have left alluvial soil behind the southern shore. These conditions explain why a Dutch account in 1822 refers to the lower reaches of the Ogan as "the thousand islands."[94] The northern shore has not, of course, been wholly immune from sedimentation, but the sediment would be in the form of coarse materials such as gravel, sand, and other heavy substances and would account for the silting of its tributary rivers to create the creeks there today.

One of the Landsat images throws into relief a detail slightly west of Karanganyar, where the somewhat higher and drier land is broken by a sizeable expanse of moist soil, and this might once have been an important watercourse and correspond with the Lami Daro river, which flows from the northeast close to Bukit Seguntang. Perhaps a harbor was here in former times.

In spite of patches of inundated land observable today in and around the Bukit Seguntang area, the terrain has not, it seems, been disturbed by major changes in the Musi waterbed. The area with numerous watercourses and small islands was a

---

[92] Ibid. Referring to the Karanganyar area, Dr. McKinnon considers that "enough remains to be seen on and in the ground to suggest that the location of an ancient seat of power in the Palembang area soon will no longer be a mystery"; McKinnon, "Early Polities in Southern Sumatra," p. 17.

[93] I again acknowledge Professor Ta Liang's assistance in interpreting the images.

[94] *De Heldheftige bevrediging van Palembang* (Rotterdam: Arbon en Krap, 1822) [by an anonymous writer], p. 16.

favorable one for permanent settlement. A royal residence somewhere here is more than likely in Sriwijayan times, and it would be what Professor Wheatley calls a "focally situated settlement."

I-ching never mentions a royal residence, although Takakusu translates him as referring to "the fortified city of Sriwijaya."[95] The closest the pilgrim gets to mentioning a residence is when he refers to the "suburbs" (郭下) in which more than a thousand monks lived.[96] Takakusu transferred to Sriwijaya the Chinese model of a walled complex of imperial palaces. The model is inappropriate. Stone, though not laterite, is in scarce supply, and laterite bricks were probably reserved for religious foundations. Wooden palisades may have been used, and their postholes could be identified. Chinese histories sometimes mention wooden palisades in Southeast Asia. *B'uân-b'uân* on the Thai isthmus is an example.[97]

The "suburbs" would represent a scattered and unwalled stretch of dwellings and fields extending indefinitely beyond the royal residence and its adjacent official buildings, and here the monks lived. The "suburbs," in my opinion, comprised the Bukit Seguntang area itself. I-ching was impressed by the size of the Buddhist community. He mentions only one larger one, and this was at Nālandā in northeastern India and the most famous center in the Buddhist world. According to him, more than three thousand monks lived there.[98] Sriwijaya would therefore be, in his judgment, the second largest Buddhist center outside India. But one should not accept his numbers too literally. One scholar suggests that I-ching overestimated the number of monks at Nālandā; the surviving archaeological remains would not accommodate three thousand and more monks.[99]

Identifying the exact site of the monks' quarters is likely to be difficult if not impossible, unless concentrations of particular types of sherds and other artifacts come to light. All the same, details in I-ching's *Record* should not be disregarded. When, no doubt drawing on his experiences in Sriwijaya, he describes the numerous fasting days in "the ten *chou* of the Southern Ocean," he states that the host of the feast at the end of the fast would go to "the monastery" (寺)," apparently a specific location, to announce that the exact time for feasting had come.[100] But I-ching also refers to the monks' "apartments" (房), the word used to signify the rooms where monks and nuns actually lived; holy images were sometimes erected in the apartments.[101] The apartments could have spread over considerable space. I follow Dra. Suleiman's view that the monks lived in flimsy wooden huts, leaving no traces behind.[102] Nevertheless one detail in the *Record* is worth noting: "What we call a

---

[95] Takakusu, *Record*, p. xxxiv and quoting I-ching's note in *Mūla*, p. 477.

[96] Takakusu, *Record*, p. xxxiv. The Taisho Tripiṭaka notes that 廍, the character in the text, means 郭. Professor Wheatley translates the term as "an enclosed settlement"; *Nāgara and Commandery*, p. 239.

[97] Wheatley, *Nāgara and Commandery*, p. 234. Dr. McKinnon, in a letter dated July 12, 1985, suggests a thick natural palisade of thorny bamboo. There would be no postholes but, instead, a line of denser organic matter where the roots were and perhaps posts at the entrance or gateways.

[98] Takakusu, *Record*, p. 154 and n. 2.

[99] S. Dutt, *Buddhist Monks and Monasteries in India* (London: Allen and Unwin, 1962), p. 340.

[100] Takakusu, *Record*, p. 46.

[101] Ibid., p. 113.

[102] Wolters, "Studying Śrīvijaya," p. 19. [See also the present volume, chapter four.—Ed.]

monastery [寺]," he writes, "is a general designation for the place of residence [for the Sangha], the whole of which may be regarded as a monastic kitchen. In every apartment raw and cooked food may be kept."[103] Kitchen utensils need not have entirely disappeared.

In this context attention should be given to what I-ching says about the use of water by those who occupied the apartments. The Buddhist discipline enjoined monks to be careful in using clean water for drinking purposes. I-ching insists on earthenware and porcelain, and he mentions *kuṇḍī*, or water jars.[104] *Kuṇḍī* were also used by the monks for washing their hands when they were about to attend feasts after they had fasted.[105] Water used for the ritual bathing of images would have come from these containers. The monks' apartments have disappeared long ago, but fairly dense concentrations of broken domestic ware and especially of water jars may point to possible sites where the monks dwelt, and the following passage is worth bearing in mind: "When earthenware utensils have been already used, they should be thrown away into a ditch."[106] We should not assume that all rubbish ended up in the Musi.

It would be surprising if the site occupied by I-ching's monks ceased to have religious associations after I-ching's day. Sriwijaya continued to be an important Buddhist center until at least the beginning of the eleventh century and probably later. Atīśa, the tantric missionary to Tibet, studied there under the renowned teacher Dharmakīrti. Sherds of a later vintage may therefore point to where I-ching's monks lived.

But in spite of these possibilities a particular circumstance will hamper the search for the monks' debris. The monks were not the only inhabitants, and it may be difficult to distinguish their sherds from those of their Malay neighbors. Laymen as well as monks would use Chinese jars for storing water if they could afford them, and especially when imports of stoneware became increasingly available in Sung times. The monks were not an isolated section of the population. For one reason, they had to beg for alms. I-ching gives an example of a young Chinese monk who sought alms when he was learning Sanskrit texts in Sriwijaya.[107] Another reason for supposing that there were close contacts between monks and their Malay neighbors was that some monks known to I-ching could speak Malay (*k'un-lun*).[108] One Chinese monk who did so decided to become a layman and remained in Sriwijaya.[109]

The *Record* gives further evidence of contacts. I-ching asked laymen why they made offerings to a Buddha image. "To earn merit," was the reply.[110] He refers to "monks and laymen" in the Southern Ocean who accompanied images on a carriage;[111] he probably saw this scene in Sriwijaya. In the same passage he describes

---

[103] Takakusu, *Record*, p. 84. I-ching writes that there were three hundred apartments at Nālandā; Takakusu, *Record*, p. 154.

[104] Takakusu, *Record*, pp. 26, 27–30, 36, 37, 48, 190.

[105] Ibid., pp. 36–37.

[106] Ibid., p. 36.

[107] Chavannes, *Mémoire*, p. 189.

[108] Ibid., pp. 63–64 (the monk decided to resume a lay life in Sriwijaya); p. 159 (the monk understood K'un-lun in Sriwijaya); p. 183 (the monk did likewise).

[109] Ibid., p. 64.

[110] Takakusu, *Record*, p. 46.

[111] Ibid., p. 45.

how girls and boys flanked the images during the fasting ceremony; these would be the children of Malay Buddhists. In the Southern Ocean, according to I-ching, monks and laymen alike chanted the *Gātakamāla*, the stories of the accomplishments of the future Buddha.[112] Or again, during the fasting ceremonies monks offered prayers on behalf of the *nāga* and spirits, and these would be local divinities.[113] In these ways, Sanskrit vocabulary and Buddhist meditative techniques, such as the use of tantras, mentioned in the Sabokingking inscription, would become familiar to the Malays.

A final point may be made about the monks. One must not assume that there were many Chinese in the Sriwijaya monastery. I-ching only mentions a few in his day. The great majority of the monks were probably Malays and Indians. For example, according to I-ching, the famous Indian teacher, Sākyakīrti, who had studied in the Five Indias, lived there.[114] He also notes that teachers from India smiled when they saw the cloth used for kneeling to perform salutations.[115] When I-ching, after returning to China for the last time, recommended that Chinese monks bound for India should first study the Buddhist rules in Sriwijaya,[116] as he had done in 671–672, the reason must be that he knew that Indian scholars were to be found there. The same reason would explain why he saw so little to distinguish Buddhist practices in Sriwijaya from those in the Five Indias. His longest digression about Southern Ocean practices concerns the celebration of fasts, and the elaborate details he records suggest that he witnessed the ceremonies and probably participated in them when he was studying and writing in Sriwijaya.

The presence of only a limited number of Chinese will probably make the search for their durable artifacts even more difficult, especially if we suppose that Indian and Malay monks also used Chinese stoneware and porcelain. On the other hand, the relationship between the Buddhist center at Sriwijaya and Indian Buddhism was probably close and continuous, and the monks' residential area is likely to have retained its identity for a considerable time and left evidence of itself on the soil.

The monks were wedged in a patchwork of straddling Malay settlements. The settlements would comprise dwellings on piles on the banks of streams behind the northern shore of the Musi and at the edges of relatively high and dry terrain. They may have been quite numerous. Abū Zayd Ḥasan, early in the tenth century reporting merchant gossip, writes that the soil [of Sriwijaya] "is as fertile as any land can be,"[117] and Wang Ta-yüan in the fourteenth century writes about the Palembang soil in similarly glowing terms.[118] Abū Zayd also records that it is worthy of belief that the cocks of this country begin to crow at dawn and reply to each other over a hundred and more *parasang* (one *parasang* is about 6.25 kilometers) because the villages are contiguous and succeed each other without interruption."[119] Arab traders were unlikely to travel far inland, and the statement may incorporate a Malay figure of speech to describe the density of population in the area. A Karanganyar inhabitant

---

[112] Ibid., p. 163.

[113] Ibid., p. 48.

[114] Ibid., p. 184.

[115] Ibid., p. 111.

[116] Ibid., p. xxxiv, quoting *Mūla*, p. 477.

[117] G. Ferrand, *L'empire sumatranais de Çrīvijaya* (Paris: Geuthner, 1922), p. 57.

[118] Rockhill, "Notes on Relations and Trade," p. 135.

[119] Ferrand, *L'empire sumatranais*, p. 57.

in the twentieth century used a similar figure of speech when he said that cats could move from Karanganyar to Batang Hari Leko, about forty miles upstream, without touching the ground.[120]

Abundant supplies of fish, prawns, and bivalves would support a considerable population. Crops would be cultivated, and palaeobotanical research may assist in identifying them. The terrain, though by no means entirely waterlogged, is sufficiently moist to preserve organic data for laboratory analysis. The whole area would resemble a garden suburb, and the monks may have chosen to live on the lower slopes around the Bukit Seguntang hill where the land was suitable for fruit trees rather than crops.

The role of the hill in Sriwijayan times cannot be determined at present. Bukit Seguntang, albeit under a hundred feet high, is the only tall landmark close to the Musi and may have been venerated in ancient times and its religious fame enhanced in Sriwijayan times as a result of Buddhism. The earliest reference to it is in the *Sejarah Melayu*, where it is the scene of the miraculous appearance of Sri Tri Buana. I once suggested that the signs of his appearance are reminiscent of a bodhisattva's attributes.[121] If this were so, the hill could have acquired Buddhist associations. Buddhist imagery and greatly disturbed old bricks, the remains of a *stūpa*, have been discovered on or near the hill.

Estimating the extent of the inhabited land in the Bukit Seguntang area when Sriwijaya was flourishing is a fruitless endeavor until extended archaeological research has been undertaken. Cultivation would increase over the centuries. Perhaps the cultivated lands in the seventh century were somewhere within a zone of approximately four miles (6.4 km) along the northern shore of the river and about two miles inland, a stretch of land that includes the site of the 684 inscription to the northwest and the land extending north, east, and southeast of Bukit Seguntang. To this heartland should be added the ridge of land lying behind the swamps of the modern city of Palembang and leading to relatively high land east of Palembang city in the shape of a spur or peninsula that extends northwards.[122] My friends and I have, perhaps prematurely, become accustomed to regarding the eastern part of the area as a "holy land." Several important religious finds have come from here: the remains of the Angsoka and Walang *candi*, a group of bronze statues, a bronze statue of Śiva, and statues of Avalokiteśvara and Gaṇeśa. The Sabokingking inscription, a shaft of votive *stūpika* and *siddhiyātra* inscriptions have also been found east of Palembang city.[123] Wang Ta-yüan wrote that there were "many brick *stūpa* along the roads."[124] If these *stūpa* were east of Palembang city, they would catch the merchants' notice when sailing up the river. Finally, in the same area an inscribed stone was found in the 1930s. The inscription would be very close in time to the period of the

---

[120] L. C. Westenenk, "Boekit Segoentung en Goenoeng Mahameroe uit de Sedjarah Malajoe," *Tijdschrift voor Indische taal-, land- en volkenkunde* 63 (1923): 223.

[121] Wolters, *Fall of Śrīvijaya*, ch. 8.

[122] I discuss this feature in "Landfall on the Palembang Coast," pp. 43–45 and map 12 facing p. 39. When I wrote this article, I still accepted Obedijn's notion of a deep inland gulf that reached Palembang from the sea.

[123] The shaft was discovered in 1974 and is described in Wolters, "Landfall on the Palembang Coast," p. 45.

[124] Rockhill, "Notes on Relations and Trade," p. 135.

Old-Malay inscription of 682 in the Bukit Seguntang area, and it refers to "the Vihara in this country [or village]."[125]

The archaeological yield east of Palembang city could suggest that the royal residence was here. I do not take this view, because the area is too close to the northeastern sweep of the Musi and would be exposed to surprise attack. Moreover, the Bukit Seguntang area has much more inhabitable land close to the river. The Sriwijayan heartland had several subcenters, each with its own function, and McKinnon has suggested that the area east of Palembang was, among other things, an assembly site.

So much for glimpses or possibilities of the heartland or "focally situated" part of the Sriwijayan polity. Where would have been its "restricted peripheral territory," over which control could be exercised?

Whatever else it was, we are dealing with a polity knit together by the tide, which affected the heartland and periphery alike. The Siraf writer of the early tenth century, Abū Zayd Ḥasan, records that the ruler's palace faced a small lake fed by tidal water,[126] as, in fact, the Karanganyar settlement site does. Communications in this part of Sumatra would be almost exclusively by river. Early in the nineteenth century *perahu* from Muara Rawas, rather more than a hundred miles upstream from Bukit Seguntang, reached Karanganyar in four days,[127] but paddlers on the lower reaches of the Musi could maximize the advantage of the tide and reduce the effect of distance. At Palembang the rate of the ebb tide is generally two knots and the flood tide from one to one-and-a-half knots.[128] The tide affects not only the lower reaches of the Musi but also some of its long tributaries, such as the Komering and Ogan, whose confluences are close to Bukit Seguntang, and their tidal reaches would be part of the "restricted peripheral territory."

The riverine polity would represent a considerable amount of space, but space within which swift tidal communications assisted the exercise of political authority. At the same time, alluvial deposition as a result of sedimentation from upstream would support a large population. One can visualize a genuine unity based on shared environmental conditions. The periphery would not be difficult to control.

Finally, Professor Wheatley in his Langkasuka model proposes "an indefinite region beyond" both the center and the periphery and a region where tribute could be exacted. Riverine communications should again be taken into account, and I shall suggest one example of what could be part of "the region beyond." In July 1984 my companions and I visited Ulu Bayat, a small village on the tidal Sungei Lalang and more than a hundred miles upstream from the Banju Asin estuary where the Lalang waters reach the sea. Ulu Bayat is about seven miles from the site of a ruined *candi* in the jungle near the Sungei Klobak, a tributary of the Sungei Lalang. The Ulu Bayat inhabitants told us that their forebears had to make special deliveries of benzoin to the Sultans of Palembang.[129] On the map the village seems closer to the Batang Hari

---

[125] De Casparis, *Prasasti II*, p. 14. Damais thought that *wanua ini* might mean "this village"; L. C. Damais, "Bibliographie Indonésienne," *BEFEO* 54 (1968): 426. Dr. McKinnon suggests that a priestly presence nearby could be an essential element in the oath-taking ceremony.

[126] Ferrand, *L'empire sumatranais*, pp. 57–58.

[127] Woelders, *Het Sultanaat Palembang, 1811–1825*, p. 180.

[128] *Eastern Archipelago Pilot*, 4 (London: Hydrographic Office of Great Britain, 1890), p. 64.

[129] Westenenk, "Boekit Segoentang," p. 225, mentions the *candi*. For a nineteenth-century reference to benzoin from the Sungei Lalang area, see W. L. de Sturler, *Proeve eener beschrijving*

river in the north, but the direction of the watershed required the people as a matter of course to look southwards towards the Sultanate on the distant Musi. Ulu Bayat may be an instance of somewhere beyond the Sriwijayan heartland whence tribute could be exacted. A study of the *candi* in the jungle might throw light on the possibility. The *Hsin T'ang-shu* notes that "the land (十) of B'juət-d'ậi has many rare aromatics," and Wang Ta-yüan lists benzoin and gharuwood among the local products of the Old Harbor, Palembang.

The location of other territories beyond the periphery can only be surmised at present. Evidently in I-ching's day Malayu was one of them. The locations of the Sriwijayan inscriptions far up the Batang Hari river system on the Merangin river and at the extreme south of Sumatra must have been within the Sriwijayan sphere of influence at that time. The inscriptions mention "those who have been invested by me" with the charge of the *dātu*, and this suggests that the local chiefs were now in vassal relationship with the Sriwijayan ruler and were probably *dātu* themselves. The upper reaches of the Musi and its long tributaries were from time to time almost certainly part of "the beyond." Fragments of brick *candi* and Hindu–Buddhist statuary at confluences of rivers such as the Batang Hari Leko and up the Lematang river indicate influences beamed upstream from the heartland to create a degree of cultural unity.[130] Those who today discuss Sriwijaya emphasize the importance of the hinterland's natural wealth and warn us not to attach exclusive weight to the entrepôt wealth of Sriwijaya, with its trade goods from the Middle East and India. Dr. John Miksic suggests that "ceremonial centers, and also inscriptions, may indicate strategic points on ancient communication and transport routes" and help us "map out a methodology which may eventually provide us with a picture of internal Sumatran political and economic institutions ..."[131]

Relations between the center and "the beyond" would be complex. Sacral ties such as a Sabokingking-type oath and the royal gifts associated with magical sanctity would represent sanctions based on the overlord's personal prestige. In 684 the Sriwijayan ruler disclosed himself to his subjects as a bodhisattva. Kinship ties would supply another and less stable form of relationship. The Sabokingking inscription frequently mentions "families" and "kin" as capable of incurring the ruler's wrath. Professor de Casparis disagrees with Professor Boechari, who argued that the ruler

---

van het gebied van Palembang (Zuid-oostelijk gedeelte van Sumatra) (Groningen: Oomirens, 1843), pp. 43 and 109.

[130] Westenenk, "Boekit Segoentung," p. 224, observed the remains of a stone edifice on a small hill near the confluence of the Leko and Musi. Bennet Bronson discusses the economic role of confluences in "Exchange at the Upstream and Downstream Ends: Notes toward a Functional Model of the Coastal State in Southeast Asia," in *Economic Exchange and Social Interaction in Southeast Asia: Perspectives from Prehistory, History, and Ethnography*, ed. Karl L. Hutterer, Michigan Papers on South and Southeast Asia, no. 13 (Ann Arbor, MI: University of Michigan Center for South and Southeast Asian Studies, 1977), pp. 39–52.

[131] John Miksic, "Classical Archaeology in Sumatra," *Indonesia* 30 (October 1980): 65. Jane E. Drakard has recently illustrated how a critical reading of Sumatran texts may contribute to the study of trading routes in the Sumatran hinterland. Her two texts are situated in Barus and the Batak interior, and their function is to elaborate arguments on behalf of the status of two princely families. The arguments reveal, among other things, claims to the loyalty of specified inland and strategically located centers for collecting camphor and benzoin, famous trade products in studies of this part of Sumatra. See Jane E. Drakard, "A Malay Frontier: The Adaptation of Malay Political Culture in Barus" (MA thesis, Monash University, 1984).

would have little to fear from his own relatives.[132] I am sure that Professor de Casparis is right, and the reason is that a ruler's relatives would include many as the result of marriage alliances with members of the families of *datu*, the most eligible and powerful of all families. The *datu* would never be prepared to accept indefinitely the political status quo enforced by the Sriwijayan rulers. Family ties in a society organized by means of cognatic kinship provided a convenient means of binding the center and "the beyond" by tributary relations but were also, at the same time, a potential threat to the ruler's authority.

I have tried to sketch the outline of a *mandala/kuo* based on Bukit Seguntang in Sriwijayan times and availed myself of guidelines provided by Professor Wheatley's Langkasuka model. I happen to believe that I have been writing about Sriwijaya itself. One should not, of course, imagine that there were ever fixed boundaries. Varying degrees of influence would be exerted from the center in different times, and the waxing and waning of Sriwijayan power is a matter for historical research. Only one feature of the geopolitical situation is likely to be permanent. There would have been a riverine core of settlements, knit together by the Musi's tidal waters.

Sriwijaya is the object of endless study. By way of conclusion, I wish to take the opportunity of revising something I once wrote on the best-known aspect of Sriwijayan history: the connection between its power and international trade. I am interested in reconsidering a passage written by Ma Tuan-lin (c. 1250–1325), the Chinese encyclopaedist, and quoted by Groeneveldt as long ago as 1876. According to Ma Tuan-lin, "the barbarians [foreigners] of the islands only brought tribute because they sought the advantage of trade and imperial presents."[133] I-ching will once more be my point of departure.

TRADE AND DIPLOMACY IN SRIWIJAYAN TIMES

Merchant ships were sailing regularly between Canton and Sriwijaya when I-ching's fellow-monks visited Sriwijaya. When Fêng Hsiao-ch'üan, a local official in southern China and I-ching's *dānapati*, introduced him to a shipowner in 671, I-ching probably assumed that Sriwijaya was an established facility for pilgrims on their way to "the Five Indias." If this were so, he would not have been disappointed when he reached Sumatras where the ruler showed him sympathy by providing shipping space to enable him to sail to Malayu and on to India. I-ching describes the king as "bestowing [a gift] at the time of departure [贈支持送]," and he uses the same term when his *dānapati*'s family in Canton "bestowed" gifts on him in 671 and when monks and laity in Canton did likewise in 689.[134] He recalls in the *Record* the famous Buddhist teacher, Nagarjuna, who dedicated a letter in verse to a southern Indian king who had been his *dānapati*.[135] I-ching does not describe the Sriwijayan ruler as a *dānapati*, but he uses language for the king's service appropriate in the context of assistance bestowed on a pilgrim. The ruler's conduct was in the hospitable tradition

---

[132] De Casparis, "Some Notes on the Epigraphic Heritage," p. 33.

[133] W. P. Groeneveldt, *Notes on the Malay Archipelago and Malacca Compiled from Chinese Sources* (Batavia: n.p., 1876), p. 61, n. 1.

[134] Chavannes, *Mémoire*, p. 119; *Ta-T'ang*, p. 7.

[135] Takakusu, *Record*, pp. 158–159.

of the Indian rulers mentioned in the *Memoir* and would not have been cultivated overnight.[136]

I-ching's continued respect for Sriwijaya is shown when he calls it "Suvarṇadvīpa." The T'ang envoy's visit in 683 is another sign of Sriwijaya's fame.[137] A pilgrim accompanied the envoy and brought gifts of *sūtra* and images. Perhaps the gifts graced the mission.[138] The ruler was evidently regarded as a worthy recipient and must have been recognized in China as the ruler of an important Buddhist polity.

Nevertheless, in spite of regular trading relations between Sriwijaya and China, the Sriwijayan rulers had not yet established tributary relations with China when I-ching was overseas.[139] This circumstance may seem surprising when we read in the *Memoir* of the special respect the ruler paid to two pilgrims when he realized that they came from the T'ang empire. The ruler valued the connection with China.[140] Yet the first verifiable mission from Sriwijaya was as late as 702; others followed in 716, 724, 728, and 742. Before I-ching's time the most recent mission from anywhere in Indonesia had been from the Javanese polity of Ho-ling, in 666.[141] Indonesian missions after Sriwijaya's in 742 were resumed by Ho-ling in 767, though one side of the Ligor inscription on the Thai isthmus and dated 775 extols the ruler of Sriwijaya's title. Sriwijaya's tributary relationship with T'ang China was brief.

But a lean tributary record need not be the only measure of the scale of Sriwijayan trade in T'ang times. In 684 K'un-lun merchants in Canton killed the governor, Lu Yüan-jui, because "he tried to cheat them of their goods,"[142] and another source states that the governor's staff was "licentious and extortionist."[143] I-ching uses the word "K'un-lun" when he refers to the Malay language spoken in Sriwijaya.[144] Again, in 695 the T'ang Court issued regulations for provisioning foreign merchants in China, and Sriwijaya and Ho-ling were among the countries to benefit.[145] Trade between Sriwijaya and China was probably continuous in the last

---

[136] Spencer makes a similar comment: "The hospitality accorded to Chinese monks in Śrīvijaya suggests that its rulers were not unaware of their realm's significant cultural, as well as geographical, position between India and China"; George W. Spencer, *The Politics of Expansion: The Chola Conquest of Sri Lanka and Sri Vijaya* (Madras: New Era Publications. 1983), p. 109.

[137] Chavannes, *Mémoire*, p. 159.

[138] The circumstances of the mission are unknown. The *Memoir* states that the mission was sent in the second year of the *Yung-chüan* reign-period. There is only one such year, and the year in question must be the single year of the next *(Hung-tao)* reign-period (February 2, 683–January 22, 684). The envoy, unnamed, could have sailed with the northeast monsoon towards the end of 682 or 683. The T'ang emperor Kao-tsung died on December 27, 683, and had lost interest in Buddhism many years earlier, but his wife, who succeeded him on the throne, had already become the patroness of Buddhism. Perhaps she sent the envoy. Alternatively, the envoy was sent by a senior official in southern China.

[139] According to the *Hsin T'ang-shu*, Po-na edition, ch. 222 C, p. 5a, Sriwijayan missions were sent from the 670–673 to the 727–750 reign-periods, but only the *Ts'ê-fu yüan-kuei* records the years when missions were sent, and these were in the first half of the eighth century.

[140] Chavannes, *Mémoire*, p. 75.

[141] Wang Gungwu, "The Nanhai Trade: A Study of the Early History of Chinese Trade in the South China Sea," *JMBRAS* 31,2 (1958): 122.

[142] Ibid., p. 75.

[143] Ibid., p. 76.

[144] See notes 108 and 109, above.

[145] *T'ang hui-yao*, ch. 100, p. 1798.

thirty years of the seventh century and before missions were sent, even though the T'ang government was tardy in realizing that suitable administrative arrangements were needed in Canton to protect its economic interests and those of foreign merchants. The T'ang response came at an unknown time before 714 when the post of Superintendent of Merchant Shipping was established in Canton.[146] Even then not all was well. The *Hsin T'ang-shu* states that sometime in the first half of the eighth century a Sriwijaya ruler complained through his envoys that the Canton officials misbehaved.[147] The complaint would have been made during one of the missions between 716 and 742.

Were, then, tributary missions and commercial exchange closely related activities as Ma Tuan-lin insisted? What happened in the second half of the seventh century does not support this view. Nevertheless, I had long supposed that the tributary system provided the mechanism for giving access to the Chinese market and that Sriwijaya's prosperity depended to a large extent on the willingness or ability of the Chinese emperors to receive missions from their "vassal." The missions, I assumed, were commercial occasions that brought wealth to the Malay rulers and helped to reassure merchants using Sriwijaya's harbors that the rulers were respected in China and that merchants would be accorded a satisfactory reception in Chinese ports. When the internal situation in China was disturbed, the rulers would no longer send missions and merchants would be reluctant to sail to China. According to Abū Zayd Hasan, many foreigners were massacred during Huang Ch'ao's rebellion in 878. The rebellion scared merchants and kept them away from China.[148]

On the basis of this hypothesis, I suggested that the operation or abeyance of the tributary trade constituted a rhythm in Malay history.[149] When the imperial government was strong, the China trade nourished the Malay overlords' power. The rhythm ended only in the twelfth century, when the expansion of the Chinese mercantile marine enabled Chinese merchants to trade with Southern Ocean centers of production at will. This development diminished the economic importance of the Śrīvijayan entrepôt. Moreover, by the twelfth century the emperors themselves were no longer interested in tributary trade. Missions petered out, the entrepôt lost its economic role, and the Malay rulers forfeited their influence in Sumatra.

My interpretation of the relationship between the tributary system and the China trade depended, however, on an arbitrary distinction or opposition between the tributary trade and Chinese private trade. I am now no longer convinced that the distinction is correct. As a result of discussions with Chinese historians during a visit to Xiamen University in the spring of 1985, I became aware that Chinese merchant ships from southern China were sailing to Southeast Asia as early as the tenth century and long before the tributary trade was falling into abeyance in the twelfth century.

The information brought to my notice is miscellaneous and lacking in geographical detail, but none the less interesting. In Xiamen, I was told that texts reveal that merchants from Fukien province in southern China were sailing south for trading purposes at the time of the Five Dynasties (907–960), during the interval

---

[146] Wang, "Nanhai Trade" pp. 99–100.

[147] Ibid., p. 97.

[148] G. Ferrand, trans., *Voyage du marchand arabe Sulaymān en Inde et en Chine ... rédigé en 851 de remarques par Abū Zayd Hasan (vers 916)* (Paris: Editions Bissard, 1922), pp. 75–76.

[149] Wolters, *Fall of Śrīvijaya*, ch. 4.

between the fall of T'ang and rise of Sung when there was no strong government in southern China.[150] One merchant, I was told, had porcelain in his cargo. The situation had not changed by the end of the tenth century. In 992 a Javanese mission to the Sung Court reported that a shipowner and important merchant, Mao Hsü from Chien-ch'i in Fukien province, had come to Java on several occasions. The Javanese ruler availed himself of the opportunity provided by the merchant's presence in Java to organize the mission of 992.[151]

Further materials are available as the result of the Sung government's reestablishment of the Superintendency of Merchant Shipping in 971 in an effort to impose an official monopoly on particularly valuable imports arriving in Chinese as well as in foreign ships. In 982 ocean-going ships of Chang-chou and Ch'üan-chou in Fukien province were prohibited from sailing elsewhere on the China coast to trade in certain goods, including frankincense.[152] In 989 the government required "merchants going out to sea to trade with foreign countries" to obtain travel documents at the Chekiang Superintendency of Merchant Shipping before being allowed to import "valuable goods."[153] Chekiang is north of Fukien on the coast.

Finally, a poem by Hsieh Li in Wang Hsiang-chih's thirteenth-century geography extends these glimpses of Chinese shipping in Southeast Asia into the middle of the eleventh century. Hsieh Li was an official in the neighborhood of Ch'üan-chou at that time.[154]

The Ch'üan-chou Song of the South

> The Ch'üan-chou population is dense. The mountains and valleys are barren.
> The people want to till, but there is no land to open up.
> To the south lies the ocean, vast and limitless.
> Every year they build ships and go to foreign lands.

The glimpses of Chinese overseas shipping are interesting for several reasons. They bring Fukien province into prominence from the early tenth century onwards, and archaeologists may be able to identify Bukit Seguntang sherds as products of Fukien kilns. Moreover, in 985[155] and 1028[156] the Sung government despatched its envoys to the Southern Ocean to persuade foreign traders to bring frankincense and other natural produce to China. The needs of the market were so considerable that

---

[150] I thank Mr. Liao Dake, of the Nanyang Institute, Xiamen University, for bringing the new information to my notice. His dissertation on the subject of early Chinese shipping in the Southern Ocean will, when published, be of considerable interest to Southeast Asian historians.

[151] *Sung-shih*, Po-na edition, ch. 489, p. 17a; Groeneveldt, *Notes on the Malay Archipelago*, p. 18.

[152] *Sung hui-yao chi-kao*, photolithographic reprint of the Chai yeh t'ang copy in the Peking Library, Chung-hua shu-chü edition, vol. 4, *chih-kuan*, 44, p. 3364.

[153] Ibid.

[154] Wang Hsiang-chih, *Yü-ti chi-sheng*, Wên-hai ch'u-pan shê, 1971 printing, vol. 2, ch. 130, p. 692. On Wang Hsiang-chih, see *A Sung Bibliography* (initiated by Étienne Balazs and edited by Yves Hervouet) (Hong Kong: Chinese University Press, 1979), p. 130. On Hsieh Li, see *Chung-wên ta tz'u-tien* (Taipeh: Chung-hua Ta-hsüeh, 1982), vol. 8, p. 1103. I am grateful to Mr. Liao Dake for bringing the poem to my notice.

[155] *Sung hui-yao chi-kao, chih-kuan*, 44, p. 3364.

[156] Ibid., pp. 3365–3366.

there would be opportunities for private as well as tributary trade. But the feature of the new evidence that concerns me is evidence of Chinese trading ships in the Southern Ocean two hundred years before about 1100, which was, I had supposed in 1983, the earliest certain time when such evidence was available.[157] Chinese private trade had overlapped with the tributary trade for about two hundred years.

The sharp distinction I formerly proposed between the tributary trade and Chinese private trade seems to be no longer tenable. There need have been no competition. Both forms of trade would benefit the Sriwijaya entrepôt, and a clear instance is provided by the *P'ing-chou k'o-t'an*, which states that, about 1100, Chinese going to the Middle East repaired their ships and exchanged goods in San-fo-ch'i. "Merchants from distant places congregate there. This country is therefore considered to be very prosperous."[158] Chinese merchants during the previous two centuries would likewise be attracted to a well-known entrepôt where frankincense was readily available from the Middle East. Almost every Chinese account of Sriwijaya associates it with the frankincense trade. The Sriwijayan rulers' own merchants[159] and foreign merchants, including Chinese, would cooperate in maintaining the trade, especially in Sung times when the Chinese government depended increasingly on revenue from imports reserved for resale under its auspices.

What, then, was the purpose of the tributary missions? The missions were certainly occasions when the rulers could trade with China, but I believe that the rulers had another and more important intention. In 1983, when I was discussing the missions from San-fo-ch'i in the last twenty years of the eleventh and in the twelfth centuries, I already suspected that these missions had diplomatic objectives. Foreign rulers in Sung times were anxious for imperial favors that signified their seniority vis-à-vis other Chinese vassals and especially those who were their neighbors and potential rivals. Distinctions of rank were part of the political culture of Southeast Asia[160] and, when granted by the emperors, helped to establish status among Southeast Asian rulers whose spheres of influence overlapped.[161]

Today, after taking into account what I-ching wrote about the multicentered situation in Sumatra, and no longer satisfied with my earlier distinction between tributary and private trade, I am coming to the view that the status associations of the missions—and not their commercial associations—were always important. Missions would be sent to enhance and verify the prestige of the rulers and not merely to demonstrate the trading pretensions of what George Spencer has called

---

[157] For my view in 1983, see "A Few and Miscellaneous *pi-chi* Jottings on Early Indonesia," *Indonesia* 36 (October 1983): 57.

[158] Wolters, "A Few and Miscellaneous *pi-chi* Jottings," p. 55.

[159] A shipowner from Sriwijaya is mentioned in 985; Groeneveldt, *Notes on the Malay Archipelago*, p. 64.

[160] Wolters, "A Few and Miscellaneous *pi-chi* Jottings," pp. 58-61. Prapañca attributes such a sentiment to Hayam Wuruk of Majapahit: "Whosoever he may be, he shall be my enemy in the world if he is an equal on earth"; Pigeaud, *Java in the 14th Century*, vol. 3, canto 51, stanza 7.

[161] In 1077 the Sung emperor, conferring a high rank on the Sriwijayan ruler, stated that he did so in order to embellish his loyal vassal's reputation and honor his country with a special favor; *Sung-shih*, Po-na edition, ch. 489, pp. 14a–b. The Malay ruler would have the same intention when he honored his own subordinates and would certainly understand the significance of the emperor's favor.

"the dominant port."[162] The missions did not in themselves create prestige any more than did the erection of temples in India during the early eleventh century for the Sriwijayan rulers.[163] Prestige was the consequence of the rulers' achievement in controlling rival Sumatran polities and surviving the dangers reflected in the Sabokingking inscription. Missions to China and temples in India projected the rulers' own notion of their relative importance among their neighbors. Thus, for example, the Sriwijayan missions from 702 to 742 would reflect the rulers' earned status in Sumatra, to which one can suppose that the subordination of Malayu and Kedah contributed more than anything else. Malayu had sent a mission to China in 644.[164]

If one thinks of missions as "diplomatic" measures against a background of a restless inter-polity situation in Sumatra itself, and not as what George Spencer calls "commercial diplomacy,"[165] some Chinese notices about Sriwijaya may make better sense. Though I-ching contradicts the *Hsin T'ang-shu*'s impression of Sriwijaya as constituting most of Sumatra,[166] this may be precisely the impression that Malay envoys wished to leave in the mind of the T'ang Court. Similarly, the invariably extravagant language used by Arab writers in the ninth and early tenth centuries to praise the "Maharaja" may reflect the ruler's own notions of his greatness. We do not know how long after the 742 mission the rulers were able to maintain their overlordship, but the missions from Jambi in 852 and 871 should not be ignored. In the middle of the ninth century Bālaputradeva describes himself in the Nālandā inscription as the ruler of "Suvarṇadvīpa."[167] Unfortunately, we do not know whether he was ruling on the Batang Hari or Musi river. The interesting detail is that he chose to invoke the illustrious name of Suvarṇadvīpa to communicate his status abroad.

When T'ang fell in the first years of the tenth century, Malay trading with southern China did not cease. Foreign and, by now, some Chinese merchants maintained it. But the rise of Sung in 960 was a favorable opportunity for the Sriwijayan rulers to advertise in China their status in Sumatra. According to the Cōḷa envoys' itinerary in 1015, the rulers' center seems at this time to be on the Musi,[168] and the sudden currency of "San-fo-ch'i" as the Chinese name for the dominant Sumatran polity may be an instance of the rulers' insistence on their unique status. "San-fo-ch'i" is not a transcription of "Sriwijaya," though the name "Sriwijaya" continued to be *en vogue*; the name appears in a southern Indian inscription of the early eleventh century.[169] Some years ago I suggested that "San-fo-ch'i" means no more than what it means literally in Chinese: "the Three Vijayas."[170] If this explanation is correct, during the mission of 960 the Malay ruler promptly identified himself as the overlord of the three parts of Sumatra or of Sumatra and the Malay

[162] Spencer, *Politics of Expansion*, p. 107.

[163] Coedès, *Indianized States*, pp. 141–42.

[164] *T'ang hui-yao*, ch. 100, p. 1790.

[165] Spencer, *Politics of Expansion*, p. 109.

[166] See note 42 above for the *Hsin T'ang-shu*'s description of Sriwijaya.

[167] See note 80 above.

[168] See note 35 above.

[169] Coedès, *Indianized States*, p. 142.

[170] Wolters, "Studying Śrīvijaya," p. 23. [See also the present volume, chapter four. —Ed.]

Peninsula that were customarily associated with the illustrious name "Vijaya" (Fo-ch'i).[171] Another instance of a Malay ruler's concern to project his local status overseas is the title he used during his mission of 1017; he describes himself as the ruler of "the Ocean Lands."[172] This was when the ruler's fame was well known. 1017 is in the period when the future reformer of Tibetan Buddhism, Atīśa, was attracted to Sriwijaya, described as "Śrīwijayanagara, in Malayagiri, in Suvarṇadvīpa."[173] The exact significance of "Malayagiri" is not clear, but the Tanjore inscription of 1031, recording the Cōla ruler's victories in Southeast Asia, distinguishes between "Sriwijaya" and "Malaiyer."[174]

In early Sung times the Sriwijayan rulers seem to have insisted on their suzerain pretensions when they sent missions to the Chinese Court, and the titles and courtesies conferred on them during the missions between 960 and 1028 suggest that they made a successful impression. We do not know whether they were facing difficulties in maintaining their local hegemony in these years. According to the *Sung shih*, between 988 and 992 Sriwijaya was invaded by Javanese. This episode may have threatened the Malay ruler. M. Shiraishi has suggested that missions from Sriwijaya had nothing to do with such conventional matters as changes in Chinese and Malay rulers, and in 1983 I assumed that the missions in early Sung times were no more than important commercial occasions.[175] But if the possibility is borne in mind that the missions were frequent when the rulers had particular reasons for affirming their reputation as overlords, one is encouraged to take into account what is known of other happenings in Sumatra and Java that could cause the rulers to be anxious.

I was already beginning to consider the diplomatic aspects of the tributary missions when, in 1983, I wrote about the final phase of the tributary system when San-fo-chli had become the Chinese name for the Malay center at Muara Jambi on the Batang Hari.[176] The first missions from the Batang Hari between 1092 and 1094, I argued, would be intended to convince the Chinese that the Muara Jambi princes occupied the status formerly enjoyed by the rulers on the Musi river. The missions of 1157 and 1178 were similar diplomatic gestures.[177]

The Musi polity of Bukit Seguntang has been the focus of this essay, and there I shall end my sketch of the tributary relationship. Chao Ju-kuo includes "Palembang *kuo*" among the fifteen "dependencies" of San-fo-ch'i.[178] Sumatran tributary trade was now a thing of the past and had been overtaken by Chinese private trade, but

---

[171] An early eleventh-century Cōla inscription describes the ruler as the king of Sriwijaya and Kaṭāha (Kedah on the Malay Peninsula); Coedès, *Indianized States*, p. 142. A mission had come from "Vijaya" in 904. Wang Gungwu suggests that it reached a port in Fukien; Wang, "Nanhai Trade," p. 86.

[172] P. Pelliot, *Notes on Marco Polo*, vol. 2 (Paris: Imprimerie nationale, 1963), p. 839. [In the original publication of this essay, the date in this sentence was misprinted as 1917.—Ed.]

[173] Coedès, *Indianized States*, p. 144.

[174] Ibid., p. 142.

[175] Wolters, "A Few and Miscellaneous *pi-chi* Jottings," p. 58.

[176] Ibid., pp. 56-57, 60-61.

[177] See Robert M. Hartwell, "Tribute Missions to China, 960-1126" (manuscript, Philadelphia, 1983), pp. 176 and 180, for a discussion of the Chinese materials for the Sumatran missions of 1079.

[178] Friedrich Hirth and W. W. Rockhill, *Chau Ju-kuo* (St. Petersburg: Imperial Academy of Sciences, 1911), p. 62.

this circumstance made no difference to the Musi emporium. The *Sejarah Malayu* makes a great deal of Bukit Seguntang. Not much evidence has been discovered of settlements in that area from the eleventh to the fourteenth centuries, but numerous sherds of later, Sung and Yüan vintage are concentrated in the eastern suburbs of Palembang.[179] Moreover, Chinese sources record the presence of many overseas Chinese in the Palembang area towards the end of the fourteenth century. Ming sailing directions of the early fifteenth century ignore the Batang Hari estuary but not the Musi estuary.[180] In 1377 the Javanese destroyed completely and utterly the Muara Jambi *kraton* and all the settlements on the lower Batang Hari, and for many years thereafter no successor government on the Batang Hari was able to attract traders.[181] The situation on the Musi was very different. The Javanese destroyed the Palembang *kraton* in the 1390s, but a sufficient number of overseas Chinese lived there to survive and fill the vacuum created by the Javanese attack. The Musi emporium had become too well established over the centuries to disappear.

I have digressed from the subject of I-ching and the Bukit Seguntang area in order to contest my earlier view that Sumatran missions to China should be accounted for simply in terms of commercial transactions. Yet I would not have done so if I-ching and the Sabokingking inscription had not persuaded me to envisage the Sriwijayan polity in its initial Sumatran setting as being on a relatively small territorial scale and, to that extent, somewhat fragile. The "Sriwijaya" of the history books tends to be seen as a far-flung and long-enduring empire and with a history not easily associated with a small-scale polity. Yet, we need not underestimate its advantages: a favorable riverine location, natural resources in its hinterland, and access to the international shipping route through the Malacca and Bangka Straits. These advantages were protected by local naval power and also by the conservatism of merchants from distant parts of maritime Asia who had become habituated to the trading amenities they could expect in the Sriwijayan harbor. The Musi entrepôt was not an ephemeral one. Nevertheless, the rulers' relations with other princely families on the island, or, more accurately, with kinship networks organized through female as well as male branches of the families, can hardly have been stable throughout the centuries. This sociological feature of the situation is why I suggest that sequences of tributary missions do not represent trading ventures but rather, as I put it, projections overseas of the Malay overlord's domestic status in Sumatra, which he maintained in spite of the multicentered character of the Sumatran political scene.

CONCLUSION

The time span covered in this essay has extended from the second half of the seventh to early in the fifteenth century, but its point of departure was I-ching. I-ching deserves the benefit of the doubt as an accurate, if limited, source of information. When he traveled in Indonesia his Buddhist training, his interest in the different schools of Buddhism, and his knowledge of India meant that he wrote systematically and therefore informatively. I tried to identify some of his writing

---

[179] The sherds were recovered during an archaeological survey in 1974; see Wolters, "Landfall," pp. 2 and 35.

[180] Ibid., p. 35.

[181] Dr. McKinnon has informed me that recent archaeological evidence suggests that several settlements in the area came to an abrupt and complete end at about this time.

conventions and especially those he used for defining geographical and political units of space. I also discussed the functions of his notes and instances of Buddhist-influenced language and figurative speech. More could be done on these lines.

I believe that I-ching's texts and the text provided by the Bukit Seguntang terrain tend to complement each other, though I have been careful to insist that a better knowledge of Sriwijaya depends on archaeologists. The terrain is now the superior text in Sriwijayan studies. Archaeology on the lower and middle reaches of the Musi river system will, I hope, one day become not only a massive undertaking but also exciting because unexpected information will come to light and encourage new lines of enquiry. I benefited from Professor Wheatley's Langkasuka model; space in the Bukit Seguntang polity seems to be similarly organized. On the other hand, one should not assume that there were no differences among the riverine settlements in the Malay world. Professor Wheatley has observed that the settlement pattern now being revealed in the Musi valley is what one would expect throughout ecosystems developed in the narrow valleys of the uplands and along the rivers and sea faces on the Sunda platform: "dwellings interrupted, typically, at infrequent and irregular intervals only by spatially restricted nuclei of administrative, religious, and service facilities."[182] Archaeologists should remember these words when they ask themselves questions about their discoveries. Does it, they may ask, make the slightest difference whether Sriwijaya was in the Musi valley or elsewhere in the Sumatran coastal lowlands? For example, would the relationships between downstream and upstream in the Musi and Batang Hari river systems have been identical? Or did the dominant polity in the Musi valley possess particular features that distinguished it in scale and coherence from the neighboring polity on the Batang Hari? Research in both valleys may contribute to the comparative study of settlement patterns in the Malay world. And if archaeologists and others eventually succeed in defining particular advantages of the Musi terrain, what would we then learn about the human agency in the local culture responsible for developing the advantages and making these particular "spatially restricted nuclei" cohere? Onerous demands will be made on archaeologists in particular, but the archaeology of "Sriwijaya" is an unusually rich subject for its own sake.

---

[182] Wheatley, *Nāgara and Commandery*, p. 245.

PART III

MAINLAND MANDALAS

CHAPTER SIX

AYUDHYĀ AND THE REARWARD PART OF THE WORLD

The Thai Kingdom of Ayudhyā endured several periods of crisis during its long history from 1350 to 1767, but the crisis that will concern us here happened in 1592. During that year the king, Nareśvara, was well aware that he lived in a hostile world of unusually wide dimensions. His behavior will be discussed as a basis for a brief consideration of Ayudhyā's attitude towards the world, a subject of more than diplomatic interest.

The background to 1592 in the Menam [Chaophraya River] basin will be recalled. The kingdom's security had improved since 1569, when the capital city of Ayudhyā was sacked by the Burman king, Bayinnaung, who appointed a descendant of the rulers of the now extinguished kingdom of Sukhodaya as his vassal prince in Ayudhyā. But neither the vassal nor the vassal's son, Nareśvara, saw their future other than in terms of the greater unity of Ayudhyā.[1] Thai sources state that in 1584 Nareśvara renounced vassal status, while documents of the Ming dynasty reveal that as early as 1575 he sent a mission to Peking to request a seal of office to replace the seal destroyed by the Burmans.[2] Thai armies were now managing to keep the Burmans at bay and punish the Khmers, who had exploited Burman pressure on Ayudhyā by raiding its eastern territories. Nareśvara succeeded his father as king in 1590 and repulsed another Burman invasion. Yet by 1592 he was still not safe. When, towards the end of that year, he was preparing to resume the campaign against the Khmers, the Burmans made their final effort, and early in 1593 a great battle took

---

[1] Their loyalty to Ayudhyā is surely one of the momentous decisions in Thai history. The decision was made in spite of the rivalry between the Thai of the two regions, suggested by Prince Damrong and exploited by the Burmans in 1569: see Prince Dhani's review of Prince Damrong's *The History of King Nareśvara the Great* in *JSS* 38,2 (1951): 74.

[2] 1575 is the date given in the *pên-chi* section of the *Ming-shih* (Po-na edition), 20, 3*a*, and with more detail in the *Shên-tsung shih-lu* (photoprint of a MS copy in the Chiang-su kuo-hsüeh t'u-shu-kuan), 39, 9*b*, and in the *Kuo-ch'üeh* (Ku-chi ch'u-pan shê edition, Peking, 1958), vol. 5, 4269. But the *Ming-shih*, *pên-chi*, 20, 2*a*, and also the *Kuo-ch'üeh*, vol. 5, 4221, refer to a mission as early as 1573. The latter text calls "the king of Siam" *Hua-chao-sung*; the last syllable of the transcription suggests "suen" in Naresuen, or Nareśvara. The Chinese evidence reveals the promptness with which Nareśvara sought to obtain Chinese recognition of Ayudhyā's independent status some years before Bayinnaung died.

place outside the walls of the Thai capital.[3] The king killed the Burman crown prince in personal combat, reconquered Tenasserim and Tavoy, and captured the Khmer capital of Lovek in 1594.

These unbroken successes, reviving Ayudhyā from the ashes of 1569, have invested Naresvara's career with epic quality, and we tend to forget that 1592 was a critical year for him. During that year he had to think promptly and boldly, and he made a decision for which he has never been given sufficient credit. His decision permits a study of the motions of one Thai mind under stress.

Danger came to him in 1592 not only from the immediate east and west of the Menam basin. His capital city was a trading centre, and with trade comes news. Moreover, bad news always travels fast and far, and the geographical setting of the king's situation that year must now be suddenly widened.

The second half of the sixteenth century saw a long period of disunity coming to an end in Japan, and from 1584 the presiding genius was Hideyoshi.[4] Hideyoshi seems to have realized that international commerce offered a means of diverting Japanese vigor and consolidating the islands' newly obtained unity. Their ships were already visiting the Philippine Islands by 1565. In 1589 a Japanese ship, carrying arms, was released by the Spaniards when they were told that it was bound for Siam. Miscellaneous references to Japanese ships in the Philippines, Borneo, and Malacca suggest that Hideyoshi's issue of trading seals in 1592 reflects his concern to expand activities already well underway. Among the ten countries that Japanese possessing seals could visit was Siam.

But Hideyoshi was interested in much more than the unity of Japan and its foreign trade. He has been nicknamed the "Napoleon" of Japan, who dreamed of conquering Asia.[5] By 1589 the maritime world of East and Southeast Asia would have heard disquieting rumors. That year the ruler of the Ryu-kyu Islands saw fit to send him tribute, while the following year he was told that "it had long been [Hideyoshi's] cherished desire to place foreign lands under [his] rule."[6] As long ago as the beginning of the fifteenth century Ayudhyā had been trading with the Ryu-kyu Islands,[7] and here was one way Japanese ambitions could have reached Siam. Hideyoshi was frank in announcing his plans. In 1591 the governor of the Philippines was informed that "Korea, Ryu-kyu, and other nations which are far away have sent their tribute-bearing envoys and paid homage to us." The Spanish governor decided to strengthen his coastal defences and request reinforcements from Mexico and Spain. Thai ships were already trading with Manila by 1586, and the

---

[3] The site of the battle according to F. H. Giles, *Selected Articles from the Siam Society Journal,* VII (Bangkok: The Siam Society, 1959), pp. 138–39. Giles noted that the Burmese account agreed with van Vliet's information.

[4] Background information on Hideyoshi has been obtained from Yoshi S. Kuno, *Japanese Expansion on the Asiatic Continent,* I (Berkeley: University of California Press, 1937); N. Péri, "Essai sur les relations du Japon et de l'Indochine aux XVIe et XVIIe siècles," *BEFEO* 23 (1923): 1–19; G. B. Sansom, *Japan: A Short Cultural History,* 2nd ed. (London: Cresset Press, 1952); Giuliana Stramigioli, "Hideyoshi's Expansionist Policy on the Asiatic Mainland," *Transactions of the Asiatic Society of Japan,* 3rd ser., 3 (December 1954): 74–116.

[5] Kuno, *Japanese Expansion,* p. 143.

[6] Ibid., p. 306.

[7] *Yung-lo shih-lu* (photoprint of a MS copy in the Chiang-su-kuo-t'u-shu-kuan), 31, 2*a*.

Spanish alarm could have been communicated to Siam.[8] And in 1591 Hideyoshi sent a letter to the Portuguese viceroy in Goa, informing him that India would in time be conquered by Japan.[9] He was waging what may be called psychological warfare, and the depression he sought to create in the maritime world of East and Southeast Asia is reflected in a statement by the compiler of the *Ming-shih* that "he was intimidating Ryu-kyu, Luzon, Siam, and the Franks."[10] His boldest disclosure of all, which was his plan to conquer China, certainly, as we shall see, reached Nareśvara's ears. The Thai king, who attached importance to accurate political intelligence, was bound to have known that the Japanese were becoming dangerous.

The Korean king had received a threatening letter in 1590, in which he was warned that he would be expected to assist in the invasion of China. On December 19, 1591, he reported to the Ming emperor in Peking that Japanese informers earlier that year had stated that Hideyoshi had brought Ryu-kyu and "the southern barbarians" into submission and was planning to attack China in the following year.[11]

And so we come to the wider implications of 1592 as a year of crisis for Ayudhyā. Another Korean report reached Peking on June 19 that the Japanese had landed at Pusan. The Korean armies were unable to hold up the invasion, and Chinese reinforcements were insufficient. By early August the Chinese court knew that Seoul was captured, that the Korean king was in flight, and that the Japanese were moving northwards. A conference was held in Peking on August 8, when the decision was taken to mobilize the Chinese forces. On September 10 the Ming court learned that Pyongyang had fallen. Everything now depended on the transfer of a powerful army from the Mongolian border to the relief of stricken Korea. Meanwhile the Minister of War played for time, and a go-between was sent to the Japanese to discuss peace.

Such was the tense situation in Peking when twenty-seven Thai envoys arrived there. The first indication of their presence is a banquet in their honor on October 31, 1592.[12] They presented their tribute on November 16.[13]

What was the occasion for this mission? The Chinese discussed with the envoys an alliance against the Japanese, and the proposal was that the Thai should attack the Japanese islands themselves. The question now arises whether Nareśvara sent the mission and proposal of his own accord or in response to a Chinese appeal for help. Professor Kuno states that on September 2 the emperor told the Korean king that instructions had been sent to foreign countries, including Siam, to invade Japan,[14] while the *Kuo-ch'üeh*, under the date of September 12, notes that Thai help was discussed in Peking; the *Shên-tsung shih-lu*, the basic official documents for this reign,

---

[8] Kuno, *Japanese Expansion*, p. 308; *The Philippine Islands, 1493–1898: Relating to China and the Chinese*, ed. E. H. Blair and J. A. Robertson (Cleveland, OH: A. H. Clark Company, 1915), vol. 7, pp. 35, 138, 221–22. In this period Thai, among other foreign invalids, were being cared for in the Franciscan convent in Manila: see *Readings in Philippine History*, ed. H. de la Costa (Manila: Bookmark, 1965), p. 32.

[9] Kuno, *Japanese Expansion*, p. 314.

[10] *Ming-shih*, 322, 18*b*.

[11] *Kuo-ch'üeh*, vol. 5, 4662.

[12] *Shên-tsung shih-lu*, 252, 10*b*.

[13] Ibid., 253, 6*a*.

[14] Kuno, *Japanese Expansion*, p. 157.

do not, however, confirm this matter.[15] On August 8 the Chinese government, suddenly aware of the grave turn of events in Korea, took the decision to mobilize its forces, but no mention is made of an appeal for outside help.[16] The only suggestion on these lines in the *Shên-tsung shih-lu* is the offering of rewards on January 18, 1593, to anyone, including "the chiefs of the islands" overseas, who killed Hideyoshi.[17] Furthermore, when on February 6, 1593 the Thai alliance was discussed by the Chinese officials, the viceroy of Kuangtung and Kuangsi specifically reported that the Thai envoys had told the Ministry of War that they wished to help the empire, and the viceroy added that they urged that an appeal should be issued to neighboring countries.[18] Though the relevant chapters of the *Shên-tsung shih-lu* may have been incompetently compiled, an appeal for outside assistance is unlikely to have been made before August 8, when the decision to mobilize was taken.[19] If the appeal had been sent to Nareśvara, it would hardly have reached Ayudhyā quickly enough to result in a response that reached Peking before the end of October. In September the southwest monsoon weakens, and it generally comes to an end off the coast of Vietnam about the first week of September. The inevitable delay in shipping communications is perhaps the chief reason for believing that the appeal never reached Ayudhyā. Finally, the Chinese records would almost certainly have made much of Nareśvara's response. That the mission was a result of Thai initiative is reflected in a statement in the *Shên-tsung shih-lu* that the envoys were indignant when their offer was rejected. An order was sent to Nareśvara to keep his ships under control, which suggests that the envoys had told the Chinese that he was ready to take action as soon as his offer was accepted. It is true that the same text describes the Chinese Minister of War as recommending that Siam should be ordered to attack Japan direct, but the passage appears in the account of the debate on the proposal on February 6, 1593, and we do not know the substance of the discussions that had already taken place between the envoys and the Ministry.

Thus no additional facts in the *Shên-tsung shih-lu* upset the understanding of the compilers of the *Ming-shih* and the *Ming hui-yao* that the alliance and strategy were proffered by the king without any prompting from the Chinese.[20] What probably happened was that Hideyoshi's well-advertised intentions reached Ayudhyā along the trade-routes. As early as September 7, 1591, Chinese coastal authorities had reported that Japan was seeking to involve the Ryu-kyu Islands in aggression against China,[21] and the news could easily have been relayed to Siam from southern China or the Philippines. The mission's arrival in Peking at the moment when the Chinese need was greatest seems to be a coincidence.

---

[15] *Kuo-ch'üeh*, vol. 4680. The *Shên-tsung shih-lu*, 251, 5b–6a, does not mention this.

[16] *Shên-tsung shih-lu*, 250, 2b.

[17] Ibid., 255, 7b.

[18] Ibid., 256, 2b.

[19] Hsia Hsieh, compiler of the *Ming T'ung-chien*, notes discrepancies in the evidence for the date of the invasion of Korea and attributes Chinese awareness of the crisis to August 23, 1592; *Ming T'ung-chien*, vol. 3, 2726 (Chung-hua shu-chü edition). Thus, in spite of inaccuracies attributed to the *Shih-lu* for this reign, there is general agreement that the Chinese government did not begin to react vigorously to the crisis before August. The forthcoming publication of the *Hung-kê* text of the *Wan-li shih-lu* may throw additional light on the events of 1592 and early 1593.

[20] *Ming-shih*, 324, 19b; *Ming hui-yao* (Chung-hua shu-chü edition, Peking, 1935), 2, 1514.

[21] *Shên-tsung shih-lu*, 238, 10b.

Naresvara was therefore prepared to send his fleet to attack Japan. Nor need we dismiss the proposal as fantastic. A major problem for the Japanese was lack of shipping to take reinforcements to Korea. The Thai fleet, if it had sailed, might have added to Hideyoshi's difficulties. The nineteenth-century Chinese writer, Wei Yüan, whose recollections of this episode will be noted below, realized that Japan was weak on the sea at this time and regretted the Ming failure to exploit this circumstance.[22]

The alliance came up for debate on February 6, 1593.[23] The viceroy of Kuangtung and Kuangsi, no doubt regarded as an expert on Southeast Asian affairs, seems to have been the chief critic. He emphasized the difficulties of logistics and doubted the Thai motives, and he expressed the hope that, whatever happened, China would not rely on the strength of these "island barbarians." The ministers then withdrew for further discussion, and the project was abandoned. The envoys, as we have seen, were indignant.

We need not concern ourselves further with the Korean war, which ended only with the death of Hideyoshi in 1598. Naresvara is the focus of our interest, and the obvious question must now be asked: why was he prepared to intervene in Northeast Asia?

Mr. Wood, in his history of Siam, suggests that this episode shows no more than that Naresvara was no longer worried by the Burmans; his intentions in making the offer remain inexplicable.[24] Certainly no evidence exists to prove that Hideyoshi's vainglorious claims over the "southern barbarians" ever meant an immediate threat to Siam, nor, in fact, do any documents known to the present writer disclose specific reasons for the king's action in 1592. He may have been inspired merely by goodwill towards the Ming dynasty, with which Ayudhyā had enjoyed good relations from the beginning of its history more than two centuries earlier. On the other hand, 1592 was hardly a suitable year in the Menam basin for so extravagant a demonstration of friendship. Moreover, Naresvara's career, and especially his conduct in face of the persisting threat from Burma, reveals him as a calculating man, intent only to preserve and strengthen his kingdom. One cannot easily picture his undertaking an overseas adventure merely out of chivalrous regard for China.

Perhaps we can begin to reconstruct his motives when we remember that for twenty-three years his single purpose had been to rebuild the kingdom. This objective required him to reinforce his base, which was the city of Ayudhyā itself. Between 1570 and 1586 he had driven off the Khmers no less than six times. In 1580 he had strengthened the defenses of the city, and in 1584, when he renounced his allegiance to Burma, he took the important step of transferring the population of his northern provinces to the neighborhood of Ayudhyā.[25]

---

[22] Ssŭ-yü Têng and John K. Fairbank, *China's Response to the West* (Cambridge, MA: Harvard University Press, 1961), p. 31.

[23] *Shên-tsung shih-lu*, 256, 2a–b.

[24] W. A. R. Wood, *A History of Siam*, rev. ed. (Bangkok: The Siam Barnakich Press, 1933), p. 146. The author is grateful to Mr. C. J. Reynolds, of Cornell, for informing him that Prince Damrong does not refer to this episode in his biography of Naresvara. In a volume dealing with Chinese documents on Siam, Prince Damrong remarked that "it is very surprising that the king should have done this."

[25] These details are from Frankfurter's translation of the "Luang Prasroeth" recension of the *Annals of Ayudhyā, JSS* 6,3 (1909): 22.

But Ayudhyā was more than a concentration of the kingdom's manpower resources. The city had access to the sea and was an important trading centre, bringing supplies and revenues to the royal treasury. The Thai had been trading with China since the middle of the fourteenth century, and glimpses of this continuing trade are available in the decades before Nareśvara came to the fore. In 1519 the Portuguese commander, d'Andrade, interfered with Thai ships in the approaches to Canton.[26] In 1522, when Thai cargo ships reached Kuangtung, a local Chinese official illegally allowed members of his family to trade with them.[27] Well-stocked Ayudhyā missions came to China in the fifth decade of the sixteenth century.[28]

The Japanese, however, were no ordinary traders, likely to swell the economic power of Ayudhyā. They were soldiers of fortune, organized by the feudal families of Japan in pursuit of wealth overseas.[29] The situation that their arrival abroad could provoke is indicated by what happened in the Philippines in 1587, when a Japanese ship's captain offered to recruit 6,000 armed men for expeditions against Brunei, Siam, or China, and then became involved in a Filipino conspiracy against the Spanish government.[30] Thai tradition states that Nareśvara had a bodyguard of 500 Japanese soldiers,[31] and the ready way Japanese residents played a ruffian role in local troubles was seen in Cambodia in the last years of the sixteenth century[32] and in Siam itself early in the following century.

Yet Nareśvara probably saw the Japanese more as a nuisance on the sea than on the land. They had been raiding the Chinese coast throughout the Ming period, latterly in cooperation with Chinese pirates.[33] In 1578 a Chinese pirate, Lin Tao-kan,

---

[26] T'ien Tse Chang, "Malacca and the Failure of the First Portuguese Embassy to Peking," *JSEAH* 3,2 (1962): 52.

[27] *Ming-shih*, 324, 19a.

[28] The Ming documents do not agree on the number of missions in the 1550s. The *Ming-shih, pên-chi*, attributes them to 1554, 1558, 1559, and 1560: 18, 7a; 9a; 9b; 10b. The *Shih-tsung shih-lu* confirms the missions of 1554, 1558, and 1559: 414, 9b; 462, 5a; 476, 4a. Certainly the single mission of 1553, mentioned in the *Ming-shi's* chapter on Ayudhyā, conceals the considerable tributary trade between Ayudhyā and China on the eve of the Burman invasion. Ku Yen-wu, in his *T'ien-hsia chün-kuo li-ping shu* (Ssǔ-pu ts'ung-k'an edition, 1936), 33, 41a–b, gives details of the wide range and great quantities of tribute offered in 1553 and 1558. A Portuguese who managed to trade with Canton in 1552 agreed to pay the "twenty per cent customs tax" paid by the Thai "who frequent these waters under licence of the Emperor of China": see J. M. Braga, *The Western Pioneers and their Discovery of Macao* (Macau: Impr. Nacional, 1949), p. 85. In 1559 the Thai envoys asked that they should be relieved of the tax in order to defray shipping expenses: *Shih-tsung shih-lu*, 476, 4a. "The licence of the Emperor of China" explains why, in 1575, Nareśvara requested the issue of new documents, replacing those destroyed by the Burmans, to facilitate his tributary missions: *Shên-tsung shih-lu*, 39, 9b. Tributary trade was apparently flourishing in the years immediately before the sack of Ayudhyā, and Nareśvara was probably anxious to revive it as soon as possible.

[29] Sansom, *Japan: A Short Cultural History*, pp. 413–14.

[30] H. de la Costa, *The Jesuits in the Philippines, 1581–1768* (Cambridge, MA: Harvard University Press, 1961), pp. 112–15.

[31] F. H. Giles, "Concerning the Japanese in Siam in the 16th and 17th Centuries," *Selected Articles from the Siam Society Journal: Relationship with Portugal, Holland, and the Vatican* (Bangkok: The Siam Society, 1959), vol. 7, p. 143.

[32] B. P. Groslier, *Angkor et le Cambodge au XVIe siècle d'après les sources portugaises et espagnoles* (Paris: Presses universitaires de France, 1958), pp. 43–44. A Japanese murdered a Catholic priest in Ayudhyā sometime after 1599: see Groslier, *Angkor et le Cambodge*, p. 33.

[33] *Ming-shih*, 322, 17.

with his base on the Kuangtung coast, attacked the "black raven" ships of the Thai. The Thai beat off the attack, inflicted heavy casualties on the pirates, and sent them flying for refuge to plan further raids on foreign shipping.[34] Before long Lin Tao-kan was back in business, and the Chinese noted that he was using Japanese.[35] The Thai victory in 1578 was sufficiently famous in China to enable a contemporary writer, Ch'ü Chiu-ssŭ, to remark that it was comparable with the Spanish defeat of the notorious "Limahong" in 1574, the victory of St. Andrew's Day that was still celebrated annually in Manila fifty years later.[36] Nareśvara was anxious to strengthen his kingdom by means of foreign trade, and his conquest of Tenasserim and Tavoy in 1593 has been interpreted as evidence of his determination to secure ports on the Indian Ocean.[37] Thus the prospect of further Japanese adventurers overseas, supported by Hideyoshi's well-advertised claim to be the overlord of Asia, is the most satisfactory explanation at present available for his decision to take part in the war against Japan. He must have had confidence in the ability of his fleet to give a good account of itself.

Nevertheless, Nareśvara could excusably have told himself that the Ming empire had much more at stake in fighting Japan. The Thai mission sailed to Peking with the monsoon in the middle of 1592. Ahead for the king lay another campaigning season, and at the moment when his envoys were in conference in Peking, he himself was probably fighting the Burmans. His circumstances in the Menam basin were such that he had every reason for minding his own business.ṃṃ

Such was Nareśvara's decision in 1592, and now we must ask ourselves whether we are dealing with a gallant but quixotic episode.

The view will be advanced that his willingness to attack Japan, communicated through a special mission of twenty-seven envoys, was a rational one, and that he was revealing himself as the confident exponent of an ancient tradition of diplomacy in Southeast Asia, much older than the Thai kingdoms but one that the Thai had fruitfully assimilated. The tradition may be defined as a facility for seeing one's place in the widest possible world. The king's conduct in 1592 was a calculated response to his assessment of the needs of the international situation.

Two texts, containing Chinese impressions of the king that year, allow us to examine more closely his processes of reasoning. T'an Ch'ien, writing about fifty years later, states:

> Hsiao Yen, viceroy of Kuangtung and Kuangsi, reported to the emperor: [the king of] Siam was angry with the *kampaku* [of Japan]. His sense of duty moved him, with neighborly sympathy, to help the emperor.[38]

---

[34] *Shên-tsung shih-lu*, 79, 4a–b. Perhaps this event explains why later that year the Thai king was given an imperial seal: ibid., 80, 4b. The "black ravens" may refer to the *haṃsa* or *garuḍa* on the ships. An excellent contemporary Japanese illustration of a Thai ship can be seen in C. N. Spinks, "Siam and the Pottery Trade of Asia," *JSS* 44,2 (1956): facing p. 82.

[35] *Shên-tsung shih-lu*, 80, 2b.

[36] Quoted in *Kuo-ch'üeh*, vol. 5, 4276. The Spaniards believed that the Chinese pirate, "Limahong," had Japanese in his force: see Blair and Robertson, *The Philippine Islands, 1493–1898*, vol. 4, p. 38.

[37] D. G. E. Hall, *A History of South-East Asia*, 2nd ed. (New York, NY: St. Martin's Press, 1964), p. 253.

[38] *Kuo-ch'üeh*, vol. 5, 4691. Hideyoshi relinquished the post of *kampaku*, or Regent, in 1591.

The compiler of the *Ming-shih* states:

> In 1592 Japan attacked Korea. [The king of Siam] requested that he should secretly send troops for a direct attack on Japan in order to embarrass [Japan's] rear.[39]

These two statements make it clear that Nareśvara was understood to have a capacious sense of international responsibilities as well as a flair for bold strategy. The Chinese skeptics in Peking, aware that Siam was a distant country not involved in the struggle between Japan and China, could not understand his motives, but one person would certainly have applauded the decision to intervene in the affairs of Northeast Asia. This person was Kauṭilya, who lived in India in the fourth century BCE and is accredited with the famous textbook on statecraft known as the *Arthaśāstra*. Kauṭilya is sometimes called the "Machiavelli" of India, the advocate of unscrupulous policies. Nevertheless, his often brutally realistic advice is based on a view of warring states that was accepted by the later Indian theorists, including the famous Manu, whose name is honored in Southeast Asian epigraphy.

Kauṭilya, in the style of Indian scientific writing, provides a comprehensive list of definitions of political phenomena and an equally comprehensive range of policies recommended for meeting the problems of a "conqueror," the king whom he is advising. The identification of predicaments to permit rapid decision is what concerns Kauṭilya. Two main categories of external relations have to be taken into account, and the sequence in which they are introduced in the *Arthaśāstra* is significant: relations with enemies and with friends.[40] For Kauṭilya, and also for Manu,

> ... the king who is situated anywhere immediately on the circumference of the conqueror's territory is termed the enemy.[41]

> The king who is likewise situated close to the enemy, but separated from the conqueror only by the enemy, is termed the friend [of the conqueror].[42]

But the international situation is more complicated than a mere confrontation of king, enemy, and friend.

> In front of the conqueror and close to his enemy there happen to be situated kings, such as the conqueror's friend, and next to him the enemy's friend, and next to the latter the conqueror's friend, and next to him the enemy's friend's friend.[43]

---

[39] *Ming-shih*, 324, 19*b*.

[40] R. Shamasastry, *Kauṭilya's Arthaśāstra*, 4th ed. (Mysore: Raghuveer Printing Press, 1951), p. 290.

[41] Shamasastry, *Arthaśāstra*, p. 290.

[42] Ibid.; *The Laws of Manu* (S.B.E., XXV) (Oxford: The Clarendon Press, 1886), VII, p. 158.

[43] Shamasastry, *Arthaśāstra*, p. 290.

Thus Kauṭilya and his successors thought in terms of an indefinitely enlarged circle of states, always unstable, for which the term was *maṇḍala*. The *maṇḍala* was the ideal organization of all relevant space. Every kingdom was, in principle, part of a single and interrelated system, and no kingdom could hope to survive by ignoring its neighbors. Independence defended by genuine neutrality was out of the question. Only vassals, forgoing the right to have their own "foreign policy," could enjoy neutrality. The king survived the exigencies of life in the circle by exploiting the advantages offered by its complex composition; the geographical pattern was matched by an equally complicated pattern of alliances. Thus the king should realize that:

> in the rear of the conqueror there happen to be situated a rearward enemy, a rearward friend, an ally of the rearward enemy, and an ally of the rearward friend.[44]

But the king was required not only to identify his location in the circle of states, recognizing his enemies and friends at varying removes from himself. He had also to decide on his priorities of attack, remembering that his enemies, like him, were involved in intra-circle warfare. Kauṭilya poses the problem of military priorities and gives an instantaneous reply:

> When two enemies, one an assailable enemy and another a strong enemy, are equally involved in troubles, which of them is to be marched against first?

> The strong enemy is to be marched against first; after vanquishing him, the assailable enemy is to be attacked, for, when a strong enemy has been vanquished, an assailable enemy will volunteer of his own accord to help the conqueror; but not so a strong ally.[45]

The bold policy of taking on one's stronger enemy first is recommended even when that enemy is less embarrassed by troubles than one's weaker enemy.

> The conqueror should march against the strong enemy under less troubles, for the troubles of the strong enemy, though less, will be augmented when attacked.[46]

But Kauṭilya was aware of a further strategic possibility, which was to attack the rear of an enemy engaged in fighting elsewhere. He devotes a chapter to this interesting technique.

> Resources being equal, he who captures the rear of one who has made vast preparations gains more advantages, for one who has made vast preparations has to put down the enemy in the rear only after destroying

---

[44] Ibid., p. 290.

[45] Ibid., pp. 303–4. An "assailable enemy" is defined as "a neighbouring foe of considerable power" who is "involved in calamities or has taken himself to evil ways": *Arthaśāstra*, p. 290.

[46] Ibid., p. 304.

> the frontal enemy ... Preparations being equal, he who captures the rear
> of one who has marched out with all his resources gains more
> advantages; for one whose base is undefended is easy to be subdued, but
> not one who has marched out with a part of the army after having made
> arrangements to defend the rear.[47]

So much for Kauṭilya. We need not imagine that Nareśvara in 1592 took out the *Arthaśāstra* from his library and consulted the appropriate chapters to meet his needs. Nevertheless, his policy that year, incomprehensible to the Chinese, is remarkably consistent with Kauṭilya's theory. The king of Ayudhyā had undoubtedly identified the components of a very extensive *maṇḍala*. His immediate and "assailable" enemies were weak Cambodia and weakened Burma. Japan was seen as a powerful "rearward" enemy, likely to become an immediate and dangerous one unless Hideyoshi were humbled. In these circumstances China was Nareśvara's "rearward" friend. A less nimble-minded man might have told himself that, when Japan struck China in its Korean rear, he had no self-evident reason to intervene; but not so, apparently, Nareśvara. Japanese ambitions merely created a new problem of priorities, which were assessed in a manner worthy of Kauṭilya. Japan, though stronger than Cambodia or Burma, was committing its armies to the massive campaign against Korea and China, its frontal enemies, thus making itself vulnerable to an attack in the rear by the "black raven" ships of Ayudhyā.

The elements in Nareśvara's strategy in 1592 have been interpreted in terms of ancient Indian statecraft. Very clearly the king had a pronounced sense of the rear side of the world of Ayudhyā, which happened to comprise Northeast Asia. How may we explain his sense of rearward situations?

The *maṇḍala* conception was an ancient and familiar one in Southeast Asia, except among the semi-sinicized Vietnamese. A remarkable illustration, seen from the Javanese point of view, is contained in a fourteenth-century poem, where Java, overlord of the archipelago, is described as "ringed" by many countries "protected by the Illustrious Prince" of Majapahit. The protected countries included the Thai kingdoms, Cambodia, and Champa. The single Southeast Asia country of "ally" status in the Javanese *maṇḍala* was Vietnam, an exception which suggests that Vietnam, with its un-Indian background, was seen as being different from the rest of the region.[48]

Centuries earlier, however, mainland Southeast Asia had known a more substantial *maṇḍala*-type situation. The founder of the first city of Angkor at the end of the ninth century, Yaśovarman I, was called

> ... the supreme master of the earth, which had for its limits the
> barbarians, the ocean, China, and Champa.[49]

A century later the world of Angkor was described in identical terms.[50] In the tenth century, in spite of references to royal successes in this *maṇḍala*,[51] the control of

[47] Shamasastry, *Arthaśāstra*, pp. 329–30.

[48] T. G. T. Pigeaud, *Java in the 14th Century: A Study in Cultural History: The Nagara-kĕrtagama*, III, (The Hague: M. Nijhoff, 1960), pp. 16-18.

[49] George Coedès, *Inscriptions du Cambodge*, IV (Paris, E. de Boccard, 1952), p. 98. Hereafter, *IC*.

[50] Coedès, *IC*, VII (Paris: E. de Boccard, 1964), p. 182.

the lands from the China Sea to the Bay of Bengal was still unrealized, but in the eleventh and twelfth centuries the Khmers made determined efforts to transform their aspiration into a reality. The climax came during the reign of the great Jayavarman VII at the end of the twelfth century and the beginning of the thirteenth, when the Menam basin and Champa temporarily acknowledged the hegemony of Angkor. Memories of this vast empire would have made a profound impression on the Thai chiefs in the Menam basin, asserting their independence and power in the thirteenth century, and even in the fourteenth century the Thai ruler of Sukhodaya remembered Jayavarman VII as the "god."[52]

But the Thai princes were influenced by more than the example of Angkor. Their predecessors in the Menam basin were Mon princes, and we should not imagine that the Buddhist Mons saw the world very differently from the Khmers. Fringing metropolitan Cambodia to the north and west were several Mon kingdoms, whose inscriptions are in Mon, Khmer, Pali, and Sanskrit, with contents referring to Brahmanical cults as well as to Buddhist monasteries.[53] These Mon rulers were certainly familiar with Indian political ideas. A northern Thai source indicates that Lopburi in the thirteenth century was where one could study secular Indian subjects,[54] while Professor Jean Boisselier has recently suggested that continuity should be seen between a tenth-century Brahmanical sanctuary tower in Mon Lopburi and the later *prang* tower of Ayudhyā, with the implication that Khmer-like features in early Ayudhyā may perhaps be attributed to an earlier Mon culture there, similar to but not necessarily derived from Angkor.[55] Early Ayudhyā, with its Mon background, would have been deeply impregnated with royal Brahmanical cults, and we need not be surprised that in 1601, when Nareśvara was still alive,

> ... statues of Śiva and Viṣṇu were received, and on one and the same day homage was paid to the four statues (of the Brahmanical gods) by being carried in procession.[56]

Śiva was the patron of learning, and with these cults would have been associated learned Brahmans, familiar with the Indian treatises. Moreover, Dr. Wyatt, in a study of Thai education, has discussed the manner in which Buddhist monasteries were themselves custodians of Sanskrit learning.[57] The learning in question included the *śāstras* on government, which dealt with the king and his relationship with the world.

---

[51] For example, Coedès, *IC*, I (Hanoi: Imprimerie d'Extrême Orient, 1937), p. 135; Coedès, *IC*, V (Paris: E. de Boccard, 1953), p. 168.

[52] George Coedès, *Recueil des inscriptions du Siam*, I (Bangkok, 1924), p. 49.

[53] George Coedès, "Nouvelles données epigraphiques sur l'histoire de l'Indochine centrale," *JA* 246 (1958): 125–42. For archaeological evidence of Brahmanical cults see J. Boisselier, "Récentes recherches archéologiques en Thailande," *Arts Asiatiques* 12 (1965): 142–43, 156.

[54] Mentioned by D. K. Wyatt, "The Beginnings of Modern Education in Thailand, 1868-1910" (PhD thesis, Cornell University, 1966), p. 10, n. 24. [Published as *The Politics of Reform in Thailand: Education under the Reign of King Chulalongkorn* (New Haven and London: Yale University Press, 1969), p. 5, n. 8.—Ed.]

[55] J. Boisselier, "Récentes recherches," pp. 131–32, 136, 143.

[56] Frankfurter's translation of the "Luang: Prasroeth" version of the *Annals of Ayudhyā, JSS* 6,3 (1909): 25.

[57] D. K. Wyatt, "The Beginnings," pp. 9–14; [*Politics of Reform*, pp. 4–6.—Ed.].

The Theravāda persuasion of the Thai did not mean a breach with the so-called "Hindu" past. Professor Coedès has observed that the Ayudhyā monarchy seems to have made every effort to continue the traditions of the rulers of Angkor instead of flouting them,[58] a circumstance that symbolizes one of the important continuities in Southeast Asian history. The monks had no special political message beyond teaching the king's role as protector of Buddhism and exemplar of moral and merciful behavior, and a record of Nareśvara's reign quotes monks as disclaiming the ability to give advice on a practical matter.[59] Perhaps the chief political consequence of Theravāda Buddhism in mainland Southeast Asia at this time was to reinforce Thai exuberance with Buddhist zeal. No longer were the heroes of the Indian epics the only models for successful kings. Aśoka and the Sinhalese kings, defenders of Buddhism, were now admired. Thus, according to Prince Damrong, Nareśvara emulated the great Sinhalese king Duttugemunu, the victor against the Tamils of the second century BCE, by building a pagoda on the spot where he fought the Burman crown prince.[60]

With this Khmer and Mon background in mind, we can move easily into the world the rulers of Ayudhyā recognized. Mainland Southeast Asia remained a geographically extensive circle of principalities. Thai initiative did not lead to a great pan-Thai kingdom. Only the Mongol threat at the end of the thirteenth century produced a short-lived alliance among the Thai leaders. Some Thai in fourteenth-century Ayudhyā were probably anxious to end once and for all the struggle with the Khmers for the control of the lands between Ayudhyā and Angkor, and thus the founder of the new city of Ayudhyā, Rāmādhipati I, captured Angkor in 1369. Other Ayudhyā Thai were concerned to extend their overlordship in the Menam basin.[61] The Chiengmai rulers in the north sought to bring their influence to bear on the foothill princes to the east and west of Chiengmai, seeing Sukhodaya as a buffer state between Chiengmai and Ayudhyā.

The Burmese wars of the sixteenth century dramatically widened the world of Ayudhyā. The Burmans, Mons, Shans, northern Thai, Lao, Khmers, and Ayudhyā Thai were now enmeshed in a vast *maṇḍala* of conflict, providing plenty of opportunity for skilful diplomacy in the Indian tradition. Manu advises the king "constantly to explore the weaknesses of his foe,"[62] and before the opportunity arose of attacking Japan in the rear, Nareśvara was attacking the Burmans by means of the Mons of Lower Burma.[63] Long before him Jayavarman VII's technique in fighting

[58] George Coedès, *The Making of South East Asia* (Berkeley: University of California Press, 1966), p. 146.

[59] U Aung Thein's translation of Prince Damrong's "Our Wars with the Burmese," *JBRS* 40,2 (1957): 170.

[60] Damrong, "Our Wars with the Burmese," p. 167. Another reference to Duttugemunu appears on an Ava inscription of 1375: Than Tun, "History of Burma, AD 1300–1400," *JBRS* 42,2 (1959): 130.

[61] For some suggestions on this subject see the present writer's "The Khmer King at Basan (1371–1373)," *Asia Major* 12,1 (1966): 83–84.

[62] *The Laws of Manu*, VII, p. 102.

[63] For example, U Aung Thein's translation of Prince Damrong's "Our Wars with the Burmese," *JBRS* 38,2 (1955): 181, 184.

Champa had been to encourage traditional antipathies between northern and southern Chams.[64] All these expedients would have delighted Kautilya.

This is the background of experience that helps to explain the diplomacy of the Ayudhyā kings in the seventeenth century. With the growing competition among European traders, new opportunities for alliances became available for Naresvara's successors, always isolated in their immediate neighborhood. The Dutch were sought against the Portuguese, and then the French were sought against the Dutch. Sometimes we may be tempted to see Nārāyana's alliance with Louis XIV as a bold improvisation in the spirit of the nineteenth and twentieth centuries. But Nārāyana was the heir of the traditions of Naresvara, who in turn inherited many centuries of Southeast Asian experience.

By the nineteenth century, the Thai were realizing that they lived in an enormously wide world of danger, and their flexible response is well known. Not surprisingly, foreigners began to recognize that the Thai possessed some special skill in the conduct of international relations. A Vietnamese, familiar with Bangkok, begged the Huê ruler to emulate the Thai in playing off one European power against another.[65] In 1910 Douwes Dekker commented on the remarkable diplomatic skill of the Thai as one of the signs of Asian revival.[66] But the compliment that is more appropriately mentioned here takes us back to 1592. Shortly after the Opium War of 1839–42, Wei Yüan took an anxious look at the perilous world encompassing China. In his book, the *Hai-kuo t'u-chih,* he recalled Siam's loyal offer of 1592. Observing that Britain had established a powerful base in Singapore, Wei Yüan invoked the proposal of 1592 and suggested that Siam, with the help of Vietnam, should be ordered to send troops to recover Malacca and Singapore from the British.[67] The Chinese mood had changed since their time of pride and skepticism at the end of the sixteenth century.

With this belated Chinese acknowledgement of Naresvara's conduct in 1592, we shall end these reflections on Ayudhyā's sense of the rearward side of its world. But Thai responses to the outside world involved much more than an agile diplomacy. By way of conclusion a wider perspective will be broached for the subject of Ayudhyā and the world. Naresvara's initiative in 1592 is only a specific illustration of a far-ranging outlook that the Thai inherited from earlier Southeast Asia and fruitfully adapted during the course of their history. Perhaps our understanding of the region and its behavior even today may require us to study certain liberal influences that have shaped the outward-lookingness of the Southeast Asian mentality over many centuries.

The world view of Ayudhyā was, in the final analysis, "Hindu," by which no more is meant than that its classical exposition is in the Sanskrit literature of India, of which Kautilya's *Arthasāstra* is a sample. This literature, from the first centuries of the Christian era, was the matrix that provided the courtly minds of Southeast Asia

---

[64] The Khmer-Cham wars of the twelfth century may have been accompanied by the expedient of stimulating internal dynastic dissensions in each other's country; on this possibility see J. Boisselier, *La statuaire du Champa: Recherches sur les cultes et l'iconographie* (Paris: École Française d'Extrême-Orient, 1963), p. 316.

[65] Le Thanh Khoi, *Le Viet-nam: Histoire et civilization* (Paris: Editions de Minuit, 1955), pp. 364–65.

[66] Douwes Dekker, *Koloniale Rundschau*, 2 (Munich, 1910), p. 566.

[67] Wei Yüan, *Hai-kuo t'u-chih*, 4, *Hai-an kao*, 3, 12*b*–14*a* (Ku-wei t'ang reprint of 1849).

with their windows on the "civilized" world. As a result, several important assumptions came easily to them.

They believed that the contents of the Sanskrit books were the gift of the gods and were therefore the possession of all civilized men, no matter whether they lived in Southeast Asia or in India. We cannot exaggerate the significance of this sense of a common culture, for it meant that men living in small countries in Southeast Asia learnt to "think big" and to see themselves, their problems, and their aspirations as being in no way different from what would be found at the most distant end of the "civilized" world. Because of this catholic outlook, ideas could be shared within the framework of a common élite culture without any feeling that one country was merely borrowing blindly from another. Again, this élite assumed that, although the basic formulations contained in the sacred Sanskrit texts had universal and eternal relevance, men were not relieved of the responsibility of exercising their reasoning faculty to ensure that the texts were interpreted so as not to conflict with contemporary needs. In the words of a modern scholar, "the ultimate test of the law of the social order" was the judgment of cultured and enlightened men.[68] Thus the Indians wrote continuous commentaries on the sacred texts, and Kauṭilya himself laid down the rule "that reasoning based on the king's law prevails in the event of its conflict with the canon."[69] The intellectual training of the Southeast Asian élite would have been such that they, too, came to accept the sensible view that elaborations of knowledge, while always contained within terms of universal application, were possible and indeed necessary. Their mental flexibility, encouraged by Indian example, would have been developed even further by the need to adapt Indian generalities to the requirements of Southeast Asian customary law. Finally, the élite believed that a fundamentally important part of this universal knowledge dealt with what we may call "the science of government," conceived as a matter of moral and academic training rather than of mere intuition.

This view of the world was an intellectual one, sustained by values that transcended linguistic or political boundaries. The view fostered self-confidence, a sense of what was practical, and a belief that modernity could be expressed in formulations of universal relevance. Its buoyant mood is reflected in the inscriptions of Angkor, a magnificent corpus that the student of Southeast Asian intellectual history cannot ignore. Here we find the emphasis on the contribution of education to good government. The Khmer kings were "drunk in the ocean of the *śāstras*" or "versed in the science of politics." "This sage," through proper implementation of the principles of government, "achieved great results."[70] A king could be described as "the artisan of the stability of the universe."[71] Nor did the Khmer scholars imagine that they were living in a borrowed civilization. The founder of the city of Angkor was described as being as clever "in all the sciences as if he had been their inventor"; their inventor was no mere Hindu but the god Śiva himself.[72] A royal teacher in

---

[68] U. N. Ghoshal, *A History of Indian Political Ideas* (Bombay: Oxford University Press, 1959), p. 11.

[69] Ibid., p. 11; Shamasastry, *Arthaśāstra*, p. 171.

[70] Coedès, *IC*, I, p. 113.

[71] Coedès, *IC*, IV, p. 253.

[72] Quoted by L. P. Briggs, *The Ancient Khmer Empire* (Philadelphia, PA: The American Philosophical Society, 1951), p. 113.

Angkor was "the envy of the sages of the other continents."[73] We can also find hints of the flexible outlook of genuine "Hinduism," which perhaps was India's greatest gift to Southeast Asia. The claim could be made on behalf of one king that "he put aside the actions practiced by the ancient sages and taught in their treatises and accomplished only what was new."[74] His son helped his subjects by skillfully "adapting" his methods.[75] Behind the conventional language of adulation we should learn to recognize ideals that expressed standards sought in times of peace, when educated men in Angkor were able to see themselves on terms of equality with the rest of the civilized world.

This outward-looking intellectual heritage, sketched all too inadequately, awaited the Thai in the Menam basin. The essence of the heritage was that books were the windows on the world, and the Thai kept the windows open.[76] Books contained the wisdom of the civilized world, and the good ruler could not afford to ignore them. Nareśvara, in his year of crisis during 1592, was able to apply old formulas concerning the rearward part of the world of Ayudhyā, and an attempt has been made to interpret the effortless way his mind worked. The same cultural heritage, evoked by the Thai genius, helped them to enter the "modern" world. But other Southeast Asian peoples are also heirs to flexible and pragmatic traditions, born of the marriage of Indian precepts and local realities. Perhaps one day historians may be able to suggest that pedagogic influences during nearly two millennia were one of the region's concealed resources in the present years of crisis.

---

[73] Coedès, *IC*, I, p. 154.

[74] Ibid., p. 133.

[75] Coedès, *IC*, 1V, 97–98.

[76] One instance of an open window has been suggested by Mr. Simmonds. Perhaps some of the stylized imagery in the dawn theme in Thai poetry during the seventeenth century may be an adaptation of Bengali poetry of the period of Govindadas and Chandidas: E. H. S. Simmonds, in *Eos: An Enquiry into the Theme of Lovers' Meetings and Partings at Dawn in Poetry*, ed. Arthur T. Hatto (London: Mouton, 1965), p. 189.

CHAPTER SEVEN

JAYAVARMAN II'S MILITARY POWER: THE TERRITORIAL FOUNDATION OF THE ANGKOR EMPIRE

Jayavarman II is the famous Khmer ruler who, in the first half of the ninth century and after a hundred years when Khmer overlordship had been in abeyance, was consecrated on Mount Mahendra "to ensure that the country of the Kambujas would no longer be dependent on Java and that there would be no more than one sovereign who was *cakravartin.*"[1] His inscriptions have never been recovered, but Khmers in later times remembered his reign as the time when their ancestors, his supporters, were rewarded with estates. Historians are today tending to regard the reign as a somewhat less significant period in Khmer history than earlier generations of historians had supposed. Its conventionally accepted length (802–850 CE) is no longer taken for granted.[2] The king's cult, inaugurated on Mount Mahendra, may not have been as innovative as was originally believed.[3] Even the extent of the king's temporal power has been revised. In 1952, Dupont, clarifying the king's chronology, came to the conclusion that his territorial authority had been exaggerated and that his bid for overlordship had failed.[4]

---

[1] George Coedès, *The Indianized States of Southeast Asia*, ed. Walter F. Vella, trans. Susan Brown Cowing (Honolulu, HI: East-West Center Press, 1968), p. 99.

[2] C. Jacques, "Sur les données chronologiques de la stèle de Tuol Ta Pec," *BEFEO* 58 (1971): 165–66.

[3] The literature on Jayavarman II's cult is surveyed in Hubert de Mestier du Bourg, "A propos du culte du dieu-roi (devarāja) au Cambodge," *Cahiers d'histoire mondiale* 11 (1968–69): 499–516. On the same subject, also see I. W. Mabbett, "Devarāja," *JSEAH* 10,2 (1969): 204–9, and Sachchidanand Sahai, *Les institutions politiques et l'organisation administrative du Cambodge ancien (VI–XIII siècles)* (Paris: Publications de l'Ecole Française d'Extrême-Orient, no. 75, 1970), pp. 40–46.

[4] P. Dupont, "Les débuts de la royauté angkorienne," *BEFEO* 46,1 (1952): 168–69. Professor Sahai has followed Dupont's reconstruction of Jayavarman II's territorial authority: Sahai, *Les institutions politiques*, p. 141.

Only one aspect of Jayavarman's reign, his military power, will be discussed in this essay. Epigraphic and Chinese evidence, unavailable to Dupont in 1952, indicate that Jayavarman was certainly as successful a warrior as any of his predecessors had been and was probably the most powerful king whom his contemporaries could recall.

Jayavarman II's career is outlined stage by stage in the Sdok Kak Thom of 1052.[5] Dupont, relating other epigraphic evidence to its succinct details, noted the Palhal inscription of 1069, which states that when, at the beginning of the reign, the king was still at Indrapura on the Mekong to the east of Kompong Cham, he conquered an enemy.[6] The king therefore emerges as a victor in southern Cambodia, and the Vat Samrong inscription, published in 1964 and probably written in the first half of the tenth century, supports this impression of his initial prowess. The Vat Samrong inscription, which comes from Ba Phnom in southern Cambodia and the site of the ancient Khmer capital city of Vyādhapura, refers to a ceremony performed by the Mratāñ Śrī Pṛthivīnarendra at the king's command to prevent Kambujadeśa from being taken over by "Java."[7] Coedès suggests that this ceremony in the south occurred before the king ruled at Mount Mahendra in the north.[8]

The performance of so important a ceremony of state means that the king's prestige in the south was considerable,[9] and further information about the Mratāñ Śrī Pṛthivīnarendra, noted below, suggests that the king's representative at this ceremony was, at a relatively early stage in the reign and perhaps at the time of the ceremony mentioned in the Vat Samrong inscription, also the commander of a powerful royal army. First, however, other consequences of Jayavarman's authority in the south may be noted. He was able to dispose of lands in the Ba Phnom region[10] and in the Kompong Thom region east of the Tonlé Sap.[11] He was also able to attract to his side two brothers, whose ancestral home was at Angkor Borei not far south of Vyādhapura.[12] The Angkor Borei area was part of the *pramān* of Vyādhapura, where, during the reign of Jayavarman's son and successor, Jayavarman III, other members

---

[5] G. Coedès and P. Dupont, "Les stèles de Sdok Kak Thom, Phnom Sandak, et Prah Vihar," *BEFEO* 43 (1943–46): 56–154.

[6] G. Coedès, "La stèle de Palhal," *BEFEO* 13,6 (1913): 33; Dupont, "Les débuts," p. 148. Indrapura's location is discussed by Coedès in *Indianized States*, p. 98.

[7] G. Coedès, *Inscriptions du Cambodge*, VII (Hanoi: Imprimerie d'Extrême Orient, 1964), p. 133. Hereafter, *IC*.

[8] Ibid., p. 129. The significance of "Java" in this context is still unknown. The country in question must surely have been in the archipelago or on the Malay Peninsula. Coedès discusses the problem in *Indianized States*, pp. 92–93. Professor Boechari, in conversation with the author, has said that a recently discovered inscription from southern Sumatra persuades him that the *bhūmi Jāva*, mentioned in the Kota Kapur inscription of Śrīvijaya, dated 686, refers to an area in the extreme south of Sumatra. On the latter inscription, see Coedès, *Indianized States*, p. 83.

[9] Professor Boisselier has noted this implication of the Vat Samrong inscription: J. Boisselier, "Les linteaux Khmers du VIIIe siècle. Nouvelles donnés dur le style de Kompong Prah," *Artibus Asiae* 30, 2/3 (1968): 141.

[10] *IC*, II, p. 144. A tenth-century legal dispute in the Ba Phnom area seems to have had its origins in Jayavarman's reign: *IC*, VII, pp. 24–25.

[11] *IC*, VI, pp. 137–38; II, p. 109.

[12] Dupont, "Les débuts," pp. 148–49, quoting the Palhal inscription.

of this family were living.[13] Jayavarman II's influence in southern Cambodia is also the likely background to the *Chên-la* missions to China in 813 and 814.[14] The *Ts'ê-fu yüan-kuei* does not supply the king's name or his reasons for communicating with the Chinese court,[15] but the missions are significant because, in the eighth century, envoys had been sent more frequently from the northern kingdom of *Mjuən-tân* than from southern Cambodia. The last certain southern mission was as long ago as 710.[16] Evidently a prince with high pretensions was ruling in southern Cambodia in 813–814.

The consequence of the changed political situation in the south is revealed in further evidence. The location of only one of the king's conquests is identified. His victim was Malyāng in northwestern Cambodia and west of the Tonlé Sap. Dupont notes that the conquest took place by 816 at the latest, which is not long after the missions to China in 813 and 814.[17] The royal general on this occasion was the same Mratañ Śrī Pṛthivīnarendra who had performed the ceremony in the Vat Samrong inscription. His birthplace is unknown, but two of his subordinates were the brothers from Angkor Borei. The general requested the king to reward them with land in the Porsat area west of the Tonlé Sap.[18]

The conquest of Malyāng was a notable achievement. In the seventh century, northwestern Cambodia had been conquered twice by would-be Khmer overlords.[19] The first occasion was by Bhavavarman I, perhaps towards the end of the sixth or the beginning of the seventh century. The region subsequently recovered its independence, and in 638 four chiefs, including the ruler of Malyāng, sent missions to China. The reconquest was by Jayavarman I, who began his campaign between January 31, 656, and June 14, 657. The campaign, which included Malyāng among its targets, was not completed until some time between 671 and 682. By 682, Jayavarman I seems to have controlled the whole of northwestern Cambodia west of the Tonlé Sap and south of the Dangreks. His triumph in this region was an important reason for his claim to be a *cakravartin*, attested in his inscription at Vat Phu. Jayavarman II, fighting in the same region, was not seen by his contemporaries as taming a weak fringe territory, perhaps important because it lay at a distance from the sea and safe from attacks by "Java." Instead he fought in a region whose subjection was necessary if he were to make good his claim to be the new Khmer overlord. He was able to

---

[13] Coedès, "La stèle de Palhal," p. 34. Members of this family were favorites of Jayavarman III.

[14] *Ts'ê-fu yüan-kuei* (1642 edition, published in Peking in 1960), 972, 11417b. Hereafter, *TFYK*. The text has been checked in the Southern Sung woodblock print at the Seikado Bunko, Tokyo. For *TFYK*'s consistent use of the term "*Chên-la*" to refer to southern Cambodia, see the author's "North-western Cambodia in the Seventh Century," *BSOAS* 37,2 (1974): 355–84. [Reprinted in *Classical Civilizations of South East Asia: An Anthology of Articles Published in the Bulletin of SOAS*, ed. Vladimir Braginsky (London and New York, NY: RoutledgeCurzon, 2002).—Ed.]

[15] Cham raids on southern Cambodia may have been one reason. On these raids, see Coedès, *Indianized States*, p. 104.

[16] *TFYK*, 970, 11404a. A southern mission may have come in 750; P. Pelliot, *BEFEO* 4,1–2 (1904): 212, n. 2.

[17] Dupont, "Les débuts," pp. 148–49, quoting the Palhal inscription. Dupont has corrected Coedès's date to read "816."

[18] Coedès, "La stèle de Palhal," p. 33.

[19] The evidence is discussed in the author's "North-western Cambodia in the Seventh Century."

impose his authority there because he had already attracted a military following in southern Cambodia.

The conquest of Malyāng was permanent, and in 893 the territory was described as a *pramān*.[20] Other principalities in northwestern Cambodia, also conquered, may be represented by the expression "all the districts," including Malyāng, which the king ordered his officials "to pacify."[21] The details of the campaigns have not been recovered, but the consequences are revealed in the subsequent decades. Jayavarman III visited Garyāk, where the two brothers from Angkor Borei had received lands.[22] Sukṣmavindu, of the family of Jayavarman II's *purohita*, was granted land in the Dangreks province during Jayavarman III's reign.[23] As late as 868, part of the Korat plateau north of the Dangreks was described as being "outside Kambudeśa,"[24] but an inscription of Indravarman I (877–889), dated 886, has been found some miles northwest of Ubon in the Mun valley.[25] By 886, a Khmer king exercised authority north of the Dangreks. Yaśovarman I (889–910/12)[26] built a monastery near Sisophon, not far south of the Dangreks,[27] and by 928 the province of Vīrendra, just north of the Dangreks at the western end of the range, had been established.[28] The momentum of Jayavarman II's campaigns in northwestern Cambodia was therefore maintained. His victories must have been regarded by his contemporaries, aware of Jayavarman I's performance in the seventh century, as a yardstick of his military prowess and a major justification for his claim to be their overlord and protector.[29]

The Malyāng campaign was over by 816 at the latest. At that time, the king was still in "the eastern district" immediately to the east of the future Angkor site. The "eastern district" is only the second of the six, consecutive royal residences attributed to the king in the Sdok Kak Thom inscription. He remained there until at least 822,[30] leaving it to reside at Hariharālaya, not far away. The duration of his residence at Hariharālaya is unknown. He then went to Amarendrapura, an unknown site.[31] Here gifts of land were made to royal supporters, and the presumption is that he was rewarding them for their help in further campaigns. The next royal residence was at Mount Mahendra in the Kulen hills northeast of the future Angkor site, where he

---

[20] *IC*, I, p. 30.

[21] Coedès, "La stèle de Palhal," p. 33.

[22] Ibid., p. 34.

[23] Coedès and Dupont, "Les stèles de Sdok Kak Thom, Phnom Sandak et Prah Vihar," p. 62.

[24] *IC*, VI, p. 85.

[25] E. Seidenfaden, "Complément à l'inventaire descriptif des monuments du Cambdoge pour les quatre provinces du Siam oriental," *BEFEO* 22 (1922): 62–63.

[26] For the revision of the length of Yaśovarman I's reign, see C. Jacques, "Sur les données chronologiques de la stèle de Tuol Ta Pec," pp. 167–68.

[27] A. Barth and A. Bergaigne, *Inscriptions sanscrites du Cambodge et du Campā* (Paris: Imprimerie nationale, 1885–1893), p. 377. Hereafter, *ISCC*.

[28] *IC*, I, p. 53. Vīrendra is located in *IC*, VII, p. 154.

[29] One need not doubt that Khmer chiefs remembered earlier conquerors. In 668 Rudravarman, of the first half of the sixth century, was compared with Viṣṇu; *ISCC*, p. 68.

[30] Dupont, "Les débuts," p. 159.

[31] Ibid., p. 161. Dupont believed that Amarendrapura was in the north, p. 126.

was consecrated *cakravartin*. He left Mount Mahendra to return to Hariharālaya, where he died in a year which is still undetermined.[32]

With the exception of Malyāng, the inscriptions do not identify the location of Jayavarman II's victories, but something can be said of those associated with him. They came from various places east of the Tonlé Sap. Aninditapura, to the east of the northern end of the Tonlé Sap,[33] was a source of support in the early years of the reign; perhaps Jayavarman's distant relationship with Puṣkara of Aninditapura, of the early eighth century, is one explanation.[34] His chief priest, Śivakaivalya, who was with him at Indrapura in 802, was connected with this place.[35] Another person from here "was chosen" for the royal entourage when the king was still at Indrapura.[36] Yet another was "at the head of the counselors."[37] Bhavapura, which in the ninth century may have been the name of a town to the east of the Tonlé Sap,[38] also provided supporters.[39] Āmalakasthala[40] and Śreṣṭhapura[41] are also mentioned as places of origin of those who were close to the king. We have already observed that two brothers came to his side from Angkor Borei.

Incomplete though this evidence is, its geographical span is sufficiently considerable to show that those who rallied to Jayavarman II came from a number of centers east of the Tonlé Sap.[42] In some cases, whole families joined him. Moreover, his supporters would have used their local influence to encourage others to seek their fortunes in the king's cause. The Mratāñ Śri Pṛthivīnarendra, for example, was a territorial chief who took care to ensure that his protégés obtained a share of the royal largesse.[43] Rewards were in the form of land, titles of honor, and posts at court. The inscriptions mention those who became generals, counselors, priests, fan-

---

[32] See C. Jacques, "Sur les données chronologiques de la stèle de Tuol Ta Pec," pp. 165–66, for a discussion of the ambiguous evidence concerning the accession date of Jayavarman's successor, Jayavarman III.

[33] For this location see Coedès, "La tradition généologique des premiers rois d'Angkor d'après les inscriptions de Yaçovarman et de Rājendravarman," *BEFEO* 28,1–2 (1928): 133.

[34] *ISCC*, p. 369. Jayavarman's parents seem to have been connected with Sambor on the Mekong, north of Indrapura, but nothing is known of the part they played in the king's career; Coedès, "La tradition généologique des premiers rois d'Angkor," p. 132.

[35] Coedès and Dupont, "Les stèles de Sdok Kak Thom," p. 104.

[36] *IC*, VII, p. 182.

[37] *IC*, V, p. 233. Another example is in Finot, "Nouvelles inscriptions du Cambodge," *BEFEO* 28 (1928): 71.

[38] See Coedès, *Indianized States*, p. 67. Professor Lévy suggests that a distinction should be made between this Bhavapura and the capital of Bhavavarman I, which he associates with Stung Treng on the Mekong. See P. Lévy, *JA* 258,1–2 (1970): 122.

[39] *IC*, VII, p. 132. The brahman remembered as teaching the *devarāja* ritual on Mount Mahendra belonged to the royal family of Bhavapura: *IC*, V1, pp. 104–5.

[40] *ISCC*, p. 109. On this site, apparently close to the future Angkor site, see Dupont, "Les débuts," p. 159.

[41] Coedès and Dupont, "Les inscriptions du Prasat Kōk Pŏ," *BEFEO* 37 (1937): 392. On the identification of this site with the Vat Phu area, see Coedès, *Indianized States*, p. 66. The supporter in question was a scholar.

[42] Dupont suggested that the art of Kulen (Mount Mahendra) reflected traditions as heterogeneous as the areas from which the king's supporters came; "Les débuts," p. 165.

[43] *IC*, VII, p. 133; Coedès, "La stèle de Palhal," p. 33.

bearers, pages, a "supervisor of the castes," a master of the bed-chamber, and a keeper of the private treasure.

Families who joined the king *en bloc* also provided him with wives, and at least seven instances of marriage alliances are found in the inscriptions left by the descendants of those who had flourished under Jayavarman II. Two wives, Sarasvatī and Steñ Devikī, came from families connected with Aninditapura. Sarasvatī's brother was a royal counselor,[44] and Steñ Devikī's father began his career in royal service as a fan-bearer.[45] Hyang Pavitrā's relatives are not recorded.[46] Teng Ayak came from Bhavapura.[47] Bhās-svāminī was a brahman's daughter.[48]

Two other marriages represented alliances with unusually important families, and something must be said of them because they have a bearing on the king's military power.

The first of these wives is Kambujalakṣmī, also known as Prana. She was related to the Mratañ Śri Pṛthivīnarendra.[49] The latter was evidently a valuable member of the royal entourage. He performed the ceremony near Vyādhapura to prevent "Kambujadeśa" from being taken by "Javā,"[50] and he conquered Malyāng by 816 at the latest, when he requested the king to reward the brothers from Angkor Borei. The king responded by bestowing lands on the brothers and by marrying their sister, Hyang Amṛta, who became known as Nṛpendradevī.[51] The years when Kambujalakṣmī's family and protégés were closely associated with the king were successful ones in the earlier years of his reign. The date of this marriage is unknown, but Kambujalakṣmī's royal name is noteworthy; it incorporates the name of Cambodia ("Kambuja").[52]

The other marriage deserves particular attention. It took place a number of years later and was even more important than Kambujalakṣmī's marriage. The queen in question is Dharaṇīndradevī,[53] and her son, the prince Jayavardhana, succeeded to the kingship over the heads of Kambujalakṣmī's son, Dharmavardhana, and other sons of the king.[54]

---

[44] *IC*, V, p. 233.

[45] *IC*, VII, pp. 182–83.

[46] *ISCC*, p. 112.

[47] *IC*, VII, p. 132.

[48] *ISCC*, pp. 108–9. Yet another wife is mentioned in *IC*, V, p. 140.

[49] *ISCC*, p. 539.

[50] *IC*, VII, p. 133.

[51] Coedès, "La stèle de Palhal," pp. 33–34.

[52] Early in Jayavarman's reign, a Cham inscription refers to the "country of the Kambujas"; *ISCC*, p. 269.

[53] The identification is based on the queen's name in Jayavarman II's sanctuary at Prah Ko, built by Indravarman I later in the ninth century; P. Dupont, "La dislocation de Tchen-la et la formation de Cambodge Angkorien (viie-ixe siècle)," *BEFEO* 43 (1943–46): 20, 35.

[54] *ISCC*, p. 370, v. 10, gives Jayavarman III's princely name of Jayavardhana. Dharmavardhana is mentioned in *ISCC*, p. 541, v. 9. The queen Nṛpendradevī had a son called Iśvarajña: Coedès, "La stèle de Palhal," p. 34. The prince Śrī Indrāyudha, another son by an unknown mother, is mentioned below.

That Jayavardhana's status was later regarded as especially privileged is indicated by two posthumous references to him as *garbheśvara* or "royal by birth."[55] Another Khmer king, Rājendravarman II (941/2–968),[56] is described in the same way. Rājendravarman, who became ruler when he was very young,[57] is referred to as *garbheśvara* in a passage in the Prè Rup inscription, which discloses that his father and also his mother were descended from royal families.[58] Jayavarman III, the former prince Jayavardhana, had similarly illustrious parents. His father was Jayavarman II, and two inscriptions of the early Angkorian period show that his mother was regarded as being of high birth. His mother's maternal uncle is said to be the "kṣatriya" Rudravarman,[59] and his maternal uncle's son is said to be Indravarman I (877–889).[60] The history of Dharaṇīndradevī's family is unknown except in the genealogies of Indravarman I and his son, Yaśovarman I, but its influence was sufficient to enable Jayavarman III, born into their family as well as into Jayavarman II's, to succeed Jayavarman II and to enable Indravarman I, another member of this family, to succeed Jayavarman III.

The date of Dharaṇīndradevī's marriage is unknown, but a fan-bearer, described as Rudravarman's grandson, was in Jayavarman II's entourage when the king was at Mount Mahendra.[61] The fan-bearer's grandfather and Jayavarman III's mother's uncle were both called Rudravarman, and it is reasonable to suppose that the same ancestor is involved. The fan-bearer, "a beloved servant of the king," was in royal service when the king was at Mount Mahendra, and his promotion would have been on the occasion of his relative's marriage to the king. The marriage probably took place when the king was at Mount Mahendra or not long before.[62] The years when the king was at Mount Mahendra are unknown, but they were later than 822, when the king was still in "the eastern district" and gave land to Kambujalakṣmī's brother-in-law.[63] The king did not immediately go to Mount Mahendra from "the eastern district." He first went to Hariharālaya and then to Amarendrapura. Perhaps he took up residence at Mount Mahendra in about 830.

And thus Mount Mahendra was not only the scene of Jayavarman's consecration ceremony but also of his alliance with Dharaṇīndradevī's family. The alliance was probably an important one, for Dharaṇīndradevī's son succeeded the king. The apparently high status of this family, together with the circumstance that his land grants have been found only in the north and west of the Tonlé Sap, were reasons why Dupont believed that Jayavarman's territorial power had been exaggerated.[64]

Two preliminary comments may be made on this interpretation of the marriage.

---

[55] *ISCC*, p. 370, v. 10 (an inscription of Yaśovarman I's reign); *IC*, V, p. 168, v. 5 (an inscription of the second half of the tenth century).

[56] Rājendravarman II's dates are based on C. Jacques, "Sur les données chronologiques de la stèle de Tuol Ta Pec," p. 175.

[57] *IC*, I, p. 75.

[58] Ibid., p. 107.

[59] *ISCC*, p. 370, v. 11.

[60] *IC*, IV, p. 98, v. 24. Also see *IC*, IV, p. 86; V, p. 168.

[61] *ISCC*, p. 134.

[62] Dupont suggests that the marriage took place on Mount Mahendra; see Dupont, "Les débuts," p. 162.

[63] Ibid., pp. 133, 159.

[64] Ibid., pp. 166–69.

In the first place, Jayavarman's early success had attracted to his side supporters from several centers east of the Tonlé Sap, and some of them can be supposed to have put their military levies at his disposal. The result was that the king was acknowledged in southern Cambodia and had conquered north-western Cambodia before he took up residence on Mount Mahendra. Dharaṇīndradevī's family can hardly have controlled such extensive lands.[65] Some chiefs may have been reluctant to acknowledge the king's overlordship,[66] but by about 830 they would have known that the conqueror of Malyāṅg and other lands disposed of great power. His land grants, whose limited span impressed Dupont, were in conquered territory[67] and not in territory whose chiefs had decided to accept his authority in order to retain possession of their ranks and estates.[68]

In the second place, Rudravarman's high status need not be taken too seriously. Though Dupont sometimes refers to him as a "king," Dupont also observed that only once is Rudravarman accorded a kingly title (*avanipālaka*).[69] It must also be borne in mind that the early Angkorian kings had every reason to exalt the status of Indravarman I's ancestor. And even if Rudravarman in his lifetime assumed a royal title, he would not have been the only Khmer chief in the eighth century to have done so. Eighth-century epigraphy discloses the existence of several "kings,"[70] but nothing leads one to believe that they were more than local chiefs. In the seventh century, when overlords were ruling in Cambodia, epigraphy mentions *mratāñs* and subordinate Sanskrit titles of rank, reserving kingly titles for the overlords. Only in the absence of overlordship during the eighth century were some chiefs able to ascribe to themselves kingly rank in order to assert their independent role as protectors of the local peace. Thus Rudravarman is said to have had "an unsullied sense of his duty" (*śuddhadharma*).[71] He is also said to have been "an incarnate portion of Viṣṇu" and therefore likened to Pṛthu, who was raised to the kingship to protect the dharma.[72] Rudravarman probably had considerable local influence before

---

[65] It is unknown where these lands were; on this subject, see Dupont, "Les débuts," pp. 149–50. Indravarman I married Indradevī, who, in terms of disclosed genealogy, was the most famous bride of the ninth century. Her ancestors included Puṣkara of Aninditapura and, through the latter's son or grandson, Rājendravarman I of Sambor, they were linked by marriage connections with the ancient overlords (*Adhirāja*) of Vyādhapura; *ISCC*, p. 369. But the date of Indradevī's marriage is unknown. If it had taken place before the king's residence on Mount Mahendra, Dharaṇīndradevī's family may have developed a substantial network of family alliances.

[66] Dupont notes the possibility of an expedition against rebels towards the end of Jayavarman II's reign; see Dupont, "Les débuts," p. 162.

[67] The Palhal inscription states that Garyāk, given to the Angkor Borei brothers, had a *tīrtha*, presumably in the possession of the previous occupants of the land; Coedès, "La stèle de Palhal," p. 33.

[68] For example, in the seventh century a chief was confirmed in his title of *mratāñ* by three successive kings: *IC*, IV, p. 30. During the same three reigns, Indrapura was the seat of a hereditary chief, whose position was probably similarly confirmed; Coedès, "Quelques précisions sur la fin de Fou-nan," *BEFEO* 43 (1943-46), p. 7.

[69] See Dupont's "La dislocation de Tchen-la," p. 36, for his reservation concerning Rudravarman as a ruler. In "Les débuts," pp. 150, 162, Dupont refers to the "royal" clan, of which Dharaṇīndradevī was a member.

[70] Dupont, "La dislocation de Tchen-la," p. 54.

[71] *ISCC*, p. 365, v. 11.

[72] Ibid., p. 134, v. 12.

Jayavarman II came into prominence, but his family's status in Jayavarman II's reign would have increasingly resembled that of an influential seventh-century chief's, vis-à-vis, for example, Jayavarman I.

Nevertheless, Dharaṇīndradevī's family and allies were able to control the kingship after Jayavarman II's death. The circumstances of Jayavarman III's succession over the heads of his half-brothers are unknown. Jayavarman II may have given his consent, which would suggest that his new relatives had insisted that a condition of the marriage to Dharaṇīndradevī was that the offspring would be regarded as the heir.[73] On the other hand, a coup d'état when Jayavarman died could have brought Jayavardhana-Jayavarman III and his mother's family to the fore. Only one fact about Jayavarman III's accession is certain: he was young at the time. An inscription states that in 850 he "enjoyed the kingship at the age of sixteen," meaning that he succeeded his father that year. But the passage can also mean that, in 850, he had enjoyed the kingship "for sixteen years."[74] He could have been born in 835, or he could have become ruler in 834.[75] In either case, he would have been young at the time of his accession and likely to be surrounded by his mother's relatives.

Before we consider further the significance of Dharaṇīndradevī's marriage, one more piece of evidence will be noted. The evidence is a comment on the power of the Khmer army in 838.

The *Ts'ê-fu yüan-kuei*, in its chapter on "raids," states that on September 19, 838, the Chinese court received news from its province of Annam that "Water *Chên-la*"[76] had sent "the king's son" with troops and horses to attack Champa and that Chinese troops were being despatched to Hoan-châu on the Cham border "to suppress the barbarians."[77] Presumably the Chinese governor feared that Hoan-châu would be the scene of fighting between the Khmers and Chams.

The *Ts'ê-fu yüan-kuei* is the only record that mentions this event, but the timing of the alarm on the borders of Vietnam is not inconsistent with other evidence. In the later T'ang period, the Chinese administration in Tonkin was frequently embarrassed by revolts,[78] but Ma Chih, the governor in 838, happens to have been a conscientious official, against whose regime revolts have not been recorded.[79] He would have

---

[73] Jayavarman III seems to have been well-educated; see Au Chhieng, *JA* 254,1 (1966): 161. There is also a reference to his guru, a protégé of Jayavarman II: see Coedès and Dupont, "Les inscriptions du Prasat Kôk Pô," p. 392. But, in view of the uncertainty about the year when Jayavarman III was born, this evidence cannot be interpreted as meaning that he was given a suitably royal education during his father's lifetime.

[74] The doubt concerning the date of Jayavarman III's accession is discussed by Professor Jacques in "Sur les données chronologiques de la stèle de Tuol Ta Pec," pp. 165–66.

[75] If we assume that his age is according to Khmer reckoning, he was fifteen years old in 850 and was born in 835. If the ambiguous evidence is construed to refer to the length of his reign in 850, his reign began in 834.

[76] This is the single instance when *TFYK* uses the term "Water *Chên-la*," but it appears in a communication from an official in Vietnam, who was probably identifying the area in Cambodia that had launched the attack. "Water *Chên-la*" is a geographical and not a political expression. On the usage of "Land" and "Water" *Chên-la,* see the author's "North-western Cambodia in the Seventh Century."

[77] *TFYK,* 995, 11688a.

[78] The numerous raids and revolts in the first half of the ninth century are listed by E. H. Schafer, *The Vermillion Bird* (Berkeley, CA: University of California, 1967), pp. 64–67.

[79] The *An-nam chí-lu-óc* (Huế: Viện Đại-học edition, 1961), p. 101, relates the response of Vietnamese to this enlightened governor. In 838, the year of his report of the Khmer invasion

enjoyed sufficient control of the province to be able to send reinforcements to Hoan-châu. Again, there is a gap in Cham epigraphy from 817 to 854, which may reflect a disturbed period in Cham history.[80] Earlier in the ninth century, the Chams had the initiative. According to a Po Nagar inscription from southern Champa, the Cham general, Senāpati Pār, ravaged Cambodia; his attacks are believed to have taken place in 813 and probably in 817 as well.[81] At that time, Jayavarman II's preoccupation was with the northwest. The Khmers had every reason for retaliating when the opportunity occurred.

The *Ts'ê-fu yüan-kuei* is not the only source which contains evidence of Khmer pressure on Champa in the ninth century. A tenth-century inscription states that Jayavarman II's son, Śrī Indrāyudha, captured a Cham leader.[82] He cannot be assumed to be "the king's son" to whom the Chinese source refers, and the inscription does not make it certain that Śrī Indrāyudha, who lived into old age, distinguished himself when his father was still alive. Nevertheless, the Chinese and Khmer sources agree that a consequence of Jayavarman's success in Cambodia was expeditions against Champa.

The Khmer army in 838 was supplied with horses, which means that it travelled overland to northern Champa. The army probably followed the route taken in 722 by the Khmer allies of the Vietnamese rebel, Mai Thúc Loan.[83] Thus, in 838 the Khmers had access to routes through territory that, in the eighth century, had been under the influence of *Mjuan-tân*,[84] the Khmer principality that helped the Vietnamese rebel in 722. The extension of southern Cambodian power northwards is not surprising. One of Jayavarman's supporters had a family connection with Śreṣthapura, the city identified with the Vat Phu area just north of the Mun-Mekong confluence, and Indravarman I's inscription of 886 from the Ubon area in the Mun valley shows that later in the ninth century a Khmer overlord ruled north of the Dangreks.[85]

Clearly the military situation in mainland Southeast Asia had greatly changed since the time when, in the eighth century, "Javā" in an undisclosed way was involved in Khmer affairs. In 838, a Khmer army was able to worry the Chinese administration in southern Vietnam. If Jayavarman II were still alive that year, his expedition would be additional evidence that he was a distinguished warrior king, controlling by conquest, capitulation, or consent the whole of Cambodia. On the other hand, if he were dead in 838, his achievement would have been even greater. In spite of his death in 834, his army's fighting capacity would have remained intact and the territorial integrity of Cambodia would have been undiminished by the presence of a minor on the throne.

---

of Champa, he was advising the T'ang court to encourage local loyalty by raising a certain region to the status of *châu*; Schafer, *Vermillion Bird*, p. 71.

[80] Coedès, *Indianized States*, p. 104.

[81] Ibid., p. 104.

[82] *IC*, VII, p. 87.

[83] H. Maspero, "La frontière de l'Annam et du Cambodge du 8 au 14 siècle," *BEFEO* 18,3 (1918): 29. If the Khmers had attacked Champa from the south, they would have had to pursue them through the entire length of Champa.

[84] i.e. *Wên-tan*, inaccurately referred to as "Land *Chên-la*."

[85] Jayavarman I, whose military career in the seventh century parallels Jayavarman II's, left an inscription at Vat Phu and appointed a brahman's son as chief at Śreṣthapura.

This essay has attempted to measure Jayavarman II's power in terms of the territory he controlled, and his conquest of Malyāng early in the reign has been suggested as a yardstick of his scale of achievement. But his territorial power cannot be explained simply in military terms. He succeeded because he could attract support, and those who helped him were not entirely motivated by the prospect of material gain. Great leaders in early Southeast Asia were perceived by their contemporaries as agents of divine power, and royal service could be valued as a source of religious merit.[86] Sooner or later his uninterrupted success would have implied that he was supported by irresistible religious power. Spiritual *rapport* between him and his supporters was part of the background to the royal cult established on Mount Mahendra.

Because his military success implied divine power, Dharaṇīndradevī's marriage is unlikely to have meant that his position was still insecure. Whether he persuaded her relatives to join his family or whether they offered him an alliance which he chose not to reject need not be important questions in determining his power. He had achieved so much before the marriage that he must have towered over his contemporaries. His new wife's family would have wished to be associated with him.

Similarly, the circumstance that Dharaṇīndradevī's relatives seized the kingship perhaps at the time of the youthful Jayavarman III's accession and certainly in 877, when Indravarman I became ruler, need not be understood to reflect Jayavarman II's weakness during his lifetime. He was a ninth-century Khmer and the product of a society whose élite practiced polygamy.[87] As a result, there were always a number of princes who could regard themselves as members of the royal family and, when the opportunity occurred, try to mobilize their mothers' families and allies in order to seize the kingship. Jayavarman II can hardly have expected to control the royal succession. But he was forward-thinking in a different way. The Sdok Kak Thom inscription states that he intended that his cult, established on Mount Mahendra, would guarantee that Cambodia henceforth always had a *cakravartin*, and he therefore entrusted its supervision to his *purohita*'s descendants. A member of this priestly family was responsible for the Sdok Kak Thom inscription. The family had every reason for keeping alive the memory of the king's intention, and we can suppose that Jayavarman believed that his reign had created new possibilities for Cambodia. And, indeed, throughout the Angkorian centuries, struggles for power were never at the expense of the kingdom. The goal of ambitious men, such as Indravarman I may be presumed to have been, was to rule over a territorially intact country. Local independence was no longer the acceptable objective as it had been in the eighth century. The integrity of the Angkorian kingdom was not in question.

Thus, no matter how the cult on Mount Mahendra is interpreted or what were the reasons for Dharaṇīndradevī's marriage, Jayavarman II, in the wake of his military victories, introduced several centuries of Khmer history when the institution of kingship retained its prestige. No doubt some of his supporters' descendants had estates in different parts of the country and therefore a vested interest in maintaining

---

[86] An inscription of Yaśovarman I asserts that "kingship should be honored by those who enjoy good works"; Coedès, "A la recherché du Yaçodharāçrama," *BEFEO* 32,1 (1932): 94, v. 27.

[87] Jayavarman II did not shed his earlier relatives on Mount Mahendra. Śrī Pṛthivīnarendra's kinsmen received additional land when he was there; Dupont, "Les débuts," pp. 161–62.

some degree of political unity. No doubt, too, careers in the service of the Angkorian rulers became materially and spiritually attractive and reinforced the institution of kingship. But one can also suggest that Jayavarman's achievements were accompanied by a heightened awareness among his contemporaries of the totality of temporal power represented by Khmer kingship, and it would not be surprising if his cult on Mount Mahendra was intended to formulate a measurement of that power in religious terms.[88]

---

[88] In this connexion, one should bear in mind Professor Filliozat's argument that *devarāja*, the name of Jayavarman II's cult on Mount Mahendra ascribed to him by the Sdok Kak Thom inscription of 1052, should be understood to mean "king of the gods," or Śiva; J. Filliozat, "New Researches on the Relations between India and Cambodia," *Indica* 3 (1966): 100–102.

CHAPTER EIGHT

KHMER "HINDUISM" IN THE SEVENTH CENTURY

This essay is a historian's comment on Cambodian protohistory, and the seventh century is a time for taking stock of developments already under way. The scene is Cambodia because Cambodian protohistory is incomparably better served with relatively continuous Chinese and epigraphic evidence than any other part of Southeast Asia during the first centuries of the Christian era. Nearly two hundred inscriptions in Sanskrit and also in Khmer have been attributed to the seventh century, and seventy-nine of them are dated or mention identifiable kings. These inscriptions supply the most important corpus of indigenous literary information so far available in the region before the end of the seventh century.

The intention in this essay is to discuss some social, political, and religious phenomena, especially visible in the seventh century, in order to enquire by way of hypothesis whether Khmers were construing what they had come to learn of Hinduism in terms intelligible to them because of their pre-Hindu experiences and beliefs. The assumption will be that, for the Khmers, Hinduism was essentially a religious phenomenon, to be examined later in the essay, and that we should think of it as coming to the Khmers originally in the form of news, traveling over trade routes. Men listen to news only when they can interpret it and can perceive that it has some meaning for them. We shall therefore be concerned with the possibility of Khmer "Hinduism," which may be a concept as valid as, for example, Chinese "Buddhism." The Chinese were able to restate the Mahāyāna,[1] and the possibility that the Khmers did likewise in respect of Hinduism need not be entirely fanciful.

Consideration must first be given to the identity of those who appear in epigraphy in an apparently Hindu religious context. We shall refer to them as members of the Khmer élite, ruling as chiefs in independent territories that may be described as principalities. The Chinese records, though not throwing light on Khmer motivation during the protohistoric period, describe some fairly normal secular situations in which this élite found itself. These situations have been known to historians as long ago as 1903, when Pelliot published his study of "Funan,"[2] but

---

[1] See Arthur Wright, *Buddhism in Chinese History* (New York, NY: Atheneum, 1968), chapters 3 and 4.

[2] P. Pelliot, "Le Fou-nan," *BEFEO* 3 (1903): 248–303.

they will be briefly recapitulated because the extension of Hindu influences did little to modify them.

In the early centuries of the Christian era, inter-territorial warfare seems to have been frequent. The location and social structure of the principalities cannot be accurately described, but one can suppose that "Cambodia" comprised an unknown number of independent centers of territorial authority that correspond with the statement in the third century *Nan-chou i-wu chih* that "all the vassal countries" of Funan "have their own chiefs."[3] Certain chiefs could sometimes muster sufficient military power to impose a hegemony over their neighbors, but hegemonies were short-lived and followed by renewed warfare. A familiar event was what the Chinese regarded as a "usurpation." No matter how extensive had been a hegemon's supra-territorial authority, there was no assurance that his chosen successor would be unchallenged. Not many "usurpations" are recorded in the Chinese texts, but we must remember that not every Khmer ruler was known to the Chinese government. One reason for believing that disturbed conditions persisted is that, as late as the seventh century, the conquering family of Bhavavarman I lost control before many decades had passed. Thereafter an interval of perhaps thirty years separated its hegemony from that of Jayavarman I. During most of the eighth century, no hegemon appeared.[4]

The Chinese records reflect an important circumstance that accompanied this warfare during the protohistoric period. Marriage alliance enabled a would-be hegemon to bind other chiefs to his side. According to the *Liang-shu*, the great conqueror *B'iwăm-*miwăn, living about 200 CE, had a sister who married someone sufficiently powerful that her son, *Tian, "who was the leader of two thousand men," could seize power from *B'iwăm-*miwăn's son.[5] But relatives by marriage were not disarmed. When the opportunity arose, they would mobilize their own allies and dependants in order to make or support a new bid for hegemony. And so *Tian was later overthrown by another of *B'iwăm-*miwăn's sons, *D'iang, "who had lived among the people ... and was able to collect good soldiers of the country." These "soldiers" would have included men from his mother's territory, where he must have taken refuge during the years of *Tian's power. But *D'iang was subsequently overthrown by one of *Tian's generals, who would have been yet another chief, with his own manpower resources. The same circumstance of marriage alliance helps to explain Rudravarman's success in the first half of the sixth century. Rudravarman is described by the Chinese as a concubine's son and his father's intended heir as "the son of the legal wife," but the Chinese, familiar with concubinage rather than with polygamy, misunderstood Rudravarman's status. He would have been the son of a woman from an important and independent princely family bound to his royal father by marriage alliance. Seventh-century epigraphy refers to the brother of

---

[3] *T'ai-p'ing yü-lan* (Han fên lou facsimile of a Sung print), Chung-ha shu-chü edition (Peking, 1960), 786, 3482b. For a description of the urban status of the chiefs' settlements, see Paul Wheatley, *The Pivot of the Four Quarters: A Preliminary Enquiry in the Origins and Character of the Ancient Chinese City* (Edinburgh: Edinburgh University Press, 1971), p. 254.

[4] Here I follow Professor Jacques's recent revision of Jayavarman II's chronology, which dates the king's rise to overlordship in the last decades of the eighth century: C. Jacques, "Études d'épigraphie Cambodgienne: VIII: La carrière de Jayavarman II," *BEFEO* 59 (1972): 205–20.

[5] Karlgren's phonology has been followed for reconstructing the names of Khmer chiefs mentioned in the Chinese sources; Bernhard Karlgren, *Études sur la phonologie Chinoise* (Leiden and Stockholm: J.-A. Lundell, 1915).

Jayavarman I's mother, who, "while not bearing the title of king, enjoyed a fortune worthy of a king."[6] Perhaps Jayavarman had discharged a debt to his mother's family, incurred when the latter helped him in his campaigns. In the eighth and ninth centuries, the great Jayavarman II contracted at least seven marriages, two of which were of considerable political importance.[7]

In this situation, we can suppose with some confidence that would-be hegemons, after giving evidence of their ability, were acclaimed as overlords by their relatives and allies. And thus, again according to the *Liang-shu*, *B'iwăm-*miwăn* "was promoted by the people of the country to be king," and similarly, perhaps, Kauṇḍinya II about 400 CE was summoned from the Malay Peninsula and "established as king."

The implication of this evidence is that the significant political event in the Khmer world was an overlordship, of temporary duration and made possible by a coalition of chiefs who recognized the capacity of the adventurer seeking the hegemony. Rewards would then be distributed, additional marriage alliances would be negotiated, and those who wished to be undisturbed in their local power would prudently hasten to have their authority confirmed by the new overlord.

The territories that were the scene of these king-making adventures cannot convincingly be described as a "kingdom," possessing its own acknowledged and permanent identity. Only the Chinese, with their sense of "dynasty," write of the existence of a "kingdom of Funan," a term that they found convenient to retain until the early seventh century.[8] Their reason was simply that the chief of *B'iu-nam* ("Funan") perhaps residing at his center of Vyādhapura, happened to be the first Khmer chief with whom they established contact as long ago as the third century. Yet there is no certainty that an overlord always resided there. In the king-making process, the practical significance of lineage probably lay in the means it provided for identifying family connections and therefore potential allies: lineage is unlikely to have compensated for an absence of the personal quality of leadership.[9] Moral stigma was not attached to what the Chinese regarded as "usurpation," for an overlord's power was not protected by the concept of a "dynasty" in a society with a plethora of half-brothers.[10] The political reality was a temporary overlordship based on this or that territorial center. A ninth-century inscription, which mentions an

---

[6] A. Barth and A. Bergaigne, *Inscriptions sanscrites du Cambodge et du Campā* (Paris: Imprimerie nationale, 1885–1893), p. 71, v(erse) 17. Hereafter, *ISCC*.

[7] In this volume, chapter 7, "Jayavarman II's Military Power."

[8] See C. Jacques, "'Funan,' 'Zhenla': The Reality Concealed by these Chinese Views of Indochina," in *Early South East Asia: Essays in Archaeology, History and Historical Geography*, ed. R. B. Smith and W. Watson (New York and Kuala Lumpur: Oxford University Press, 1979), pp. 371–79, for a discussion of the epigraphic reasons for rejecting the conception of a "kingdom of Funan." The present author, in "North-western Cambodia in the Seventh Century," *BSOAS* 37,2 (1974): 355–84, examined some Chinese preconceptions that required them to think in terms of a "kingdom of Funan." [Reprinted in *Classical Civilizations of South East Asia: An Anthology of Articles Published in the Bulletin of SOAS*, ed. Vladimir Braginsky (London and New York: RoutledgeCurzon, 2002).—Ed.]

[9] I gratefully acknowledge my indebtedness to my colleague in anthropology, Professor A. Thomas Kirsch, for discussions on the phenomenon of alliance within the Southeast Asian social context.

[10] The *Sui-shu* (Po-na edition), 82, 6b, records the Khmer practice of killing or mutilating brothers of a new king on the day of his accession.

eighth-century chief, Rajendravarman, states that he was descended on his mother's side from the overlords (*adhirāja*) of a particular center, Vyādhapura.[11]

Because the chiefs did not understand the notion of a "kingdom," with its supra-territorial demands on their loyalty, "kingship" remained essentially a personal achievement. Those who acclaimed someone as "king" realized that he was endowed with extraordinary qualities, which we shall call "prowess." The essential nature of his "prowess" will be considered later in this essay. No more need be suggested here than that the adventurer was able to mobilize his coalition not because he could claim to be the descendant of an earlier overlord but because his supporters were able to perceive that he was distinguished by personal qualities of leadership and self-confidence, which guaranteed the success of his enterprise. Provided that he gave evidence of prowess, subordinate adventurers, living in a society that probably practiced bilateral kinship as it does today and in which the establishment of new households was customary, would have been waiting in the wings for chances of bettering their fortunes. According to the *Sui-shu*, containing information brought to China during a mission in 616:

> When a man's marriage ceremonies are completed, he takes a share of his parents' property and leaves them in order to live elsewhere.[12]

Enterprising men, not bound by parental ties, could therefore travel to seek their fortunes by putting themselves under the protection of chiefs of promise. The seventh-century inscriptions reflect this society in their references to brothers in control of separate territories and to pairs of brothers who made good in apparently independent careers.[13] When a man of prowess was perceived, families could mobilize their own independent resources and also those of their relatives in order to rally around him *en bloc*, as happened in the reign of Jayavarman II.[14] The more relatives a supporter had, the greater would be his contribution to the royal adventurer's enterprise.[15]

We can now attempt a general comment on these aspects of Khmer protohistory. Part of the experience of the princely élite and their entourages was an awareness that society was composed of men with greatly different capacities for achievement. The overlordship was the symbol of the highest achievement, and what we would define as "the kingdom" was no more than the territorial measurement of a particular overlord's prowess. Territories within an overlordship were defined not

---

[11] *ISCC*, p. 364, v. 3.

[12] *Sui-shu*, 82, 6b.

[13] *ISCC*, pp. 68–72; G. Coedès, *Inscriptions du Cambodge*, I (Hanoi: Imprimerie d'Extrême Orient, 1937-1966), p. 11; IV, p. 31; V, p. 37, 43. Hereafter, *IC*.

[14] In this volume, chapter 7, "Jayavarman II's Military Power."

[15] The importance of relatives, albeit elsewhere in Southeast Asia and later in time, is well illustrated in the following passage in the Achinese *Hikatjat Malen Dagang*, brought to my attention by Professor James Siegel:

> He has many relatives of both sides, there are many to help him as general.

> He has many older and younger brothers, there are many to take his place as general [if he should be killed].

> Counting all his relatives on both sides there are three hundred strong ones.

> They are [willing to] follow, all [willing to] die ...

by geographical boundaries but by the behavior of those who, for the time being, acknowledged the ruler's personal authority. The overlordship could not be won and the kingship seized until the would-be hegemon's fellow chiefs were able to recognize his prowess in the field of endeavor most familiar to them, which was warfare. Important changes in the status quo would therefore be bound to be accompanied by a sensation of rapport between leaders and supporters. In general, Khmer protohistory would have been the story of human inequality in terms of prowess but also of profitable dependent relationships at a time when the quickening of international trade through Southeast Asia was increasing the means and rewards of warfare.

These chiefs will now be considered as they appear in the epigraphy of Khmer protohistory and especially in seventh-century inscriptions. Their "Hindu" professions will be seen to be by no means inconsistent with their behavior as it is reflected in the fragmentary Chinese records, but their motivation now becomes explicit, though expressed by means of the Sanskrit vocabulary of Hinduism. Their modes of worship are, as Bosch insisted in a discussion of the Hinduisation of Indonesia, those of Śivaite devotionalism.[16]

The influence of this doctrine is reflected in the definitions of Śiva's attributes, proclaimed by the invocations of the seventh-century inscriptions. He is "the creator."[17] He is "omniscient"[18] and "the first of the ascetics."[19] An inscription of 624, a statement of Śivaite doctrine, represents Śiva as a personal god of grace, with inherent qualities, and also as absolute brahman.[20]

The modes of worship, extolled in the inscriptions, are also those of Śivaite devotionalism. The worshipper is required to give "undiverted" thought and devotion.[21] Śiva is "accessible to sages through meditation exclusively concentrated on him."[22] Sense control must be practiced.[23] One of Śiva's worshippers claims to be "without pride."[24] Asceticism in honor of Śiva, the first of the ascetics, is particularly emphasized. Ascetics are placed in charge of temples.[25] Land is granted to ascetics.[26] An ascetic, ablaze with Śiva's *śakti*, or divine energy, is in charge of a grotto for other ascetics.[27]

Ascetics are referred to under several terms, including *muni*,[28] and among them are the Pāśupatas, mentioned on two occasions. The Pāśupatas were the ascetics *par*

---

[16] F. D. K. Bosch, *Selected Studies in Indonesian Archaeology* (The Hague: M. Nijhoff, 1961).

[17] *IC*, I, p. 14, v. ii.

[18] *IC*, III, p. 172, v. i.

[19] *IC*, II, p. 150, v. i.

[20] *ISCC*, p. 36; Kamaleswar Bhattacharya, "La secte des Pāçupata dans l'ancien Cambodge," *JA* 243 (1955): 479–90, and his *Les religions brahmaniques dans l'ancien Cambodge* (Paris: EFEO, 1961), pp. 57–58.

[21] *ISCC*, p. 70, v. 13; *IC*, I, p. 15, v. vii.

[22] *IC*, V, p. 43, v. i.

[23] *ISCC*, p. 70, v. 16; *IC*, I, p. 11, v. xv.

[24] *ISCC*, p. 70, v. 16.

[25] *ISCC*, p. 19, v. 33; *IC*, IV, p. 32, v. viii.

[26] *IC*, II, p. 12, v. iv.

[27] *IC*, V, p. 13.

[28] *ISCC*, p. 50, v. 3.

excellence in this period, and they were in the confidence of kings. Īśānavarman I entrusted one of them with the care of a temple,[29] and Bhavavarman employed another as a poet; he practiced asceticism according to the Śaiva rule (*vidhi*).[30]

The Pāśupatas are the only Śivaite sect known in the *Mahābhārata*, and they are mentioned in an inscription of Mathurā of the fourth century CE.[31] Kauṇḍinya, who wrote a commentary on the *Pāśupata-sūtra*, is believed to have lived between the fourth and sixth centuries.[32] Hsüan-tsang observed Pāśupatas in several parts of India during the first half of the seventh century. He also saw them in Afghanistan, and they may have traveled as far east as Khotan in Turkestan,[33] where a "heretic covered with cinders" advises a king. Thus, they were to be found on or near the trans-Asian continental trade route, and their appearance in Cambodia near a trans-Asian maritime route is not altogether surprising.

We need not doubt that Śivaite devotionalism was established among the Khmer élite in the seventh century. By that time Khmer-language inscriptions are using important Sanskrit terms as part of the vocabulary for honoring Śiva.[34] The antiquity and first origins of this situation will not be discussed here, though we can note that the Buddhist Nāgasena had observed a royal Śiva cult in Cambodia in 484.[35] The term *bhakti*, albeit in the context of the worship of Viṣṇu by a king's son, appears in an inscription of the second half of the fifth century.[36]

The feature of Hinduism in Cambodia by the seventh century that must now be emphasized is that Śivaite devotionalism, implicitly individualist in its goal of personal union with Śiva, was also practiced within the social context of Khmer overlordship. Although many of the inscriptions make no reference to the contemporary political situation, those in the names of kings or the kings' followers reveal that devotionalism had taken into account the distinction between a man of prowess and those over whom he had asserted his hegemony. The hierarchy of temporal prowess, reflected in Chinese evidence of king-making adventures against a background of independent principalities, is complemented by a devotional hierarchy. The hierarchy is maintained in spite of the circumstance that both overlords and their "servants" (*bhṛtya*) subscribe in their invocations to the same doctrinal beliefs concerning Śiva. They respect ascetic practices, and they erect *liṅgas* or statues to Śiva.[37]

---

[29] L. Finot, "Nouvelles inscriptions du Cambodge," *BEFEO* 27, 1–2 (1928): 46, v. xii; *IC*, IV, pp. 17–19.

[30] *IC*, I, p. 5, v. iv and viii.

[31] Bhattacharya, *Les religions brahmaniques*, pp. 43–44.

[32] H. Chakraborti, *Pāśupata Sūtram with Panchārtha-bhāsya of Kaundinya* (Calcutta: Academic Publishers, 1970), p. 14.

[33] Chakraborti, *Pāśupata Sūtram*, p. 15; Samuel Beal, *Buddhist Records of the Western World*, reprint ed. (Delhi: Oriental Books Reprint Corp., 1969), under "Pāśupata" and in Book II, pp. 310–11.

[34] Pūjā ("homage"), *IC*, II, p. 11; Pradāna ("donation"), *IC*, II, p. 27, l. 16; Satra ("offering"), *IC*, V, p. 57, l. 3; *IC*, V, p. 76, face B, l. 4; Yajamāna ("he who offers gifts to a god"), *IC*, VII, p. 130, l. 1; Punya ("merit"), *IC*, II, p. 45, l. 2.

[35] Bhattacharya, *Les religions brahmaniques*, pp. 12–13.

[36] G. Coedès, "Deux inscriptions sanskrites du Fou-nan," *BEFEO* 31,1–2 (1931): 7.

[37] For example of a royal cult, *IC*, IV, p. 11. The servants are noted below.

The overlord did not emerge in a social vacuum. He was only a territorial chief, whose private military resources were never sufficient to enable him to dispense with the need for allies, attracted to him by his abnormal powers of leadership. Now, in a "Hindu" guise, the overlord's superior prowess can be measured. He is seen as one whose soul (*ātman*) had achieved the closest possible relationship with Śiva by virtue of his ascetic efforts in devotion to Śiva, the first of ascetics. As a result, he enjoys Śiva's *śakti* and therefore spiritual and physical power. Bhavavarman II is described as "possessing unshakable self-control as a result of his austerities [*tapas*]."[38] A king who may be Bhavavarman I is "able to conquer the six vices."[39] Bhavavarman I had "seized the kingship by means of his personal *śakti*," a statement that epitomizes the "Hinduised" man with the most prowess in Khmer inter-territorial relations.[40] Īśānavarman I recalls Śiva as living among the ascetics,[41] and he himself "took pleasure in the company of sages";[42] his sages can be assumed to include ascetics. Not surprisingly, Īśānavarman I is ascribed with *śakti*.[43] Jayavarman I, who came to the fore after some decades when overlordship was in abeyance,[44] is "an incarnate portion [*anśa*] of the god, who is Śiva."[45] He, too, would have possessed *śakti*.

These kings apparently welcomed to their entourage religious ascetics, including Pāśupatas. Other Śivaite ascetics as well as Pāśupatas would have been represented, but they can be expected to have had much in common with the Pāśupatas, differing only in ritual and religious practices.[46] Because the language of the invocations reflects Pāśupata doctrine as set forth in the *Pāśupata-sūtra*'s commentary by Kauṇḍinya, Kauṇḍinya's text may throw some light on religious influences within Khmer royal courts, represented by the Pāśupatas.

These startling ascetics, covered with ashes, are bound to have made an impression. The commentary states that they share all Śiva's power with the exception of the power of creation.[47] They are, in fact, warned not to take too much delight in the attainment of miraculous power, placing them beyond Śiva's jurisdiction.[48] Even more impressive would have been their conception of the guru's status. The guru represents Śiva. "There is no doubt that Śiva becomes worshipped by him who worships the teacher always in all circumstances."[49] Or again, "the disciple becomes powerful by [the power of] the *guru* ..."[50] The guru at court would

---

[38] *IC*, II, p. 70, v. i.

[39] *ISCC*, p. 17, v. 4. Professor Jacques has suggested that certain inscriptions, conventionally attributed to Bhavavarman II, should be attributed to Bhavavarman I; *Annuaire, 1971–1972* (École pratique des Hautes Études, IVe Section), p. 608.

[40] *ISCC*, p. 69, v. 5.

[41] *IC*, V, p. 31, v. i.

[42] Ibid., p. 26, v. ii.

[43] *IC*, IV, p. 9, v. ix.

[44] Wolters, "North-western Cambodia in the Seventh Century."

[45] *IC*, I, p. 10, v. iii.

[46] J. Gonda, *Les religions de l'Inde*, vol. 2 (Paris: Payot, 1965), p. 237.

[47] Chakraborti, *Pāśupata Sūtram*, p. 28.

[48] Ibid., p. 107.

[49] Ibid., p. 72.

[50] Ibid., p. 89.

have been the royal disciple's most accessible link with the god, who could link his disciple to god. The overlords therefore had opportunities and encouragement for cultivating their own close relationship with Śiva, bringing them limitless spiritual power and the temporal implications of such power.

The presence of Pāśupatas in the royal entourage tells us something more about Khmer "Hinduism." The Pāśupatas belonged to the religious élite in the sense that they were brahmans, but they were wayward brahmans who were not interested in Vedic sacrifices and believed that Śiva's grace prevailed over the law of *karma*. In India, they turned their back on society and behaved as "lunatics" for God's sake.[51] Their willingness to cross the ocean may be another sign of their indifference to brahmanical conventions and of their zeal in incurring hardship for Śiva's sake. These Indian representatives of Hinduism in Cambodia are unlikely to have insisted that some form of brahmanical society should be reproduced there.

In Khmer "Hinduism" the man of prowess, with his ascetic advisors, was now Śiva's foremost worshipper. What can be said of the "Hinduism" of his "servants," those who had come under his influence?

Their inscriptions are much less numerous than those of Śiva-worshippers who mention no overlord in their inscriptions and whose political relationships are not disclosed. On the other hand, a general consistency appears in the contents of the royal "servants" inscriptions; their inscriptions reveal the significance they attach to various kinds of royal gifts in the context of their devotion to Śiva, a devotion sometimes explicitly in support of their hope for a superior death status.

Four kinds of royal gifts are mentioned. The first kind comprises a wide range of posts with honorable responsibilities, including the posts of special counselor, president of the royal council, governorships of towns, and head of the royal oarsmen. These posts are bestowed as signs of royal confidence in the recipients,[52] and they justify ascribing the officeholders with specific spiritual qualities.[53] Royal service is also seen as protecting the *dharma*.[54] The second type of gift is in the form of presents from the ruler.[55] The third is the gift of titles of honor.[56] Fourthly, the ruler confirms secular and religious privileges.[57]

The gift-recording inscriptions are undertaken when the recipient erects a *liṅga* or statue to demonstrate his devotion (*bhakti*) to Śiva.[58] In one instance the royal gifts seem actually to be offered to the recipient's cult.[59] Sometimes the intention in founding the cult is unambiguously expressed in the hope of a superior death status, described in conventional terms of a fortunate rebirth or entering Śiva's abode,[60] and

---

[51] Ibid., p. 140.

[52] *IC*, I, p. 11, v. xvi, xx; *IC*, I, p. 15, v. vi; *IC*, III, p. 163, v. xiii; *ISCC*, pp. 18–19, v. 22–24; *ISCC*, p. 71, v. 17.

[53] *IC*, II, p. 151, v. iii; *IC*, III, p. 163, v. xiii; *ISCC*, p. 18, v. 22; *ISCC*, p. 70, v. 16.

[54] *ISCC*, p. 19, v. 30; *ISCC*, p. 25, v. 12; *ISCC*, p. 70, v. 14–15; *IC*, III, p. 163, v. xiii.

[55] *ISCC*, p. 25, v. 6 and 9; *IC*, I, p. 15, v. vi.

[56] *IC*, IV, p. 32, v. iv; *IC*, IV, p. 30. *IC*, IV, p. 30, refers to an *ācārya*, who states that three successive kings had conferred on him the title of *Mratān An*.

[57] *IC*, VI, p. 8, v. vi; *ISCC*, p. 71, v. 18.

[58] *IC*, II, p. 151, v. iv; *ISCC*, p. 19, v. 32.

[59] *IC*, I, p. 15, v. viii–ix.

[60] *IC*, I, p. 12, v. xxiii; *IC*, II, p. 151, v. iv.

all these foundations can be assumed to be with this purpose in mind unless another intention is clearly stated.[61]

The overlord was evidently seen as a spiritual influence on his servants' lives and hopes of salvation. Not surprisingly, overlords attracted personal loyalty, described in one case as *bhakti*.[62] As gestures of homage, servants offer presents to the ruler's temple or erect statues of the god in the ruler's honor.[63] But gifts to brahmans, not described as ascetics, are rare in the extant inscriptions.[64] Brahmans would have benefited from their superintendence of the chiefs' temples, for which revenue was made available, but they do not seem to have been honored because of the rituals that they performed in India on behalf of society. In inscriptions of the Gupta period, the *Mahābhārata* is frequently quoted to emphasize the importance of gifts to brahmans, but not in the Khmer inscriptions. In Gupta times, brahmans, because of gifts specially made to them, were becoming wealthy landowners, but in Cambodia merit is earned by personal achievement and not by honoring brahmans.[65]

Khmer "Hindu" practices are always on behalf of the worshipper, layman as well as ascetic, and those in royal service are seen as having most to offer their god. The secular and hierarchical structure of Khmer inter-territorial relationships is not modified by the presence of a brahman class on top of society. Instead, it is complemented by the hierarchical modes of Śivaite devotionalism. The members of the élite continue to perform their customary roles, and their secular performance on behalf of men of prowess enables them to earn additional merit and enhance their prospects after death.

The question may now be asked whether the Khmers were emphasizing certain features of available Hinduism to reflect pre-Hindu beliefs. Paul Mus has already proposed that Śiva's creative and fertilizing powers, cosmic in scale, permitted Southeast Asians to identify their stones in honor of gods of the soil with the Śiva-*liṅga*.[66] Perhaps additional pre-Hindu beliefs are echoed in Khmer "Hinduism."

If Khmers were construing Hinduism in comprehensible terms, they may have instinctively accommodated two pre-Hindu assumptions. Gifts from above may already have been seen as possessing a religious quality, from which the recipient was believed to benefit. This assumption would explain the importance the "servants" attached to symbols of royal favor in their death wish inscriptions. Secondly, gifts may already have been regarded as spiritually efficacious only when the recipient had earned them by his own achievements. The overlord practiced asceticism, and his servants exerted themselves by accepting and following royal leadership.

---

[61] For example, one's merits could be transferred to one's father; *ISCC*, p. 71, v. 22. See *IC*, IV, p. 25, v. vi for a queen's death wish.

[62] *IC*, V, p. 29, v. xii.

[63] Ibid.; G. Coedès, "Études cambodgiennes, XXXI: A Propos du Tchen-la d'Eau: trois inscriptions de Cochinchine," *BEFEO* 34 (1936): 9.

[64] *IC*, IV, pp. 61–63; *ISCC*, p. 47, v. 4.

[65] Nevertheless, the penalty for damaging a private cult is said to be equivalent to that for murdering a brahman; *IC*, II, p. 125, face B, pp. 12–14.

[66] P. Mus, "Cultes indiens et indigènes au Champa," *BEFEO* 33 (1933): 367–410. Śiva's fertilizing power explains the undecaying vegetation on his holy hill, reported by Nāgasena in 464; Pelliot, "Le Fou-nan," p. 260. The hill is in Cambodia.

But these two assumptions would have been sustained by a further one, representing the essence of pre-Hindu religious experience. Society, seen as the scene for exhibiting various capacities for personal achievement with religious as well as secular significance, would also have been perceived as the scene of relationships between those with different capacities for achievement, enabling the man of superior prowess to provide those of lesser prowess with opportunities for achieving within their capacity.

Gupta and Pallava epigraphy, though a record of merit-earning and often in honor of Śiva, does not seem to articulate these assumptions as clearly and insistently as the Cambodian inscriptions of the seventh century do. In particular, the king-servant relationship, expressed in terms of honorable gifts, is not starkly elaborated. The social setting of religious beliefs in other cultures may resemble Khmer "Hinduism" more closely.

For example, the inscriptions of bronze vessels in early Chou times "advertise the honours conferred [by king or feudal prince] on the person responsible for the casting of the bronze."[67] These bronzes were used in sacrifices to the recipients' ancestors, to be "treasured perpetually" by their descendants,[68] and Professor Watson has suggested that the religious and political purposes recorded in the inscriptions belong equally to the uninscribed bronzes buried in the tombs.[69] Perhaps the Khmer death-wish inscriptions, also commemorating honors conferred by kings, are not dissimilar in religious intent: in both cultures, gifts have significance in the afterlife.

Another similarity may exist between Khmer "Hinduism" and beliefs held in ancient China. The Chinese quality of *tê* has been understood to include the notion of potentiality, latent power, and the virtue inherent in things.[70] *Tê* was a quality shared by the patricians, who had inherited it from the ancestors of their clans.[71] The Chinese king, like the Khmer overlord, was the first among the princes, and his *tê* won him the favor of Heaven. But his *tê* also influenced others. As Granet puts it, "the special genius (*tê*)" of the Chinese overlord was of a "religious and magic nature. This genius rules and regulates all things by immediate action, the action of spirit upon spirit. It acts by contagion."[72] Or again, because of the princely virtue, "le coeur des hommes va droit au devoir."[73]

This understanding of the nature of *tê* resembles, at least superficially, the Khmer "Hindu" conception of the soul (*ātman*). The prowess of the overlord's soul, having won Śiva's favor in the form of *śakti*, creates conditions whereby his followers can perform roles on behalf of the *dharma*. Perhaps the coalitions on behalf of chiefs, recorded by the Chinese as early as in the third century of Cambodian protohistory,

[67] William Watson, *Ancient Chinese Bronzes* (London: Faber; Rutland: Tuttle, 1962), p. 76. Sometimes the princes bestowed the bronze, p. 78.

[68] William Watson, *Early Civilization in China* (London: Thames and Hudson, 1966), p. 100.

[69] Watson, *Ancient Chinese Bronzes*, p. 68.

[70] Arthur Waley, *The Way and its Power: A Study of the Tao Te Ching and its Place in Chinese Thought* (London: George Allen & Unwin, 1934), pp. 31–32.

[71] Henri Maspero, *La Chine Antique*, Nouvelle edition (Paris: Imprimerie Nationale, 1955), p. 100.

[72] M. Granet, *Chinese Civilisation* (London: Kegan Paul, 1930), pp. 250–51.

[73] M. Granet, *La Religion des Chinois* (Paris: Presses Universitaires de France, 1951; reprint ed.), p. 41.

were motivated by the chiefs' belief that the souls of lesser men could respond beneficially to those of their leaders.

The possibility that a pre-Hindu system of beliefs enabled Khmers to interpret Śivaite devotionalism is not contradicted by what is known of the tribesmen in the highlands of mainland Southeast Asia. Professor Kirsch has attributed to the tribesmen a theory of "unequal souls."[74] They seem to identify in themselves a quality similar to *mana*, expressed by the procedure of feastgiving. "The successful feaster is actually demonstrating his 'innate virtue,' showing his 'internal potency,' and his control over external supernatural forces."[75] We can interpret in this way the reverence paid to the Khmer overlord's gifts by his subordinates. The overlord has clearly displayed proof of his potency, and his association with "external supernatural forces." Again, we can note that among the Iu Mien-yao, for example, merit-making investments in the world of men ensure the individual's status in the spirit world.[76]

Here, then, are some possibilities in support of the hypothesis that, when the Khmer élite began to hear of Hindu devotionalism, they brought to it as much as they took from it. Indeed, they may even have been recognizing some primitive notions in Hinduism that Hinduism shared with many peoples. The implication of the hypothesis is that Hindu ascetic practices tended to throw into sharper relief Khmer assumptions about an uneven distribution of prowess and the religious rapport that bound leaders and led.

Elsewhere in this volume[77] references are made to graves known to have been occupied several millennia ago. These graves may one day be seen to yield evidence of the beliefs of those who occupy them. The time may not be premature for prehistorians to be asking themselves three questions. Are they in the presence of evidence that throws light on very early Southeast Asian conceptions of the afterlife? Are there grounds for supposing that a connection was assumed between temporal achievement and a superior death status? To what extent does the evidence indicate

---

[74] A. Thomas Kirsch, *Feasting and Social Oscillation: Religion and Society in Upland Southeast Asia* (Ithaca, NY: Southeast Asia Program, Cornell University, 1973), p. 15.

[75] Ibid.

[76] P. Kandre, "Autonomy and Integration of Social Systems: the Lu Mien ('Yao' or 'Man') Mountain Population and their Neighbours," in *Southeast Asian Tribes, Minorities, and Nations*, ed. Peter Kunstadter, vol. 2 (Princeton, NJ: Princeton University Press, 1967), p. 596. We need not suppose that the social setting of Khmer "Hinduism" was only on the scale of overlordship. Some inscriptions suggest that a chief's cult could become a focus of homage in the neighborhood. In 685, the Mratān Devasvāmi performed a "great cult ceremony" at which no less than twenty-two others are said to be present as witnesses; IC, II, p. 124; Bhattacharya, *Les religions brahmaniques*, p. 149. In the same century, twenty-five persons gave gifts to the god of the Lord of Tamandarapura, whose elder brother was the Lord of Rudrapurī; IC, V, pp. 37–38. Ten contributed gifts to a tower built by Kṛṣṇamitra's grandson; IC, II, pp. 27–28. Gifts to cults were also made by wives and mothers-in-law; ISCC, p. 58, v. 3; IC, II, p. 201. Kṛṣṇamitra's brother-in-law gave land to Kṛṣṇamitra's *liṅga*, which was for the sake of the "family"; IC, II, pp. 27–28. The same inscription states that the grandson of these two chiefs, who had himself been the chief of a certain area since his youth, erected the tower on behalf of his two grandfathers. These scraps of information suggest that a considerable amount of inter-family alliance, reflected in cult worship, took place when families entered into marriage relationships. The network of alliances at regional level was a source of military power, available to a man of prowess with kingly ambitions.

[77] ["This volume" refers to *Early South East Asia*, ed. Ralph Smith and William Watson (Oxford: Oxford University Press, 1979), in which "Khmer 'Hinduism'" originally appeared.—Ed.]

that hierarchy was associated with religious attributes? In dealing with these questions, the prehistorian has one advantage over the protohistorian. Those who have left evidence of themselves in prehistoric times are anonymous and can be studied without having to be classified as "kings" or "chiefs." The protohistorian, on the other hand, has to avoid being misled by epigraphic distinctions of ranks. Hinduism was not something that only attracted would-be kings; it was essentially a religious experience of individuals in chieftain society. Moreover, if this experience were as much Khmer as "Hindu," Hinduism would not inevitably have created a religious wedge between that society and the rest of the population. Śiva's procreative role, as Paul Mus foresaw, would have been understood not only by chiefs but by peasants in the monsoon-controlled lands of Cambodia.

But, if and when the day comes when indigenous elements in Khmer "Hindu" evidence are more distinct, we must be careful not to react too strongly against the view that Hinduism swamped the Khmer outlook. Although Khmer "Hinduism" has been discussed in this essay in terms of personal religion, feeding on circumstances of Khmer society and perhaps shaped by pre-Hindu beliefs, we shall suggest, by way of conclusion, that Śivaite devotionalism also brought in its train something that distinguishes protohistory from prehistory. The chiefs came to have a new perception of the environment in which their personal cults flourished. Continuing to perform their ancient roles, they, like the inhabitants of peninsular India, came to see themselves as living in a "Hindu world." They were not "Hindus" only in their moments of worship.

By "Hindu world" is meant less the actual world of the regional polities in India, visited by or described to Khmers, than the world of the gods and heroes as it is set forth in Indian sacred literature and perhaps, above all, in the *Mahābhārata*, known in parts of Southeast Asia from at least as early as the fifth century.

The Khmers would not have had much difficulty in identifying some prominent similarities between the "Hindu world" and Cambodia. The assumption in Indian sacred literature is that all experience is an expression of universal truths, valid everywhere, and Khmers could verify the assumption from their own environment. For example, the *śāstras* assume that all space is organized in *maṇḍalas*, comprising warring polities sometimes brought under the influence of a "king of kings," and the concept would have corresponded accurately with the Khmer tribal situation. Similarly, happenings in the past as recorded in the *Mahābhārata* would not have perplexed them. The epic does not describe the gradual expansion of a great "kingdom." Instead, it renders the past as a record of the continuous expansion and contraction of righteous living, when men beloved by the gods appear from time to time, and Khmers would have observed that heroic princes and warriors often practiced asceticism to win divine support. The epic world would have been mirrored in Khmer tribal experience, with its series of overlordships and their collapses. The feat of holding together a number of independent territories by the Khmer chief closest to Śiva could readily be seen as keeping the dharma intact. Again, Indian literature, extolling examples of excellent religious conduct, does not disguise the co-existence of "barbarians." Cambodia also had its population living beyond the chiefs' domains. There were "horrible forests, the abode of savage men."[78]

---

[78] *IC*, I, p. 11, v. xiv.

In other words, the world of the epic would not have made impossible demands on the Khmer imagination. The Khmer chiefs, hearing about other parts of the Hindu world, would not have felt that they were living in a greatly different environment. They, too, were in the lands of the monsoons. The Indian texts' lists of general categories of phenomena, illustrated by examples classified under comprehensive headings, would more often than not have allowed Khmers to identify their own known facts within a framework of experience assumed in the texts to be universal. Hindu law acknowledged the importance of local customs. The Indians are likely to have had a Sanskrit word for most things familiar and important in Cambodia, enabling Khmer literati to invoke Indian texts, carrying great prestige, as ratifications of what they already knew to be true. Manu's seven constituents of government would have sounded as common sense.[79]

But a general comparability of experience does not necessarily mean that Khmers saw themselves as living in the Hindu world. Is there any evidence that they did in fact do so and by conviction? If so, why and how did they do so?

Two pieces of evidence indicate that they came to see themselves inside the Hindu world and not in its extension overseas. The first of these is that, when they observed certain stone mountain tops, they believed that they were seeing Siva's natural *lingas* (*svāyambhuvalingas*), fashioned in crude stone. These are the most prestigious of all *lingas*. Bhavavarman's Pāśupata poet, on a pilgrimage, visited mountains and, in a dream, Śiva brought him to a *linga*. When he woke up, he saw the *linga* on the top of a hill.[80] A follower of Jayavarman I also venerated a natural *linga*; he, too, would have seen himself in the Hindu world.[81] Similarly, Tamils could apprehend these *lingas* in their own country.

The second piece of evidence concerns something that happened in the shadow of the natural *linga* at Vat Phu, and it shows not only that Cambodia could be seen as part of the Hindu world but also how this perception was possible.

A king Devānīka, perhaps a Cham conqueror, visited this region in the fifth century.[82] He was installed in supreme power by "the blessed Śrī Lingaparvata," the natural *linga* that dominated the region. He then resolved to found a *tīrtha* in the form of a tank. He gave his tank the name of "Kurukṣetra," the name of the famous *tīrtha* in the region of Delhi and of the great civil war in the *Mahābhārata*. His tank's name therefore evokes the associations of a site that is in the very center of the Hindu world as that world is portrayed in the epic. He undoubtedly had in mind the "Kurukṣetra" of the epic, for verses from the epic concerning "Kurukṣetra" are quoted in his inscription.[83] And so the inscription states: "May the celestial fruit, proclaimed formerly in the Kurukṣetra and celebrated by the Devarṣi, find itself here in the new Kurukṣetra; ...may the fruits obtained in the thousand *tīrtha* of Kurukṣetra find themselves present here and complete."

Is Devānīka identifying the epic's tank in Cambodia in the sense of locating it there or is he merely transferring it? For him there could be only one "Kurukṣetra," and it was the epic's tank, now to be found in Cambodia as a result of his pious

---

[79] i.e. king, capital, ministers, army, treasury, countryside, allies.

[80] *IC*, I, p. 5, v. vi–vii.

[81] Ibid., p. 15, v. vii.

[82] G. Coedès, "Nouvelles donnés sur les origines du royaume khmer: la stèle de Vat Luong Kau, près de Vat P'hu," *BEFEO* 48,1 (1956): 209–20.

[83] C. Jacques, "Notes sur l'inscription de la stèle de Vat Luong Kau," *JA* 250,2 (1962): 250–52.

intention. In the words of his inscription, he "had created on earth the best of the *tīrtha*," and the reason why it was possible to execute such an intention tells us something about how he, and Khmer "Hindus," could apprehend their environment as part of the world of the cosmic gods and therefore part of what we are calling "the Hindu world."

The *Tīrtha yātrā parvan*, the section of the epic that deals with Kurukṣetra and also the section quoted in the Vat Phu inscription, assures its reader or listener that "he that is inspired with the desire of beholding all *tīrthas* should sojourn to them even in imagination … Men of piety and learning are able to visit these *tīrthas* by reason of their purified senses, their belief in Godhead, and their acquaintance with the Vedas."[84] And of Kurukṣetra, it is said: "O foremost of warriors, the sins of one that desireth to repair to Kurukṣetra even mentally are all destroyed."[85]

Devānīka was aware of the efficacy of traveling to Kurukṣetra in his mind. The reason need not necessarily be because he had obeyed the recommendation of the *Mahābhārata* concerning mental travel. Instead, he could have used the imaginative faculty which *gurus* were teaching their disciples as the means of strengthening an awareness of being in their god's presence. Devānīka states that he had just been installed in supreme power by the Śrī Liṅgaparvata, a manifestation of Śiva, and he, together with other Śiva-worshippers, may have been familiar with meditative techniques for willing states of mind that encouraged them to apprehend divinity in all its forms, and everywhere. The world was Śiva's creation,[86] and his worshipper would wish to learn to see the world in this way. Moreover, at the beginning of his inscription, Devānīka invokes his many merits, and he probably considers himself qualified to perform what amounts to an "Act of Truth (*satya*)," with the power to visit mentally all holy sites and therefore the one and only Kurukṣetra in the shape of the tank he has just built.[87] In this way, he can invest the region with Kurukṣetra's sanctity. A holy site in the epic has, as a feat of pious volition, become part of Cambodian reality. By virtue of his own merits, the king can project and leave behind him a permanent mark of his privileged perception of the "Hindu" world. Not surprisingly, this part of the Vat Phu region was still known as "Kurukṣetra" at least as late as the eleventh century.[88]

Meditative techniques need not have been more difficult than remembering that even a criminal, pronouncing the god's name without knowing it, obtained salvation or at least forgiveness of his sins before the judge of the dead.[89] According to a seventh-century inscription, hearing Śiva's name destroyed all sins.[90] Śiva could

---

[84] P. C. Roy, trans., *Mahābhārata*, vol. 2 (Calcutta: Bharata Press, 1884), *Tīrtha yātrā parvan*, p. 284.

[85] Ibid., p. 250.

[86] One of Iśānavarman I's inscriptions refers to the erection of a statue of Nṛtteśvara, the Śiva who dances the world into being; *IC*, IV, p. 11, v. xxxiii.

[87] His reason for invoking the name "Kurukṣetra" may be because he had just been consecrated as "king of kings," with the appropriate rites to which his inscription refers. He would therefore have undergone the *rājasūya* ceremony, bathed with holy water no doubt from the *liṅga* mountain. The epic says that, "by repairing to Kurukṣetra in a pious frame of mind, one obtaineth the fruits of the *Rājasūya*."

[88] *IC*, VI, p. 267.

[89] J. Gonda, *Les religions de l'Inde*, p. 240.

[90] *IC*, I, p. 11, v. xiii.

always be approached by speech. Listening to the recitation of the holy texts had particular efficacy; the listener earned merit and could, perhaps, identify himself with what was being recited. The *Mahābhārata, Purāṇa,* and *Rāmāyaṇa* were deposited in a seventh-century Khmer temple for the purpose of recitation.[91]

The *guru's* techniques for teaching the worship of personal gods were therefore also those that enabled the worshipper to reinforce his quest for the omnipresent god by seeing around him a zone of holy sites, which he could himself enlarge as Devānīka had done. These holy sites were the landmarks of the Hindu world, and the center of that world was always where the Hindu, be he Indian or Khmer, worshipped in the presence of his god.

But everything not connected with personal cults and the accompanying perception of zones of holiness had nothing to do with the Khmers' sense of being in the Hindu world.[92] The veneer of Indian literary allusions in their inscriptions is no more than a metaphorizing of their situations and heroes and a comment on the quality of their scribes' education. Kings are compared with Viṣṇu and Pṛthu, who was impregnated by Viṣṇu, but only to emphasize their courage. "Viṣṇu" is the metaphor for describing the military qualities of an overlord and his spiritual and Śiva-like qualities that account for his heroism. Īśānavarman I is said to be "like another Viṣṇu."[93] Sometimes the royal metaphors are condensed into the single expression that the king is the "compendium (*varṇamuṣṭi*) of the kings" in the sense of embodying all kingly qualities. Bhavavarman is such a person.[94] Īśānavarman I is the *varṇamuṣṭi* "of the kings of the first of the *yugas.*"[95]

The process of "Hinduization," as sketched above, can now be summarized. The process was one of empathy, and, because it was possible through the cultivation of mental aptitudes taught by devotional pedagogy, was essentially one of self-Hinduisation. It was a matter of imaginative intention, and the intention that supplied the underlying impulse was that of tapping cosmic power for personal ends. The process was a continuing one, in which generation after generation of local chiefs and those influenced by the chiefs' life-style willed their way ever more confidently into the universal reality in which their death wish could be most hopefully expressed. Perhaps times of king-making adventures were when there was a lively sense of achievement and therefore a sense of religious well-being.[96] But self-Hinduization was always against a background of inter-territorial relations. As the centuries passed, a more spacious measurement of the performance of royal prowess no doubt became available, but the consequence was never the establishment of the concept of a Khmer kingdom as something with its own identity. There was only a cult of kingship in the form of the personal cult of the man who had seized the

---

[91] *ISCC,* p. 31, v. 4.

[92] The Khmers were not, of course, finding a place for themselves in a world dominated by "India." Their inscriptions show that they were aware only of regions in "India." They knew of Dakṣiṇapatha (*IC,* IV, p. 27, v. iii), Kāñcipura (*IC,* p. 10, v. iv), Madhyadeśa (*IC,* IV, p. 61, v. iii), and Malava (*IC,* V, p. 39, v. ii).

[93] *IC,* I, p. 15, v. iv.

[94] *IC,* II, p. 70, v. i.

[95] Finot, "Nouvelles inscriptions du Cambodge," 45, v. iv.

[96] In this context, we can note the Chinese statement about Kauṇḍinya II, who was acclaimed about 400. He is said to have "changed again the system and used Indian laws"; Pelliot, "Le Fou-nan," p. 269. The alliance of kings and chiefs may have generated a mood of religious rapport in which everything could be seen in Hindu terms.

kingship. Political allegiance, expressed by personal loyalty, was no more than the sum total of the personal religious concerns of the territorial chiefs who believed that an overlordship was providing them with additional means of earning merit and satisfying their death wishes. For them Cambodia was not a "kingdom" but a holy land in the Hindu world, linked by networks of pilgrimage sites. Their past was lost in the origins of mankind and was adorned more recently by instances of devout warriors, performing great deeds. The present was always the time that mattered, when merit-earning achievement was possible. The future lay in the rewards beyond the tomb.

PART IV

VIETNAMESE HISTORIOGRAPHY AND LITERATURE

CHAPTER NINE

HISTORIANS AND EMPERORS IN VIETNAM AND CHINA: COMMENTS ARISING OUT OF LÊ VĂN HƯU'S HISTORY, PRESENTED TO THE TRẦN COURT IN 1272[*]

I shall discuss two perceptions of the past. The first is, as far as one who is not a sinologue can discern it, that of Chinese literati who wrote histories. Their perspective was conveyed by their books to Vietnamese literati, including Lê Văn Hưu, an examination graduate of 1247 and, at one stage in his career, an official in the Han Lam academy. The other perception is Lê Văn Hưu's. The Vietnamese annals (*Đại Việt Sử Ký Toàn Thư*) state that he was commissioned to edit the historical records of Vietnam and was congratulated when he submitted his completed *Đại Việt Sử Ký* to the Trần throne early in 1272. He had been ordered to cover the period from Triệu Đà's reign to the end of the Lý dynasty, a span of time extending from the end of the third century BCE to the early thirteenth, when the Trần dynasty succeeded the Lý.

The Chinese and Vietnamese perceptions of the past that will be my point of departure concern a theme of significance to Vietnamese in medieval times: the meaning of the Sino–Vietnamese tributary relationship. Hưu, as we shall see, incorporated information from Chinese historical records concerning the conventions of the relationship, and the possibility arises that he was influenced by Chinese historiographical models and intentions. The Trần rulers of the thirteenth century were devoutly Buddhist, subscribing to the Dhyāna school of the Mahāyāna, but they also employed a bureaucracy and appointed literati to subordinate posts. To this extent, the court may have been more susceptible, though not necessarily always hospitable, to sinic influences than any other sector in Vietnamese society at the time.

[*] I am indebted to the Guggenheim Foundation for a Fellowship during 1972–73 that enabled me to study early Vietnamese history. I am grateful to Professors James Siegel and Charles Peterson and to Dr. David Elliott for discussing drafts of this essay.

Before I compare the form, treatment, and purpose of Lê Văn Hưu's history with corresponding features in a Chinese history, I shall summarize the disturbing contemporary background in Vietnam that gave special significance to the subject of Vietnam's relations with China. In the years immediately after the first unsuccessful Mongol invasion of 1257, Kublai Khan increasingly suspected his Vietnamese "vassal's" fidelity, and he exerted immoderate diplomatic pressure in order to supervise the Trần court. He frequently sent envoys to Vietnam and even posted his own representative to the capital of Thăng-long. Towards the end of 1270, Kublai despatched an angry message that denounced the Trần court's haughty protocol when it received Mongol edicts and entertained Kublai's envoys. He had recently realized that, during the past decade, the Trần ruler persisted in according Mongol envoys the courtesies appropriate in an independent ruler's court. In 1271 the Trần ruler replied to the edict. His memorial was humbly phrased and suppressed references to his pretensions, though the imperial status of the Vietnamese rulers, asserted within their own territories, is at least as old as 1057, when bricks excavated in modern times are dated according to the reign period of "the third emperor of the Lý family." But the Trần ruler insisted in his reply to Kublai that his court protocol was in accordance with his country's ancient customs.

Such was the disturbing background when Lê Văn Hưu was ordered to compile the Vietnamese annals, and the question is whether he wrote an ingenious history that should be regarded as a Chinese-modeled counter-history, with the same range of topics and treatment that one finds in a Chinese history but adapted to sustain a Vietnamese interpretation of the tributary relationship. After all, he was constructing a history of dynasties as Ssŭ-ma Kuang did; the Tzu-chih t'ung-chien covers a roughly comparable span of time. Moreover, Hưu's research among Chinese sources for information about the tributary relationship implies that he was familiar with the organization, purposes, and outlook of Chinese historians.

I shall first define briefly some essential features of the Chinese perception and presentation of the past. Because Hưu is interested in the Sino–Vietnamese past as seen through Vietnamese eyes, I shall also note how the Vietnamese past was seen through Chinese eyes.

Chinese history, written by scholars of the "Confucian persuasion," was seen as a record, generation by generation, of mankind's performance in living up to the moral standards taught by the sage rulers of high antiquity. Chinese historians contemplated a golden age of the sage rulers, whose moral principles supplied canons for interpreting the behaviour of subsequent generations of rulers and subjects. The inevitable consequence was that the historians, usually officials, paid special attention to the role of government as the agency for protecting morality. The Chinese were convinced that Heaven had ordained the rule of a given dynastic line in recognition of its superior *virtus (tê)* and for the purpose of achieving harmony among human beings. The dynasty, supported by its Mandate, was seen as being in the orthodox line of succession (*cheng-t'ung*) from the sage emperors, who did not found dynasties, and the three dynasties of Hsia, Shang, and Chou that succeeded to the Mandate. The dynastic line of succession was the mechanism whereby primeval wisdom was, despite setbacks, transmitted to the living generation. The Han and subsequent dynasties could be seen, with more or less verisimilitude, as the successors of the Chou.

Obviously a special emphasis was given to the phenomenon of the orthodox line of succession as a consequence of the historian's need to justify his own dynasty's right to be recognized as the recipient of Heaven's Mandate after the preceding dynasty had forfeited it. Obviously, too, the compiling and reviewing of the record of the past were opportunities for commending admirable examples of persons outside the imperial families who chose to lead moral lives or for criticizing those who did otherwise. The performance of dynasties and officials became valuable teaching aids for instructing the present generation. Ssŭ-ma Kuang, preparing to write his great history, informed the Sung emperor, Ying-tsung, that he had wanted to write a chronological history that embodied:

> all that a prince ought to know—everything pertaining to the rise and fall of dynasties and the good and ill fortune of the common people, all good and bad examples that can furnish models and warnings.[1]

He was writing at a time when the emperors were beginning to hold seminars, attended by readers-in-waiting, to lecture on the classics or to read history. In this way, current policy questions could be discussed in the light of relevant historical analogies.[2] Here, too, was an opportunity for historians to influence the present generation of rulers and officials by displaying their sophistication and their by no means unobjective attitude towards the past.

The same perception of the past, with its emphasis on moral excellence and cultural continuity, shaped Chinese perceptions of the Sino–Vietnamese relationship. Chinese scholars were able to read in the Shih-chi that Chiao-chih, the Western Han name for Vietnam and perhaps the corruption of an indigenous name,[3] lay within the sphere of influence of Kao-yang, the fifth of the great sage emperors of antiquity.[4] But only in China did dynasties inherit the Mandate of Heaven.

The Chinese imperial heirs of the sages were seen as being able to attract automatic obedience from vassals in distant lands, and ancient Chinese literature was believed to supply them with an example that, over the centuries, could be cited as an allusion to the way in which Vietnam in early times had been attracted by Chinese civilization. The Hou Han-shu mentions what came to be regarded as the first tributary mission from Vietnam, sent in early Chou times. The mission was sent from Việt-thường. The envoys said that they had come a great distance because they knew that China had a sage.[5] This event became the symbol of an ancient gesture of homage to China and, in later times, part of the cultural justification for Vietnam's political submission. From early T'ang times a body of classicist opinion in the Chinese court was able to recall the benign influence of the sage emperors and kings as an argument for adopting pacific policies towards Vietnam, and they could justify

---

[1] E. G. Pulleyblank, "Chinese Historical Criticism: Liu Chih-chi and Ssu-ma," in *Historians of China and Japan*, ed. W. G. Beasley and E. G. Pulleyblank (London: Oxford University Press, 1961), pp. 153–54.

[2] R. M. Hartwell, "Historical Analogism, Public Policy, and Social Science in Eleventh- and Twelfth-Century China," *The American Historical Review* 76,3 (1971): 701.

[3] Nguyễn Phúc Long, "Les nouvelles recherches archeologiques au Vietnam (Complement au Vietnam de Louis Bezacier)," *Arts Asiatiques*, Numéro special 31 (1975): 14. The suggestion is that *Chiao-chih* originally meant "the territories occupied by the peoples who worshipped the *Kiao long* (the crocodile-dragon totem)."

[4] E. Chavannes, *Les Memoires Historiques de Se-ma Ts'ien*, vol. 1 (Leiden: E. J. Brill, 1967), p. 37. The year of this legendary emperor's accession corresponds to 2435 BCE.

[5] *Hou Han-shu* (Po-na edition), ch. 116, 7b–8a

their case on military grounds by quoting the Việt-thường envoys' account of the distance that separated the two countries.[6]

Triệu Đà (207–137 BCE), who, as we shall see, was an important figure in Lê Văn Hưu's conception of Vietnamese history, was a contemporary of the early Han emperors and had seized a satrapy for himself in southern China, where he ruled from Canton and exercised minimal influence in Vietnam. The Han records show that he had acknowledged the sage-like Han emperors as his suzerains, and he was always remembered in China as an obedient vassal. Sĩ Nhiếp provided the Chinese with a different kind of exemplary figure in the Sino–Vietnamese past. He was the Eastern Han's representative in Vietnam during the last decades of Han rule at the end of the second century CE and the beginning of the third. Though of Vietnamese origin, he had been educated in China and attempted to rule Vietnam as a Chinese-style official.

So much, then, by way of a summary of the Chinese perception of the past. Vietnamese history, subsumed by Chinese dynastic chronology, becomes an opportunity for moralistic observations by Chinese emperors and scholar-officials and lends itself as a foil for the historians' didactic purpose in their effort to teach the principles and consequences of good government. Vietnamese history is no more than a pale reflection of the sequel to the cultural glow at the dawn of Chinese history, a glow that is fanned from time to time when good emperors are ruling in China. The tributary relationship is regarded as the Vietnamese vassals' privileged occasion for communicating with the Chinese emperors, always the source of cultural excellence.

We can now return to Lê Văn Hưu and inquire to what extent he seems to adapt Vietnamese history to a similarly organized view of the past in order to write a counter-history based on a Chinese-modeled dynastic form. He uses dynastic history in Vietnam as the skein for his narrative and, as we shall see, he is by no means hesitant in assigning praise and blame in his comments. Yet there are several odd features in his treatment of the past.

He does not specifically mention the Chinese primeval golden age—when the sages were ruling—though his comments show that he is familiar with the sages. Instead, he begins his history with Triệu Đà's reign in the third and second centuries BCE. Triệu Đà was a Chinese adventurer from Chen-ting in Hopei. According to the Shih-chi and the Mien Han-shu, he assumed and retained the title and style of the Han emperors, even though he also accepted Han suzerainty on two occasions.[7] The Chinese admission finds its way into the Vietnamese annals under the date of 144 BCE and enables Hưu, who was certainly responsible for introducing the Chinese texts about Triệu Đà into the annals, to write a eulogizing comment on him. Triệu Đà's *virtus* is compared with that of Shun and Wen Wang, ancient sage rulers. He is described as the successful diplomat who preserved as well as founded the Vietnamese imperial institution.

> He inaugurated the imperial institution in our country. His achievement may be judged to be great. If the later emperors could have emulated Triệu Vũ in sealing off the frontier, establishing the country's army, following the correct way in

---

[6] The argument was also used by the Trần court to justify the ruler's refusal to visit China to receive investiture.

[7] *Shih-chi* (Po-na edition), ch. 113, 3b; *Ch'ien Han-shu* (Po-na edition), ch. 95, 12a.

their relations with neighbouring countries, and safeguarding their throne with benevolence, they would have preserved the country for a long time, and the Northerners would not again have been able to gaze on us with covetous eyes.[8]

Vietnam's golden age is depicted not in terms of cultural excellence but of imperial independence, when the court's style was exactly the same as that of the Han court. Here is a reconstruction of a golden age that seems to caricature the Chinese view of the most ancient past. Even more odd is Hưu's treatment of the centuries from the tenth to the early thirteenth, when Vietnam recovered and maintained its independence. While China's past, seen by its historians, is the record of the transmission of a cultural heritage, Vietnam's past is always the record of a very imperfect matching of Triệu Đà's achievement. Nothing in Vietnamese history is equivalent to the waxing and waning of moral excellence that enabled the Chinese to organize their perception of the past and chronicle the succession to the Mandate of Heaven. On the contrary, Vietnamese history, seen in Hưu's comments, by no means illustrates the more or less continuous expression of imperial status and *virtus* after independence had been recovered in the tenth century.

Surprisingly, Hưu refuses to acknowledge Ngô Quyền as being in the line of succession from Triệu Đà, and the reason is simply that Ngô Quyền did not proclaim himself as "emperor." Hưu's denial of status is in spite of this ruler's defeat of the Chinese in 938, which Hưu acknowledges in handsome terms. Đinh Tiên Hoàng in 968 became Triệu Đà's first successor because he styled himself "emperor" and introduced a system of court officials. Hưu hails this event:

> Was it not, indeed, Heaven's will that our country should again produce the sages' wisdom so that Triệu vương should have a successor?[9]

Thereafter, Vietnam had heroic diplomat–rulers who could manipulate the tributary relationship in order to maintain their imperial status in Vietnam, and no ruler was more successful than Lê Hoàn (980–1005). Hưu, always concerned to show that the tributary relationship was compatible with Vietnamese independence, again quotes from Chinese texts to verify his contention. He incorporates, with appropriate modifications, passages that reveal that Lê Hoàn behaved as an independent monarch in the presence of Sung envoys.[10] He also quotes a Chinese text that states

---

[8] *Đại Việt Sử Ký Toàn Thư* [Complete Book of the Historical Record of Great Viet] under date of 137 BCE. I have translated in the past tense because I believe that Hưu had in mind the opening of the frontier by the last ruler of Triệu Đà's dynasty, whom he criticizes in his comment under the date of 111 BCE. Triệu Đà had sealed the frontier. Triệu Đà styled himself Vũ-đế (the martial emperor). [A copy of the *Đại Việt Sử Ký Toàn Thư*, the consolidated annalistic history of Vietnam compiled at the end of the seventh century, which is in itself a copy of the Kong-yon-kim Library text, is available at the Tōyō Bunka. It was collated by Ch'en Chingho (Tokyo: Tokyo Daigaku Tōyō Bunka Kênkynjo, 1984–86). Hereafter *TT*.—Ed.]

[9] *TT* under date of 986. Hưu's reference to "the sages' wisdom" and to the "succession" persuade me that he has Triệu Đà and not Triệu Việt-vương in mind. The latter led the resistance against the Chinese in the sixth century but did not interest Hưu. "Vương" (king) is the prestigious title attributed to the rulers of the Three Dynasties (Hsia, Shang, and Chou).

[10] According to *TT* under date of 990, Lê Hoàn pretended to be wounded to avoid having to dismount from his horse and pay respect to the Sung envoys. His pretext is mentioned in Li T'ao, *Hsu tzu-chih t'ung-chien ch'ang-pien* (Chung-kuo hsueh-shu ming-chu series) (Taipeh, n.p.,

that Lê Hoàn insisted that there was no reason for the Sung court to send missions to Vietnam.[11] Here was historical evidence that showed that the Sung emperors, unlike Kublai Khan, connived at the Vietnamese construction of the tributary system.

But, according to Hưu, the Vietnamese emperors were wanting in other essential respects. They were unable to make proper arrangements for transmitting the throne to their descendants.[12] Again, their court style, unlike Triệu Đà's, did not satisfactorily exemplify the proposition, so dear to Hưu, that in its symbolic and ritual features the Vietnamese court was the peer of the Chinese imperial court. This proposition was of central importance in Hưu's rendering of Vietnamese independence.

Also surprising in the work of a scholar who was familiar with Chinese historical writing is Hưu's attitude towards the founders of the Lý dynasty, the first long-lived one in Vietnam, which is critical. Founders of new dynasties are tenderly treated in Chinese histories. According to Hưu, however, only in one respect do they supply exemplary figures. These are the second and third Lý rulers, and the reason is that they avenged earlier Cham attacks across the southern borders.

Hưu's criticisms are inspired to a large extent by the Buddhist values and behaviour of the Lý court, and his prejudice may lead us to suppose that he is deploring the absence of Confucian influence in the seat of government. The implication would be that he associates himself with the ideology and perspectives of Chinese historians.

I believe that this is a mistaken interpretation of his concern. The term he uses for non-Buddhist scholars is *nho* (儒). When used in Chinese contexts before the late twelfth century, the term should not be translated as "Confucianist" in the sense that such a person was sincerely committed to advocating Confucian principles in framing governmental policies. "Classicist" is a better translation,[13] and the Lý period context in which the *nho* appear is consistent with this rendering of the term. The *nho* were merely expected to have read and to be familiar with the contents of Chinese classical literature, known to Hưu as the "learning of antiquity."[14] Hưu is interested in the "learning of antiquity" rather than in the *nho*, and his interest had nothing to do with moralistic doctrines. The *nho*, with their special expertise, could and should have cited this learning to help the court fulfill more effectively its essential role of safeguarding the country's independence. Moreover, and equally important, they could and should have advised the rulers on matters of court style that would have enabled the court to match the style of the Chinese court. If these

---

1961), ch. 31, 1. The two accounts of the episode are identical except that the *TT* admits that Lê Hoàn was being deceitful.

[11] *TT* under date of 986. His request is in Li T'ao, ch. 27, 20. According to *TT* under date of 990, Lê Hoàn obtained the Sung emperor's agreement that diplomatic correspondence should be exchanged on the border. Li T'ao is silent on this matter.

[12] I have discussed Hưu's views on dynastic succession in "Lê Văn Hưu's Treatment of Lý Thần Tôn's Reign," in *Southeast Asian History and Historiography: Essays Presented to D. G. E. Hall*, ed. C. D. Cowan and O. W. Wolters (Ithaca, NY: Cornell University Press, 1976), pp. 203–26.

[13] I am following Hartwell, "Historical Analogism, Public Policy," p. 690, n. 4.

[14] See *TT* under date of 970, where Hưu refers to the "learning of antiquity." His comments under the dates of 1028 and 1039 refer to the lack of "learning" of the ruler and the *nho*. His comments under dates of 1034 and 1130 quote Confucius and the Book of Songs respectively. His comment on 1129 deplores the ignorance of "rites," an element in the old learning.

two spheres of appropriate *nho* influence are borne in mind, we need not be misled by Hưu's strictures on Buddhism.

Space permits only two examples of occasions when Hưu criticizes the *nho* for their failure to strengthen the court with their learning. The absence of their advice explains why in 1043 the second Lý ruler showed undue mercy towards the rebel Nung ruler in the northern mountains. According to Hưu, the emperor practiced the "lesser benevolence" (小仁) of Buddhism and forgot his "major duty" (大義) to the states.[15] "Benevolence" and "duty" are concepts that *nho* should have understood. But, because they were ignorant or obsequious, they did not supply this kind of muscle to the dynasty. The other example of Hưu's criticism of the *nho* is in the context of his criticisms of the insufficiently imperial style of the Lý court. His comment under the year 1009 compares unfavourably the titles conferred by the first Lý ruler on his parents with those conferred by the founders of the Chou and also, it should be noted, of the contemporary Sung.[16] He has already likened Triệu Đà's *virtus* to that of Shun and Wen Wang, and he is not being inconsistent when he invokes other Chinese precedents to emphasize the identical status of the Vietnamese and Chinese courts during Triệu Đà's rule, which was later diminished by Lý court practices.

Lê Văn Hưu's notion of the "learning of antiquity" is very different from that of Ou-yang Hsiu (1007–1072), compiler of the Hsin T'ang-shu and another critic of Buddhism. Ou-yang Hsiu was worried by the failure of Confucianism to make headway among the Buddhist masses, for the reason that the whole social and cultural environment was indisposed to Confucianism.[17] But Hưu is not interested in transforming the population by Confucian teachings. He soft-pedals the Chinese view, and also the view of later Vietnamese historians, that Sĩ Nhiếp, the Eastern Han governor of Vietnam, should be admired as a good cultural influence. His comments never suggest that Vietnam had a tradition of good government that depended on secular doctrines to which rulers and subjects should subscribe. Government is good only when the ruler can rally the country behind him in times of external danger and can strengthen the dynastic succession procedures. A few rulers had achieved the former objective, but no ruler satisfactorily achieved the latter.

Lê Văn Hưu's treatment of Vietnamese history is hardly the kind of treatment one would expect of a Chinese historian of Chinese dynasties. Nevertheless, his craftsmanship and didactic bias may give the impression that he was adapting a history after the Chinese model in order to present a Vietnamese counter-history on the theme of independence and the means of preserving it. He begins with a golden age, dominated by the first emperor, Triệu Đà. He issues warnings on how the empire, the exemplary institution of the golden age, should have been protected by later generations of rulers. The orthodox succession (*chính thống*) is resumed in the tenth century and maintained thereafter, even though the succession is always threatened by succession disputes. Hưu's history does not reflect a Confucian-style tension between good and bad moral influences, but the tension between Chinese and Vietnamese renderings of the tributary relationship gives interpretative

---

[15] *TT* under date of 1043. Also see comment under date of 1154 for another reference to "duty."

[16] *TT* under date of 1009.

[17] W. T. de Bary, "Some Common Tendencies in Neo-Confucianism," in *Confucianism in Action*, ed. D. S. Nivison and A. F. Wright (Stanford, CA: Stanford University Press, 1959), p. 34.

significance to his work. And even if he seems to find bad rather than good lessons from the past, he remains a teacher of the lessons of history to whom such terms as *virtus*, duty, and benevolence are familiar. He attacks Buddhism, though on the grounds that it weakens the court and wastes the country's revenue and manpower.[18] Are we, then, dealing with a Chinese-structured perception of the past that came naturally to him when he disclosed his own perception of the Vietnamese past or are we in the presence of an altogether different conception of history?

In spite of apparent similarities between a Chinese history and Huu's history, I have come to the conclusion that Huu did not share the outlook of a Chinese historian, and doubt begins to arise when we consider some implications of the most curious episode in his view of the past, which is the foundation of the empire by Triệu Đà. Huu had searched Chinese texts and was well aware that Triệu Đà was only a Chinese adventurer; indeed, his treatment of the adventurer was regarded as extravagant by the historian Ngô Thì Sĩ in the eighteenth century.[19] Perhaps Huu was aware of an ancient Vietnamese folk tradition that accepted Triệu Đà as a patriot, whose surname was adopted by heroes in later wars of resistance against the Chinese.[20] On the other hand, Triệu Đà is conspicuously absent among the tutelary spirits honored by the Trần rulers and described in the *Việt điện u linh tập*, the collection of folk legends compiled in the early fourteenth century. Moreover, there is no evidence that Huu was interested in the Vietnamese background to Triệu Đà's intervention in Vietnam; Triệu Đà had overthrown An-dương of Cổ-loa, who had overthrown the last Hùng king. On the contrary, Huu's comment on Triệu Đà, the first of his comments, reads as though he was deliberately giving effect to the Trần court's order that his work should begin with Triệu Đà in order to prove that the Vietnamese empire was founded by this ruler. Triệu Đà does not lead him backwards into folklore but enables him to interpret the sequel of Vietnamese imperial history.[21]

Triệu Đà's function is to introduce the "imperial" history of independent Vietnam. He is the diplomat who manipulated the tributary relationship so that he could preside over a Chinese-style court that was the Chinese court's equal and therefore independent. None of his successors down the centuries had discharged all these responsibilities to Huu's satisfaction. But the Trần court, which ordered Huu to introduce his history with Triệu Đà, was putting up a brave diplomatic front against Kublai Khan's assault on the conventions of the tributary relationship as they had evolved in Sung times and had allowed the Vietnamese ruler to sustain the title of "emperor." Huu may have been using Triệu Đà as a peg on which to hang his conception of the ideal Vietnamese emperor, an ideal that became a reality only in the person of Trần Thái-tôn (1225–1277), the reigning emperor. The possibility

---

[18] *TT* under date of 1010.

[19] Ngô Thì Sĩ, *Việt Sử Tiêu Án* (Saigon: Văn-hóa Á-châu, 1960), pp. 33–36. Ngô Thì Sĩ cut Triệu Đà down to size by criticizing him for introducing the period of Chinese domination and for contributing nothing to the cultural well-being of Vietnam.

[20] Dr. Keith W. Taylor has discussed Triệu Đà's position in "The Historical Self-image of the Vietnamese People." See Keith W. Taylor, "The Rise of Đại Việt and the Establishment of Thăng-long," in *Explorations in Early Southeast Asian History: The Origins of Southeast Asian Statecraft*, ed. Kenneth R. Hall and John K. Whitmore (Ann Arbor, MI: Center for South and Southeast Asian Studies, University of Michigan, 1976), pp. 161–63.

[21] Triệu Đà's status as the inaugurator of Vietnamese imperial history is explicit or implied in Huu's comments of 137 BCE, 42, 184, 210, and 968 CE.

becomes more likely when we note what Hưu would have known during his lifetime and especially the dominating influence of Thái-tôn, the patron of Hưu's history.

Hưu would have seen two exciting phenomena. The court was increasingly acknowledging the usefulness of the *nho* and was recognizing as never before that the "learning of antiquity" could contribute to the well-being of the state. Secondly, the empire was showing the promise of being able to survive in the face of unprecedented danger, and, as we shall see, the court's imperial style was, because of its debt to the "learning of antiquity," even helping to supply the empire with its maximum strength.

The "learning of antiquity," in the form of the Four Books and the Six Classics, was being expounded by *nho* under court auspices since 1253. Examinations for public service were being regularly held. Court style was improving. The ruler was being addressed by a term (*quan gia*) that carried Chinese classical allusions and was superior to the different terms used in Lý times, to which Hưu objects.[22] In 1237, when Trần Thái-tôn remarried, his previous wife was reduced to the rank of princess; no longer did the ruler possess two or more consorts of the same rank, another un-Chinese Lý practice that Hưu deplores. In 1267, according to the Vietnamese annals, *nho* graduates were being appointed to the administrative bureaux and a beginning was made in displacing illiterate eunuchs in positions of power. Finally, and much more exhilarating for Hưu, *nho* were actively helping the court by traveling on dangerous missions to face Kublai Khan with memorials written to defend Vietnamese court protocol or explain why Kublai's orders had been disobeyed. Other *nho* were defending independence by drafting replies to Mongol edicts in the Hàn Lâm or Tập Hiền Offices, where the Chinese texts that Hưu so skillfully exploited were stacked.

But Hưu was also writing at a time when the "learning of antiquity" was making a much more notable contribution to the country's strength.

Before we examine this development, we must remember that, during the dangerous years in the middle of the thirteenth century, Vietnam's security in the final analysis depended on the Trần family's nerve and unity. But all had not been well in the family. In 1237, Thái-tôn had married his brother's wife. His brother rebelled and would have been executed if Thái-tôn had not intervened. The brother remained aggrieved, and his son tried to escape to Sung China not long before the first Mongol invasion in 1257. In these unhappy times, the behaviour of the Trần princes was of decisive importance, and the greatest test of their unity was likely to arise when Thái-tôn died and a princely struggle for the throne might erupt, as happened in 1028 when the founder of the Lý dynasty died. The struggle could then become Kublai Khan's opportunity for intervening on behalf of a disloyal prince. Indeed, two Trần princes were to defect to the Mongols during the second invasion in the 1280s and one of them allowed himself to be made puppet emperor.

Bearing in mind this threat to Vietnam's security, we shall now consider a remarkable event that took place in 1258, not long after the withdrawal of the Mongol army. Early that year Thái-tôn appointed his son Hoàng as "emperor" and withdrew to the Northern Palace. This was the first occasion that the question of the succession had arisen since the Trần dynasty was founded in 1225. Reign periods

---

[22] *TT* under date of 1369 shows that the Trần rulers were addressed as *quan gia*. In 1277 the ruler congratulated a prince for explaining the classical origin of the term. Is the *TT*'s reference to *quốc gia* (under date of 1250) an error for *quan gia*?

and edicts were now announced in the name of the new emperor, known after he died as Thánh-tôn. Thái-tôn became the "senior emperor" (上皇), the title held by his father who died in 1234. Thái-tôn remained the ultimate source of authority but was able to share some of the chores of government with his son. The Trần family maintained the same procedure, and the continuing integrity of the senior emperor's authority is illustrated in 1299, when Thái-tôn's grandson, now senior emperor, warned his son, the "emperor," that a new emperor could be appointed if he continued to misbehave. Thái-tôn in 1258 was evidently making known whom he intended to succeed him and whom he proposed to train in imperial responsibilities. The Lý rulers had also indicated their preference in selecting heirs and giving them responsibilities, but, as Hưu regrets, the formal appointment was always postponed until the rulers were dying. Thái-tôn expressed his choice when he was still in the full vigour of life and could protect his son's claim to the throne. The heir was now "emperor," and his dispossession of the throne when Thái-tôn died would be an act of treason.

The significance of the succession procedure of 1258 is enhanced when we observe that the procedure was presented under the guise of the "learning of antiquity." Thái-tôn's new honorific title incorporated the following words: "the emperor who is manifesting Yao's sage(-like) old age." The expression is an allusion to the teachings of Mencius (c. 371–289 BCE).

According to Mencius, the sage emperor Yao in his old age associated Shun, who was not of his family, with "the joint running of the empire." Shun had become known to Yao because of his extraordinary filial piety. Yao was not abdicating; he was seeking assistance in ruling. Shun proved to be a worthy assistant, and Yao, before he died, ignored his own worthless son and "presented Shun to Heaven" as the person best suited to succeed him. Shun withdrew from court during the three years of mourning, but the feudal lords did not hail Yao's son as the new emperor when the three years were over. Instead, they turned to Shun, who assumed the dignity of Son of Heaven.

Mencius, the first Chinese philosopher to develop the theme of the succession of sages, attaches great importance to this episode. He explains that Yao did not give the empire to Shun. Only Heaven could do so, and Heaven made its will known through the people's approval of Shun's conduct when he was assisting Yao. Mencius can therefore utter his famous statement that Heaven sees as the people see. But Mencius does not commit himself to the view that an emperor should always be succeeded by a worthy minister. Instead, he quotes Confucius as saying that the succession from father to son was also according to the concept of duty (義) in the sense perhaps that the father was not inappropriately indulging himself by appointing a worthy son to succeed him. Confucius had in mind the three dynasties of Hsia, Shang, and Chou.

The literal understanding of the incorporation of Yao's name in Thái-tôn's new title can only be that Thái-tôn was making it known that his son was being cast for the role of Shun and that, if all went well, the son would be a worthy successor. The father would satisfy himself that the son deserved to succeed him. Then, according to Mencius's scenario, the Trần princes would turn to the son as enthusiastically as the feudal lords had turned to Shun when Yao died.

I have described the scenario of 1258 because it raises the crucial question of the authority and function of Chinese texts, culled from the "learning of antiquity," when they were invoked in support of Vietnamese decision making. Lê Văn Hưu respected the "learning of antiquity" and was at home in Chinese historical literature. Vietnamese attitudes, generated over many centuries, towards these texts seem to lie at the core of our understanding of Hưu's cultural identity when he was writing history.

Thái-tôn's invocation of Mencius in 1258 is not an isolated example of the use of a Chinese text to reinforce an imperial succession. The sanctity of the Vietnamese dynastic institution could not be taken for granted during the Lý period (1009–1224),[23] and what happened more than a century earlier is so strikingly similar to the scenario of 1258 that it suggests Chinese texts were believed to provide some special security to the imperial succession.

In 1127, the fourth Lý ruler, Nhân-tôn, was dying. Because he was childless, some years earlier he had adopted his brother's son. The heir was still young, and his youthfulness as well as the circumstance that this was the first occasion in Lý dynastic history when the ruler would not be succeeded by a natural son made it more than possible that difficulties would arise.[24] Indeed, when Nhân-tôn died, special policing precautions were taken in the imperial city. In this situation, the outcome of which Nhân-tôn could not confidently predict, he issued a remarkable edict to formalize his choice of heir, and the Vietnamese annals record the measures adopted after his death to execute it. The edict, which survives in the annals, contains the assurance that the heir is well qualified to succeed and orders the publication of Nhân-tôn's final instructions. The dying emperor also expresses his wish that the mourning rites should be as frugal as those of Han Wen-ti (180–157 BCE).

Nhân-tôn's edict is, in fact, a recognizable adaptation of Wen-ti's own death-bed edict, preserved in the *Ch'ien Han-shu*.[25] The vocabulary is not always identical, but the contents and mood are unmistakably similar, though the Vietnamese version has to break new ground by referring to Nhân-tôn's heir and to Wen-ti. Here, then, is another instance of the use of a Chinese text to support a specific and urgent Vietnamese purpose. The occasions in 1127 and 1258 concern the dynastic succession; the only difference is that Thái-tôn was not dying in 1258.

Within minutes of Nhân-tôn's death, his executors in the court, anxious to find out the details of Wen-ti's mourning, would discover (if they had not already known) that they were reading an edict that emphasized the prestige of Wen-ti's imperial ancestors, homage that was now being transferred to Nhân-tôn's. They would then realize that Nhân-tôn on his death bed was mobilizing the prestige of his imperial family (as Wen-ti had done) to reinforce a succession that members of the Vietnamese court might have suspected was unorthodox because the heir was only a nephew. But why was the style of Wen-ti's edict selected to adorn Nhân-tôn's? Some court officials, versed in Chinese historical literature, would recall that Wen-ti, at the beginning of his reign in 179 BCE, had stressed the importance of his being

---

[23] See my "Lô Văn Hưu's Treatment of Lý Thần Tôn's Reign," in *Southeast Asian History and Historiography*, ed. Cowan and Wolters.

[24] According to the *TT*, the *Nhân vương* sutra was recited in 1126. This sutra (*Jen wang*) invokes the Buddha's protection of the country.

[25] A translation of Nhân-tôn's edict, incorporated in *TT*, will be found in Duong Đình Khuê, *Les Chefs d'oeuvre de la Littérature Vietnamienne* (Saigon, [Kim lai ấn-quán, 1966]), pp. 10–11. Wen-ti's edict is in the *Ch'ien Han-shu*, ch. 4, 17a–18b, which is translated by Burton Watson in *Anthology of Chinese Literature*, ed. C. Birch, vol. 1 (New York: Grove Press, 1965), pp. 86–87; and by Homer H. Dubs, ed. and trans., *The History of the Former Han Dynasty; vol. 1, Translation* (Baltimore, MD: Waverly Press, 1938), pp. 266–72.

succeeded by a worthy heir and was persuaded to nominate his own son.[26] Nhân-tôn, too, had given special thought to his heir's identity, which is why his edict stresses the heir's qualities. Thus, provided that the Chinese model carried weight, Nhân-tôn's edict would be read as conveying the assurance that the succession would be as legitimate and auspicious as the succession of Wen-ti's heir had been. The "learning of antiquity" would have validated and communicated the assurance. Similarly Trần Thái-tôn, by assuming the name of Yao, would have been validating his son's succession by invoking Mencius, who taught the need for prudent succession procedures. He, unlike Nhân-tôn, would be conveying the additional assurance that he recognized his obligation to train an heir who would deserve to be hailed as ruler when his father died, but both Nhân-tôn and Thái-tôn were invoking the "learning of antiquity" to influence the future by recommending suitable heirs to protect their dynasties.

The invoking of Chinese texts to reinforce Vietnamese decisions was not, however, limited to the occasions of imperial successions. According to the annals, in 1010 Lý Thái-tổ, the founder of the Lý dynasty, transferred his capital from Hoa-lư in the south to Thăng-long on the site of present-day Hanoi. He announced his decision in a decree that began by citing examples of ancient Chinese rulers who had also changed their capitals but only when there were good reasons for doing so. He then explained why he was doing so. Here, then, is another example of the apparently validating effect of Chinese textual precedents in Vietnamese decision making.[27]

Lý Thái-tổ, a fervent Buddhist whose initial support had come from the monks, is not the only Buddhist in medieval times who strengthened his argument by means of Chinese texts. According to a Buddhist source, Lý Thần-tôn (1127–1137) asked Viên Thông to explain the causes of stability and instability in the state. Viên Thông's reply draws on ideas attributable to Confucius and Mencius. He has Mencius in mind when he advises Thần-tôn to win the people's hearts,[28] and he is following Confucius when he says that one must "cultivate in oneself the capacity for easing the lot of the whole populace."[29] In 1202, according to the annals, another monk quoted from the *Book of Songs* to castigate Lý Cao-tôn's negligent conduct of affairs. Finally, we can note a detail in Trần Thái-tôn's account of his flight from the capital in 1236 in order to meditate in the mountains. A Master of Dhyāna supports Thái-tôn's uncle in urging Thái-tôn to resume his official duties, urging him to bear in mind that rulers must identify themselves with the wishes and hearts of the empire. This sentiment is reminiscent of Mencius's urging rulers to share their happiness with the people.[30]

In all these instances, we have been observing how Vietnamese cited Chinese texts in support of specific courses of action in secular affairs. The quotations or

---

[26] Dubs, *The History of the Former Han Dynasty*, pp. 233–36.

[27] A striking, though late, example of this use of Chinese texts is in David G. Marr, *Vietnamese Anticolonialism, 1885–1925* (Berkeley, CA: University of California Press, 1971), pp. 49–51.

[28] *Đại-Nam thuyền uyển truyền đăng tập lục* (EFEO microfilm no. 2767), p. 62a; M, IV A, 9, i. For a discussion of textual problems arising out of the records of the Vietnamese Masters of the Dhyāna, see E. Gaspardone, "Bibliographie annamite," *BEFEO* 34,1 (1934): 140–43.

[29] *The Analects*, p. 14, xlv. Arthur Waley's translation is in *The Analects of Confucius* (London: Allen and Unwin, 1938), p. 191.

[30] "Trần Thái-tôn ngự chế khóa hư" (preface to the *Thuyền* [Thiền?—Ed.]-*tôn chi-nam*), q. 1, 26, printed in *Việt-nam Phát dien* [triển?—Ed.] *Tùng-khan* (Société Asiatique copy, Ann 1916–1917) (Hanoi: n. p., 1943), p. 7; M, I B, 4, iii.

allusions always seem to communicate and reinforce authority. What, then, would have been the authority that a Chinese text was seen to possess?

I believe that the text's authority stemmed from the Vietnamese conviction that it embodied the well-tested experience of hallowed antiquity. The experience written into the texts concerned spheres of human activity that had been the insistent concern of the ancient Chinese sages rather than of the teachers of the Mahāyāna. In particular, the texts were seen to contain valuable practical guidance on matters connected with the welfare of rulers. The original sages had been rulers, and Confucius and Mencius tirelessly advised rulers. And so Vietnamese had long ago developed the habit of identifying and invoking passages in the Chinese books that professed to aid in the successful exercise of power.

The texts were invoked because they embodied the practical experience of antiquity. But the same texts also reflected the profound respect of the Chinese themselves for antiquity, a point that would not have been lost on the Vietnamese. The Chinese approached the texts with the reverence accorded to a literary record of the revelation of the eternal Tao by the ancient sage rulers and their successors. Furthermore, the circumstance that the divine wisdom had been written down meant that for the Chinese, and also for the Vietnamese, it was always available and could therefore be regarded as timeless wisdom.[31] To this extent literate Vietnamese were bound to absorb the Chinese respect for antiquity. But a special circumstance enhanced the Vietnamese respect for antiquity and therefore the authority of a classical text. For the Chinese, and especially as a result of the influence of Han Yu and the Sung neo-Confucian philosophers, the ancient texts became the *point d'appui* for affirming the cultural identity of the Chinese people and for interpreting significant developments in their history. The effects of the ancient learning over the centuries were as important to Chinese scholars as was the ancient learning itself. For the Vietnamese, on the other hand, the ancient texts could not be read as the sacred overture to Vietnamese history. As late as the thirteenth century, they did not discern in Chinese antiquity the germs of an internal movement that was to assume the shape of Vietnamese cultural history and link them with antiquity. Instead, antiquity remained self-contained as well as immensely remote, contributing experience of timeless and universal validity when Vietnamese chose to tap it. Because the texts were not the *point d'appui* for understanding Vietnamese history, they were not seen as supplying a critique for later human behaviour. Their contents did not furnish a system of ideas that, in their entirety, formed a blueprint for the moral order of the universe and the social order of mankind. The texts were not read in order to study a "Confucianist" ideology. Instead, they would have been seen as resembling an encyclopaedia of recorded wisdom that the Vietnamese could consult in ways that seemed relevant in recognizing specific situations, such as an imperial succession, and the specific measures that those situations seemed to require. A discriminating assessment of the relevance of the sages' teachings, eschewing unreal moralizing

---

[31] I am grateful to Professor Wang Gungwu for his observation during the colloquium on the consequence in a literate society of recording wisdom in texts. All texts, no matter when they were actually written, became, simply because they were written, part of the record of antiquity and equally distant from the present, always available, and to this extent therefore timeless. In one of his writings, Trần Thái-tôn mentions Han Yu (768–824) as well as Lao-tzu, Confucius, and the Buddha; see "Trần Thái-tôn ngự chế khóa hư" [Exhortation on Resolution], q. 1, 11a. He ignores the historical context of these teachers for the reason that their teachings have been recorded and therefore absorbed into the great fund of ancient wisdom.

concerns, would have come easily to those who had been brought up in a vigorous Buddhist tradition and who envisaged sublime goals in ways that were unacceptable to the Chinese philosophers.

The Chinese texts embodied timeless and authoritative experience on matters that happened to concern the Vietnamese. But why did invoking this limited amount of experience come easily to them? After all, they were surrounded by Buddhist influences, encouraged by the Lý and Trần courts, and they were fiercely aware of their independence from China whenever China, as in Kublai Khan's day, challenged their independence. I believe that there were two reasons why they were able to invoke the texts selectively. In the first place, they were familiar with them simply because the texts would have been read by those who wanted to become literate in order to be chosen to occupy subordinate posts in the administration. But another reason for paying attention to Chinese texts was supplied by Trần Thái-tôn and shows why he invoked Mencius in staging the succession procedure in 1258.

Thái-tôn, Lê Văn Hưu's contemporary, states in his preface to the *Thiền-tôn chi-nam* (A Guide to the Dhyāna):

> Those who transmitted rules through the generations and laid guidelines were greatly honoured by the former sages. For this reason, Hui-neng [the sixth patriarch of the Dhyāna school of Buddhism in southern China] once said that there was no difference between the sages and the great Buddhist teachers. I can draw on the example of the former sages when I transmit the teachings of Buddhism. Cannot I make the responsibility of the sages my own responsibility in teaching Buddhism?[32]

Thái-tôn is explaining his role as a Buddhist teacher by comparing it with the teaching function of the sages, whose special characteristic he sees as laying down rules to influence later generations. He, a devout Buddhist and indifferent to the sages' moral values, readily acknowledges a particular quality of the ancient learning: its teachings were concerned with plans for the future. Thus, in the setting of the scenario of 1258, he is recognizing Mencius as the teacher who recommended prescience in selecting a suitable imperial heir. In his preface to the *Thiền-tôn chi-nam*, he states that planners were honoured by the sages, and he is no doubt confident that he is making arrangements in 1258 that Mencius would have approved. He is responding to the sage's teachings by appointing a worthy person, his son, as his associate in order to try out his capacity as the future ruler. By assuming the new style of "Yao," he is communicating an authoritative assurance, based on the experience of antiquity, in order to win support for his decision.

I have attempted to explain what Vietnamese literati believed to be the authority and function of Chinese texts when they quoted from them for their own purposes, and I shall now return to Lê Văn Hưu's cultural identity as a historian. His attitude towards the "learning of antiquity" need no longer be ambiguous. He is as familiar with Mencius as Thái-tôn is, and Mencius is the classical writer whom he seems to invoke most frequently in order to validate the observations he makes in his comments on Vietnamese history.

---

[32] "Trần Thái-tôn ngự chế khóa hư," q. 1, 27a.

He quotes Mencius in his eulogy of Triệu Đà when he observes that rulers with *virtus* need not come from a particular part of the world.[33] This statement, based on antiquity, is the basis for his claim that Vietnam is an independent country under its sage ruler. He can therefore compare Triệu Đà with Shun and Wen Wang; the three rulers exhibited *virtus*, benevolence, and a sense of duty. Similarly, he has Mencius in mind when he assumes that all genuine rulers must be sages.[34] He shares Mencius's concern, and also Thái-tôn's, with the influence of rulers on the future.[35] He is quoting Mencius when he says that the family is the "root" of the state, a proposition that he invokes to insist that an imperial father should be succeeded by his son.[36] He even arms himself with Mencius's teaching on the deposition of rulers when he states that a Vietnamese ruler who opens the frontiers to China must be replaced.[37]

What are Hưu's intentions when he validates his comments with quotations from Mencius? Under cover of and reinforced by the teaching of antiquity, he seems to be promoting two assertions of extraordinary importance in his own lifetime.

His first assertion, as we have frequently seen, is that the Vietnamese court is the court of an empire that is as independent and imperial as the Chinese empire and had been so since the beginning of the Han period in Chinese history. The assertion is made at a time when Kublai Khan is trying to demolish Vietnamese court protocol. Hưu is able to demonstrate his assertion by construing Mencius's teaching to render Triệu Đà as the founder of an empire and by quoting Han and Sung texts with devastating effect to show that Triệu Đà and Lô Hoàn had presided over an independent court with Chinese connivance, in spite of the tributary relationship. Both these rulers relied, as Thái-tôn did, on diplomacy to retain the substance of independence. He clinches his validation of Vietnamese independence by enclosing his comments in a literary form sufficiently adorned with such Chinese historiographical features as a golden age, dynastic sequence, a concern with orthodox imperial succession, and didactic comments that it resembles the type of history that could be appropriately submitted to an imperial court. He has the same respect for the authenticating style of documentation that marks Nhân-tôn's edict, the parallel version of Wen-ti's. His respect matches his own comment on the importance of an embellished imperial text.[38]

The assertion of the Vietnamese court's equality with the Chinese court is an exegesis on the reality of the independence that Thái-tôn and his heir were heroically defending. Hưu's second assertion is as important as his first one, and it is an exegesis on Thái-tôn's prescience: Vietnam will always be in great danger if its ruler neglects Mencius's advice on regulating the succession. And so Hưu shows the result

---

[33] *TT* under date of 137 BCE; *M*, IV B, 1, i–iv.

[34] *TT* under date of 184 and especially of 968. On Mencius's identification of sages and emperors, see Fung Yu-lan, *A History of Chinese Philosophy*, trans. D. Bodde, vol. 1 (Princeton, NJ: Princeton University Press, 1952), pp. 115–17.

[35] *TT* under dates of 981 and 1154. Mencius has much to say on the continuing influence of sage rulers; see, for example, *M*, I B, 14, iii; *M*, II B, 13, iii; and *M*, IV B, 22, i.

[36] *TT* under date of 1129; *M*, IV A, 5.

[37] *TT* under date of 111 BCE; *M*, V B, 9, i. Hưu's comment also refers to I Yin, who banished a bad ruler. For information on I Yin, see *M*, VII A, 31, i.

[38] *TT* under date of 1028. Hưu regrets that the *nho* could not embellish the name of the first Lý ruler's tomb. For "embellishing," he uses an expression in *The Analects* (p. 14, 9) where Confucius describes the four stages in preparing official decrees. "Embellishment" is the final stage.

of disregarding the experience of antiquity. Vietnamese dynasties had either been short-lived, brought down by feuding (which enabled the Sung to exploit the situation in 980),[39] or had been insecure because the Lý rulers had postponed their heirs' appointment until the rulers were dying. Only prescient rulers, by invoking the experience of antiquity, can avoid imperiling the country in this way. Those in the Trần court who read Hưu's history would be left in no doubt that the scenario of 1258 commanded the acceptance of Thái-tôn's authoritative assurance that the dynasty would survive and continue to provide leadership in defending the country from the Mongols.

Did Hưu make these two assertions because he had been ordered to do so when he was commissioned to edit Vietnamese history? I believe that this is an unreal question. Learning for a *nho* was always in support of the state, and the great contemporary issues of independence and the succession were issues on which the authoritative guidance of antiquity was abundantly available. Moreover, sufficient rapport already existed between the ruler and the *nho* to encourage Hưu to invoke the "learning of antiquity" when he commented on Vietnamese history. The court's appeal to "ancient customs" in its memorials to Kublai Khan, which the *nho* helped to draft, was an open invitation for Hưu to assemble the texts that validated the court's sense of precedents; diplomatic exigency may well have been the specific reason why Hưu was ordered to edit Vietnamese history. But Thái-tôn's recognition in 1258 of Mencius's wisdom was also an open invitation for Hưu to mobilize textual authority on behalf of Thái-tôn's heir. Assurances based on antiquity had therefore already been communicated to Hưu, and his obedient response was inevitable. While he was the Trần spokesman, he was also the spokesman of the *nho* in support of the Trần.

E. Balazs, discussing Chinese historical literature, asks: "Qui est l'auteur et qui sont ses lecteurs? La réponse est nette: l'histoire est écrite par des fonctionnaires pour les fonctionnaires."[40] Hưu is not this kind of historian. His readers are imperial princes and not the Vietnamese people in general. But he is also in a cultural tradition that permits him to handle Chinese forms without being influenced by Chinese perceptions of the past. He appropriates Mencius in order to show that the past has, with the exception of Triệu Đà, yielded nothing that provides a faultless model for the imperial institution before Thái-tôn's reign. Dominating his attitude towards the past is the living example of Thái-tôn, a Vietnamese sage emperor, for whose foreign and domestic policies Hưu's history is not only a transparent tribute but also an authoritative validation.

Hưu's *Đại Việt Sử Ký* seems to have made some impact on the Trần court. The evidence is in the subsequent prestige of that singular figure, Triệu Đà. When the Hưng-đạo prince, the hero of the Mongol wars, was dying in 1300, the "emperor" Anh-tôn visited him and asked what measures should be taken if the "northern bandits" attacked again. The prince replied by referring to Vietnamese heroes who had successfully resisted invaders, and the first name in his list is that of Triệu Đà. There is also an inter-linear note in the Vietnamese annals immediately after the

---

[39] The *TT*, under date of 980 and incorporating a Chinese source, quotes a Chinese border official as advising the Sung court that dynastic confusion in Vietnam was China's opportunity for recovering the province.

[40] E. Balazs, "L'histoire comme guide de la pratique bureaucratique...," in Beasley and Pulleybank, *Historians of China and Japan*, p. 82.

notice of Triệu Đà's death in 137 BCE, which states that the later Trần, who tried to recover power after Hồ Quý Lý's family was defeated by the Ming army in 1407, conferred on Triệu Đà the grandiloquently imperial title of *Khai-thiên thể đạo thành vũ thần triệt hoàng đế*.[41] Finally, Hưu's influence is seen in a passage of probably the most famous work of medieval Vietnamese literature. I am referring to Nguyễn Trãi's *Bình Ngô Đại Cáo* (Great Proclamation upon the Pacification of the Wu), issued in 1428 on behalf of the founder of the Lê Dynasty after he had defeated the Ming occupation army.

> Mountains and rivers have demarcated the borders [of our country]. The customs of the North [China] and the South [Vietnam] are also different. We find [in antiquity] that the Triệu, Đinh, Lý, and Trần [dynasties] built our country. Alongside the Han, T'ang, Sung, and Yuan [dynasties], the rulers [of our dynasties] ruled as emperors over their own part [of the world represented by the North and South].[42]

Much had happened in the century and a half that separated Nguyễn Trãi from Lê Văn Hưu, but Hưu's textually validated assertion of the coexistence and equality of the Vietnamese and Chinese "empires" was as acceptable and timely to the Lê court as it had been to the Trần court. Lê Lợi, the founder of the Lê dynasty, was as determined to maintain his country's independence in face of the Ming invaders as Thái-tôn had been to maintain it in face of Kublai Khan's intimidating edicts. And so Trai readily prolongs the sequence of Vietnamese imperial dynasties from Triệu Đà into the period that corresponded in time with the Mongol Yuan dynasty, the predecessor of the aggressive Ming dynasty.

Trãi would never have imagined that Hưu needed to justify his country's status by appealing to Chinese historical records. Kublai's bullying did not call forth a Chinese-style history of Vietnamese independence that had to be neatly documented by chronologically apt quotations from Chinese sources or reflect the cyclical framework that enabled Chinese historians to organize their perception of dynastic and cultural time. Instead, the Mongol challenge mobilized a very different approach to the function of texts that had evolved over the centuries within a Vietnamese cultural tradition and came instinctively to Lê Văn Hưu. Hưu discloses what he sees as the function of texts when he quotes Mencius to justify the ancient imperial status of the Vietnamese court or to criticize the weaknesses of the Lý court in a manner that can only mean that he regards Thái-tôn as a safe ruler and is validating Thái-tôn's succession procedure of 1258. Its appeal to Mencius matches that of the Buddhist Thái-tôn in 1258. Thái-tôn and Hưu, and, I believe, all Vietnamese *nho* at that time, recognized the texts of antiquity not as a source of historical evidence but

---

[41] Translated: "The emperor who opened the Way of Heaven's blessings by his sage-like military power and holy wisdom."

[42] *Ức Trai Tập*, q. 3, 9a (1868 printing in the library of the Société Asiatique). Also see Truong Buu Lam, *Patterns of Vietnamese Response to Foreign Intervention: 1858–1900*, Yale Southeast Asia Studies, Monograph Series no. 11 (New Haven, CT: Yale University Southeast Asia Studies, 1967), pp. 34–35. For a fifteenth-century poem on Triệu Đà, based on the Chinese textual information exploited by Hưu, see Lý Tử Cau's [Lý Tử Tấn?—Ed.] poem in Bùi Bích [Bùi Huy Bích?—Ed.], *Hoàng Việt thi tuyển* (H.M. 2214 in the library of the Société Asiatique), q. 3, 6a. Cau was a famous *nho* in the first half of the fifteenth century. His poem refers to Triệu Đà's imperial court and the Lạc country (Vietnam)'s resolve to resist China.

as an authoritative reservoir of recorded experiential knowledge that was contextually neutral and therefore of universal and timeless validity, and was also always available to supply and communicate persuasive assurances that Vietnamese decision-making exemplified considerations that commanded the maximum respect.

CHAPTER TEN

Phạm Sư Mạnh's Poems Written While Patrolling the Vietnamese Northern Border in the Middle of the Fourteenth Century*

I recently discussed the response of Phạm Sư Mạnh and other fourteenth-century Vietnamese officials to signs of peasant unrest when the Trần dynasty (1226–1400) weakened.[1] I suggested that the officials were witnessing social and political conditions that compelled them to abandon their habitual sense of being the emperors' obedient subordinates and, instead, reluctantly to assume the responsibility of defining norms of good government. Their unwonted behaviour led me to believe that important changes were under way in fourteenth-century Vietnam. Educated men, under pressure of events, were beginning to become monitors of government even though they served and wanted to protect the Trần autocracy.

The officials, whom I described as "witnesses," were also accomplished poets. They wrote poetry in the Chinese literary language according to the complex rules of T'ang "new style" verse. About 450 poems by more than fifty poets survive.[2] Together with a volume of folktales,[3] the annalistic history known as the *Việt sử lược*, and the so far largely unstudied inscriptions, these poems, the majority of which are in T'ang "new style" verse, comprise a substantial contribution to the surviving contemporary Vietnamese written material of the fourteenth century. Moreover, T'ang-style Vietnamese poems begin to survive in considerable numbers only from this century.

---

* This paper was originally presented at the Eighth Conference of the International Association of Historians of Asia, held in Kuala Lumpur in August 1980.

[1] O. W. Wolters, "Assertions of Cultural Well-Being in Fourteenth-Century Vietnam: Part two," *JSEAS* 11,1 (1980): 74–90.

[2] They are published in the *Thơ Văn Lý-Trần*, vol. 3 (Hanoi: Khoa Học Xã Hội, 1978).

[3] *Lý Tế Xuyên, Việt Điện U-Linh Tập* (École Française d'Extrême Orient, A47). Perhaps some of the tales in the *Lĩnh Nam Trích Quái* were compiled in the later years of the fourteenth century.

I am inclined to explain the sudden outburst of poetic activity as the result of two influences in the wake of the Mongol invaders' final defeats in the 1280s. In the first place, by the beginning of the fourteenth century, educated men were more frequently promoted to senior posts in the Trần court. In the competitive official environment of that time, they were anxious to distinguish themselves in the eyes of the rulers and their colleagues. Writing acceptable T'ang-style verse displayed their literary qualifications and confirmed their status as *nho*, or the lettered members of society. One *nho*, Nguyễn Trung Ngạn (± 1289–± 1368), an official and poet who rose high in the imperial service, was eulogized by a fellow poet as "composing poetry on horseback" when he was sent on a mission to China in 1314.[4] Even Trần Khắc Chung, a hero in the Mongol wars who later earned the evil reputation of being an ambitious and ruthless imperial counselor, was inspired by the famous Chinese poet T'ao Ch'ien to write a poem on the chrysanthemum.[5]

The other influence that may account for the sudden vogue of T'ang-style poetry is connected with proud memories of military achievements, still fresh in the early fourteenth century. Educated Vietnamese had always claimed that their country possessed sovereign status equal with what was attributed by the Chinese to the Middle Kingdom. They had also been accustomed for more than a millennium to thinking of the world in terms of "South" and "North." Perhaps they were now determined to write Southern poetry as excellent as Northern poetry. Literate Vietnamese from as early as the tenth century had skillfully conformed to the Chinese protocol of exchanging poems of welcome and farewell, written in Chinese verse, when Chinese envoys visited Vietnam, and in the thirteenth century the Trần emperors manipulated the same protocol to convey polite but firm diplomatic messages to Kublai Khan's envoys. The tradition of measuring by Chinese standards Vietnamese poetry written by Vietnamese in Chinese was well established before the fourteenth century, and it is not implausible to suppose that literati in the ebullient post-war years took the tradition a stage further by writing Chinese-style poetry not only for their own enjoyment but also to demonstrate successfully that their countryside lent itself to Chinese-style poetry as admirably as the Chinese countryside did. Chinese models were often adapted to serve Vietnamese purposes; the Vietnamese imperial institution is the most striking example. Writing Chinese-style poetry about Vietnam would be a similar act of homage to "the country of the rivers." "Poetry follows fine scenery," wrote one poet.[6] Sometimes poets appropriated the Chinese poetic convention of writing about the landscape as though they had seen it in a beautiful picture. Chu Văn An, Phạm Sư Mạnh's teacher, wrote:

Line upon line of blue mountains, they are massed into a painted screen.[7]

Poems on Vietnamese themes would, however, render homage only when the poets were particularly careful to compose poetry that read exactly as though it were Chinese poetry written in China. The poets paid meticulous attention to the number

---

[4] Nguyễn Sưởng, *Toàn Viêt thi lục* (HM 2319 in the library of the Société Asiatique, Paris, undated preface), q. 3, pp. 14a–b. Hereafter, *TVTL*.

[5] *TVTL*, q. 2, p. 10b. He also flaunts his knowledge of Ch'ü Yüan.

[6] Nguyễn Tử Thành, *Thơ văn Lý Trần*, vol. 3, p. 21. Hereafter, *TV*.

[7] Ibid., p. 56.

of lines and syllables, the tone endings in the even lines, and parallelisms in the second and third couplets in poems of eight lines. Sometimes their poems incorporated snatches of verse from famous Chinese poets such as Ch'ü Yüan, Chuang-tzŭ, T'ao Ch'ien, and Tu Fu. Occasional allusions to the Chinese classics and histories adorned their poems. For them, as for the Chinese, the oriole sang in lonely places, and the flying seagull signified happy abandon. Scrupulous attention to poetic language was essential in order to ensure the maximum effect in appropriating Chinese verse forms for Vietnamese ends. Similarly, the thirteenth-century historian, Lê Văn Hưu, wrote a Vietnamese history that exhibited the appearance of a Chinese annalistic history.

In this essay, I am interested in some of Phạm Sư Mạnh's poems. Mạnh, one of the witnesses, was remembered by the fifteenth-century annalist as a disciple of the renowned and public-minded scholar Chu Văn An (1292–1370). Mạnh's recorded career as a court official spans the period from the 1340s to the 1360s. The dates of his birth and death are unknown, but he wrote several poems in 1369 to welcome a Ming envoy to Vietnam. Thirty-nine of his poems have so far been identified.[8]

In the second part of my recent article, I called attention to Mạnh's poem which refers to the place-name "Văn Lang" in the context of his administrative tour of northwestern Vietnam. I suggested that, in Mạnh's mind and in the minds of the other witnesses, the kingdom of Văn Lang, briefly noticed in early Chinese accounts of Vietnam, represented Vietnam's golden age, when the ruler's benign authority was signified by the expression "writing and chariots." I quoted *The Doctrine of the Mean*, which states that it is the prerogative only of the Son of Heaven to standardize writing and width of chariot rims. The *Li-chi* also uses the expression: "Now throughout the empire chariots have the same axles, books are in the same script, and conduct is according to the same principles."[9] The expression "writing and chariots" signifies the notion of standardization and unity within a territory and therefore the notion of authority. In fourteenth-century Vietnam, the witnesses associated this state of affairs with ancient Văn Lang as an indigenous achievement that had nothing to do with Chinese cultural influence, and they were able to conclude that, when the Văn Lang rulers presided over Vietnam's golden age, Vietnamese customs were "simple and pure."[10] The impulse behind this construction of the past was the witnesses' concern about the contemporary deterioration in the people's behaviour and the government's effectiveness. In the Văn Lang period, the rulers had provided leadership and the people were obedient and contented.

---

[8] They are published in *TV*.

[9] S. Couvreur, *Li Ki*, 2nd edition, vol. 2 (Ho Kien Fou: Impr. de la Mission Catholique, 1913), p. 469.

[10] The cultural significance of the expression "writing and chariots" is illustrated in one of Nguyễn Trãi's poems, composed in honour of Lê Lợi's victory in 1432 over tribal rebels at Lai Châu in the extreme northwestern part of Vietnam. Trãi was related by marriage to Nguyễn Đán (1326–90), one of the fourteenth-century witnesses. Trãi states that Lê Lợi pitied the customs of distant people and concludes his poem:

> From now within the four seas chariots and script will be uniform

> This is similar to the abundant virtue and magnificent achievement of remote
>   antiquity.

Trãi sees Lê Lợi's victory as a civilizing mission and, by implication, comparable with the achievement of the Văn Lang rulers; *Ưc-Trãi tập* (HM 2210 in the Société Asiatique; first preface dated 1825), q. 1, p. 12b–13a.

In my earlier essay, I used Mạnh's poem because it documented his association of Văn Lang with a well-governed state in antiquity and helped me to reconstruct a synoptic account of developments in the fourteenth century. I used the poem alongside different types of documents, such as the fifteenth-century compilation of the Trần annals, a history of Vietnam written towards the end of the fourteenth century, the recollections of a Vietnamese exile in China during the early fifteenth century, folktales, and poems by other fourteenth-century officials. I did not, however, approach Mạnh's poem as a "poem" that deserved to be read simply as a poem.

In order to "read" this poem, I have ventured to experiment with an approach borrowed from the field of structuralist poetics. I have tried to read the poem not as a "document" but as a "text." A document refers to something outside itself, and I had treated the poem as a document because it referred to the Văn Lang toponym, which I brought into relationship with other documented fourteenth-century Vietnamese references to antiquity. A text, on the other hand, refers to nothing outside itself. When one reads a text, its author and one's own subjective response to its contents have to be suppressed. One is not interested in what words signify. Instead, one is interested in the words simply as signifiers. The signifiers supply a "literary message" by means of particular combinations of words, selected from a repertoire with equivalent meanings or associations. The combinations provide the structure for the poet's flow of linguistic units. As a literary critic has put it, the study of the message is concerned "not with content but with the process by which content is formulated."[11]

Mạnh was writing a poem and not a documentary record for historians to consult. He knew that his poem was bound to call attention to itself as a poem because of its often strange language, organized according to the complex set of poetic conventions drawn from T'ang "new style" prosody. Nevertheless, the particular combinations of linguistic units were his decision, and the combinations therefore sustain his "Vietnamese" literary message.

In this essay I shall try to repair my neglect of the poem as a "poem" and shall read it alongside eight other poems written by Mạnh when he was touring the northern border. Three were written when he was in the northwest and six in the Lạng Sơn area farther east. I shall consult the collated versions of Mạnh's texts in the *Thơ-văn Lý-Trần* published in Hanoi, where the contents sometimes differ from the versions previously available to me.

But, first, I wish to revise what I wrote in my earlier essay about the circumstances and time when these "border" poems were written. I suggested that they were written in the 1360s when military precautions were being taken on the northern border to safeguard Vietnam from consequences of the civil war in southern China on the eve of the Ming dynasty's accession in 1368. I now believe that I was mistaken. I had disregarded an editorial note attached to one of Mạnh's poems on Lạng Sơn in an eighteenth-century compilation of Vietnamese poetry. The note states that perhaps Mạnh wrote this poem when he was serving as *Kinh lược* in Lạng Giang, the administrative unit that included Lạng Sơn.[12] Officials in Trần times had this title when they were entrusted with special duties in trouble-stricken provinces;

---

[11] Terence Hawkes, *Structuralism and Semiotics* (Berkeley and Los Angeles, CA: University of California Press, 1977), p. 158.

[12] I am referring to Bùi Bích's *Hoàng Việt thi tuyển*. See *TV*, vol. 3, p. 115, n. 1.

Trương Hán Siêu, one of the "witnesses," held the title in Lạng Giang in 1342, and Nguyễn Trung Ngạn likewise in Lạng Giang in 1355. According to the annals, disturbances broke out in 1351 at Thái-nguyên in the northwest and at Lạng Sơn, and troops were sent to both places. In 1354 disturbances broke out in Lạng Giang and the neighbouring area of Nam Sách.

Trương Hán Siêu and Nguyễn Trung Ngạn are, with Phạm Sư Mạnh, the senior court officials most prominently mentioned in the annals during the first sixty years of the fourteenth century. The annals do not state that Mạnh was sent to suppress revolts, though revolts were already beginning in the 1340s. On the other hand, Mạnh is described in 1346, 1358, and 1362 as serving in the *Khu Mật Viện*, an organ of government with military responsibilities in the fourteenth century. Mạnh's "Lạng Sơn" poems show that he was in charge of troops. He says that he has been involved twenty times in plans to "pacify" the border and that he has "grown old" in service in the Lạng Sơn area. Moreover, according to the version of his "Văn Lang" poem in the *Thơ văn Lý Trần*, he is suppressing banditry in the northwest.

For these reasons, I now believe that Mạnh wrote his "border" poems in the 1350s or perhaps in the early 1360s when he was engaged in measures to restore order in the northern regions. We need not doubt that he was often close to the border, but his major concern lay on the Vietnamese side of the border.

I shall now translate three of the six "Lạng Sơn" poems, and I shall then discuss their poetic structure. My translations are intended to throw light on the meaning rather than to adorn an anthology.[13]

I. The Northern Part of the Border[14]

1. I have been entrusted with the imperial order that the army must march I dare not tarry.
2. Beneath my oil-painted green pennant, I grasp my halberd.
3. The border mountain is called Lão Thử Lâu Lại.
4. It is raining and snowing on Thượng Ngao's peak in Lộc Châu.
5. Powerful cavalry to the east and west are urged on by drums and horns.
6. Flags to the left and right inspire the brave troops.
7. In my lifetime twenty times I have been [involved] in plans to pacify the border.
8. A loyal heart glows through my white hair.

II. Thượng Ngao[15]

1. Generals and officers surround and guard the camp gate.
2. On their left they grasp bows and swords. On their right they carry the quivers.
3. Ten thousand horses and a thousand foot soldiers patrol the border from end to end.
4. Lofty flags and great banners shine on Khâu Ôn.

---

[13] I have used the texts collated by the editors of *TV*. I thank Professors Jonathan Culler, Harold Shadick, and James Siegel for their criticism of an earlier draft of this essay.

[14] *TV*, vol. 3, p. 107.

[15] Ibid., p. 112.

5. The barrier mountain's strong points determine our strategy.
6. Streams, mountain torrents, and a screen of tribesmen provide a far-flung defence.
7. Grown old serving in Lạng Châu, a fearsome suppressor of [disturbances].
8. A loyal heart protects the world.

III. On the Way to Quảng Lăng[16]

1. By day sun shines on the patrol's saddles. Moon gleams on the riders' crops.
2. In the west wind the flags and pennants are constantly fluttering.
3. There are a multitude of peaks above Quảng Lăng's grottos.[17]
4. There are ninety-three twists in Lâu Lại's stream.
5. The army's muster and deployment comply with the sage's (the ruler's) stratagem.
6. The tribal villages and settlements protect the border's extremities.
7. I am trying with a court's official's hand
8. To draft the first chapter of the *Pacification of the Western Barbarians*.

In each of these poems, as we shall see, the four couplets present a common sequence of elements. The first couplet always contains words that signify the ruler's initiative or the movement of officials and troops in response to the ruler's initiative. Movement is signified in a variety of ways: not daring to tarry; movement in time (sun and moon); grasping weapons, cavalry, and fluttering flags. Another Lạng Sơn poem begins:

Unworthily exercising supreme military command, I mount the general's reviewing stand.
When the north has its troubles, dare I decline hardship?[18]

The second couplets are in parallel verses and describe the scene and space where the movement occurs. Notions of defence enter, but the emphasis is on the outline of the natural scene. There is profuse topographical precision: six place-names are mentioned. Height and depth are indicated by the peaks and streams of the contorted landscape. The Lộc Châu peak is so high that it is raining and snowing there. Lofty flags shine on Khâu Ôn. Extensive space is indicated by a patrol of ten thousand horses and a thousand soldiers, by multitudinous peaks, and by the many twists in Lâu Lại's stream. Another Lạng Sơn poem states in its second couplet:

A thousand layers of cloud conceal the Khâu Môn post.

---

[16] Ibid., p. 113.

[17] The *TV* text gives "miasmas" instead of "peaks." The text in the HM copy in Paris gives "peaks," and I follow it here because I believe that Mạnh's imagery is not influenced by the Chinese convention that the Vietnamese northern mountains were characterized by miasmas. I give below two references to "miasmas," one to Nguyễn Trung Ngạn and the other by Mạnh. Ngạn is following the convention but Mạnh associates miasmas with the Chinese side of the border.

[18] *TV*, vol. 3, p. 109.

Ten thousand miles of sky enclose the Công Mẫu mountain?[19]

Two more place-names are mentioned.

The third couplet in each poem, also in parallel verses, concerns occupation and control of the space just described. Occupation is effected by cavalry "to the east and west" and by "brave troops to left and right." Control is effected by resourceful use of topographical and human features. The poetic structure is similar in the third couplets of two other poems:

> For the control of the world, the flags must be unfurled.
> Only when the barrier mountains are cleansed do the horns begin to chill.[20]

"Cleansed" is an equivalence of "control." Or, again,

> The Lâu Lại ravine is deeper than the bottom of a well.
> Chi Lăng's perilous heights are level with the sky.[21]

Here is another way of referring to the screen of strong points provided by the barrier mountains in the poem on Thượng Ngao.

The final couplets identify Mạnh as an aged, experienced, brave, and loyal servant of the ruler who has been entrusted with the weighty responsibility of supervising the occupation and control of the space in question. One is left in no doubt that Mạnh's role is a major one. He has been twenty times on this kind of mission. He is "protecting the world." He is beginning "to pacify the Western Barbarians." In another Lạng Sơn poem, he writes in his final couplet:

> On this expedition I am not just seizing the tribes' provisions.
> I shall take and hold Lộc Châu with all its mountain lands.[22]

This passage supports the view that he was engaged in restoring law and order in the northern province of Lạng Giang rather than guarding the frontier. Another poem ends:

> Facing the wind, the horses plod on. High up, they toss their heads.
> They are lofty peaks of blocking barriers, with clouds and mist trailing westward.[23]

Mạnh is not mentioned. He is represented by the plodding horses.

The structure of these poems is uniform and simple. The flow of language is intended to describe ruler-sponsored military movement through rugged landscape, the occupation of which is entrusted to the faithful Mạnh.

I shall now translate another "Lạng Sơn" poem. The poetic language is different, but the meaning behind the structure is the same.

---

[19] Ibid.

[20] Ibid.

[21] Ibid., p. 114.

[22] Ibid., p. 109.

[23] Ibid., p. 114.

IV. The Tam Thanh Grotto[24]

1. Drawing a girdle, the Seven Streams surround Thượng Ngao.
2. The rocks are a strong border. The water is a moat.
3. The terrain separates South from North, as forbidding as a fortified citadel.
4. When Heaven created spirits and immortals, their grotto abode was [and is] in these heights.
5. The Celestial Emperor's Pure Capital is close at hand.
6. The pool of the immortals and [the sage emperor] Vũ [Yü]'s Cave are within easy reach.
7. When the troops are stationed on the border, naturally they climb here to survey.
8. In close formation they tread lightly, each of them grasping his sword.

In this poem, vaguely Taoist associations inspire the language. Immortal beings have their home in nature. Only the final couplet introduces mortals in the persons of the troops, though Mạnh does not appear. Nevertheless, language flows as in the other poems. In the first couplet, "drawing a girdle" signifies the movement that happened at the beginning of time when the region was created as a border of rocks and moat. In the other poems, "generals and officers surround and guard the camp gate," mounted patrols move forward, the ruler issues orders, and Mạnh obeys. The second couplet describes the divinely created and defended space in question, where spirits and immortals reside in a terrain "as forbidding as a fortified citadel." The space is especially privileged. Vietnam is separated from China by spirits and immortals.

In their third couplets, the other poems describe activities connected with the occupation and control of space. In this poem there is an allusion to the magical activity associated with divine rulers.[25] One of the other poems refers in its corresponding couplet to "the sage," who is the Vietnamese ruler. The final couplet locates the troops in the scene; they are in enchanted and therefore secure territory. Other poems locate Mạnh, though one of them ends with "the plodding horses" in the heights.

The Tam Thanh poem develops the language of spiritual power to indicate that the border is under divine protection rather than under the ruler's protection, but the poetic structure is identical with that of the other poems. The Tam Thanh poem

---

[24] Ibid., p. 110.

[25] Professor James Siegel observes a contrast in these poems between Mạnh's vivid military details and the unsubstantiality of the physical border. He merely names the peaks and ravines. Miasmas are excluded. Color is reserved for the flags. He is interested in movement near the border but, when he looks at the border itself, he never seems to see it. The Tam Thanh poem emphasizes the border's invisibility by referring to celestial sites "close at hand" or "within easy reach" but never seen. Yet the border contains a celestial capital and is a centre surrounded by a girdle of streams and a moat. A celestial capital is necessarily invisible, and this is what gives substance to things outside it, such as flags and troops. The flags and troops compensate for what is not seen; they supply presence to make up for absence on the border itself. The Celestial Capital creates a physical gap, and the gap represents the border.

supports the conclusion that Mạnh organizes all his "Lạng Sơn" poems in a similar manner.

We can now summarize the poems' structure. The ruler of Vietnam or of the spirit world initiates movement within a particular scene. The movement leads to the occupation and control of the scene. Mạnh dutifully participates in the control. The most frequent linguistic units are those of "grasping" weapons, flying flags, heights and depths, patrolling troops, words signifying control, and Mạnh's loyal heart and white hair. The lively imagery is evoked by the authority of an absent ruler or of hidden spirits.

Three general comments may be made on the "Lạng Sơn" poems.

In the first place, Mạnh never pauses to enjoy or fear. A notable omission in his vocabulary is references to "miasmas" in the mountain valleys.[26] The Chinese and also the Vietnamese poetic convention was that the mountains of northern Vietnam and southern China were miasma-infected, cold, and damp. Nguyễn Trung Ngạn, for example, writes of the Công Mẫu mountain, mentioned by Mạnh:

> Eyes look up at the flying birds beyond the setting sun.
> Yet my body is trailing long grass in the miasmas and mist.
> I am away on active service, sadly chanting and unbearably confused.
> Always facing this mountain to console my misery.[27]

Ngạn was familiar with the modern border when he crossed it on his mission to China in 1314. He wrote several poems about his experiences and emphasizes the physical hardship he endured for the sake of a "meritorious name":

> A meritorious name gained in this fickle world is in one's mind.
> Only half my attention is on loyalty and filial piety.
> In spite of all this, although marching and fording on this journey are arduous,
> It is still better than being at home in the company of my daughters and sons.[28]

Mạnh's poems are free of self-pity.

In the second place, Mạnh is not interested in what lay beyond the border or in differences between South and North. For him the Vietnamese side of the border resembles a screen. Barrier peaks disappear into the sky and clouds. China is never glimpsed. He can also lower his gaze and find deep ravines, and he looks into the picture and finds grottos. Posses of patrolling soldiers etch the contour when they climb into the heights. As in a Chinese painting, the details are sparse but the scene is complete.

Mạnh knew, of course, that China lay behind the border, and my third comment is that, in spite of this fact, his poems lack any kind of historical reference. A timeless atmosphere pervades them even though in his days the Lạng Sơn region had played an important strategic role in Vietnamese history. During the eleventh and thirteenth centuries, Northern soldiers began their unsuccessful invasions from passes in or

---

[26] See note 14, above.

[27] *TVTL*, q. 2, p. 26a.

[28] Ibid., p. 33b.

near this region. Khâu Ôn was involved in the Mongol invasion of 1285. The tribal chief of Lạng Giang distinguished himself during the third Mongol invasion of 1288. Yet the only time when Mạnh refers to the North is in his poem on the Tam Thanh grotto where he states that "the terrain separates South from North. It is as forbidding as a fortified citadel." Heaven created protecting spirits here, and Heaven signifies timelessness. Mạnh's conception of Vietnam's security by divine intention can be likened to Lý Thường Kiệt's in the eleventh century, when he wrote a famous poem on the occasion of a Chinese invasion:

> In the Southern country's mountains and streams the Southern emperor resides.
> A clear division is fixed by Heavenly writ.

I shall now discuss Mạnh's three poems on the northwestern part of the border. One of them mentions Văn Lang, the kingdom at the dawn of Vietnamese civilization. I am concerned to discover whether what we have gathered about the structure of the "Lạng Sơn" poems enables us to be better informed when reading these three poems.

V. Inspecting the Thao River Province[29]

1. Here are the frontier river's ten thousand miles. I am constantly in my campaigning attire.
2. The gods of the rain and wind drive away the miasmas and mist.
3. The customs include those of the Nhiêm Bàng and Bặc Bắc tribes.
4. The north adjoins Thiên Thiện and Vân Nam (Yünnan).
5. For me, with my loyal heart and white hair, the heavenly gates are nine.
6. With its blue water and purple mountains, the border commanderies are three.
7. On behalf of the court I am enquiring into the people's suffering.
8. I shall extirpate corruption and evil practices and eliminate treachery and extortion.

VI. On Patrol I Inspect Chân Đăng Châu[30]

1. Heaven opens and the Earth splits asunder: this is the province of the Three Rivers.
2. How marvellous is this journey, such as I have never known before.
3. Beyond the border the hundred tribes are an ancient encircling rampart.
4. In the western part of our country the great stronghold is the powerful Chân Đăng.
5. Pools from an earth-banked moat; rocks make the town's breastwork.
6. The houses are like thatched nests; the towers rise like bean stalks.
7. I want to climb the Côn Luân [K'un Lun] mountains and visit the magic orchard.
8. Soaring on the wind for ten thousand miles, happily flying like the roc.

---

[29] *TV*, vol. 3, p. 98.
[30] Ibid., p. 101.

The structure of these two poems is by no means unfamiliar, though the language is different. The context is no longer that of a military operation under way, yet the first couplets still deal with movements of the ruler's representative. The first couplet in the Chân Đăng poem contains Mạnh's only outburst of aesthetic delight in the border landscape. The first couplet in the Thao river poem mentions "miasmas" driven away by the gods of the rain and mist. Here is another equivalence of movement, always a theme in the first couplets. Miasmas are conventionally associated with the mountains of northern Vietnam and southern China, but Mạnh removes them from the Vietnamese landscape. The miasmas are only in China. On the Vietnamese side of the border the elements are working in Vietnam's favour, just as the spirits in the grottos do in the Lạng Sơn area.

The second couplets describe the scene, and here, as usual, place-names are mentioned. The scene in the Thao river poem alludes to China for the first time in the "border" poems, though China continues to be excluded from the scene just as its miasmas are. Thiện Thiện (Shan-hsi) is the name of a state in central Asia during the Han period. Nhiêm Bàng and Bặc Bắc are believed to be archaic names of tribes in southeastern China,[31] and the tribes at the extremity of the Vietnamese side of the border are seen by Mạnh as being similar. The northwestern border seems to be more porous than the Lạng Sơn border. Chân Đăng is a settlement in the Lâm thao district of Phú-thọ province in northwestern Vietnam, and it is the first Vietnamese place-name in these poems that does not refer to a natural feature; it is the name of a fortified place. Chân Đăng is mentioned in the Lý annals under the dates of 1033, 1068, 1113, and 1140. Its chiefs, always loyal, were in marriage alliance with the early Lý ruler. Moreover, Chân Đăng lay in a prestigious area. A shrine of the Hùng kings existed in the Lâm-thao district from at least as early as the beginning of the fifteenth century. According to the *Việt Sử Lược*, a late-fourteenth century Vietnamese history, the Hùng kings were the rulers of Văn Lang. I believe that Mạnh's interest in Chân Đăng is derived from its famous neighbourhood in ancient times.

The third couplets continue to refer to the occupation of space, though the language is different from what it is when Mạnh is leading patrols in the Lạng Sơn area. In the Thao river poem, control of space is represented by man-defined commanderies. Mạnh also thinks of the "heavenly gates"; Taoist imagery has appeared in the Tam Thanh poem, when he refers to the Celestial Emperor's capital and the pool of the immortals. Space in the Chân Đăng poem is controlled by a moat, a breastwork, houses that resemble nests, and towers. He is now thinking of a network of fortifications and settled human occupation rather than of mobile troops and strategic physical features. Moreover, another archaism appears in the third couplet of the Chân Đăng poem. "Houses like nests" is a Chinese convention for dwellings in ancient times. Perhaps the expression is introduced because Mạnh knows that he is in a region associated with Văn Lang. The first tale in the *Lĩnh Nam Trích Quái*, a compilation of the late fourteenth or early fifteenth century, tells that in Văn Lang the people built wooden houses to protect themselves from tigers and wolves.[32] Elevated houses are reminiscent of nests. The archaism is apt in a region that contains the temple of the ancient Hùng kings. A porous frontier, indicated by a

---

[31] Ibid., p. 99, n. 2.

[32] I have consulted the 1960 editions by Lê Hữu Mục and by Đinh Gia Khánh and Nguyễn Ngọc San.

similarity of customs on either side, may be another archaic allusion in a poem written about a region that was famous long before the Chinese emperors consolidated control of their southwestern lands and fixed the border. The witnesses believed that Văn Lang flourished for centuries before the First Emperor of China conquered southern China in the third century BC.

The final couplets situate Mạnh. In the Thao river poem, he seems to be performing civilian rather than military duties, and in the Chân Đăng poem he permits himself a reverie. The reason must be, as the second line tells us, that he is amid "marvellous" scenery.

The "border" structure is still recognizable in these two poems, but Mạnh's presence in the northwest is accompanied by new imagery. Movement is conveyed in non-military terms, the place-names allude to man-defined space, space is rendered as ancient space, and Mạnh is elated in a manner not disclosed in the sterner Lạng Sơn poems.

We now have some preparation for rereading the poem that mentions Văn Lang. I have modified my translation in accordance with the Chinese text provided by the editors of the *Thơ văn Lý-Trần*.

VII. Patrolling the Province[33]

> 1. I moor my boat by a rock in the river, facing the clear waves.
> 2. The river guards race to hail the official's pennant as it passes by.
> 3. There are tribal stockades along the Lô river and the Thao river's settlements.
> 4. Here Văn Lang's sun and moon once shone upon Thục's mountains and rivers.
> 5. Then, when over ten thousand miles there was writing and chariots, the frontier soil was peaceful.
> 6. But for a thousand years there have been disorders in the world.
> 7. I am favoured with the imperial order to control the border lands.
> 8. I shall expel and subdue robbers and bring warfare to an end.

We do not know whether Mạnh wrote this poem before or after he was in the Lạng Sơn region, but the structure is identical with that in the other "border" poems. The first couplet deals with movement set in train by the ruler. The "pennant" signifies the ruler's travelling official as it does in the Lạng Sơn poem on "the northern part of the border." The river guards are moving when they "race to hail the pennant"; they are the equivalence of assembled troops, flags, and pennants in the other poems. The second couplet describes the scene. Place-names, including Văn Lang, are again registered. The "bamboo fences" and "settlements" take the place of the "mountains," "valley," "barrier," and "fortified citadel" in the Lạng Sơn poems or of the "great fortress" of Chân Đăng. The "border" poems never describe the Chinese side of the border; even in the Thao river poem the tribesmen are only

---

[33] *TV*, vol. 3, p. 99.

"adjoining" Shan-hsi and Yünnan. For Mạnh, as for modern Vietnamese historians, Thục is firmly associated with Vietnamese soil.[34]

The third couplet, as elsewhere, deals with the exercise of royal authority and the occupation and control of space. In Văn Lang's day, "the frontier soil was peaceful." The ruler's authority is signified by "writing and chariots," the archaic linguistic unit that refers to the standardization of measurements in Vietnam's golden age. The final couplet inevitably places the loyal Mạnh in the scene. He is proud to be helping to control the border on the ruler's behalf.

The common structure, elaborated in various ways, is always intact in the "border" poems, even though the imagery changes when Mạnh is in the northwest. This is the conclusion I reach after trying to read the "Văn Lang" poem not as a document among other documents, most of which are not poems, but as one poem among several "border" poems by the same author. The structure of the "Văn Lang" poem consistently supports the "message" in all the poems: action happens when the ruler ordains it, and the consequence is the control of territory. The structure is appropriate for a fourteenth-century official who is doing his duty in serving the Trần autocracy. When we read these poems, we are made aware of notions taken for granted at the time. The poems bring to life an aspect of public service in the middle of the fourteenth century, and their message is spontaneous and authentic. Mạnh could not write otherwise because he was a Vietnamese who was living at a particular time in his country's history. The notion of royal authority was so engrained that he could take it for granted and concentrate his skills on poeticizing it. So simple is his notion of royal authority that he must have been conceptualizing the ruler not as the "emperor" (*đế*), a term derived from the Chinese vocabulary and used in Vietnamese court protocol, but as the *vua*, the Vietnamese word for the father-figure who led his people.

I have sought to discover the poetic structure in Mạnh's "border" poems. I shall now suggest reasons why his "literary message" may interest a historian.

In the first place, we have seen that Mạnh uses a particular imagery in the northwest. In the Chân Đăng poem and especially in the Văn Lang poem, royal initiative and the control of space are shown within the setting of antiquity and supported by appropriate archaic language. The expression "writing and chariots" shows that Mạnh is aware that he is beholding "cultural" as well as "military" space, once controlled by Văn Lang's sage-like rulers. The topographical associations of the northwest compel him to introduce "history" in the relevant part of his structure. The historical allusions are not a parade of his learning. The northwest had special significance for educated men in the fourteenth century and required Mạnh to use this language.

We can also contrast Mạnh's sense of historical association in the northwest with the timeless atmosphere in his Lạng Sơn poems. I believe that, for him, the "past" means a real past preserved in folklore and organized around stories of tutelary spirits written during the fourteenth century. All Vietnamese venerated the spirits because the spirits protected specific localities and put their space-protecting spiritual power at the ruler's disposal. The northwest was rich in such folklore, and no spirits would have been more prestigious than the Hùng kings, rulers of ancient

---

[34] Vietnamese historians believe that Thục is not a toponym but the patronym of a ruler of a federation of Âu Việt tribes; Nguyễn Khắc Viện, *Le Vietnam traditionnel — quelques étapes historiques, Études vietnamiennes* 21 (1969): 21.

Văn Lang.[35] But in Mạnh's day the Lạng Sơn area does not seem to be remembered in this fashion, and this is why Mạnh, in his Tam Thanh poem, substitutes supernatural protection in the persons of the timeless spirits of the grottos.

The "border" poems suggest something more. China is always blocked out, whether by the landscape or by loyal tribesmen. Mạnh is concerned only with the Vietnamese side of the border, and the reason must surely be that he is suppressing revolts on behalf of the ruler. In my earlier essay I believed that he rejoiced that Trần authority was accepted in the northwest. I now think otherwise. Mạnh's single and unambiguous reference to "robbers" happens to be in the Văn Lang poem. The contrast between the authority of the Văn Lang rulers and that of his own ruler must have been striking and poignant. Space in his day had to be recovered from rebels. His poem is a glimpse of the fourteenth-century nostalgia for Văn Lang's golden age.

Finally, we can note the bold language Mạnh uses to describe his own role. He is dealing with "the control of the world" and is "protecting the world." He is a "fearsome suppressor" and is exercising "supreme military command." He is "drafting the first chapter of *The Pacification of the Western Barbarians*." He is "occupying all the mountain lands of Lộc Châu." Earlier in Trần times, the emperor Minh-tôn led expeditions against invaders in the 1330s, and Minh-tôn's father and grandfather did likewise. The Trần family had taken the lead in the wars against the Mongols. But now Mạnh was leading the troops in the last years of Minh-tôn's reign (1320–57) or under Minh-tôn's feckless son, Dụ-tôn (1357–69). The *Lĩnh Nam Trích Quái* tells us that in the Văn Lang kingdom, "rulers and officials" were established "in order of precedence,"[36] but by the middle of the fourteenth century the rulers had come to depend on their officials to an extent that never happened before during the Trần dynasty or in Văn Lang times. Mạnh knew that he was shouldering responsibilities that the rulers themselves should have done, and this is probably why his poems, unlike those composed earlier in the fourteenth century, never justify his conduct on the grounds that he is earning a "meritorious name." Unlike his predecessors, who competed for recognition by energetic rulers, he was providing indispensable services. The experience of heavy responsibility explains why he and other witnesses were reluctantly daring to offer advice to the rulers about the way authority should be exercised. Although the "message" in Mạnh's poems is that all initiative comes from the rulers, he and his colleagues were taking the initiative in military campaigns and in memorials to the throne. After reading Mạnh's poems, I remain confident that the fourteenth century was a time of cruel contradictions for the witnesses and a watershed in Vietnamese history.

---

[35] In another poem, Mạnh mentions Phong Khê, associated with An-dương, who overthrew the Hùng kings in the third century BCE. In yet another poem, he mentions Ông Trọng, a hero of the third century BCE who became a Vietnamese tutelary spirit. Ông Trọng's shrine is noted in the poem. In both cases, Mạnh is alluding to sites in the neighbourhood of Hanoi.

[36] In the first tale.

CHAPTER ELEVEN

ON TELLING A STORY OF VIETNAM IN THE THIRTEENTH AND FOURTEENTH CENTURIES

My essay in celebration of the *Journal of Southeast Asian Studies*'s anniversary sketches what may be the concluding chapter in a study of Vietnam in the thirteenth and fourteenth centuries, when the Trần dynasty reigned (1226–1400). In 1225, the Trần family overthrew the last emperor of the previous dynasty, the Lý (1009–1225), and hitherto the only long-lived one. The Lý imperial line, in fact, lasted nearly fifty years longer than its successor. Nevertheless, the Trần is unquestionably the most renowned of all Vietnamese dynasties on account of its victories when Kubilai Khan's armies attacked three times in the thirteenth century. Yet one has to ask what kind of dynasty it was and how the country it ruled should be defined. Should one look to China, the source of the dynastic institution, for guidance, or should one look elsewhere? An event in 1237 suggests ambiguity. That year officials were required to offer betel and tea to the emperor when he was departing from the Eastern Pier near the capital. "Betel and tea" bring Southeast Asia as well as China into the picture.

My concluding chapter will be written as a chronologically constructed and, I hope, not too narrowly focused narrative history. An account of a unit of time as important as the Trần centuries needs room. Another merit of narrative history is that the historian is continually encouraged to ask questions about how and why things actually happened in a particular and maybe changing cultural context. The historian should also have space for reflecting on problems that arise and be challenged to experience with effective narrational devices and craftsmanship in general.

The final chapter will be preceded by five others which seek to unravel my sources' textual properties. A chapter-by-chapter analysis of the sources will, I hope, relieve me of the problem I had foreseen if a historian tried to combine a narrational approach with the requirements of textual criticism and continually had to slow down his pace in order to ask questions about a text's form as well as its contents.[1] "The mind is refrigerated by interruptions," remarked Dr. Johnson, and so, too, would be narrative history.

---

[1] O. W. Wolters, "Engaging J. D. Legge: Narrating the Fall of the Lý and the Rise of the Trần Dynasties," *Asian Studies Association of Australia Review* 10,2 (1986): 24–25.

By the sources' "textual properties" I refer to no more than patterned literary features and structures that bid for recognition to allow the sources to be endowed with meaning over and above specific items of information. A source's textual meaning represents how Vietnam "appeared" to its author, or its style. My own narrative of Vietnam in the concluding chapter would take into account the sources' competing "appearances," in which they illuminated each other, and also instances of how they sometimes sounded alike. What I write cannot help being yet another "appearance," though, perhaps, it may be closer to a "countenance," or substance, behind the various "appearances." By "countenance," derived from the Latin *continentia* (the way one holds oneself together), I understand the extent to which Trần Vietnam "held together."

Writing narrative history is telling a story with a plot. The plot comprises the way a story's parts and effects cohere. My sources can be read as stories with plots responsible for their meanings and "appearance." For a long time I have believed that the fourteenth century situated a watershed in Vietnamese history, but I did not sense the drama until I knew more about the thirteenth century. Thus, the sweep of Trần time has suggested a subject for the plot in my concluding chapter: simply a dynasty which was already disintegrating within a century of spectacular military triumph. The story and its plot, sketched in this essay, reflect some considerations to be borne in mind when I come to write my concluding chapter. The essay resembles, as it were, one of Henry James's prefaces that tells the story of a story.

In my first chapter, I would have furnished a historical background to the Trần period and explained my intentions. But my final chapter would need what I had come to regard as an appropriate setting for Trần history, and, for this purpose, I would take note of several sources. One of them, and perhaps in the final analysis the most interesting, would be what I would refer to as "the voices," by which I mean Trần period prose or verse preserved in the *Thơ văn Lý Trần* compilations, published in Hanoi in 1978 and 1989, and also in the Vietnamese annals mentioned below. The "voices" help us hear how people in Trần times expressed their immediate and various concerns. Though elitist, they are fairly diverse: those of rulers, princes, monks, generals, poets, different types of officials, and landowners. Chinese records are another, and by no means trivial or untrustworthy, source, even though the "appearance" they convey is of a politically and culturally backward country, distant and isolated from the fount of civilization in China.[2] "Voices" and Chinese sources must not be ignored when, as so often has to happen, one falls back on yet another and famous source, the *Đại Việt Sử Ký Toàn Thư* or Trần annals, compiled in the middle of the fifteenth century and the source invariably accorded the status of the "master text" for this period on account of its relatively abundant detail. The annals, with frequent pauses contrived by the annalist himself to underscore the significance of his entries, tell the story of the Trần family as a shifting relationship of princes and subordinates and give Vietnam the "appearance" of being run by and for the ruling family, though its plot, I shall suggest, is disclosed only within the context of the early fourteenth century. I have found myself continually having to resist the annals' influence and to remind myself that it provides only one of several "appearances" of Trần Vietnam.

---

[2] Ch'en Fu, "Chen gang zhong shi za," *Si-ku quan-shu chen-pen ba-ji*, no. 159; *An-nan zhi-yuan*, ed. L. Arrousseau (Hanoi: École Française d'Extrême-Orient, 1932).

The following setting would enable my story to get under way, and I would be less concerned with dense description than with a few features that seem, in my opinion, to affect what happens. I would begin with the Trần family's elaborate hierarchy, over which presides a "Son of Heaven," the source of all initiatives and hailed as a Chinese-style emperor and dynastic head. According to Ch'en Fu, a Chinese envoy in 1293, only important people in this meticulously ranked society used silver platters for their betel. Nothing in the records of the previous Lý dynasty suggests quite so elaborate and exclusive a Court as the one rapidly established by this ruthless family of former fishermen from the Red River delta and perhaps of Chinese origin. I would allude to my chapter on the annals to recall how, by a series of bold improvisations to deal with unforeseen emergencies, the family had been able to guarantee that a ruler's eldest son would succeed him and marry a woman who herself belonged to the Trần family. Furthermore, the same source would show that the emperors were assisted by their uncles and brothers, on whom they showered privileges and bestowed the highest offices. In 1266 the emperor authorized the members of the imperial family to assemble the landless and open up vacant territory. The princes would become increasingly wealthy. Ch'en Fu knew only of princely estates in the countryside and not of towns. Here, then, would be a tightly knit and pampered family. A thirteenth-century "voice"—that of the emperor Thánh-tôn (died 1290) during a family feast in 1268—intones: "The empire is our ancestors', and those who inherit it [i.e. himself] should share the enjoyment of riches and status with his brothers in the family." In 1370 a Trần princess, rallying her supine male relatives against an usurper, arrogantly reminds them that "the empire was the ancestors'. Why should we surrender it to another?"

The chain of command extended from the ruler and princes to trusted subordinates, known as *hành-khiển* and often eunuchs, and thence to junior executive staff. Everything depended on the ruler and his entourage of princes and *hành-khiển* and not on a bureaucracy. Affairs would be conducted in an informal and relaxed manner. The sign that one belonged to the imperial entourage was when, for some reason or other, one caught the ruler's eye and was "appointed" to a responsible post. For example, in 1299 a young scholar was lucky enough to have the opportunity of composing the drunken heir's letter of apology to his father. His career was now launched. But this casually organized polity was also capable of severity, as Ch'en Fu observes.

The rulers' personal supervision of their government becomes plausible when one notes that a Chinese source, the *An-nan zhi-yuan*, describes Vietnam in Lý and Trần times as a "small and accessible" country, where only runners are necessary to travel by foot from the capital to Lạng Sơn on the northern border or to Thanh Hóa on the coast. Chinese sources deploy every possible narrational device to emphasize that the Trần realm was no more than a diminutive "corner of the ocean" with abundant riverine communications that gave the rulers easy access to remoter areas. Every source is coloured by references to rivers. Rivers are the scene of naval manoeuvres, warfare, floods, dykes, canals, commercial transport, rafting, markets and entertainment held on bridges, princely escapes and escapades, legends, and landscape poetry. In 1241 Thái-tôn (died 1277) audaciously crossed the Kuangtung border in a river boat. Inevitably, a boat's appurtenances can signify imperial rank.

I would go on to introduce what I regard as an essential aspect of the setting, and "voices" now claim my attention. A story of Trần times has to consider the influence of the *dhyāna*, or meditational Buddhism, on the emperors' mood. Those who ruled until 1357, less that half a century before the dynasty fell, have left a considerable body of Buddhist literature, and we learn from it that they made a virtue of avoiding prejudice or partiality, of reconciling opposite points of view, and of tolerating the simple devotional expedients (*upāya*) of the majority of their subjects. But they did not neglect their official duties. Thái-tôn claims that he has to work hard but manages to steal leisure to study none other than *The Diamond Sūtra*, a major source for the *dhyāna*'s basic teachings on mindlessness, the perception of one's Buddha-nature as a void, the practicability of immediate enlightenment, and the relativity of all phenomena. Those who absorb these teachings can ignore distinctions and especially the distinction of past, present, and future. Thánh-tôn, in a poem on the Buddha nature, writes: "there is no past or future, loss or gain." The past is relevant only in terms of the present. "Now" is when flashes of spiritual enlightenment are achievable and bad karma avoided. This serene outlook would be compatible with a present-minded and relaxed mode of government, and one would expect those who had mastered meditative techniques to possess immense reserves of confidence in their ability to cope with every situation.

The setting established, a swiftly paced story would get under way. The new dynasty quickly establishes itself. In 1299 the last rebel from Lý times prepares to surrender, and the annalist observes that "the empire was united." In 1237 Thái-tôn's uncle, thinking ahead but only to safeguard the imperial succession, addresses his nephew thus: "It is necessary to risk marrying [your brother's pregnant wife] in order to have confidence in the future." Thái-tôn reluctantly agrees, and the bitter family feud is resolved in 1258 when the offspring of this arrangement marries the outraged brother's daughter. The dynasts would now seem to enjoy a foolproof autocracy, and the annalist, always interested in the princes' story, pauses to comment on the family feast given by Thánh-tôn in 1268: "Thus, at this time the princes were entirely peaceful, in harmony with each other, and respected the ruler." In another passage of contrived narrative after an entry about the filling of vacant offices in 1246, the annalist pauses to note that "at this time the country had no problems. The people were content and officials had occupied their posts for a long time. The highest offices at Court were in the hands of wise and educated members of the ruling family."

But in 1257 the Mongol's invaded for the first time and were defeated after a riverine battle. Thereafter, until 1288, when, at the Bạch Đằng river, the Vietnamese were victorious for the third time, the story would be full of exciting details. Because the Vietnamese victories are famous, I would be careful to show that there were close shaves, near disasters, and even instances of treachery. More important than anything else, however, I would contrive to allow "voices" to be regularly heard in order to provide, as it were, their running commentary, chronologically organized, on what was happening. By this means I would hope to develop the theme that I believe to be crucial for understanding the thirteenth century and also the drama of Trần dynastic history. The theme is mounting confidence in the face of peril. The Vietnamese would come to believe that their leaders possessed expedients for success on every occasion.

Shrewd diplomacy is one expedient. "It was Heaven's Will that our country should again produce sage-like wisdom," exclaims the Court historian, Lô Văn Hưu, in 1272 when he records how Đinh Thiôn Hoàng in 968 styled himself "emperor," a title first assumed by Triệu Đà in the second century BCE. The title is a metaphor for Vietnamese independence from China, the other empire. The rulers also believe that a "dynastic" Court will help to supply the strength they associate with China. In Trần times, good government means no more than strong government. But Triệu Đà and the Vietnamese rulers in the tenth century and thereafter protect their independence by prudently and repeatedly sending humble tributary missions to China to forestall the despatch of inquisitive Chinese envoys. Unfortunately Kubilai Khan, a Mongol, is eccentric and demands that his "vassals" should come to China to pay homage in person, and the Trần family has to fight to uphold its own version of the tributary relationship. After 1288 the relationship is resumed intact.

Trần diplomacy eventually prevailed, but wartime successes under Trần princes would, more than anything else, convince Vietnamese that they were invulnerable. A diviner, later to be appointed to the imperial entourage, correctly predicted the Mongols' defeat when they invaded for the second and third times in the 1280s. But no one was better qualified to be confident in the lessons of experience than Trần Quốc Tuấn, the commander-in-chief and son of the affronted prince whose wife Thái-tôn had taken in 1237. When he is dying in 1300, Quốc Tuấn reviews the age-long and repeatedly successful record of Vietnamese resistance to China in order to enjoin on the rulers, their senior assistants, and "the little people" the need to cooperate. He assures them that guerrilla tactics would compensate for the lack of superior numbers. Already in 1286, on the eve of the third invasion, he had been so confident that he promised that he would "certainly" win.

For further evidence of Vietnamese confidence in their experience, I would allude to Lý Tế Xuyên's compilation in 1329 of tales of the country's tutelary spirits, the *Việt Điện U-Linh Tập*, discussed in the third chapter of my study.[3] Many spirits were honored for their help during the Mongol invasions, and the specific services of two are recorded. The tales' plots are simple and often uniformly structured: the invariably successful relationship between Vietnamese rulers, frequently eleventh-century ones, and the local spirits but only if the ruler alertly apprehends a spirit's presence, if necessary testing it, appoints it to a post of military responsibility, and rewards it for its contribution to victory. The spirit, who always salutes the ruler, now joins the entourage. When this procedure is followed, victory is "certain." Vietnam's "appearance" in the tales is that of a supernaturally protected land with fine scenery. The landscape, too, is a source of confidence in dangerous times. According to Vietnamese poets, experience shows that the mountains astride their northern border, considered by the Chinese to be a wild and unhealthy zone, have furnished a protective screen from time immemorial.

The confidence in the future that Thái-tôn's uncle urges in 1237 seems justified throughout the thirteenth century. The imperial succession is secure. The emperor's carefully educated and trained eldest sons by mothers of the Trần family invariably become suitable heirs. Senior princes, generation by generation, are monotonously appointed to and distinguish themselves in the highest posts. Regularly despatched tributary missions, omens, guerrilla warfare, riverine battles, tutelary spirits, and the landscape repeatedly—so the sources insist—protect the country. I would now recall a "voice" discussed in my fourth chapter and in the form of an eulogistic and moving inscription of 1291 in honor of a dead Trần princess, Trần Phụng Dương, Trần Quang Khải's wife. Quang Khải was Thái-tôn's son and chief minister during the second and third invasions. Loyal and brave women are part of the Trần story. The inscription seems to illustrate recurring themes in the thirteenth century so

---

[3] Lý Tế Xuyên, "Việt Điện U-Linh Tập," *École Française d'Extrême-Orient* A47.

convincingly that it could stand in for "the whole text" of the thirteenth century in the sense that the themes are connected up with each other through the Trần family.[4] The inscription embodies the family's notable features: continuous inter-marriage, princely government, *dhyāna* Buddhism, habitual use of China-derived metaphors to supply images of themselves (because of her lack of envy and gentle manner of admonishing, the princess is likened rhetorically to a Confucian "Gentleman of old"), and wartime heroism (she throws her body on top of her husband to protect him when they escape by river). This plucky woman symbolizes her family's ability to cope confidently with emergencies. The inscription praises her adaptability by the device of enumerating no less than fifteen roles, spelt out in detail, in which she excelled. In particular, she handles onerous household problems arising from her marriage to a busy wartime prince who neglects her and his family. Her husband is an administrator, diplomat, general, and poet. Other princes are similarly versatile. Affairs of state do not depend wholly on the emperors. The talented and energetic Trần family provides a reservoir of prowess for all contingencies. Disaster is averted because the family always manages to hold together.

The major theme in my story so far is that the Vietnamese, no matter what happens, have reason to become increasingly confident. The country's internal affairs are not unmanageable, the country is apparently invincible when attacked from without, the ruling family is able to hang together effectively, and there is no reason to suppose that the situation will change adversely. On the contrary, everything in Vietnamese experience would seem to be predictable. The resumption of tributary missions to Peking would certainly convince the Trần Court that the Mongols were no longer to be feared. The emperors Nhân-tôn (died 1308), who preaches Buddhism in the countryside, Anh-tôn (died 1320), and Minh-tôn (died, 1357) practice meditation. Poets, using Chinese literary forms, rejoice in their "land of rivers" and employ the language that the famous Chinese poets in T'ang times used to extol their landscape. "The river coils," writes Nguyễn Sưởng, "and the aged general [Trần Quốc Tuấn] discusses the battle scene." The annals describe Minh-tôn as a vigorous ruler who selected and managed his officials with "discernment." Now, too, the annalist, recording the reigns of Anh-tôn and Minh-tôn, discloses his plot, which is how good government is conducted (and what prevents it) as it was in the first decades of the fourteenth century, when educated men were appointed to the imperial entourage. His prescription is reminiscent of the *Việt Điện U-Linh Tập*'s description of the relationship between a good ruler and the spirits; in both cases the ruler has to take the initiative and the consequences are beneficial. The annalist's prescription, like that of the tales, is structured as a syntactically recognizable and repetitive statement: the ruler appoints as officials honorable men who perform well, earn a good reputation, and enjoy his favors.[5] The annalist is unmistakably signifying an entourage; the ruler personally "appoints" and rewards his staff.

Another detail in the annals suggests stability during the first half of the fourteenth century. In a pause contrived under the date of 1323, the annalist states that, at this time, thirteen admirable men succeeded each other in the rulers' service.

---

[4] I am influenced by Valentine Cunnigham, *British Writers of the Thirties* (New York, NY, and Oxford: Oxford University Press, 1988), p. 2. He refers to "a connected field, whole text, or set of diverse signs adding up, more or less, to a single semiotic." This may be an unattainable enterprise for the historian, but it beckons all the same.

[5] O. W. Wolters, "Possibilities for a Reading of the 1293–1357 Period in the Vietnamese Annals," *Vietnam Forum* 11 (1988): 97–102.

These, and rarely eunuchs, represent *hành-khiển* in the fourteenth century. Some are active as late as the 1360s. The government should have been in good hands even though not all of these admirable men are known to be examination graduates.

But this is not the whole story. My narrative will begin to portray aging officials continually travelling on urgent business and writing poems in honor of each other's professional accomplishments, maybe likening their colleagues to famous Chinese officials. Some are mentioned in the annalist's list under the date of 1323. And, as the century moves on, poems describe suffering in the countryside. Poets may now be whistling to keep up their spirits when they no longer salute their mountains as a protective screen but as the abode of immortal beings, as though, in spite of temporary troubles, they still hope that their country will survive. I shall also begin to consider startling entries in the annals. In 1328, Minh-tôn, anxious to appoint an heir as soon as possible, executed his Trần father-in-law for advising him to be patient. This is the single deed for which the annalist criticizes him. And, much more ominous, the annals from 1343 onwards repeatedly refer to uprisings in the countryside, sometimes prolonged ones, and dependents of the princes and monks are mentioned as being among the rebels. In 1389 a monk raised an army of vagabonds, assumed a title, appointed *hành-khiển*, and occupied the capital for three days. Uprisings continued until the end of the century. Information about them is meagre yet enough to throw village behavior into sharper relief and suggest traits the Court and village sub-cultures have in common. Local leaders rally followers, attract entourages, and arrogate to themselves imperial rank and Court symbols. Originally the Trần family had done likewise. Rebels also tap sources of supernatural power.

Mongol China is now in decline, but so, it would seem, is Vietnam. What has happened so suddenly? I would suspend my narrative.

Maybe Minh-tôn, born in 1300, was aging. His grandfather and father had died when they were fifty and forty-four years old, respectively. His poems reveal that he was haunted by his crime of 1328. Unlike his predecessors, he was never assisted by a competent heir. His first heir died prematurely and the next was sexually impotent and pleasure-seeking. The senior princes were no longer able men. His poems unambiguously identify him as practicing meditation. The annals describe him as testy and standing on his dignity. Minh-tôn may be the story's only "round character" who, as E. M. Forster would put it, is "thicker than a gramophone record."[6] Perhaps Minh-tôn's personality helps to explain what was happening in the countryside, but for me, this would only be a matter of contingency. My narrative, with its bias towards entrenched characteristics of Trần history, pulls me in a different direction. The conjuncture of two aspects of the Trần system of family government are now causing grave problems. The first is Minh-tôn's religious outlook, detached from phenomenal things such as rural unrest. The annalist tells us that members of his entourage complained that people were illegally forsaking their villages and that officials were not taking up their duties. "Why worry?" is the gist of his reply, a vivid glimpse of the Trần family's relaxed management of affairs.

But I believe that another aspect of the Trần system exacerbated the situation immeasurably. The annals hint that Minh-tôn and his family were "generous" to their relatives and lenient when they misbehaved. These traits could cause them to

---

[6] [From *Aspects of the Novel*, the Clark-series lectures delivered by E. M. Forster at Trinity College, Cambridge, in 1927.—Ed.]

be excessively indulgent in allowing their relatives to appropriate State land and in tolerating their rapacious encroachment on the villagers' farming land.[7] The rulers' habit of endowing pagodas and conferring gifts of land on favored members of their entourage would cause additional economic pressure on the countryside. Moreover, the Trần princes' behavior was bound to set a bad example to greedy officials. Under the date of 1377, the annals praise the censor Trương Đỗ because he was "honest" and did not have "an estate." Hồ Tôn Thốc at the end of the century, on the other hand, and accused of harming the people, retorts: "as soon as a son receives an imperial favor, the whole family enjoys his salary."

I would have to ask why the emperors permitted such irresponsible behavior. Maybe the practice of inter-family marriages generated what the annals record as an almost obsessive sense of being apart from the rest of the population, and this could make them insensitive to happenings outside their narrow circle. Perhaps, too, they considered that nothing was more necessary than retaining their relatives' loyalty and support. The famous generals and administrators of the previous century were either princes or members of princely households. But family obedience could not be taken for granted. The thirteenth-century story would furnish instances of quarrels, feuds, and treason.

I would not pretend to be omniscient to enable me to maintain narrational flow, but I would take a great deal of trouble in contriving to illustrate the sheer scale of upheaval that had come to pass by the middle of the fourteenth century. To this end, I would present a dramatic contrast between the unchanging, predictable, and manageable Vietnam of the thirteenth century and the subsequent maelstrom. This is precisely the contrast that evidently oppressed thoughtful and always loyal men of affairs—usually officials—from the middle of the century onwards. They would be dismayed by the difference between the heroic, obedient, and apparently foreseeable world of the previous century and unprecedented and widespread disaffection in their own day. The drama of Trần history is the effect the contrast between stability and social upheaval had on these men. They were so pained that they felt compelled to rewrite, revise, or even subvert what Vietnamese experience had hitherto taken for granted, and what they rewrote impinges on nothing less than the core of traditional Vietnamese experience: notions concerning time and security. They were discreetly proposing new expedients for dynastic survival, though they would never have dared to upgrade their own status and role in public life. They had to write because they grew up in a cultural tradition that placed a high value on words written in the Chinese classical language and even, I suspect, considered something to have force only when it was in writing.[8]

A century of successful warfare is therefore followed by a century when Vietnamese experience has to be restated. Sanguine assumptions give way to anxious preoccupations, and my narrative will have to supply signs of the contrast in the form of fourteenth-century voices as their commentary on momentous developments.

Time is now conceptualized differently. Whereas there was indifference to the past, Vietnam is at last attributed with an antiquity, the golden age of Văn Lang

---

[7] For studying rural unrest in the fourteenth century, I have benefited from essays in *Tìm hiểu xã hội Việt Nam thời Lý-Trần* (Hanoi: Khoa-học Xã-hội, 1981).

[8] I prefer "rewriting" to Eric Hobsbawm's "invention of tradition," which, according to him, is what happens in time of rapid social change.

when "customs were pure." The reason for the fiction is that Văn Lang, originally an obscure toponym in two early Chinese records about northwestern Vietnam, is seized on as a nostalgic metaphor for what was assumed to be a traditionally disciplined Vietnamese society. Social discipline is henceforth government's major concern. The first known reference to Văn Lang is, appropriately, in a poem by Phạm Sư Mạnh, mentioned in the 1323 list of excellent men, written when he is policing the northwest in the middle of the century. The metaphor, because it has been committed to writing, can become a historical act, as it is by the end of the century. The thirteenth century historian, Lê Văn Hưu, needed Triệu Đà, the first "emperor," as a metaphor for Vietnamese independence in defiance of Kubilai Khan's fury, but Văn Lang was to become sufficiently important in its own right to justify the efforts of archaeologists in the 1960s to recover its artefacts. Today Văn Lang is the metaphor for the birth of the nation.

Changing conditions have made a nonsense of the notion of changelessness. Vietnam now requires a past as a critique of the present and to define its goals for the future. Lê Quát, Mạnh's friend, criticizes Buddhists of all social classes because, "when they entrust something to a temple or pagoda, they are as happy as if their reward is guaranteed tomorrow."[9] "Guaranteed" belongs to the thirteenth century's semiotic field for signifying predictability: "Heaven's Will," "certainly," "natural barriers," repetitive literary structures. Quát can no longer share this confident mood.

Furthermore, time can be organized differently when the notion of linearity, implied by Vietnam's newly found antiquity, is established.[10] Educated Vietnamese may now have become more and more convinced that the Chinese division of time into dynastic cycles corresponded with their own experience when the Trần dynasty was in decline. In the thirteenth century, Lê Văn Hưu, commenting under the date of 1005 on the bad last ruler of the family preceding the Lý, is familiar with the Chinese dogma of the "rise and fall" of dynasties, but the reason is simply that he was compiling a history appropriate for an imperial Court and therefore in the style of the Song historian Si-ma Guang (died 1086) and was bound to adopt the Chinese historiographical convention of the dynastic cycle. Not so Trần Nguyên Đán (died 1390), a descendant of Quang Khải and the heroic princess Phụng Dương, when he challenges his negligent colleagues by reminding them that "the rise and fall [of dynasties] throughout time certainly provides warning examples [of dynasties threatened with collapse]." Though the expression "throughout time" may be a rhetorical flourish, he is referring to a dynastic rhythm that belongs to Chinese and not Vietnamese historical experience.

Thus, when time is in a state of flux and Vietnamese experience no longer a reliable guide, one is required to deliberate on how best to use time. Unprecedented decisions are now feasible. In 1377 the emperor Duệ-tôn dies in battle when trying to punish the Chams beyond Vietnam's southern borders for their devastating raids, which even threaten the Vietnamese capital and send the Court flying for safety. Dynastic dogma has hitherto held that successful campaigns against foreign enemies reinforce authority at home. Thirteenth-century confidence had, in fact, largely depended on military success. Though irresolute when faced with internal problems,

---

[9] The annals under the date of 1370, when Lê Quát died.

[10] That there were two fourteenth-century instances of calendar reform may not be coincidental.

Minh-tôn was prompt in 1329 and 1335 to lead his army against invaders from the northwest. But times have now changed and traditional values have to be abandoned. Confidence has sunk so low even before the Cham campaign that Duệ-tôn's wife and his officials dare to urge him to reverse his priorities and not go to war until he has restored order at home. An essay denouncing warfare is written about this time. A few years later Trần Nguyên Đán recommends an extraordinary repudiation of past experience when he advises Nghệ-tôn (died 1394) "to respect the Ming ruler as a father and to love the Cham ruler as a brother." Đán's ancestors would be appalled. The Chinese and Vietnamese were of equal status.

A literal example of rewriting the past under stress of changed circumstances is provided by an updated version of the *Việt Điện U-Linh Tập* in which heroic spirits are now also honored for controlling evil influences in the villages.[11] In 1379, a rebel close to the capital, using magical arts, styles himself "king." The revised text is a further response to what is perceived as an urgent need to restore order in the countryside. Predictably, the proposal is made in 1397 to establish village schools for teaching family obligations, the intention no doubt being to persuade villagers not to roam and join rebel gangs. Lê Quát had deplored the absence of such schools. The conviction is gaining ground that ethical discipline is necessary in addition to routine punitive campaigns against rebels.

During the last few years before the dynasty's collapse in 1400, the Trần family is itself involved in rapid changes that help to destroy it. When Minh-tôn dies in 1357, he is, until 1394, succeeded by three sons. Only the first of them, the impotent and dissolute Dụ-tôn (died 1369), is the son of Minh-tôn's senior wife, the daughter of the uncle he murdered in 1328. The dynastic succession is now a shambles. Duệ-tôn dies in battle, and the hapless and increasingly desperate emperor Nghệ-tôn breaks with tradition by forsaking his family's policy of relying on its kinsmen and, instead, entrusts himself and his Court to a relative by marriage, Lê Quý Ly. In 1388 the aged Nghệ-tôn, born in 1321, finally throws in his lot with Ly, kills his nephew and heir, and confides his very young son to Ly's protection. An exaggerated respect for Nghệ-tôn's dynastic authority causes the unfortunate nephew to order his supporters to lay down their arms. In 1392, it is Ly's turn to rewrite the past, in this instance Chinese tradition, in order to promote the Duke of Zhou to a sage status above that of Confucius; the Duke of Zhou is the exemplary protector of a young ruler and Ly's current self-image. His charade explains why, just before Nghệ-tôn dies in 1394, a twelfth-century protector of a young Lý ruler, Tô Hiến Thành, is granted special posthumous honors. Thanh is ignored in the tales of the heroic spirits. The past is again being rewritten. About this time, too, I believe, the author of the Việt sử-lược drastically revises the reign of the last Lý ruler, Huệ-tôn (1210–25), to glorify the role of that ailing monarch's protector. The protector happens to be the founder of the Trần family's fortunes, but what is surely pertinent is the protector's marriage relationship with the Lý ruler and the contrived sequel, which is the peaceful and honorable accession of the protector's young relative to the throne. In both respects the text pointedly prepares the ground for legitimating Lê Quý Ly's

---

[11] O. W. Wolters, *Two Essays on Đại-Việt in the Fourteenth Century*, The Lac-Viet Series, no. 9 (New Haven, CT: Yale Center for International and Area Studies, 1988), pp. xx–xxii.

usurpation.[12] The annals describe the last Lý reign very differently. Thái-tôn's uncle compels Huê-tôn to hang himself and murders his family.

My narrative account of the fourteenth century would end with the blood bath in 1400 that overwhelmed the Trần family, destroyed the dynasty, and brought Lê Quý Ly to the throne. The pedantic, fumbling, and cowardly Nghệ-tôn would be contrasted with the determined, crafty, and cruel Lê Quý Ly. The narrative would also describe the formation of Ly's entourage. These men represent those who are not "thoughtful men of affairs," oppressed by change.[13]

Having on these lines sketched the scale of the contrast between the thirteenth and fourteenth centuries, I would now be able to return to the subject of my plot: a dynasty that was already disintegrating within a century of spectacular military triumph.

I would suggest that my story of the thirteenth and fourteenth centuries showed that the Trần state was flawed because it was encumbered with a dynasty. Its dynastic style and "appearance" might seem to promise continuity and stability, and a small territory should have been relatively easy to govern. But its Chinese "appearance" and the Trần annalist's appropriation of the Chinese convention of a dynastic cycle raise unreal expectations. Only two aspects of Vietnam can be seen as being "sinic." Its emperors knew that borders were fixed and not porous and that they would be judged by their ability to defend them, and some literati believed sufficiently in the authority of the written word that, when they were faced by grave changes, they felt bound to commit to writing what experience now revealed. But the Vietnamese dynastic institution was, in fact, fragile. The substance of government, or what I regard as Vietnam's "countenance"—its capacity to hold together—as distinct from its "appearance," depended on circumstances other than the prestige of the dynastic institution and its supposed guarantee of durability. It certainly did not depend on ideology formed of inter-related ethical, social, and political values and obligations. The final chapter of my study, if it is to succeed, would foreground such aspects of indigenous behavior as a preference for quick expedients to solve immediate problems rather than planning for the future, recourse to supernatural protection, a personal and informal exercise of government, the indispensable assistance of the rulers' uncles and brothers, an expansive ruling family, an obedient entourage, the rulers' favors, instances of the officials' loyalty but also their anxiety to achieve merit for the sake of professional rewards, and hints of a bilateral kinship system that militated against permanent residence in villages and the cultivation of Chinese-style social obligations, a kinship system against which the Trần family protected itself by marrying its relatives. The Chinese observers were quick to spot and deplore the essential feature of the cultural situation: the absence of schools for instilling "proper social relations and civic virtues." In these circumstances, the Trần state could be expected to hold together only when the ruling family was united and competent and could manipulate to its advantage what I have described as indigenous behavior. This is what happened from 1226 to 1357, though things were already going wrong in Minh-tôn's later years.

---

[12] Wolters, "Engaging J. D. Legge: Narrating the Fall of the Lý and the Rise of the Trần Dynasties," pp. 25–27.

[13] In my proposed final chapter, I would consider other instances of fourteenth-century change, such as an apparently expanded use of the Vietnamese *nôm* script and Vietnam's participation in the international ceramics trade.

Thereafter the dynasty declined suddenly and rapidly without signs that it could recuperate. Resourceful emperors, capable of improvising responses to emergencies, were no longer on the scene. Loyal officials might recommend policies, but an organized bureaucracy was unavailable to help fill the vacuum when the princes ceased to be capable and undertake reforms to postpone the end, as could happen in China in later T'ang times and subsequently. Instead Trần authority was temporarily shored up by a disloyal "protector."

Vietnam in the thirteenth and fourteenth centuries never enjoyed the relative stability of the Chinese empire but, at the same time, it was denied a "Southeast Asian" political flexibility, when regimes, sometimes enduring for no more than a generation or so, could disappear in rapid succession but without inflicting the prolonged misery that the declining Trần inflicted on Vietnam. There would be more frequent changes at the top, but life below would not deteriorate into a tension between villagers and those who wanted to impose order on them. If one were to retort that the dynastic institution had protected Vietnam in the thirteenth century, one would have to explain why in the tenth century, before the hereditary dynastic principle was established, China was held at bay and the protocol of the tributary system defined and functioned to maintain "a good relationship" with China, the annalist's euphemism for the system. Men and women, not institutions, had mattered in the tenth and thirteenth centuries.

A novel has been described as "a machine for generating interpretations."[14] The same may be said of historical narrative, though, unfortunately, its readers are not usually as magnanimous as those who read novels. Perhaps writers of narrative history should frankly admit to being provocative rather than definitive. And so, to conclude my final chapter, I would invoke yet another source, the work of Ngô Sĩ Liên, a late fifteenth-century commentator on the Trần annals and a convinced Confucianist, whom I discuss in my penultimate chapter under the title of "Hardly a proper imperial state: a fifteenth-century Vietnamese judgment." Liên, too, rewrites the experience of the Trần period but in order to mock it and write it off as worthless and even dangerous.[15] Liên might agree with me and, also ironically, with the Chinese sources I take into account that Trần Vietnam, dynastically speaking, could not hang together. The difference between us is that he wanted to harness the Confucian ethic to strengthen the dynastic institution, its policies, and its staff, whereas I would tell the story of the tragic consequences the institution was bound, sooner or later, to bring in its wake.

---

[14] Umberto Eco, *Reflections on The Name of the Rose* (London: Secker & Warburg Limited, 1985), p. 2.

[15] Oliver Wolters, "What Else May Ngo Si Lien Mean? A Matter of the Distinctions in the Fifteenth Century," in *Sojourners and Settlers: Histories of Southeast Asia and the Chinese in Honour of Jennifer Cushman*, ed. Anthony Reid (St. Leonards, NSW: Allen & Unwin for Asian Studies Association of Australia, 1996), pp. 94–114.

SOUTHEAST ASIA PROGRAM PUBLICATIONS

Cornell University

Studies on Southeast Asia

Number 43   *Early Southeast Asia: Selected Essays*, O. W. Wolters, ed. Craig J. Reynolds. 2008. 255 pp. ISBN 978-0-877277-43-9 (pb).

Number 42   *Thailand: The Politics of Despotic Paternalism* (revised edition), Thak Chaloemtiarana. 2007. 284 pp. ISBN 0-8772-7742-7 (pb).

Number 41   *Views of Seventeenth-Century Vietnam: Christoforo Borri on Cochinchina and Samuel Baron on Tonkin*, ed. Olga Dror and K. W. Taylor. 2006. 290 pp. ISBN 0-8772-7741-9 (pb).

Number 40   *Laskar Jihad: Islam, Militancy, and the Quest for Identity in Post-New Order Indonesia*, Noorhaidi Hasan. 2006. 266 pp. ISBN 0-877277-40-0 (pb).

Number 39   *The Indonesian Supreme Court: A Study of Institutional Collapse*, Sebastiaan Pompe. 2005. 494 pp. ISBN 0-877277-38-9 (pb).

Number 38   *Spirited Politics: Religion and Public Life in Contemporary Southeast Asia*, ed. Andrew C. Willford and Kenneth M. George. 2005. 210 pp. ISBN 0-87727-737-0.

Number 37   *Sumatran Sultanate and Colonial State: Jambi and the Rise of Dutch Imperialism, 1830-1907*, Elsbeth Locher-Scholten, trans. Beverley Jackson. 2004. 332 pp. ISBN 0-87727-736-2.

Number 36   *Southeast Asia over Three Generations: Essays Presented to Benedict R. O'G. Anderson*, ed. James T. Siegel and Audrey R. Kahin. 2003. 398 pp. ISBN 0-87727-735-4.

Number 35   *Nationalism and Revolution in Indonesia*, George McTurnan Kahin, intro. Benedict R. O'G. Anderson (reprinted from 1952 edition, Cornell University Press, with permission). 2003. 530 pp. ISBN 0-87727-734-6.

Number 34   *Golddiggers, Farmers, and Traders in the "Chinese Districts" of West Kalimantan, Indonesia*, Mary Somers Heidhues. 2003. 316 pp. ISBN 0-87727-733-8.

Number 33   *Opusculum de Sectis apud Sinenses et Tunkinenses (A Small Treatise on the Sects among the Chinese and Tonkinese): A Study of Religion in China and North Vietnam in the Eighteenth Century*, Father Adriano de St. Thecla, trans. Olga Dror, with Mariya Berezovska. 2002. 363 pp. ISBN 0-87727-732-X.

Number 32   *Fear and Sanctuary: Burmese Refugees in Thailand*, Hazel J. Lang. 2002. 204 pp. ISBN 0-87727-731-1.

Number 31   *Modern Dreams: An Inquiry into Power, Cultural Production, and the Cityscape in Contemporary Urban Penang, Malaysia*, Beng-Lan Goh. 2002. 225 pp. ISBN 0-87727-730-3.

Number 30   *Violence and the State in Suharto's Indonesia*, ed. Benedict R. O'G. Anderson. 2001. Second printing, 2002. 247 pp. ISBN 0-87727-729-X.

Number 29   *Studies in Southeast Asian Art: Essays in Honor of Stanley J. O'Connor*, ed. Nora A. Taylor. 2000. 243 pp. Illustrations. ISBN 0-87727-728-1.

Number 28   *The Hadrami Awakening: Community and Identity in the Netherlands East Indies, 1900-1942*, Natalie Mobini-Kesheh. 1999. 174 pp. ISBN 0-87727-727-3.

Number 27   *Tales from Djakarta: Caricatures of Circumstances and their Human Beings*, Pramoedya Ananta Toer. 1999. 145 pp. ISBN 0-87727-726-5.

Number 26   *History, Culture, and Region in Southeast Asian Perspectives*, rev. ed., O. W. Wolters. 1999. Second printing, 2004. 275 pp. ISBN 0-87727-725-7.

Number 25   *Figures of Criminality in Indonesia, the Philippines, and Colonial Vietnam*, ed. Vicente L. Rafael. 1999. 259 pp. ISBN 0-87727-724-9.

Number 24   *Paths to Conflagration: Fifty Years of Diplomacy and Warfare in Laos, Thailand, and Vietnam, 1778-1828*, Mayoury Ngaosyvathn and Pheuiphanh Ngaosyvathn. 1998. 268 pp. ISBN 0-87727-723-0.

Number 23   *Nguyễn Cochinchina: Southern Vietnam in the Seventeenth and Eighteenth Centuries*, Li Tana. 1998. Second printing, 2002. 194 pp. ISBN 0-87727-722-2.

Number 22   *Young Heroes: The Indonesian Family in Politics*, Saya S. Shiraishi. 1997. 183 pp. ISBN 0-87727-721-4.

Number 21   *Interpreting Development: Capitalism, Democracy, and the Middle Class in Thailand*, John Girling. 1996. 95 pp. ISBN 0-87727-720-6.

Number 20   *Making Indonesia*, ed. Daniel S. Lev, Ruth McVey. 1996. 201 pp. ISBN 0-87727-719-2.

Number 19   *Essays into Vietnamese Pasts*, ed. K. W. Taylor, John K. Whitmore. 1995. 288 pp. ISBN 0-87727-718-4.

Number 18   *In the Land of Lady White Blood: Southern Thailand and the Meaning of History*, Lorraine M. Gesick. 1995. 106 pp. ISBN 0-87727-717-6.

Number 17   *The Vernacular Press and the Emergence of Modern Indonesian Consciousness*, Ahmat Adam. 1995. 220 pp. ISBN 0-87727-716-8.

Number 16   *The Nan Chronicle*, trans., ed. David K. Wyatt. 1994. 158 pp. ISBN 0-87727-715-X.

Number 15   *Selective Judicial Competence: The Cirebon-Priangan Legal Administration, 1680–1792*, Mason C. Hoadley. 1994. 185 pp. ISBN 0-87727-714-1.

Number 14   *Sjahrir: Politics and Exile in Indonesia*, Rudolf Mrázek. 1994. 536 pp. ISBN 0-87727-713-3.

Number 13   *Fair Land Sarawak: Some Recollections of an Expatriate Officer*, Alastair Morrison. 1993. 196 pp. ISBN 0-87727-712-5.

Number 12   *Fields from the Sea: Chinese Junk Trade with Siam during the Late Eighteenth and Early Nineteenth Centuries*, Jennifer Cushman. 1993. 206 pp. ISBN 0-87727-711-7.

Number 11   *Money, Markets, and Trade in Early Southeast Asia: The Development of Indigenous Monetary Systems to AD 1400*, Robert S. Wicks. 1992. 2nd printing 1996. 354 pp., 78 tables, illus., maps. ISBN 0-87727-710-9.

Number 10   *Tai Ahoms and the Stars: Three Ritual Texts to Ward Off Danger*, trans., ed. B. J. Terwiel, Ranoo Wichasin. 1992. 170 pp. ISBN 0-87727-709-5.

Number 9   *Southeast Asian Capitalists*, ed. Ruth McVey. 1992. 2nd printing 1993. 220 pp. ISBN 0-87727-708-7.

Number 8   *The Politics of Colonial Exploitation: Java, the Dutch, and the Cultivation System*, Cornelis Fasseur, ed. R. E. Elson, trans. R. E. Elson, Ary Kraal. 1992. 2nd printing 1994. 266 pp. ISBN 0-87727-707-9.

Number 7   *A Malay Frontier: Unity and Duality in a Sumatran Kingdom,* Jane
            Drakard. 1990. 2nd printing 2003. 215 pp. ISBN 0-87727-706-0.

Number 6   *Trends in Khmer Art,* Jean Boisselier, ed. Natasha Eilenberg, trans.
            Natasha Eilenberg, Melvin Elliott. 1989. 124 pp., 24 plates.
            ISBN 0-87727-705-2.

Number 5   *Southeast Asian Ephemeris: Solar and Planetary Positions, A.D. 638–2000,*
            J. C. Eade. 1989. 175 pp. ISBN 0-87727-704-4.

Number 3   *Thai Radical Discourse: The Real Face of Thai Feudalism Today,* Craig J.
            Reynolds. 1987. 2nd printing 1994. 186 pp. ISBN 0-87727-702-8.

Number 1   *The Symbolism of the Stupa,* Adrian Snodgrass. 1985. Revised with
            index, 1988. 3rd printing 1998. 469 pp. ISBN 0-87727-700-1.

SEAP Series

Number 23   *Possessed by the Spirits: Mediumship in Contemporary Vietnamese
            Communities.* 2006. 186 pp. ISBN 0-877271-41-0 (pb).

Number 22   *The Industry of Marrying Europeans,* V_ Tr_ng Ph_ng, trans. Thúy
            Tranviet. 2006. 66 pp. ISBN 0-877271-40-2 (pb).

Number 21   *Securing a Place: Small-Scale Artisans in Modern Indonesia,* Elizabeth
            Morrell. 2005. 220 pp. ISBN 0-877271-39-9.

Number 20   *Southern Vietnam under the Reign of Minh Mạng (1820-1841): Central
            Policies and Local Response,* Choi Byung Wook. 2004. 226pp. ISBN 0-0-
            877271-40-2.

Number 19   *Gender, Household, State: Đổi Mới in Việt Nam,* ed. Jayne Werner and
            Danièle Bélanger. 2002. 151 pp. ISBN 0-87727-137-2.

Number 18   *Culture and Power in Traditional Siamese Government,* Neil A. Englehart.
            2001. 130 pp. ISBN 0-87727-135-6.

Number 17   *Gangsters, Democracy, and the State,* ed. Carl A. Trocki. 1998. Second
            printing, 2002. 94 pp. ISBN 0-87727-134-8.

Number 16   *Cutting across the Lands: An Annotated Bibliography on Natural Resource
            Management and Community Development in Indonesia, the Philippines,
            and Malaysia,* ed. Eveline Ferretti. 1997. 329 pp. ISBN 0-87727-133-X.

Number 15   *The Revolution Falters: The Left in Philippine Politics after 1986,* ed.
            Patricio N. Abinales. 1996. Second printing, 2002. 182 pp. ISBN 0-
            87727-132-1.

Number 14   *Being Kammu: My Village, My Life,* Damrong Tayanin. 1994. 138 pp., 22
            tables, illus., maps. ISBN 0-87727-130-5.

Number 13   *The American War in Vietnam,* ed. Jayne Werner, David Hunt. 1993.
            132 pp. ISBN 0-87727-131-3.

Number 12   *The Voice of Young Burma,* Aye Kyaw. 1993. 92 pp. ISBN 0-87727-129-1.

Number 11   *The Political Legacy of Aung San,* ed. Josef Silverstein. Revised edition
            1993. 169 pp. ISBN 0-87727-128-3.

Number 10   *Studies on Vietnamese Language and Literature: A Preliminary Bibliography,*
            Nguyen Dinh Tham. 1992. 227 pp. ISBN 0-87727-127-5.

Number 8   *From PKI to the Comintern, 1924–1941: The Apprenticeship of the Malayan
            Communist Party,* Cheah Boon Kheng. 1992. 147 pp. ISBN 0-87727-125-9.

Number 7   *Intellectual Property and US Relations with Indonesia, Malaysia, Singapore, and Thailand,* Elisabeth Uphoff. 1991. 67 pp. ISBN 0-87727-124-0.

Number 6   *The Rise and Fall of the Communist Party of Burma (CPB),* Bertil Lintner. 1990. 124 pp. 26 illus., 14 maps. ISBN 0-87727-123-2.

Number 5   *Japanese Relations with Vietnam: 1951–1987,* Masaya Shiraishi. 1990. 174 pp. ISBN 0-87727-122-4.

Number 3   *Postwar Vietnam: Dilemmas in Socialist Development,* ed. Christine White, David Marr. 1988. 2nd printing 1993. 260 pp. ISBN 0-87727-120-8.

Number 2   *The Dobama Movement in Burma (1930–1938),* Khin Yi. 1988. 160 pp. ISBN 0-87727-118-6.

Cornell Modern Indonesia Project Publications

Number 75   *A Tour of Duty: Changing Patterns of Military Politics in Indonesia in the 1990s.* Douglas Kammen and Siddharth Chandra. 1999. 99 pp. ISBN 0-87763-049-6.

Number 74   *The Roots of Acehnese Rebellion 1989–1992,* Tim Kell. 1995. 103 pp. ISBN 0-87763-040-2.

Number 73   *"White Book" on the 1992 General Election in Indonesia,* trans. Dwight King. 1994. 72 pp. ISBN 0-87763-039-9.

Number 72   *Popular Indonesian Literature of the Qur'an,* Howard M. Federspiel. 1994. 170 pp. ISBN 0-87763-038-0.

Number 71   *A Javanese Memoir of Sumatra, 1945–1946: Love and Hatred in the Liberation War,* Takao Fusayama. 1993. 150 pp. ISBN 0-87763-037-2.

Number 70   *East Kalimantan: The Decline of a Commercial Aristocracy,* Burhan Magenda. 1991. 120 pp. ISBN 0-87763-036-4.

Number 69   *The Road to Madiun: The Indonesian Communist Uprising of 1948,* Elizabeth Ann Swift. 1989. 120 pp. ISBN 0-87763-035-6.

Number 68   *Intellectuals and Nationalism in Indonesia: A Study of the Following Recruited by Sutan Sjahrir in Occupation Jakarta,* J. D. Legge. 1988. 159 pp. ISBN 0-87763-034-8.

Number 67   *Indonesia Free: A Biography of Mohammad Hatta,* Mavis Rose. 1987. 252 pp. ISBN 0-87763-033-X.

Number 66   *Prisoners at Kota Cane,* Leon Salim, trans. Audrey Kahin. 1986. 112 pp. ISBN 0-87763-032-1.

Number 65   *The Kenpeitai in Java and Sumatra,* trans. Barbara G. Shimer, Guy Hobbs, intro. Theodore Friend. 1986. 80 pp. ISBN 0-87763-031-3.

Number 64   *Suharto and His Generals: Indonesia's Military Politics, 1975–1983,* David Jenkins. 1984. 4th printing 1997. 300 pp. ISBN 0-87763-030-5.

Number 62   *Interpreting Indonesian Politics: Thirteen Contributions to the Debate, 1964–1981,* ed. Benedict Anderson, Audrey Kahin, intro. Daniel S. Lev. 1982. 3rd printing 1991. 172 pp. ISBN 0-87763-028-3.

Number 60   *The Minangkabau Response to Dutch Colonial Rule in the Nineteenth Century,* Elizabeth E. Graves. 1981. 157 pp. ISBN 0-87763-000-3.

Number 59   *Breaking the Chains of Oppression of the Indonesian People: Defense Statement at His Trial on Charges of Insulting the Head of State, Bandung, June 7–10, 1979*, Heri Akhmadi. 1981. 201 pp. ISBN 0-87763-001-1.

Number 57   *Permesta: Half a Rebellion*, Barbara S. Harvey. 1977. 174 pp. ISBN 0-87763-003-8.

Number 55   *Report from Banaran: The Story of the Experiences of a Soldier during the War of Independence*, Maj. Gen. T. B. Simatupang. 1972. 186 pp. ISBN 0-87763-005-4.

Number 52   *A Preliminary Analysis of the October 1 1965, Coup in Indonesia (Prepared in January 1966)*, Benedict R. Anderson, Ruth T. McVey, assist. Frederick P. Bunnell. 1971. 3rd printing 1990. 174 pp. ISBN 0-87763-008-9.

Number 51   *The Putera Reports: Problems in Indonesian-Japanese War-Time Cooperation*, Mohammad Hatta, trans., intro. William H. Frederick. 1971. 114 pp. ISBN 0-87763-009-7.

Number 50   *Schools and Politics: The Kaum Muda Movement in West Sumatra (1927–1933)*, Taufik Abdullah. 1971. 257 pp. ISBN 0-87763-010-0.

Number 49   *The Foundation of the Partai Muslimin Indonesia*, K. E. Ward. 1970. 75 pp. ISBN 0-87763-011-9.

Number 48   *Nationalism, Islam and Marxism*, Soekarno, intro. Ruth T. McVey. 1970. 2nd printing 1984. 62 pp. ISBN 0-87763-012-7.

Number 43   *State and Statecraft in Old Java: A Study of the Later Mataram Period, 16th to 19th Century*, Soemarsaid Moertono. Revised edition 1981. 180 pp. ISBN 0-87763-017-8.

Number 39   Preliminary Checklist of Indonesian Imprints (1945-1949), John M. Echols. 186 pp. ISBN 0-87763-025-9.

Number 37   *Mythology and the Tolerance of the Javanese*, Benedict R. O'G. Anderson. 2nd edition, 1996. Reprinted 2004. 104 pp., 65 illus. ISBN 0-87763-041-0.

Number 25   *The Communist Uprisings of 1926–1927 in Indonesia: Key Documents*, ed., intro. Harry J. Benda, Ruth T. McVey. 1960. 2nd printing 1969. 177 pp. ISBN 0-87763-024-0.

Number 7   *The Soviet View of the Indonesian Revolution*, Ruth T. McVey. 1957. 3rd printing 1969. 90 pp. ISBN 0-87763-018-6.

Number 6   *The Indonesian Elections of 1955*, Herbert Feith. 1957. 2nd printing 1971. 91 pp. ISBN 0-87763-020-8.

Translation Series

Volume 4   *Approaching Suharto's Indonesia from the Margins*, ed. Takashi Shiraishi. 1994. 153 pp. ISBN 0-87727-403-7.

Volume 3   *The Japanese in Colonial Southeast Asia*, ed. Saya Shiraishi, Takashi Shiraishi. 1993. 172 pp. ISBN 0-87727-402-9.

Volume 2   *Indochina in the 1940s and 1950s*, ed. Takashi Shiraishi, Motoo Furuta. 1992. 196 pp. ISBN 0-87727-401-0.

Volume 1   *Reading Southeast Asia*, ed. Takashi Shiraishi. 1990. 188 pp. ISBN 0-87727-400-2.

Language Texts

INDONESIAN

Beginning Indonesian through Self-Instruction, John U. Wolff, Dédé Oetomo, Daniel Fietkiewicz. 3rd revised edition 1992. Vol. 1. 115 pp. ISBN 0-87727-529-7. Vol. 2. 434 pp. ISBN 0-87727-530-0. Vol. 3. 473 pp. ISBN 0-87727-531-9.

Indonesian Readings, John U. Wolff. 1978. 4th printing 1992. 480 pp. ISBN 0-87727-517-3

Indonesian Conversations, John U. Wolff. 1978. 3rd printing 1991. 297 pp. ISBN 0-87727-516-5

Formal Indonesian, John U. Wolff. 2nd revised edition 1986. 446 pp. ISBN 0-87727-515-7

TAGALOG

Pilipino through Self-Instruction, John U. Wolff, Maria Theresa C. Centeno, Der-Hwa V. Rau. 1991. Vol. 1. 342 pp. ISBN 0-87727—525-4. Vol. 2., revised 2005, 378 pp. ISBN 0-87727-526-2. Vol 3., revised 2005, 431 pp. ISBN 0-87727-527-0. Vol. 4. 306 pp. ISBN 0-87727-528-9.

THAI

A. U. A. Language Center Thai Course, J. Marvin Brown. Originally published by the American University Alumni Association Language Center, 1974. Reissued by Cornell Southeast Asia Program, 1991, 1992. Book 1. 267 pp. ISBN 0-87727-506-8. Book 2. 288 pp. ISBN 0-87727-507-6. Book 3. 247 pp. ISBN 0-87727-508-4.

A. U. A. Language Center Thai Course, Reading and Writing Text (mostly reading), 1979. Reissued 1997. 164 pp. ISBN 0-87727-511-4.

A. U. A. Language Center Thai Course, Reading and Writing Workbook (mostly writing), 1979. Reissued 1997. 99 pp. ISBN 0-87727-512-2.

KHMER

Cambodian System of Writing and Beginning Reader, Franklin E. Huffman. Originally published by Yale University Press, 1970. Reissued by Cornell Southeast Asia Program, 4th printing 2002. 365 pp. ISBN 0-300-01314-0.

Modern Spoken Cambodian, Franklin E. Huffman, assist. Charan Promchan, Chhom-Rak Thong Lambert. Originally published by Yale University Press, 1970. Reissued by Cornell Southeast Asia Program, 3rd printing 1991. 451 pp. ISBN 0-300-01316-7.

Intermediate Cambodian Reader, ed. Franklin E. Huffman, assist. Im Proum. Originally published by Yale University Press, 1972. Reissued by Cornell Southeast Asia Program, 1988. 499 pp. ISBN 0-300-01552-6.

Cambodian Literary Reader and Glossary, Franklin E. Huffman, Im Proum. Originally published by Yale University Press, 1977. Reissued by Cornell Southeast Asia Program, 1988. 494 pp. ISBN 0-300-02069-4.

HMONG

White Hmong-English Dictionary, Ernest E. Heimbach. 1969. 8th printing, 2002. 523 pp. ISBN 0-87727-075-9.

VIETNAMESE

Intermediate Spoken Vietnamese, Franklin E. Huffman, Tran Trong Hai. 1980. 3rd printing 1994. ISBN 0-87727-500-9.

* * *

Southeast Asian Studies: Reorientations. Craig J. Reynolds and Ruth McVey. Frank H. Golay Lectures 2 & 3. 70 pp. ISBN 0-87727-301-4.

Javanese Literature in Surakarta Manuscripts, Nancy K. Florida. Vol. 1, *Introduction and Manuscripts of the Karaton Surakarta*. 1993. 410 pp. Frontispiece, illustrations. Hard cover, ISBN 0-87727-602-1, Paperback, ISBN 0-87727-603-X. Vol. 2, *Manuscripts of the Mangkunagaran Palace*. 2000. 576 pp. Frontispiece, illustrations. Paperback, ISBN 0-87727-604-8.

Sbek Thom: Khmer Shadow Theater. Pech Tum Kravel, trans. Sos Kem, ed. Thavro Phim, Sos Kem, Martin Hatch. 1996. 363 pp., 153 photographs. ISBN 0-87727-620-X.

In the Mirror: Literature and Politics in Siam in the American Era, ed. Benedict R. O'G. Anderson, trans. Benedict R. O'G. Anderson, Ruchira Mendiones. 1985. 2nd printing 1991. 303 pp. Paperback. ISBN 974-210-380-1.

To order, please contact:

Cornell University
Southeast Asia Program Publications
95 Brown Road
Box 1004
Ithaca NY 14850

Online: http://www.einaudi.cornell.edu/southeastasia/publications/
Tel: 1-877-865-2432 (Toll free – U.S.)
Fax: (607) 255-7534

E-mail: SEAP-Pubs@cornell.edu
Orders must be prepaid by check or credit card (VISA, MasterCard, Discover).

Lightning Source UK Ltd.
Milton Keynes UK
UKHW051103021222
413180UK00012B/483